MULTINATIONALS AND HUMAN RIGHTS IN ASIA

This book investigates the availability in Asian jurisdictions of civil remedies against multinational businesses for human rights abuses. Various means have been developed in Europe and elsewhere to hold businesses accountable to victims for human rights abuses. Techniques include legislating due diligence requirements for companies operating abroad, broadening court jurisdiction to include foreign companies having subsidiaries within a country, expanding international jurisdiction, promoting universal jurisdiction, and implementing international conventions and sanctions.

On the 15th anniversary of the 2011 UN Guiding Principles on Business and Human Rights, the book assesses whether the norms of the UN Guiding Principles have taken root in Asia, which has only had a mixed record for upholding human rights. The book first considers the international state of play in the field. It moves on to case studies of corporate governance and human rights in Asia (especially Japan, South Korea, India, Thailand and the Philippines). It then examines emerging issues (environmental damage and climate change, crimes against humanity, and compliance programs and corporate criminal responsibility), and considers how Asia has dealt and can deal with corporate responsibility in connection with those matters. By way of conclusion, the book offers an action plan for implementing the UN Guiding Principles in Asia.

Volume 15 in the series Studies in Private International Law – Asia

Studies in Private International Law – Asia

Editor: Anselmo Reyes
Advisory Editor: Paul Beaumont
Assistant Editors: Kazuaki Nishioka and Wilson Lui

Much has been written about private international law in the EU and the US. Less is known about the conflict of laws in Asia. Thus, little attention has been paid so far to the modernisation of private international law codes and rules that has been taking place over the last decade all over Asia. That trend continues. Now is the time to take stock of those reforms that have already taken place and suggest further improvements for the future.

Published under the celebrated series *Studies in Private International Law*, this monograph sub-series provides a forum for discussion and analysis of private international law in Asia. The series is not solely a survey of jurisdictions for practitioners. Comprising both in-depth thematic and country-specific studies, each volume considers the private international law of Asian countries from a variety of perspectives. An underlying assumption is that private international law in different jurisdictions follows broadly discernible patterns. Each volume in this sub-series highlights those patterns and discusses how rules in different Asian jurisdictions are either converging with, or diverging from, the patterns identified. Such an analytical framework will assist academics, judges, lawyers and legislators to envisage ways in which laws affecting cross-border relationships can be harmonised across jurisdictions and be made more responsive to the needs of citizens in Asia and elsewhere.

Volume 1: Recognition and Enforcement of Judgments in Civil and Commercial Matters
Edited by Anselmo Reyes

Volume 2: Indonesian Private International Law
Afifah Kusumadara

Volume 3: Chinese Private International Law
Edited by Xiaohong Liu and Zhengyi Zhang

Volume 4: Direct Jurisdiction: Asian Perspectives
Edited by Anselmo Reyes and Wilson Lui

Volume 5: Japanese Private International Law
Kazuaki Nishioka and Yuko Nishitani

Volume 6: Indian Private International Law
Stellina Jolly and Saloni Khanderia

Volume 7: Treatment of Foreign Law in Asia
Edited by Kazuaki Nishioka

Volume 8: Choice of Law and Recognition in Asian Family Law
Edited by Anselmo Reyes, Wilson Lui and Kazuaki Nishioka

Volume 9: Private International Law in East Asia: From Imitation to Innovation and Exportation
Edited by Olivier Gaillard and Krista Nadakavukaren Schefer

Volume 10: Overriding Mandatory Rules in International Commercial Disputes: Korean and Comparative Law
Min Kyung KIM

Volume 11: Privacy and Personal Data Protection Law in Asia
Edited by Adrian Mak, Ching Him Ho and Anselmo Reyes

Volume 12: Hong Kong Private International Law
Wilson Lui and Anselmo Reyes

Volume 13: Choice of Forum Clauses in Asia
Lemuel D Lopez

Volume 14: Cambodian Private International Law
Nobumichi Teramura

Volume 15: Multinationals and Human Rights in Asia
Edited by Jason Ho Ching Cheung and Kazuaki Nishioka

Multinational and Human Rights in Asia

Edited by
Jason Ho Ching Cheung
and
Kazuaki Nishioka

•HART•
OXFORD • LONDON • NEW YORK • NEW DELHI • SYDNEY

HART PUBLISHING

Bloomsbury Publishing Plc

Kemp House, Chawley Park, Cumnor Hill, Oxford, OX2 9PH, UK

1385 Broadway, New York, NY 10018, USA

Bloomsbury Publishing Ireland Limited, 29 Earlsfort Terrace, Dublin 2, D02 AY28, Ireland

HART PUBLISHING, the Hart/Stag logo, BLOOMSBURY and the Diana logo are trademarks of Bloomsbury Publishing Plc

First published in Great Britain 2026

A catalogue record for this book is available from the British Library.

A catalogue record for this book is available from the Library of Congress.

Library of Congress Control Number: 2026933591

ISBN: HB: 978-1-50998-040-6
ePDF: 978-1-50998-038-3
ePub: 978-1-50998-039-0

Typeset by Compuscript Ltd, Shannon

For product safety related questions contact productsafety@bloomsbury.com

To find out more about our authors and books visit www.hartpublishing.co.uk. Here you will find extracts, author information, details of forthcoming events and the option to sign up for our newsletters.

SERIES EDITORS' PREFACE

Multinationals and Human Rights in Asia is the fourth monograph in Hart's *Studies in Private International Law – Asia* series.

It is also one of several volumes in the series which seek to explore (or possibly expand) the remit of private international law. Many standard accounts of the conflict of laws (including many within the present series) routinely describe the field as encompassing four topics: (1) jurisdiction, (2) choice of law, (3) the recognition and enforcement of foreign judgments or awards, and (4) the harmonisation of private international law rules. But the underlying premise of this book and others like it within the series is that such delineation of the boundaries of private international law is too narrow. Private international law should also study the ways in which domestic laws can have extraterritorial effect and affect the lives of individuals and communities across borders for better or worse.

Enforcing compliance with human rights among multinational businesses operating across Asia, the topic of this monograph, is one area where the extraterritorial operation of domestic legislation is bound to be controversial. Few will quibble about the importance of human dignity and human rights in today's world. Thus, over 170 countries have subscribed to the International Covenant on Civil and Political Rights. But this fact does not guarantee that the instrument is uniformly applied or interpreted in every member jurisdiction. Far from it. When it comes to cross-border relations, there is a heightened scope for disparity and disagreement. For example, developed countries may seek to apply the more rigorous human rights standards of the Global North (for example, in respect of the reduction of carbon emissions for the promotion a healthy living environment) to the operations of subsidiaries of multinationals operating in developing countries. This is typically perceived by the countries of the Global South (including within Asia) as unfairly reducing their competitive advantage and thwarting their ambitions of rapid economic growth to raise their citizenry out of poverty. On the other hand, developed countries may complain that the absence of labour laws gives the Global South an unfair advantage in the production of economic goods, to the detriment of workers in the Global North. On this view, it would be right for the domestic laws (including economic sanctions) of the Global North to be applied with extraterritorial effect to ensure that all workers are treated to the same human rights standard wherever they might be. Inevitably, national interests and politics enter into the equation, and it cannot be for lawyers alone (let alone private international law specialists) to resolve the many bones of contention among countries. But that is not a reason for the conflict of laws to refrain from mapping out the contours of the multi-faceted debate.

All this means that this volume will not make for comfortable reading. It has sought not merely to be descriptive, but also to be prescriptive. The several contributors have not simply opined on whether a country will (or will not) have jurisdiction over a particular matter, but whether a country should assert jurisdiction and (if so) on what basis. The contributors have not merely listed available options for applicable law, but have considered what human rights norms may come into play and how they may be enforced across borders. They have not contented themselves with dealing with recognition and enforcement as a purely academic exercise, but have looked into how the law might have teeth transnationally. Finally, they have delved into how the law of human rights due diligence can be harmonised as far as the regulation of multinational businesses is concerned. Not everyone will agree with everything in this book. Many will almost certainly disagree with much. But this volume's function is to inform rational debate, serving as a modest step towards making this world a better place in which to live.

The Editors
Kyoto
7 October 2025

ACKNOWLEDGEMENTS

With its preparation phase beginning during the COVID-19 pandemic, and the chapters primarily written in the post-pandemic period amid ongoing and shifting global politics (in Asia and elsewhere), this book bears witness to the evolving landscape of human rights and international affairs. Far from representing the conclusion of this field of inquiry, we view this volume as a continuing contribution to the study of multinationals and human rights. We are deeply grateful to all the contributors for their commitment and continued support throughout this project. We would also like to thank Yasuaki Takeuchi for initiating this project. Unfortunately, due to his many other commitments, he was unable to remain as co-editor until the completion of this volume. However, without his tremendous groundwork, Kazuaki Nishioka would not have been able to step in and complete this volume as co-editor at short notice. Moreover, we would like to thank those who supported or referred us to contributors: Min Kyung Kim, Junhyok Jang, Surya Deva, Adrian Mak, Timothy Webster, Laura Tartakoff, and the late Paul E Schroeder. Special thanks go to Yuri Mukoji and Rachel Chi Lam Choi for their valuable editorial assistance. This book could not have come to fruition without the help of all those named above. Jason Cheung would also like to express his heartfelt thanks to his parents and his wife, Aya, for their unwavering support and encouragement throughout the editing of this book.

The Editors
Tokyo and Kobe
27 July 2025

CONTENTS

LIST OF CONTRIBUTORS

Ebony Birchall is a Lecturer at Macquarie Law School and Deputy Director of the Business and Human Rights Access to Justice Lab (A2J Lab). She has been a human rights lawyer for 15 years and acted in several landmark Australian human rights cases.

Antonia Burke is the Founder and Director of Sea of Nations.

Shaati Chandramour is an Assistant Professor at Thammasat University, Thailand.

Jason Ho Ching Cheung is a Hong Kong barrister and New York attorney practicing from Albert Luk's Chambers, Hong Kong and Yodoyabashi & Yamagami LPC, Japan. He is also a part-time lecturer at the Graduate School of Law and the Institute for the Liberal Arts at Doshisha University, Japan.

Antony Crockett is a Partner at Herbert Smith Freehills Kramer, Hong Kong.

Swaril Dania is an Assistant Professor at University School of Law and Legal Studies, Guru Gobind Singh Indraprastha University, Delhi, India.

Daichi Ishii is a current graduate student at the Institute of Science Tokyo, and a researcher at the Ministry of Defense, Japan.

Jonathan Ip is a Hong Kong barrister practicing from ALSC Chambers, Hong Kong.

Jay Koon is a Hong Kong barrister practicing from Bernacchi Chambers, Hong Kong.

Jong Hyeok Lee is an Associate Professor at Seoul National University School of Law, South Korea.

Koh Matsuki is the CEO of Proxy Watcher, Japan.

Shin Matsuzawa is a Professor at the School of Law, Waseda University, Japan.

Yuri Mukoji is a juris doctor candidate at Doshisha University, Japan.

Kazuaki Nishioka is a specially appointed associate professor at Kobe University, Japan and an arbitrator and mediator at Anselmo Reyes KK.

Jefferi Hamzah Sendut is an Associate at Herbert Smith Freehills Kramer LLP, London

Daniel Linden is a Ph.D. Candidate (Public International Law) and Research Assistant at Waseda University, Japan.

Tamio Nakamura is a Professor of Law at the School of Law, Waseda University, Japan.

Ziqing Ruan is a PhD student at Waseda University, Japan.

Manoj Kumar Sinha is the Vice-Chancellor of Dharmashastra National Law University, Jabalpur, Madhya Pradesh, India.

Youngsu Suh is a Judicial Research Officer at the Supreme Court of Korea, South Korea.

Aaron Tang is a Senior Associate at Herbert Smith Freehills Kramer, Hong Kong.

Kenneth Tsui is a graduate of BSSc, LLB and PCLL of the University of Hong Kong, and a research assistant to Professor Anselmo Reyes and Professor Lusina Ho.

Ruby Rosselle 'Ross' Tugade is a PhD researcher at the Faculty of Law & Justice, University of New South Wales supported by an Australian Government Research Training Program scholarship. She also lectures at the University of the Philippines College of Law.

Matthew Wong is a third year BBA & LLB student at the University of Hong Kong.

TABLE OF CASES

Argentina

Australia

Canada

China

European Court of Justice

TABLE OF CASES

Argentina

Australia

Canada

China

European Court of Justice

France

Germany

Hong Kong

International Court of Justice

International Criminal Court

Japan

Netherlands

Philippines

Senegal

South Korea

Thailand

United Kingdom

Trial Chamber of the International Criminal Tribunal for the Former Yugoslavia

United States

PART I

Introduction

1

Introduction

JASON HO CHING CHEUNG

I. Purpose[1]

This introductory chapter highlights the core ideas of analysing multinational business in Asia and the human rights issues that follow in an 'Asian' context. While compiling this book, contributors have expressed worry, and perhaps, even difficulties, in researching case precedents in Asia. This intriguing feedback raises concern regarding whether there is a simple lack of human rights issue in Asia. This obviously should not be the case. For instance, customers are concerned about whether their purchase involves child labour, and businesses are wary of whether their production line sponsors the same.[2] Cross-border transactions lead to these worries being shared throughout Asia, if not globally. The reason for the lack of (legal) case precedents, which some of the chapters will touch upon, may be the underdeveloped jurisprudence in this part of the world, as compared to, for instance, its European counterpart.[3]

The only legally binding system for business has been national laws, with enforcement depending on each state's jurisprudence.[4] The dynamic of international business operations changed when the 2011 United Nations Guiding Principles on Business and Human Rights (UNGPs) were adopted by the UN Human Rights Council by Resolution 17/4 on 16 June 2011.[5] The 31 principles listed in the UNGPs attempt to clarify the duties and responsibilities of governments and states and to 'serve as a key international standard for responsible business practice and a common platform for accountability against which the conduct of both governments and businesses can be assessed'.[6]

[1] The author would like to thank Mr Yuri Mukoji of Doshisha University for his assistance in the preparation of this chapter.

[2] R Smith, *International Human Rights Law*, 10th edn (Oxford, Oxford University Press, 2022) 454.

[3] International Court of Justice, 'Thailand: Barriers persist in access to justice for victims of human rights abuses involving Thai transnational corporations abroad' (ICJ report, 11 February 2021) see www.icj.org/resource/thailand-barriers-persist-in-access-to-justice-for-victims-of-human-rights-abuses-involving-thai-transnational-corporations-abroad-icj-report/?utm_source=chatgpt.com; International Court of Justice, Access to Justice: human rights abuses involving corporations in China, 2010, see www.icj.org/resource/access-to-justice-human-rights-abuses-involving-corporations-3/?utm_source=chatgpt.com; International Court of Justice, Access to justice: human rights abuses involving corporations in Philippines, 2010, see: www.icj.org/resource/access-to-justice-human-rights-abuses-involving-corporations-in-philippines/?utm_source=chatgpt.com.

[4] Smith (n 2) 455.

[5] UN Human Rights Council, *Guiding Principles on Business and Human Rights: Implementing the United Nations 'Protect, Respect and Remedy' Framework*, UN Doc A/HRC/17/31 (21 March 2011).

[6] United Nations Development Programme, *Guiding Principles on Business and Human Rights* (13 September 2022) see www.undp.org/laopdr/publications/guiding-principles-business-and-human-rights#.

This book marks the 15th anniversary of the UNGPs.[7] It is high time to investigate the availability in Asian jurisdictions of civil remedies against multinational businesses for human rights abuses. Various means have been developed in Europe and elsewhere to hold businesses accountable to victims for human rights abuses.[8] Techniques include legislating due diligence requirements for companies operating abroad, broadening court jurisdiction to include foreign companies having subsidiaries within a country, expanding international jurisdiction, promoting universal jurisdiction, and implementing international conventions and sanctions. This book assesses whether the norms of the UNGPs have taken root in Asia, which has up till now had a mixed record for upholding human rights.

The series on *Studies in Private International Studies* provides a forum for discussion and analysis of 'private' international law in Asia. One may wonder if international human rights law, which is often referred to in this book, shall be regarded as a topic of 'public' international law and therefore not fitting in the areas of private international law studies. As Hernandez in his discussion on the redemptive potential of human rights law mentioned: 'if the protection and promotion of individual rights are … to become the heart of public international law …',[9] the bundling of human rights with public but not private international law appears to be a popular linkage. Perhaps it should be suggested that readers take a step back from the title of this book: 'Multinational and human rights in Asia'. The title suggests a broader approach to the issues of human rights, while not limited to 'international law' (and in fact, the title does not mention 'law' at all) and places the relationships with 'multinationals' up front. This book may be unauthentic compared to its peers in the same series (some of which serve as both academic and practitioner texts), but nonetheless it draws us back to discerning patterns across various Asian jurisdictions on a specific topic. As the readers may realise across some of the following chapters, contributors refer to the implementation of international legal instruments such as UNGPs into a domestic context, such as domestic legislation or local case law, or by real-life practices of government policies. The nature of human rights protection concerning private individuals against multinational businesses situates the studies as both 'private' and 'public'. A straightjacket approach of limiting references to either the arena of public international law or the rules of private international law may not be as great a fit as it once was.[10] By embarking on the journey of exploration of multinational and human rights, one ultimate question the author would post to the readers is: is the arbitrary division between private and public international law necessary (at least in the human rights context)? The author wishes this book could generate some ripples in the readers' minds.

To briefly summarise, the book first considers the international state of play in the field and explores 'conceptual' issues. It moves on to case studies of corporate governance and human rights in Asia (especially Japan, South Korea, India, Thailand, and the Philippines). It then examines emerging issues (environmental damage and climate change, crimes against humanity and corporate crime and compliance programmes) and considers how Asian jurisdictions have dealt and can deal with corporate responsibility in connection with those matters. By way of conclusion, the book offers an action plan for implementing the UNGPs in Asia.

[7] Office of the United Nations High Commissioner for Human Rights, *Guiding Principles on Business and Human Rights* (16 June 2011) see www.ohchr.org/sites/default/files/documents/publications/guidingprinciplesbusinesshr_en.pdf.

[8] C Koenig, *Human Rights or Private Rights? – Effective Protection of Victims in Global Supply Chains* (16 December 2024) see www.cambridge.org/core/journals/american-journal-of-international-law/article/human-rights-or-private-rights-effective-protection-of-victims-in-global-supply-chains/9E912DAF8B293B6034F77E2C2664A338?utm_source=chatgpt.com.

[9] G Hernandez, *International Law*, 2nd edn (Oxford, Oxford University Press, 2022) 471.

[10] A Mills, 'Connecting Public and Private International Law' in D French, K McCall-Smith and VR Abou-Nigm (eds), *Linkages and Boundaries in Private and Public International Law* (Oxford, Hart Publishing, 2018) 33–53.

II. The Challenges in Asia

As of the writing of this chapter, China and Japan remain the second and third largest world economies.[11] Together with the four Asian Tigers and other growing economies in Asia, such as Thailand and the Philippines, foreign investment by multinational businesses remains prominent in the region. Would these multinational businesses follow the UNGPs and other related international human rights legal principles while conducting themselves in the region? What are the legal and cultural differences that these businesses face in conforming with international human rights laws? On the other hand, from the state's point of view, do Asian states follow the same or similar legal principles and patterns in protecting international human rights as their Western counterparts? These questions all remain to be explored.

The author suggests there are four main challenges that need to be focused on: (i) 'what is the (scope of the) law', (ii) 'who are the parties', (iii) 'how to protect', and (iv) 'is the law working'.

A. What is the (Scope of the) Law?

Professor Malcolm Shaw indicates the salient basic rule of international law, being that states have no right to encroach upon the preservation of other states' internal affairs, derived from the principle of equality and sovereignty of states.[12] However, in the human rights arena, reinterpretation may be allowed, resulting in states no longer being able to raise concerns from the international community towards their internal human rights situation.[13] The current trend in international law also includes certain human rights that may be regarded as becoming part of customary international law under state practice, or constitute an obligation *erga omnes* for human rights established under treaty.[14] In other words, human rights law opens the door to potential interference in a state by other states and the international community. It is worth seeing to what extent the law is able to extend its reach towards an individual state's traditional domestic jurisdiction. The following chapters shall guide the readers through the journey in search of the nature of the laws in this area and the laws' edges.

B. 'Who' are the Parties?

The traditional approach of international law was that private persons or individuals were not regarded as subjects, and they did not possess international legal personality.[15] But since the 1970s, there have been discussions as to whether the traditional approach should be loosened in terms of the human rights context so that non-state actors shall assume human rights obligations.[16] In particular, if some non-state actors such as multinational corporations are much wealthier

[11] 'The top 10 largest economies in the world in 2025' (*Forbes India*, 28 April 2025) see www.forbesindia.com/article/explainers/top-10-largest-economies-in-the-world/86159/1.

[12] M Shaw, *International Law*, 9th edn (Cambridge, Cambridge University Press, 2021) 246; as mirrored in article 2(7) of the United Nations Charter.

[13] ibid 246–47.

[14] ibid 252.

[15] I Bantekas and L Oette, *International Human Rights Law and Practice*, 4th edn (Cambridge, Cambridge University Press, 2024) 852.

[16] ibid 853; A Clapham, *Human Rights Obligations of Non-State Actors* (Oxford, Oxford University Press, 2006) 29–56.

and have the largest economic influence across borders, should they be subject to certain legal obligations to ensure human rights principles are followed?[17] Conversely, with private individuals not regarded as subjects under an orthodox view of international law, how should they be involved as a protected party of the international legal regime? The cherry-picking approach of human rights as to whether non-state actors possessing an obligation creates uncertainty has been criticised, which in turn encourages violations of some non-state actors and allows states to 'blur their own commitment'.[18]

Whether it is true remains debatable in the international legal community. Nevertheless, for the book's purposes, a broader question will then be: do Asian socio-political and legal cultures affect how multinational and private individuals evolve as subjects of international law? In light of the aforementioned issues, the following chapters shall provide analysis as to how multinationals and individuals become parties of owning human rights obligations to the other.

C. 'How' to Protect?

Bantekas and Oette posited multinational corporations enjoy a wide range of rights under international law but with different corresponding obligations. In particular there are three issues concerning multinational corporations: (i)international treaties do not as a rule confer obligation on multinational corporations, (ii) the corporate and other laws of the home state do not as a rule apply to the operations of multinational corporations abroad, and (iii) the laws of the host state may be curtailed by the terms of the contract with the foreign multinational corporations.[19] Whether or not these indications hinder the development of international law in binding multinationals may not be within the scope of this book. They do however, indicate the unsettled and developing nature of the law in regulating multinational corporations. The following chapter shall delve into the mechanism and method in protecting human rights in light of the multinational business context.

D. Is the Law Working in Asia?

The last challenge is built on the assumption that after a functional mechanism or jurisprudence exists to protect human rights in the context of multinationals, is that a universal applicable approach regardless of different socio and legal traditions? The author admits that this is a bold question; it is however suggested that Asia has, perhaps, a different perception of human rights.[20] One reason may be related to Asian countries' resistance to the western attempt to 'tie the implementation of human rights to development aid and the use of human rights as an instrument of political pressure'.[21] The implication would then be whether a human rights jurisprudence that often recognised *jus cogens* could be practised in the same way in Asia.[22] When performing human rights due diligence and imposing criminality on human rights violations, how do Asian countries practice differently (if at all)? The following chapters shall cover the practical

[17] Bantekas and Oette (n 15) 853.
[18] ibid 857.
[19] ibid 859.
[20] A Gunawardan, 'An Asian Perspective of Human Rights' (1994) *Singapore Journal of Legal Studies* 521.
[21] ibid 531.
[22] J Tasioulas, 'Custom, jus cogens, and human rights' in C Bradley (ed), *Custom's Future: International Law in a Changing World* (Cambridge, Cambridge University Press, 2016).

implications of multinationals and human rights in Asia, including but not limited to the enforcement mechanisms and challenges that arise from Asian jurisprudence's legal culture.

III. Structure of the Chapters

The following chapters are broadly divided into three main parts. Part I serves the purpose of an introduction to the concept of 'multinational and human rights in Asia'. Readers will be able to grasp the nature of human rights jurisprudence in Asia. There are four themes in Part I: 'why', 'what happened', 'what has happened and may happen', and 'what about Asia?'.

Chapter two takes a step back to discuss the reasons 'why' human rights and multinationals in Asia matter. The authors include both human rights legal practitioners and entrepreneurs who are active in the environmental, social and governance (ESG) industry. This chapter opens the Part I of the book by framing the key motivations and disincentives for multinational corporations (MNCs) to enforce human rights within their global operations. It begins by outlining positive drivers – ESG investment trends, reputational risk management, regulatory pressures (eg, the EU Corporate Sustainability Due Diligence Directive (CSDDD), and long-term business advantages – encouraging companies to integrate human rights protections. The chapter then turns to the structural and practical challenges companies face, including complex supply chains, limited transparency, weak enforcement in host jurisdictions and subcontracting that evades oversight. The chapter's second half focuses on Free, Prior and Informed Consent (FPIC) – a principle grounded in international law (eg, the United Nations Declaration on the Rights of Indigenous Peoples (UNDRIP))[23] as a critical but often disregarded component of corporate responsibility toward indigenous communities. First hand testimonies from the indigenous population in Australia highlight their suffering, resulting from the activities of multinationals. Drawing lessons from this case, the chapter emphasises the crucial role that institutional investors and pension funds shall play in ensuring human rights compliance.

Building on the practical experiences reflected in Chapter two, Chapter three discusses the reasons 'why' in a conceptual sense and focuses on how human rights are enforced in international jurisdiction. Serving as the theoretical lynchpin of the volume, this chapter examines how the international legal order addresses the challenge of ensuring access to remedies for human rights abuses committed by transnational corporations. It introduces and analyses three central legal tools – universal jurisdiction, extraterritorial application of law and targeted sanctions – within a structured framework that aims to bridge the 'normative application gap' and 'enforcement gap' identified under the UNGPs. The chapter begins by unpacking the three dimensions of jurisdiction under international law – prescriptive, adjudicative and enforcement jurisdiction – and shows how they constrain or enable transnational litigation. It provides a comparative analysis of national rules on international jurisdiction in the US, the EU, the UK and Japan. The chapter also reviews non-judicial grievance mechanisms, including the Bangladesh Accord,[24] the National Contact Points (NCPs) to monitor the implementation of the OECD Guidelines for Multinational Enterprises[25] and other corporate-level remedies, while noting persistent limitations in their scope and accessibility. It also provides a comparative analysis of regional

[23] United Nations Declaration on the Rights of Indigenous Peoples (New York, 13 September 2007), see undocs.org/A/RES/61/295.

[24] Accord on Fire and Building Safety in Bangladesh (Dhaka, 15 May 2013) see bangladeshaccord.org/.

[25] OECD Guidelines for Multinational Enterprises on Responsible Business Conduct (Paris, 25 May 2011) see www.oecd.org/daf/inv/mne/.

approaches across Asia, which serves as a connection with Part II of this book. Overall, this chapter offers a comprehensive conceptual map of the fragmented and evolving ecosystem of transnational corporate accountability. It serves as the procedural and normative bridge between the international frameworks introduced in Part I and the jurisdiction-specific analyses that follow in Part II.

Chapter four focuses on the history of the drafting of UNGPs regarding 'what happened' during the last several decades. The author traces the historical development and normative architecture of the UNGPs, highlighting their emergence as the most influential international framework in regulating multinational corporate conduct. The UNGPs begin with a critical account of earlier, failed regulatory efforts – such as the 1990 UN Draft Code and 2003 Draft Norms – before detailing the methodology of John Ruggie, the Special Representative who pioneered the UNGPs through what he termed 'principled pragmatism'.[26] The chapter explains the UNGPs' three-pillar framework – state duty to protect, corporate responsibility to respect and access to remedy – and elaborates on the extensive consultations and compromises that shaped the final document. The transformative role of the UNGPs in establishing human rights due diligence (HRDD) as a normative standard is highlighted, which influences numerous regulatory initiatives globally, including the OECD Guidelines for Multinational Enterprises, ISO26000[27] and EU mandatory due diligence laws. The author also highlights critics of UNGPs, with indications of possible derailment from the International Bill of Rights.[28]

Chapter five discusses the present form of the development of UNGPs. The authors review and pinpoint the development over the last few decades, in particular the efforts involved in turning UNGPs into binding law. This chapter provides a comprehensive and nuanced examination of the UN Human Rights Council's ongoing efforts to create a legally binding international treaty on business and human rights (LBI) – a project launched in 2014 via Resolution 26/9 and spearheaded by Ecuador. The authors critically assess a decade of negotiations within the Open-ended Intergovernmental Working Group, identifying enduring divisions over the treaty's scope, legal obligations, and its relationship to the non-binding UNGPs. It details how Ecuador has shifted its approach in recent years, seeking compromise through procedural innovations like the 'Friends of the Chair' group, draft language revisions, and most recently, the UNHRC's Decision 56/116, which enables intersessional consultations supported by legal experts.[29] The authors also explore how external developments – including the EU's Corporate Sustainability Due Diligence Directive (CS3D),[30] rising global ESG expectations and regulatory reforms – are shaping the LBI debate and increasing pressure on Asian jurisdictions to engage meaningfully.

[26] J Ruggie, *The Past as Prologue? – A moment of Truth for UN Business and Human Rights Treaty* (8 July 2014) 5, see www.hks.harvard.edu/sites/default/files/centers/mrcbg/programs/cri/files/Treaty_Final.pdf.

[27] International Organization for Standardization, *ISO 26000: Guidance on Social Responsibility*, 1st edn (ISO, 2010).

[28] E Birchall, 'The UN Guiding Principles: A Significant Step but not yet Delivering the Promised Corporate Respect for Human Rights' ch 4 of this volume. The term 'International Bill of Rights' refers collectively to the following three core UN human rights instruments: Universal Declaration of Human Rights (Paris, 10 December 1948), see www.un.org/en/about-us/universal-declaration-of-human-rights; International Covenant on Civil and Political Rights (New York, 16 December 1966) see treaties.un.org/doc/Treaties/1976/03/19760323%2006-17%20AM/Ch_IV_04.pdf; International Covenant on Economic, Social and Cultural Rights (New York, 16 December 1966) see treaties.un.org/doc/Treaties/1976/01/19760103%2009-57%20PM/Ch_IV_03.pdf.

[29] UN Human Rights Council, Decision 56/116 on the intersessional consultation on business and human rights, UN Doc A/HRC/DEC/56/116 (11 July 2024).

[30] Directive (EU) 2024/1760 of the European Parliament and of the Council of 13 June 2024 on corporate sustainability due diligence and amending Directive (EU) 2019/1937 and Regulation (EU) 2023/2859 [2024] OJ L 168/1.

Chapter six zooms in to look into 'what about Asia'.[31] Asia is a vast land with various countries and cultures. Taking a comparative approach, this chapter discusses the challenges that lie in implanting a 'universal' if not 'western' driven normative assumption on the rule of law into the Asian context plus the challenges of implanting an EU normative assumption on the rule of law into the Asian context. This chapter critically analyses the CSDDD and its projected impact on human rights and environmental standards in Southeast Asia, particularly within ASEAN member states. While the CSDDD aims to fill global regulatory gaps by imposing legally binding due diligence obligations on large companies (EU and non-EU) operating within the EU market, the author explores whether these obligations can function effectively in regions where the rule of law, regulatory enforcement and rights protections are uneven or weak. The chapter begins by explaining the structure and intent of the CSDDD: to transform the UNGPs' soft-law expectations into binding obligations, requiring businesses to identify, prevent, mitigate, and remediate adverse human rights and environmental impacts across their supply chains. It covers both human rights and climate obligations, along with mechanisms for enforcement, notably civil liability and mandatory public oversight. The author then focuses on the ASEAN context, examining why these mechanisms may face friction, and assesses whether the CSDDD's private governance model – including supply chain engagement, stakeholder consultation and third-party verification – can realistically operate in ASEAN countries, where legal gaps, cultural resistance and weak enforcement mechanisms persist.

Part II of the book then brings forward several Asian jurisdictions to analyse the development of human rights jurisdictions. The author wishes to state that this comes with a caveat that the countries included in this edition are by no means exclusive (and conclusive). It is, however, the wish of the authors that the selected jurisdictions can shed some light on demonstrating the challenges and uniqueness of Asia as a continent with diverse and different legal (and social) cultures.

Chapter seven discusses Japan and examines the evolving relationship between multinational corporate conduct and human rights protection within the Japanese legal and policy framework. It begins by outlining Japan's constitutional commitment to human rights – particularly through Article 13 of the Constitution – and explores how these guarantees interact with private corporate actors. The chapter then considers the growing influence of international and soft law instruments, such as the UNGPs and the OECD Guidelines for Multinational Enterprises, which have shaped Japan's increasingly global-facing posture. Particular attention is paid to Japan's recent legal and policy initiatives, including the 2020–2025 National Action Plan on Business and Human Rights, the 2022 Guidelines on Respecting Human Rights in Responsible Supply Chains and recent amendments to disability discrimination law. Through a structured exploration of domestic litigation, administrative guidance, ministerial tools and private international law, the chapter illustrates both the normative potential and practical limitations of Japan's current approach. It also considers Japan's cautious stance on extraterritoriality, offering comparative reflections on emerging European jurisprudence concerning parent company liability and human rights due diligence. Readers can expect a comprehensive and critical analysis of how Japan balances international alignment with domestic legal and cultural traditions, and how these dynamics shape the country's role in the global corporate accountability landscape.

Chapter eight on South Korea explores the special feature of corporate law in the country and offers a detailed and systematic analysis of South Korea's evolving legal framework for holding

[31] The law stated in this chapter is as of 30 September 2025. As of 30 September 2025, there are some moves to amend CSDDD under the so-called Omnibus proposals. They are still under discussion, and it remains uncertain how CSDDD would be amended.

MNCs accountable for human rights and ESG-related harms, especially in cross-border contexts. The authors evaluate how domestic substantive law, private international law and emerging ESG regulation interact to shape the legal landscape for corporate accountability in the country. The chapter begins by examining the unique structure of Korean corporate groups, in which real decision-making power often lies with informal or unincorporated entities (eg, group headquarters or dominant shareholders), complicating the attribution of legal responsibility. The special features of Korean corporate laws are further explored on issues relating to director's duty of care in corporate groups, director's liability and the business judgement rule, director's liability to third parties etc. In particular, this chapter evaluates how the Korean Commercial Code addresses this through doctrines such as quasi-director liability, veil-piercing and the business judgement rule, with increasing emphasis from the Supreme Court on directors' duties to monitor and establish internal control systems. The authors turn also to ESG-specific laws and attempt to find the approach of ESG governance in the country, together with a comprehensive overview of private international law aspects in Korea.

Chapter nine on the Philippines explores the Filipino legal framework that accommodates the standards contained in the Guiding Principles, including remedies for business-related human rights abuses. The chapter begins with a review of the 1987 Constitution, particularly its bifurcated structure: the Bill of Rights (Article III) and Social Justice provisions (Article XIII). It explains how the constitutional framework has enabled courts and the Commission on Human Rights (CHR) to adopt expansive interpretations of rights protection, including a social justice-based rationale that may extend to private actors. The chapter analyses the CHR's landmark National Inquiry on Climate Change – a novel attempt to apply the UNGPs domestically despite jurisdictional ambiguities. Several litigation strategies are then discussed in detail, with special attention to areas such as the 'Human Relations' chapter of the Civil Code of the Philippines, protective writs of *amparo* and *habeas data* against threats to life, liberty, or security, and 'expanded certiorari jurisdiction' of the Supreme Court to allow rights-based constitutional review. Sector-specific challenges are examined within this chapter, including extractive industries and mega-projects, platform labour and gender equality.

Chapter ten on Thailand provides a comprehensive legal and philosophical reflection on Thailand's adoption and implementation of the UNGPs, emphasising both doctrinal development and cultural resonance. Thailand stands out as the first country in Asia to adopt a National Action Plan (NAP) on Business and Human Rights – first in 2019, followed by a second NAP in 2023 – making it a significant case study in the region. The chapter traces the institutional role of the Department of Rights and Liberties Protection (DRLP) under the Ministry of Justice, which was charged in 2017 with developing and coordinating Thailand's BHR agenda.[32] The two NAPs reflect the UNGP's three-pillar framework (ie, state duty to protect, corporate responsibility to respect, access to remedy), with specific focus on labour rights, environmental protection and land rights, human rights defenders and cross-border investments and multinationals. The author emphasises the structural and legal coherence of the Thai approach, noting how the NAP aligns with a range of domestic policy instruments – such as the 13th National Economic and Social Development Plan and the National Security Policy – and international instruments including the ICCPR,[33] CEDAW[34] and the OECD Guidelines for Multinational Enterprises.

[32] Please also refer to ch 9 on the Philippines, in which the author points out a consolidated NAP has yet to materialise there.

[33] International Covenant on Civil and Political Rights (New York, 16 December 1966).

[34] Convention on the Elimination of All Forms of Discrimination against Women (New York, 18 December 1979).

India's chapter (Chapter eleven) takes a similar but slightly different approach in surveying the Indian jurisprudence through a review of chronologic development of landmark cases. This chapter states that the Indian judiciary has exhibited a progressive and inventive stance in dealing with intricate legal matters, encompassing both domestic legislation and international legal standards, as seen by its interpretation. It offers a rich and expansive examination of India's judicial response to human rights violations by MNCs, highlighting how Indian courts have deployed constitutional values, international legal principles and creative doctrinal development to protect vulnerable communities from corporate abuse. The chapter opens with a theoretical discussion of the power asymmetry between corporations and individuals, noting that weak enforcement, corruption and regulatory gaps often create environments where profit is prioritised over rights. Against this background, it traces India's growing judicial activism in enforcing corporate responsibility, especially in environmental, labour and health-related harms.

Part III of the book delves into specific issues concerning human rights violations and protection in Asia. These issues may not at face value be regarded as 'human rights' in an orthodox sense, the goal is to take a broader scope to see how 'in practice' certain topics are litigated and/or discussed in the region. While it is the goal of the author to cover as great a number of topics on human rights and multi-nations in Asia as possible, several prominent and perhaps 'trendy' topics are solicited herein to provide a taste of the present day challenges of the region.

Chapter twelve concerns climate change and environmental damage in Asia. This chapter investigates the emerging field of climate change litigation between private parties in Asia, situating Asian legal developments within the broader context of global trends. The author points out Japan, China, South Korea and other Asian states are bound to the internationally accepted temperature limits, similar to jurisdictions that have already experienced court rulings in favour of climate activists. Instead of focusing on many well-known administrative or constitutional cases brought against states, this chapter focuses exclusively on civil cases between non-state actors – especially those involving multinational corporations, financial institutions and NGOs. The first part of the chapter introduces the conceptual and doctrinal challenges in private climate litigation, including a lack of explicit rights to climate protection in most constitutions, procedural hurdles around standing and justiciability, causation and burden of proof issues under national tort law, and difficulties in classifying greenhouse gases (GHGs) emissions as 'nuisance' or 'pollution' for civil liability. The core of the chapter then presents a jurisdiction-by-jurisdiction survey of private climate litigation in Japan, China, and South Korea, currently the only Asian jurisdictions where such cases have been filed.

Chapter thirteen explores the notion of crimes against humanity. This chapter offers a doctrinally rich and regionally anchored analysis of crimes against humanity as defined in international law, with a particular focus on Asia's engagement – or absence thereof – with this body of norms. It begins by tracing the legal evolution of the concept, from its early articulation in the Nuremberg and Tokyo trials through to its modern codification in Article 7 of the Rome Statute and the 2019 Draft Articles on the Prevention and Punishment of Crimes Against Humanity developed by the International Law Commission (ILC). The chapter explores the customary status of crimes against humanity, the definitional elements of the offence – including the requirement of a widespread or systematic attack against a civilian population pursuant to a state or organisational policy – and the two critical contextual elements of knowledge and connection to such an attack. These doctrinal discussions are carefully linked to evolving jurisprudence in international criminal tribunals, such as the International Criminal Court (ICC). The author also discusses Asia's limited participation in the Rome Statute system, noting that only a small number of Asian states are parties to the International Criminal Court, and that engagement with ICC proceedings has been sporadic. It surveys ICC activity relating to the region, including investigations and proceedings involving Afghanistan, the Philippines, and Myanmar, and provides an overview of the ICC's institutional structure, jurisdictional scope and principle of complementarity. The chapter also details the various stages of ICC proceedings – from preliminary examination to trial and appeal – thereby providing readers with a comprehensive procedural context.

Chapter fourteen is on the notion of corporate crime, compliance programmes and criminal law. Readers may find that rather than approaching the 'human rights' law perspective, the authors took the approach of addressing corporate criminality from the perspective of criminal law and focusing on embodying the UNGPs by analysing two prominent economies in Asia: China and Japan. This chapter offers a comparative legal analysis of how Japan and China have integrated corporate human rights responsibilities – particularly under the UNGPs – into their criminal law systems, focusing on the regulation and punishment of corporate crimes. It examines not only doctrinal debates on corporate criminal liability but also the role of compliance programmes as mechanisms for crime prevention and sentencing mitigation. In the Japanese context, the authors trace the evolution from traditional German-influenced scepticism about corporate criminal responsibility to a more 'positive theory', which acknowledges the criminal agency of legal persons. In the Chinese context, the authors chart the development of corporate criminal liability since the 1997 Penal Code revisions, noting both broad legislative scope and restrained judicial practice. China's evolving criminal law now recognises over 128 corporate offences, yet enforcement remains weak due to ambiguous decision-making attribution, lenient sentencing and institutional hesitation to impose punitive damages on corporate entities. The chapter explores China's innovative 'compliance and non-indictment system', launched in 2018 and expanded in 2023, which allows prosecutors to defer or drop charges against corporations that adopt and implement effective compliance programmes.

IV. Summary

The UNGPs consist of three main parts: the state duty to protect human rights, the corporate responsibility to respect human rights, and access to remedy. Taking reference from these three main parts of the UNGPs as a basis, this book shall, through the forum for discussion and analysis provided by this series, discern the patterns in Asia for protection and violation of international human rights by in-depth thematic and Asian country-specific analysis. Through discerning an 'Asian' pattern on multinational businesses and human rights, the books will then go on to answer the series' central question: how has the modernisation of private international law codes and rules that have been taking place over the last decade all over Asia progressed?

2

Litigation against Corporations – Why Enforce Human Rights against Multinationals?

KOH MATSUKI AND ANTONIA BURKE

I. Introduction: What are Encouraging Multi-national Companies to Enforce Human Rights?

In a world where Environmental, Social, and Governance ('ESG') investing is becoming mainstream, multinational companies are increasingly expected to strengthen their commitment to human rights within their business operations.[1]

There are several key reasons for this shift:

A. Investor Expectations and ESG Criteria

ESG investors prioritise companies that demonstrate responsibility toward environmental sustainability, social welfare, and strong governance practices.[2] A core component of the 'S' in ESG is respect for human rights, which includes labour practices, community engagement, and ensuring that business activities do not harm vulnerable populations. Investors are pushing companies to address human rights more thoroughly because companies with strong ESG profiles often show better long-term financial performance, resilience, and lower risks.[3]

B. Reputational Risk and Consumer Demand

In the digital age, transparency is critical. Consumers are more aware of the ethical practices of companies and are increasingly choosing to support businesses that align with their values.

[1] R Tanaka, 'Challenges and Future Initiatives Regarding Business and Human Rights and Human Capital – Insights from an Investor's Perspective' (2023) *Japan Economic Research Institute*, www.jeri.or.jp/survey/ビジネスと人権・人的資本に関する課題と今後の/.

[2] EY, 'Why ESG performance is growing in importance for investors' (2023) *EY Insights*, www.ey.com/en_gl/insights/assurance/why-esg-performance-is-growing-in-importance-for-investors.

[3] V Agbakwuru, OB Onyenahazi, BO Antwi and K Oyewale, 'The Impact of Environmental, Social, and Governance (ESG) Reporting on Corporate Financial Performance' (2024) 5(9) *International Journal of Research Publication and Reviews* 3629–44, DOI: 10.55248/gengpi.5.0924.2710, www.researchgate.net/publication/384533952_The_Impact_of_Environmental_Social_and_Governance_ESG_Reporting_on_Corporate_Financial_Performance.

Human rights abuses such as forced labour, child labour, and violations of Indigenous rights can lead to significant reputational damage if exposed.[4] Social media amplifies these risks, meaning that a company's involvement in human rights violations can lead to public backlash, reduced consumer trust, and potential boycotts.

C. Regulatory Pressures

Governments and international organisations are implementing stricter regulations around human rights and corporate responsibility. For example, the European Union's proposed Corporate Sustainability Due Diligence Directive mandates[5] that companies take responsibility for addressing human rights and environmental impacts within their operations and supply chains. Non-compliance can result in legal penalties, making it financially crucial for companies to adopt a proactive approach to human rights issues.

D. Global Frameworks and Guidelines

Global frameworks such as the United Nations Guiding Principles on Business and Human Rights (UNGPs)[6] and the Organisation for Economic Co-operation and Development (OECD)'s Guidelines for Multinational Enterprises[7] set standards for how companies should address human rights in their operations. These guidelines urge businesses to conduct human rights due diligence, ensuring that they are not causing or contributing to human rights violations, directly or through their supply chains. Multinational companies, especially those with global supply chains, are expected to integrate these standards into their business practices to meet global expectations.

E. Long-term Financial Benefits

Companies that incorporate human rights into their core business practices often experience long-term financial benefits.[8] Ensuring good labour practices, fair wages, and safe working conditions leads to a more motivated workforce, lower turnover rates, and fewer disruptions from strikes or legal battles. Furthermore, companies with strong ESG practices are more likely to attract ESG investors, who represent a growing segment of the investment market.[9]

[4] BlackRock Investment Stewardship, 'Our Approach to Engagement on Corporate Human Rights Risks' (January 2025), www.blackrock.com/corporate/literature/publication/blk-commentary-engagement-on-human-rights.pdf.

[5] European Commission, 'Corporate Sustainability Due Diligence' (25 July 2024), commission.europa.eu/business-economy-euro/doing-business-eu/sustainability-due-diligence-responsible-business/corporate-sustainability-due-diligence_en.

[6] United Nations Office of the High Commissioner for Human Rights, 'Guiding Principles on Business and Human Rights: Implementing the United Nations "Protect, Respect and Remedy" Framework' (2011), www.ohchr.org/sites/default/files/documents/publications/guidingprinciplesbusinesshr_en.pdf.

[7] Organisation for Economic Co-operation and Development (OECD), 'OECD Guidelines for Multinational Enterprises on Responsible Business Conduct' (2023), www.oecd.org/en/publications/oecd-guidelines-for-multinational-enterprises-on-responsible-business-conduct_81f92357-en.html.

[8] K Marslev, 'Doing Well by Doing Right? Exploring the Potentials and Limitations of a Business Case for Human Rights' (2020) www.humanrights.dk/files/media/document/Rapport_DoingWell_tilg%C3%A6ngelig.pdf.

[9] R Kräussl, T Oladiran and D Stefanova, 'A review on ESG investing: Investors' expectations, beliefs and perceptions' (2023) 38(2) *Journal of Economic Surveys* 476–502. doi.org/10.1111/joes.12599.

As ESG investing becomes more prevalent, multinational companies must enhance their focus on human rights to meet investor expectations, avoid reputational risks, comply with regulations, and leverage the financial benefits of responsible business practices. Failing to address human rights can result in legal penalties, financial losses, and a damaged brand,[10] while taking proactive measures can lead to better sustainability and long-term success in global markets.

II. What Discourages Multinational Companies from Enforcing Human Rights?

On the other hand, multinational companies often fail to detect human rights risks in their supply chains or among their customers when implementing business and human rights initiatives. There are several reasons for this.

A. Complexity and Multi-Tiered Structure of Supply Chains

Many companies, especially large multinational corporations, have extremely complex and multi-layered supply chains.[11] These supply chains often extend across multiple countries and involve various subcontractors, making it difficult for companies to trace where products and services are coming from or how they are produced.[12] With so many tiers in the supply chain, it becomes challenging to detect human rights abuses, such as forced labour or unsafe working conditions, particularly when companies rely on lower-tier suppliers who may not be subject to the same scrutiny as first-tier suppliers.

B. Lack of Transparency and Information

In many cases, suppliers may not be forthcoming about the labour conditions in their operations or the practices of their own subcontractors.[13] For instance, Apple's major supplier, Foxconn, has faced multiple allegations regarding poor labour conditions, excessive overtime, and underage workers in its factories in China. Reports from organisations like China Labor Watch and *The New York Times* revealed that some factories had dangerous working conditions, forced student labour, and underreported violations.[14] This lack of transparency can make it difficult for companies to assess risks and ensure that human rights standards are being upheld throughout the supply chain. Moreover, some countries where suppliers operate may

[10] KPMG International, 'Addressing Human Rights in Business: Executive Perspectives' (December 2016), assets.kpmg.com/content/dam/kpmg/xx/pdf/2016/11/addressing-human-rights-in-business.pdf.

[11] N Peacock and T Mohin, 'Why Companies Must Address Human Rights in Their Supply Chains' (27 June 2024) www.bcg.com/publications/2024/addressing-human-rights-in-supply-chains.

[12] I McKinnon, 'The Growing Importance of Sustainability in Construction Supply Chains' (17 November 2020) www.chas.co.uk/blog/sustainable-construction-supply-chains/.

[13] P Hasle et al, 'Supply Chains' Role in Promoting Safety and Health in Construction and Agriculture: The LIFT-OSH Project' (2024) osha.europa.eu/sites/default/files/documents/Supply-chains-role-promoting-safety-and-health-in-construction-and-agriculture-LIFT-OSH_EN.pdf.

[14] C Duhigg and D Barboza, 'In China, Human Costs Are Built Into an iPad' (*The New York Times*, 25 January 2012) www.nytimes.com/2012/01/26/business/ieconomy-apples-ipad-and-the-human-costs-for-workers-in-china.html.

lack strong labour regulations or oversight, leading to a greater risk of human rights violations going unnoticed.

C. Geographical and Legal Barriers

Human rights risks often occur in countries with weak legal frameworks or enforcement mechanisms, making it harder for companies to monitor and address abuses. Legal systems in certain countries may not have strong protections for workers, Indigenous communities, or vulnerable populations, which allows for human rights violations to persist without legal consequences.[15] Additionally, geographical distance from headquarters or main markets complicates efforts to detect these issues in remote or politically unstable regions.

D. Subcontracting and Informal Work

The use of subcontractors and informal labour arrangements adds another layer of complexity. Subcontracting relationships are often less visible to the primary company, which can lead to difficulties in ensuring compliance with human rights standards. Workers in informal sectors, such as day labourers or temporary workers, are often at higher risk of exploitation because they fall outside formal legal protections. In fact, reports from Amnesty International and The Guardian revealed[16] that thousands of migrant workers from countries like Nepal, India, and Bangladesh were working in exploitative conditions to build Qatar's World Cup infrastructure. The primary companies and contractors had little oversight over these workers due to layers of subcontracting. The workers lacked proper contracts, had their passports confiscated, and faced wage theft.

E. Resource Constraints and Limited Auditing

Even when companies attempt to audit their supply chains, the sheer scale and cost of doing so comprehensively can be prohibitive. Many businesses do not have the resources or capacity to conduct thorough audits across all tiers of their supply chains. In addition, audits are often scheduled in advance, which can lead suppliers to temporarily improve working conditions to pass inspections, masking the true risks present in everyday operations. In fact, Fabio Roia, President of the Court of Milan, told Reuters that companies don't invest enough in their control systems and don't normally question the extremely cheap prices contractors offer to provide goods or services regarding a incident, in which a sub-contractor of Manufactures Dior tasked with the production of leather items was accused by Italian prosecutors in June of being a front for an operation that exploited workers.[17]

[15] A Shimbun, 'What Are Human Rights? Explanation of Their Relationship with the Constitution and SDGs, and Examples of Everyday Human Rights Issues' (April 2023) www.asahi.com/sdgs/article/15216166.

[16] P Pattisson, 'Revealed: 6,500 Migrant Workers Have Died in Qatar Since World Cup Awarded' *The Guardian* (23 February 2021), www.theguardian.com/global-development/2021/feb/23/revealed-migrant-worker-deaths-qatar-fifa-world-cup-2022.

[17] E Anzolin, E Parodi and S Ognibene, 'Inside Luxury Goods' Broken Audit System' (*Reuters*, 31 December 2024) www.reuters.com/business/retail-consumer/inside-luxury-goods-broken-audit-system-2024-12-31/.

F. Customer Risks and Data Gaps

When it comes to customers, companies may also fail to identify risks due to data gaps. For instance, businesses may lack information about how their products are being used by customers, which can lead to unintended human rights consequences. A lack of real-time data or the inability to track customer activities across jurisdictions can make it difficult to detect potential abuses, such as the misuse of technology or resources that could harm communities or individuals.

To sum up, detecting human rights risks in supply chains and among customers is a complex challenge for companies due to factors such as the multi-tiered nature of supply chains, lack of transparency, geographical and legal barriers, and resource limitations. As ESG investing and global expectations for corporate responsibility grow, businesses are increasingly pressured to find solutions to these challenges, which include greater transparency, better auditing practices, and collaboration with stakeholders to uphold human rights standards.

III. A Key Framework

In this section, we would like to introduce a practical case around business and human rights in Australia, Japan and Korea. Before we step into the discussion though, we ought to introduce the notion called Free, Prior, and Informed Consent (FPIC),[18] which often becomes a main discussion point in business and human rights.

International companies must follow the FPIC of Indigenous peoples because it is a fundamental human rights principle that ensures respect for their self-determination, cultural heritage, and land rights. The FPIC process empowers Indigenous communities by granting them the right to give or withhold consent for projects that affect their lands, territories, waters or resources. This is essential in preserving their livelihoods and cultural practices, which are often deeply tied to the land they inhabit.

FPIC is part of international human rights law, enshrined in documents such as the United Nations Declaration on the Rights of Indigenous Peoples (UNDRIP),[19] which asserts that Indigenous peoples must have the opportunity to participate in decision-making processes and provide or withhold consent for activities that impact their territories and way of life. Failure to comply with FPIC can result in conflicts, legal challenges, and reputational damage for corporations, while adherence demonstrates a commitment to ethical business practices and sustainable development.

Moreover, by respecting FPIC, companies can avoid disruptions in project timelines and foster stronger relationships with local communities, ultimately contributing to more successful and socially responsible business operations. FPIC also ensures that projects are carried out in a way that mitigates environmental harm, particularly in sensitive areas like forests, where Indigenous peoples often play a critical role in conservation efforts.[20]

[18] Institute for Human Rights and Business, 'What is Free, Prior and Informed Consent (FPIC)?' (13 December 2022), www.ihrb.org/resources/what-is-free-prior-and-informed-consent-fpic.

[19] United Nations Global Compact, 'The Business Reference Guide to the UN Declaration on the Rights of Indigenous Peoples' (2013), unglobalcompact.org/library/541.

[20] National Forestry Council and UN-REDD Programme Indonesia, 'Policy Recommendation: Free, Prior and Informed Consent (FPIC) Instrument for Indigenous Communities and/or Local Communities Who Will Be Affected by REDD+ Activities' (2011) www.un-redd.org/sites/default/files/2021-10/FPIC%20English%20version.pdf.

By adhering to FPIC, international companies not only align with legal obligations but also help support broader goals of environmental sustainability and social justice. This approach is increasingly important in a global context where responsible corporate behaviour is scrutinised by consumers and investors alike. However, FPIC of Indigenous peoples is often overlooked in the realm of business and human rights for several reasons:

A. Lack of Legal Enforcement

One of the primary reasons FPIC is ignored is the lack of legally binding mechanisms to enforce it at the international level. While FPIC is recognised in international frameworks like the United Nations Declaration on the Rights of Indigenous Peoples (UNDRIP), it is not universally enforced by domestic laws. Specialists point out that many governments such as the United States,[21] Australia[22] and New Zealand[23] have yet to fully integrate FPIC into their legal frameworks, making it easier for businesses to bypass this principle without immediate legal repercussions.

B. Economic Pressures and Business Interests

For many companies, the potential economic benefits of accessing Indigenous lands for resource extraction, infrastructure development, or commercial activities outweigh the perceived risks of not obtaining FPIC. In sectors like mining, forestry, and agriculture, where large-scale land use is necessary, businesses often prioritise short-term profits over the long-term ethical responsibility to engage Indigenous communities. This focus on profit can lead to companies pushing ahead with projects without adequately consulting or gaining the consent of affected communities.[24]

C. Complexity of Implementation

Implementing FPIC is a complex and resource-intensive process. It requires companies to invest time, money, and effort into understanding local contexts, providing information in culturally appropriate formats, and conducting consultations with potentially diverse Indigenous groups. Many companies, particularly smaller ones or those with limited experience working in areas with Indigenous populations, may lack the resources or expertise to properly navigate FPIC. As a result, they may either neglect the process entirely or conduct superficial consultations without genuinely seeking consent.

[21] A Page, 'Indigenous Peoples' Free Prior and Informed Consent in the Inter-American Human Rights System' (2004) *Sustainable Development Law & Policy*, digitalcommons.wcl.american.edu/cgi/viewcontent.cgi?article=1374&context=sdlp.

[22] Corrs Chambers Westgarth, 'FPIC in the Australian Context: Now and into the Future' (2022) www.corrs.com.au/insights/fpic-in-the-australian-context-now-and-into-the-future.

[23] A Feinstein and B Welna, 'The United Nations Declaration on the Rights of Indigenous Peoples and Climate Change' (Georgetown University Law Center, 2021) www.law.georgetown.edu/wp-content/uploads/2021/04/UNDRIP-Presentation-Andrew-Feinstein-Ben-Welna.pdf.

[24] Food and Agriculture Organization of the United Nations (FAO), 'Free Prior and Informed Consent: An Indigenous Peoples' Right and a Good Practice for Local Communities' (2016) openknowledge.fao.org/handle/10986/1232.

D. Conflicts with Government and Corporate Interests

In some cases, governments themselves may prioritise national development goals over the rights of Indigenous peoples, creating conflicts of interest that complicate the implementation of FPIC. Amazon Watch, a non-profit group, points out[25] that Governments across the Americas have been reported to prioritise economic gains over the physical and cultural survival of Indigenous peoples. This approach often leads to the approval of projects on Indigenous lands without proper consultation or consent, undermining the principles of FPIC. This dynamic makes it difficult for businesses to engage in meaningful consent processes, as they may feel they have already received governmental approval to proceed.

IV. From Case Study in Australia (and Japan) an Indigenous Group Filed a Human Rights Grievance Complaint against International Finance Institutions Regarding the Project in the Tiwi Islands

As FPIC is often ignored or inadequately implemented in the business and human rights arena, particularly in the Global South as the International Fund for Agricultural Development (IFAD) points out,[26] affected communities frequently find themselves forced to actively advocate for their rights against powerful multinational companies. This dynamic arises due to several factors.

On 4 April 2023, Traditional Owners of Tiwi Islands in the Northern Territory of Australia filed human rights grievances[27] against financial institutions supporting the Barossa gas project operated by Santos Ltd located in waters off northern Australia.

The group claimed that the syndicated loan provided by the banks could be used for Barossa gas field developments in waters off the Northern Territory in Australia that are causing and will cause adverse human rights impacts on the Tiwi Claimants and their communities (Impacted Tiwi Communities). The claimants urged the financial institutions to not provide support for the Darwin LNG extension project.

According to the claimants, the human rights complaints were sent to the following banks for an apparent failure to undertake adequate human rights due diligence for the US$1 billion loan in addition to breaches of policy and international human rights standards, including the failure to obtain Free, Prior and Informed Consent (FPIC):

- Australia and New Zealand Banking Group Limited ANZ (Australia)
- Commonwealth Bank of Australia CBA (Australia)
- Westpac Banking Corporation (Australia)
- National Australia Bank NAB (Australia)
- ING (Netherlands)

[25] Amazon Watch, 'Governments Prioritize Profit Over Indigenous Peoples' Rights' (8 August 2012) amazonwatch.org/news/2012/0808-governments-prioritize-profit-over-indigenous-peoples-rights.

[26] International Fund for Agricultural Development (IFAD), 'Indigenous Peoples' Leaders from the Global South Assert Their Right to Self-Determination' (10 February 2025), www.ifad.org/en/w/news/indigenous-peoples-leaders-from-the-global-south-assert-their-right-to-self-determination.

[27] Equity Generation Lawyers, 'Human Rights' (2023), equitygenerationlawyers.com/human-rights-2/.

- DNB Bank (Norway)
- Citigroup (USA)
- Royal Bank of Canada (Canada)
- DBS Bank (Singapore)
- Mitsubishi UFJ Financial Group (Japan)
- Sumitomo Mitsui Banking Corporation (Japan)
- Mizuho Financial Group (Japan).

Antonia Burke, an Indigenous human rights advocate, highlighted the environmental risks and the destructive legacy of Santos' projects across the country. Some of the Tiwi Islanders, along with other traditional owners, are calling on superannuation funds to withdraw their investments from Santos to prevent further harm to their lands and communities.

Antonia testifies:

> In the late 1960s the Australian Federal government gave permission for seismic testing and exploration drilling to be done in the Timor Sea just off the coastline of the Tiwi Islands.[28] More than 2 decades later the government gave permission for an offshore gas project to go ahead within 6km of the Tiwi Islands coastline. The entire system that operates around these decisions were aware of these activities, yet Tiwi people who are the residents of the Tiwi Islands, were not considered 'relevant people' to be consulted or have any rights to express their concerns about the impacts on their entire way of life. They were completely ignored.
>
> In May 2021 I was facilitating a gathering of over 260 Indigenous women from across the Northern Territory, I shared with everyone that I was from the Tiwi Islands. One of the women came to me and said 'oh you're from the Tiwi Islands, how do you feel about Barossa?' I said 'what's Barossa?' She seemed shocked that I didn't know what she was talking about. She said that when we leave the gathering I should look into it, but she didn't tell me what it was.
>
> When I returned home I went on a search for information about this 'Barossa' to find out what they were talking about. I learned that Santos had been given permission by our government to drill for gas just off the coastline of our home. After a few google searches and phone calls to gather information, my first question was 'what do Tiwi people say about this?' and the responses I got were the same, no-one actually knew how Tiwi people felt or if they even knew about it.
>
> I called a family member who is a Regional Councillor for our community, and asked if they knew anything about it, and they said no. So I flew home and I walked around our whole community asking everyone if they knew about it, and everyone I spoke to said 'karlu' which means 'no' in Tiwi language. They knew nothing, except one person who said they had heard rumors about something happening offshore a long time ago. There are approximately 350 residents in our community, a considerable portion of the residents are representatives on the Tiwi Land Council, Tiwi Islands Regional Council, and are Trustees of the 8 Clan Groups from across the Tiwi Islands. One of the people I asked was the Mayor of the Tiwi Islands at the time. They said they didn't know anything about it and asked me to go and find out more information. I also asked Directors of the Munupi Aboriginal Corporation (Munupi is the name of the land and people from our community called Pirlangimpi), Tiwi Resources and members of the Tiwi Land Council. The same answer came 'karlu' we don't know about this.
>
> I then did thorough research about the entire project. I learned that there would be drilling, a pipeline, an FPSO, that the project was originally owned by ConocoPhilips and then bought by Santos, that the Australian Federal Government and the Northern Territory Government had been planning this for

[28] See public.neats.nopta.gov.au/nopims.

decades and that there is over 59,000 square kilometers of offshore acreage sold off to overseas buyers right off the Tiwi Islands coastline.

I went back to my community and shared this information at the monthly community meeting where all residents attend to talk about what's happening in the community. The reaction of people at the meeting was sad to watch. Elders, leaders, community members standing up waving their hands in the air, saying why don't they know about it, asking each other who knew, pacing back and forward, worried, angry, scared and full of questions. The overwhelming response was that they didn't want this to happen and why weren't they told about it.

Elders, leaders and clan group members asked me to go and find people who could help get answers to their questions. And so I did. I contacted several people across the country who were also responding to similar situations. We found a local organisation called Environment Centre Northern Territory who are the peak community sector environment organization in the Northern Territory of Australia, and asked if they could support us with community education and would they be willing to have a meeting with the community. Thankfully they said yes. For the next 10 months a group of us travelled to all communities across the Tiwi Islands speaking to as many people as we could who make up the population of approximately 2,500 people, to provide project information, maps, getting everything translated from English into Tiwi language. Our group included local Tiwi people such as the Mayor, regional Councilors, cultural leaders, elders, teachers, Clan group leaders and trustees.

Tiwi peoples response was consistent. Why haven't Santos come to talk to us about this? Why didn't the Federal or Northern Territory governments tell us before they sold off our sea country? Who is paying for this? Who is buying this gas? Do they know that we are here? Do they know that we will be affected? Is there anything we can do about it? We want them to come and talk to us.

Elders and leaders asked for legal representation to see if they had a case to gain the right to be consulted. Although the right to consultation is enshrined in international law, the Elders and leaders were ready to use the legal system for this right in Australian courts.

In March 2022 Tiwi elders joined Larrakia Indigenous coastal community members and took the South Korean government's export credit agencies to court saying they have not given their free, prior and informed consent, that the Barossa gas project will damage their pristine sea country, threaten local marine life which play a central role in Tiwi culture, ceremonies and the local ecotourism industry.

The intention of this legal challenge was to prevent the South Korean Government from lending approximately \$AU964 million to the Barossa gas project via its export credit agencies, the Export-Import Bank of Korea (KEXIM) and the Korea Trade Insurance Corporation (K-SURE).

Tiwi Island clan leaders started to use their voices and demand that their human rights be respected.

One clan member and plaintiff said: 'Under Australian law and in accordance with Aboriginal tradition, the Jikilaruwu clan is the owner of the sea country where that gas pipeline will go through. We are the decision makers for that sea country. Santos did not fully explain their plans to build a gas pipeline along our coast. Santos did not explain any of the risks. We were told briefly about the pipeline in 2018 [by previous owners ConocoPhillips] and we said "No" to the project. They said it wasn't happening. Now we find out they went behind our back. Santos wants to lay the pipeline through our sea country without our consent. By taking the South Korean Government to court to stop this gas project, we are protecting our family and our land. This gas project puts our way of life at risk.'

Another Senior Tiwi Traditional Owner said: 'The pipeline is too close to Cape Fourcroy. There is a reef there with lots of turtles and dugongs. The turtles lay their eggs on that beach and we go hunting in that area. We use that coastline for camping and fishing. In the dry season we take our children there every week. We teach them about our culture and dreaming stories. I was taught there on that sea country and on that land country the same way by my father and grandfather.'

A Senior Larrakia Traditional Owner said: 'The Barossa project is devastating for us and our future. It will have a big impact, especially for Aboriginal people. This kind of thing has been happening to Dangalaba and Larrakia people for over forty years. Dangalaba people do not want more heavy industry in Darwin harbour. The mangrove systems in Darwin harbour are important to our sea life – it's where we go to do our hunting, fishing and gathering. We take fish from the harbour, and oyster, crabs, prawns, mussels, longbums from the mangroves and we use mangrove worms for important medicine. There are many sacred sites around Darwin harbour – both on land and in the water. The most important site for Dangalaba and Larrakia people is the site of Darramarrangamanidj (our creator). She resides at a place on Cox Peninsula, but the gas pipeline through the harbour cuts right through her dreaming track.'

All three elders said: 'We hope that we win this case and that no one will want to give any more money to Santos. If they do, we will be ready to fight them too. We should have been consulted about this project. If they don't want to speak to us face to face, we will keep saying, "No". We do not want this project to go ahead.'

Tiwi and Larrakia people were ignored and the finance went ahead. Not one of the people involved in this process spoke to the community members, not one of them had ever been to the Tiwi Islands or connected with where their money was going. Tiwi peoples rights to free, prior and informed consent were pushed aside.

I was then instructed by the Elders and leaders to invite lawyers who specialise in environmental law to come and help with gaining the right to be consulted. We learned that if community members and residents wanted to be consulted, we could write a letter to Santos, and to the government regulator to request consultation. And so we did that, we wrote a letter asking to be consulted. They ignored us.

By this stage Santos had already had the drill rig sent from overseas and they were in place just off the coastline. When we went to the Federal Court for the hearing, the drill rig had already started drilling, they still pushed ahead and ignored the impacted communities.

By September 2022, we won our case. Santos had to pull their drill rig out of the sea bed, pack it up and come and consult with all Tiwi clan groups. They stated that they appealed the courts decision out of responsibilities to their investors, with absolutely no regard for Indigenous people.

What this case did was show Indigenous Australians that there was already a law that existed that said 'if you're going to be impacted by offshore projects you have a right to be consulted about it. And you are considered a relevant person to be consulted along with the long list of other relevant people.'

What this exposed was that the fossil fuel industry and the Australian Federal Government Regulator National Offshore Petroleum Safety & Environment Management Authority (NOPSEMA) didn't include Indigenous coastal communities in their environment plans, therefore, when companies apply for finance they can say that Indigenous people aren't going to be impacted by the money being loaned.

When we won the court case, we made the assumption that this would trigger a response from all stakeholders and investors to comply with their human rights policies; that Australian banks and investors would comply with their Reconciliation Action Plans; that banks and other investors would follow their due diligence processes to consult with affected Indigenous coastal communities; we assumed that this would be relevant for coastal communities of Timor-Leste and Indonesia as both countries are in the environment that may be affected (EMBA). However, none of this happened and we realized we would have to continue to do the government, industries and investors work for them, to make them accountable.

The Australian Federal Government invested millions of dollars to review and implement consultation guidelines for offshore regulations. They sent out a notification to the entire fossil fuel industry in Australia which said that everyone needed to attend a briefing on what this change to the regulations means. We assumed this would be the same for banks, superannuation funds, investors and stakeholders.

Fossil fuel companies were extremely unhappy and government lobbying increased to wind this back as it was causing delay and financial loss to their projects. They were only interested in looking after their investors to maintain the relationships.

I sat with Tiwi people and wrote consultation guidelines with the terms and conditions of how they wanted to be consulted. We sent these guidelines to Santos and the government regulator. Santos completely ignored those guidelines, so we notified the federal regulator of this, and the regulator said that they can't tell mining companies how to do their consultation.

We learned that when a fossil fuel company is applying for finance, there is a question about whether Indigenous people will be impacted by their operations. We were told in our meetings with Australian and international banks that Santos had said no to this question in their loan applications. Based on this, we expected that the banks would review their loan contracts as they were now fully aware about the Australian Federal Court outcomes.

None of this happened.

So again, Tiwi and Larrakia people engaged lawyers who specialise in human rights and international law to ask if there was anything we could do about it. This led to writing and lodging human rights complaints to 15 banks and export credit agencies and 25 superannuation companies.

Every single one of them rejected the complaint. We learned that a bank receives the complaint, and they can only action the complaint if their client accepts the complaint against them. Santos did not accept the complaints and therefore Tiwi and Larrakia people were ignored. All of the power sits with the fossil fuel companies. The banks said they couldn't discuss anything with Tiwi people because they had to maintain the confidentiality of their client.

Tiwi people were very upset about this. In the human rights complaints, the elders invited all investors to come to the Tiwi Islands to have a meeting, and to connect with the environment that their investment was having an impact on. They all ignored this invitation. So we travelled to Brisbane and Sydney to attend the annual general meetings of the banks so we could speak directly to the CEO's and directors in front of their shareholders, to ask them why they keep ignoring us. Three of the four big Australian banks later agreed to visit the Tiwi Islands. At the time of writing this, only one CEO has come, and another will come in a few weeks. The others have said they won't come.

It appears that the only reason they've come is because of the public embarrassment and that it made them look bad in the media, not because they felt a responsibility to do the right thing.

The Japanese and South Korean stakeholders in the Barossa Gas Project wouldn't communicate with Tiwi people at all, so we flew to Tokyo and Seoul to meet with them.

A Tiwi elder said: 'We feel so insignificant. Like we don't matter. What else could we possibly do or say to make the banks re-think what they're doing by investing in companies that are destroying our world. They don't care enough to take us seriously, if they did care they would consult with Indigenous people to see if we are ok with what's happening. They don't live here, we do. We have a right to protect and maintain our environment, our economy, and our ancient cultural and spiritual practices and beliefs.'

I believe that the power still sits with the people. That when enough people come forward to stand up for their rights, we can create positive change, to protect our homes, our environment, and our cultural heritage. When people are connected to a place, they make better and more informed decisions, otherwise it's just a transaction.

A. Barossa Gas Project: What's been Discussed

The Barossa gas project[29] is a major offshore development located in the Timor Sea, about 300 kilometers north of Darwin, Australia. It is operated by Santos, an Australian oil and gas company, in partnership with SK E&S, a Korean energy company, and JERA, a Japanese power company. Its primary goal is to replace the dwindling output of the Bayu-Undan field to ensure a continuous supply of natural gas to the Darwin liquefied natural gas (LNG) plant, which Santos also operates.

Integral to this project is the construction of a Floating Production, Storage, and Offloading (FPSO) facility. The plans include drilling up to eight subsea wells in the Barossa field. A subsea

[29] Offshore Technology, 'Barossa Project, Australia' (22 March 2024), www.offshore-technology.com/projects/barossa-offshore-development-project/.

pipeline will also be constructed to transport the processed gas from the FPSO to the Darwin plant. The project is expected to produce 3.7 million tonnes of LNG annually over its 25-year lifespan.

The intended effects of this project[30] include enhancing Australia's position in the global LNG market, creating jobs, maintaining energy security, and supporting the local and national economy through LNG exports.

However, civil society organisations such as Japan Center for a Sustainable Environment and Society (JACSES) points out[31] that even though FPIC should be obtained from the communities, Tiwi islanders have not been meaningfully consulted at all plus the project is quite problematic also from a human-rights perspective.

According to A Business Reference Guide of United Nations Declaration on the Rights of Indigenous Peoples,[32] FPIC is fundamental to the UN Declaration as a measure to ensure that Indigenous peoples' rights are protected. The UN Special Rapporteur on the Rights of Indigenous Peoples made clear[33] as well that consultation and consent together are a special requirement safeguarding substantive human rights firmly enshrined in international law including the right to self-determination.

A Business Reference Guide of United Nations Declaration on the Rights of Indigenous Peoples also clarifies that 'consultation and consent together are a special requirement safeguarding substantive human rights firmly enshrined in international law, including the right to self-determination.'

However, in practice, the FPIC process often takes place at the same time as other processes. The guidebook clarified that 'Business should remember that FPIC is not a mere formality to be obtained. FPIC should be obtained before the proposed activity starts (recognizing that the timeline for obtaining FPIC can interfere with government timelines for issuing licenses and approvals), and is only valid if obtained after all relevant information has been provided to indigenous peoples.'

JACSES points out that not obtaining the FPIC for affected Indigenous peoples from Tiwi violates the JBIC Guidelines for Confirmation of Environmental and Social Considerations and the Equator Principles, which private banks should comply with when providing financing.

B. How International Financial Institutions are Reacting to Human Rights Complaints?

i. Australian Banks

Peter King, CEO of Westpac, kept his promise to consult with the Indigenous leaders of Tiwi. According to a report from the Australian Financial Review,[34] Mr King had originally offered

[30] Santos, 'Barossa Gas Export Pipeline Fact Sheet' (October 2023) www.santos.com/wp-content/uploads/2023/10/Barossa-GEP-Fact-Sheet-October-2023.pdf.

[31] Japan Center for a Sustainable Environment and Society (JACSES), 'Joint Statement: NGOs urge Japanese financial institutions to stop developing/supporting the Scarborough gas field in Australia' (28 March 2024), /jacses.org/en/414/.

[32] United Nations Global Compact, 'The Business Reference Guide to the UN Declaration on the Rights of Indigenous Peoples' (2013), unglobalcompact.org/library/541.

[33] SJ Rombouts, 'Consultation and Consent Norms under ILO Convention No. 169 and the UN Declaration on the Rights of Indigenous Peoples Compared' (2017), www.ohchr.org/sites/default/files/Documents/Issues/IPeoples/EMRIP/FPIC/RomboutsSJ.pdf.

[34] Australian Financial Review, 'Westpac's Peter King keeps his promise on Tiwi Islands consultation' (3 October 2024), www.afr.com/companies/financial-services/westpac-s-peter-king-keeps-his-promise-on-tiwi-islands-consultation-20241003-p5kfkq.

to consult via a video call with the Indigenous community, but he visited Tiwi Island in person in September 2024 to meet with Indigenous leaders about Santos' $5.8 billion Barossa gas project.

On 30 September 2024, he met members of the Larrakia Nation in Darwin, and then travelled to the Tiwi Islands on 1–2 October 2024, which is 30 minutes north of Darwin by light plane.

Mr King and the Commonwealth Bank's Matt Comyn and ANZ chief executive Shayne Elliott had implied in 2023 that they would visit Tiwi Islands to meet with Indigenous leaders and understand the impact of the project.

At the stage of 30 September, the Australian Financial Review reported that ANZ rejected this complaint in May 2024 because Santos had 'declined to participate in the mechanism's process', according to a letter the bank sent the firm last month.

ii. Japanese Banks

Almost a year after the complaints were lodged, the Tiwi Islanders also visited Japan in February 2024 as three major banks including Mitsubishi UFJ Financial Group (MUFG), Sumitomo Mitsui Financial Group (SMFG), and Mizuho Financial Group (Mizuho FG), agreed to meet with them.[35] The Tiwi Islanders stated that it poses a threat to their human rights, cultural heritage and environment. Pirrawayingi, a Tiwi Islander elder along with Therese Bourke and Antonia Burke, aimed to raise awareness about their deep spiritual, cultural and environmental connection to the ecosystem, sea and land that the project would impact.

By meeting with three Japanese banks in person in Tokyo (MUFG on 22 February 2024, SMFG on 20 February 2024, and Mizuho on 21 January), exchanging thoughts at banks' headquarters, the Tiwi Islanders told banks to reconsider the finance of the projects due to its failure to adequately address human rights concerns and the environmental risks it posed. They emphasised the importance of sustainable practices and the protection of their traditional way of life, which relies heavily on the sea and its resources.

iii. Court Case Regarding Santos Barossa Gas Project

Tiwi Islanders also engaged in the local jurisdiction system in the case of *Munkara v Santos NA Barossa Pty Ltd (No 5)*.[36] On 30 October 2023 Simon Munkara, a member of the Jikilaruwu clan, filed proceedings and applied for an urgent injunction to prevent Santos commencing pipeline work on the Barossa gas project. The Tiwi Traditional Owner claimed that Santos has not properly assessed submerged cultural heritage along the route of its Barossa export pipeline. On 15 January 2024, the judge dismissed the case.

a. Timeline

In 2019 Santos submitted an environmental plan to (NOPSEMA) to construct the Barossa offshore field to an LNG processing facility in the Northern Territory. The government regulator (NOPSEMA) on 9 March 2020 accepted Santos' environmental proposal to construct the pipeline.

[35] Market Forces, 'Tiwi traditional owners take on Japan's biggest banks' (n.d.), stories.marketforces.org.au/tiwi-traditional-owners-take-on-japans-biggest-banks.

[36] [2024] FCA 717.

In September 2022 Santos was forced to stop drilling at the field roughly 130 km from the Tiwi Islands coastline in northern Australia after the Federal Court ruled it had failed to consult Indigenous people on the nearby Tiwi Islands sufficiently. On 4 April 2023, Traditional Owners, Elders and clan members filed human rights grievances against financial institutions.

In October 2023, proceedings were commenced by three applicants from the Tiwi Islands of the Jikilaruwu, Munupi, and Malawu clans (Applicants) alleging that there was a 'significant new environmental risk' to their cultural heritage, caused by the project, that was not accounted for in the original environmental plan.

On 1 November 2023 Santos was ordered to stop constructing their underwater gas export pipeline north of Darwin, due to an emergency injunction sought by a Tiwi Islands traditional owner named Simon Munkara.

On 15 November 2023, the Australian Federal Court extended an earlier injunction that forced pipelaying operations for the Barossa project to stop until there was a hearing of claims over the approval process. However, the latter injunction only applied to a certain part of the pipeline infrastructure as it runs southward from the Timor Sea past Melville Island to the Darwin LNG project.

On 15 January 2024, the Australian Federal Court rejected the claims made by a Tiwi Island group that Santos' underwater gas pipeline (Project Barossa) would damage the sea country and anger two creatures of their Dreaming stories.

In February 2024, Santos and its Barossa joint venture partners announced an investment of up to $10 million in Northern Territory coastal Aboriginal communities and homelands as the development phase of the project progresses.

V. Conclusion

Disregard for the FPIC in the business world, particularly in dealings with Indigenous communities and those in the Global South, highlights the critical role that institutional investors and pension funds must play in demanding greater accountability from companies. In fact, BlackRock[37] was the subject of an OECD complaint for investing in companies accused of violating Indigenous land rights and environmental standards in the Amazon. This case illustrates how investors ignoring FPIC risks can face formal accountability challenges. As large investors wield considerable influence, they can act as a powerful force for ensuring that corporations respect human rights and environmental standards, particularly regarding the treatment of vulnerable communities.

A. Institutional Investors' Role in ESG and Human Rights Accountability

With the rise of ESG investing, institutional investors, such as pension funds and asset managers, are increasingly expected to consider not just financial returns but also the broader impact of their investments on society and the environment. Human rights, including FPIC, are a crucial

[37] *The Guardian*, 'BlackRock under pressure over climate and human rights record' (20 November 2024), www.theguardian.com/environment/2024/nov/20/blackrock-climate-human-rights.

part of the 'S' (Social) in ESG. When companies fail to uphold FPIC for example, they are not only violating ethical norms but also exposing themselves to legal, financial, and reputational risks. Institutional investors must hold these companies accountable to mitigate these risks and ensure long-term sustainable returns for their beneficiaries

B. Fulfilling Fiduciary Duty

Asset managers and pension funds, which manage the retirement savings of millions of workers, have a fiduciary duty to act in the best interests of their beneficiaries. This duty extends beyond short-term financial gains to include the management of long-term risks associated with issues such as climate change and human rights. The Government Pension Fund Global (GPFG) of Norway provides[38] a compelling example of how responsible investment strategies can align with fiduciary duty. According to Norges Bank Investment Management, the fund's risk-based divestments – many of which are linked to concerns over human rights and climate change – have not only mitigated ethical and reputational risks but have also enhanced financial performance. In fact, these divestments increased the cumulative return on equity management by 0.64 percentage point since 2012, with climate-related and human rights-related divestments contributing 0.30 and 0.16 percentage point respectively. This evidence underscores that integrating ESG considerations into investment decision-making is not only ethically prudent but financially sound, reinforcing the broader interpretation of fiduciary duty in today's investment landscape.

Institutional investors, including pension funds, are therefore in a unique position to push companies to adopt more responsible business practices. By requiring better disclosure on human rights issues, they ensure that companies align with global sustainability goals. This approach not only protects beneficiaries' long-term interests but also contributes to a more just and equitable global economy, according to PRI.[39]

C. Alignment with International Standards and Best Practices

Institutional investors and pension funds have a responsibility to ensure that the companies they invest in adhere to internationally recognised frameworks, such as the UN Declaration on the Rights of Indigenous Peoples (UNDRIP)[40] and the OECD Guidelines for Multinational Enterprises.[41]

According to the OECD Guidelines for Multinational Enterprises, institutional investors are expected to carry out due diligence to identify, prevent, and mitigate adverse impacts on human rights, including those of Indigenous Peoples. The Guidelines emphasise that investors should use their leverage to influence investee companies to respect internationally recognised human rights standards.

[38] Norges Bank Investment Management, *Responsible Investment 2024*, www.nbim.no/contentassets/ad990bb856b94063aa2165c3715a7a85/gpfg-responsible-investment-2024.pdf.

[39] Principles for Responsible Investment, *Making Voting Count: Investor voting practices and shareholder proposals on climate change* (2023), www.unpri.org/download?ac=19441.

[40] United Nations Department of Economic and Social Affairs, *United Nations Declaration on the Rights of Indigenous Peoples* (n.d.), social.desa.un.org/issues/indigenous-peoples/united-nations-declaration-on-the-rights-of-indigenous-peoples.

[41] OECD, *Responsible Business Conduct for Institutional Investors* (2017), mneguidelines.oecd.org/RBC-for-Institutional-Investors.pdf.

D. Shaping Corporate Behaviour Through Shareholder Engagement

As large shareholders, institutional investors can engage directly with company management to demand that human rights to be fully integrated into business strategies and operations. This can take the form of filing shareholder resolutions, voting against boards that do not prioritise human rights, or engaging in dialogues to encourage stronger corporate policies. Shareholder engagement is a powerful tool, as companies are more likely to listen to the demands of their largest investors, who have the financial leverage to influence corporate behaviour (Conservation International). Additionally, pension funds and institutional investors can collaborate with other shareholders, NGOs, and advocacy groups to exert collective pressure on companies that fail to respect FPIC. This coalition-building amplifies the voice of investors and ensures that companies are held to higher standards of corporate responsibility.

E. Long-Term Impact on the Global South and Indigenous Communities

The importance of protecting human rights of Indigenous peoples and local communities in the Global South cannot be overstated. These communities are often disproportionately affected by corporate activities such as mining, logging, and large-scale agriculture. Without FPIC, they face the risk of losing their lands, livelihoods, and cultural heritage. When institutional investors demand greater accountability from companies on FPIC, they help protect the most vulnerable populations from exploitation and displacement.

Furthermore, by prioritising FPIC, investors can contribute to the broader goal of achieving sustainable development. The UNEP Finance Initiative (UNEP FI)[42] report *Nature-Related Finance and Indigenous Peoples* states that engaging the financial sector in Indigenous-led conservation efforts is both a rights-based obligation and a practical strategy to reduce investment risks and increase the long-term sustainability of projects. The report highlights that Indigenous lands overlap significantly with the world's biodiversity priority areas. Respecting the rights of Indigenous communities is closely linked to environmental conservation, as these communities often serve as stewards of some of the world's most biodiverse regions. Therefore, ensuring that companies adhere to FPIC not only protects human rights but also promotes environmental sustainability.

Institutional investors and pension funds play a crucial role in promoting corporate accountability, particularly in the context of human rights. By demanding greater transparency, engaging in shareholder advocacy, and insisting on compliance with international standards, these investors can help protect Indigenous peoples and vulnerable communities in the Global South. In doing so, they fulfil their fiduciary duties, mitigate financial and reputational risks, and contribute to a more equitable and sustainable global economy.

[42] UNEP Finance Initiative, *Nature, Finance and Indigenous Peoples* (2025), www.unepfi.org/wordpress/wp-content/uploads/2025/04/43-Nature-Finance-and-Indigenous-Peoples-2.pdf.

3

International Jurisdiction, Universal Jurisdiction, Extraterritoriality and the Enforcement of Human Rights Across Borders (Including the Use of Sanctions)

DAICHI ISHII

I. Introduction: Purpose of this Chapter and its Position in this Book

This chapter explores the fundamental question of how to ensure access to remedy, which serves as the key to making the state's duty to protect (Pillar 1) and the corporate responsibility to respect (Pillar 2) set forth in the United Nations Guiding Principles on Business and Human Rights (UNGPs)[1] effective in a cross-border context.

Two fundamental barriers – the 'normative application gap' and the 'enforcement gap' – prevent victims of human rights abuses by transnational corporations operating globally from obtaining effective remedies.[2]

The purpose of this chapter is to systematically organise the three main legal and institutional tools developed by the international community to fill these gaps, namely (1) universal jurisdiction, (2) extraterritorial application of law, and (3) targeted sanctions, and to analyse their theoretical foundations, institutional characteristics, and inherent limitations. In the overall structure of this book, this chapter serves as a theoretical and procedural 'bridge' for understanding the specific case studies of each country, which will be described in detail in Part II. The analytical framework presented in this chapter is intended to provide an overview of the multi-layered accountability ecosystem necessary to achieve the effective remedies sought by the UNGPs.

II. Basic Concepts and Analytical Framework

As a prerequisite for discussing accountability for transnational human rights violations, it is necessary to first understand the basic structure of the scope of state authority, ie, 'jurisdiction,' and the challenges it faces.

[1] United Nations, 'Guiding Principles on Business and Human Rights: Implementing the United Nations 'Protect, Respect and Remedy' Framework' (2011) UN Doc A/HRC/17/31.

[2] JG Ruggie, 'Business and Human Rights: The Evolving International Agenda' (2007) 101 *American Journal of International Law* 819.

A. Three Aspects of Jurisdiction

The authority of the state is traditionally classified into three distinct aspects under international law.[3] These aspects are interrelated but differ in nature and the geographical scope in which they are permitted, and understanding this distinction is essential for grasping the legal challenges of transnational human rights issues.

First, prescriptive jurisdiction is the authority of a state to enact and apply its laws to specific acts, relationships, or statuses. This represents the most extensive form of jurisdiction, and states may assert the applicability of their laws to acts occurring outside their territory or to foreign nationals if there is a certain connecting factor (eg, acts committed by their own nationals = personal jurisdiction, effects on the state = effects doctrine).[4] For example, the EU's Corporate Sustainability Due Diligence Directive (CS3D), which requires companies outside the EU to conduct human rights and environmental due diligence across their entire global value chain, is a classic example of the extraterritorial extension of legislative jurisdiction.[5]

Second, adjudicative jurisdiction refers to the authority of a country's courts or administrative agencies to hear and decide specific cases. This is narrower than legislative jurisdiction and is only recognised when there is a close connection between the specific case and the forum, as established by domestic law or international treaties.[6] For example, the fact that the defendant's principal place of business is located within the country or that the consequences of a tort occurred within the country may form the basis for adjudicative jurisdiction. In cross-border human rights litigation, the existence of adjudicative jurisdiction determines which country's courts the victim can turn to for redress.

Third, enforcement jurisdiction is the authority to physically enforce one's own laws or judicial decisions (eg, arresting suspects by police or seizing assets by court officers). Among the three types of jurisdiction, enforcement jurisdiction is the most strictly subject to the principle of territoriality and, as such, is generally limited to a country's own territory due to the risk of directly infringing upon another country's sovereignty.[7] For example, a police force from one country conducting investigations or arrests within another country's territory without its consent is clearly regarded as a violation of sovereignty under international law. This strict territoriality of enforcement jurisdiction is the direct cause of the 'enforcement gap' discussed later.

B. Jurisdiction in International Civil Litigation: Routes and Hurdles

The first and most important hurdle in ensuring access to judicial remedies as required by UNGP Pillar 3 is establishing 'international jurisdiction,' ie, determining in which country's courts a company can be sued. The realistic route for victims seeking civil remedies for human rights violations is largely determined by the jurisdiction rules of major legal systems, where intense legal battles unfold between victims engaging in 'forum shopping' (the strategy of selecting a

[3] MN Shaw, *International Law*, 8th edn (Cambridge, Cambridge University Press, 2017).
[4] C Ryngaert, *Jurisdiction in International Law*, 2nd edn (Oxford, Oxford University Press, 2015).
[5] European Union, 'Directive (EU) 2024/1760 of the European Parliament and of the Council on Corporate Sustainability Due Diligence' [2024] OJ L 2024/1760.
[6] GB Born, *International Civil Litigation in United States Courts*, 6th edn (Alphen aan den Rijn, Kluwer Law International, 2018).
[7] M Akehurst, 'Jurisdiction in International Law' (1972–1973) 46 *British Yearbook of International Law* 145.

venue for litigation in pursuit of more favourable judgments or procedures) and companies employing '*forum non conveniens* (FNC)' (the defence of inconvenient venues).[8]

i. High Hurdles and the FNC Barrier in the United States

The US system is particularly complex. Under each state's 'long-arm statutes,' courts must establish 'minimum contacts' between the defendant and the forum state, and the exercise of jurisdiction must not violate the constitutional requirement of 'due process.'[9] This applies only when the defendant company is deemed to have 'substantial domestic activity' in the state (general jurisdiction) or when the cause of action arises from the defendant's activities in the state (special jurisdiction), making it an extremely high hurdle for lawsuits involving overseas conduct. Furthermore, even if formal jurisdiction is recognised, the defendant may assert the FNC doctrine to seek dismissal of the lawsuit.[10] In the cases of the Bhopal chemical plant accident in India and the Chevron environmental pollution case in Ecuador, US companies skillfully utilised the FNC doctrine, citing the presence of 'much of the evidence and witnesses in the local area,' to avoid trial in US courts and successfully transfer the proceedings to host countries with weaker judicial systems.[11]

ii. Predictable Route in the EU (Brussels I Regulation)

Within the EU, the amended Brussels I Regulation governs jurisdiction in civil and commercial cases.[12] The basic principle is that the defendant may be sued in the court of their domicile (or the location of their principal place of business for corporations). However, in cases involving torts (including human rights violations), jurisdiction may also be recognised in the court where the damage occurred. This 'place of damage' may be interpreted as either the place where the harmful act was committed or the place where the harmful consequences occurred, thereby providing the plaintiff with flexibility in choosing the most favourable jurisdiction. This rule provides a relatively clear and predictable framework.

iii. New Developments in the UK (Consideration of 'Substantial Justice')

In recent years, the UK Supreme Court has adopted a more progressive approach in its FNC rulings, considering not only mere convenience but also whether 'substantial justice' can be achieved in the host country.[13] In the *Vedanta* case, the Supreme Court recognised that there was a real risk that the plaintiffs would not be able to obtain substantial justice in Zambia due to the absence of mechanisms to cover litigation costs (such as contingency fee agreements) and access to specialised legal counsel, and thus permitted the case to proceed in the UK.[14] This is a groundbreaking decision affirming jurisdiction in the home country based on

[8] AS Bell et al, *Forum Shopping and Forum Non Conveniens: A Comparative Study* (Oxford, Oxford University Press, 2019).

[9] *Daimler AG v Bauman* 571 US 117 (2014).

[10] *Piper Aircraft Co v Reyno* 454 US 235 (1981).

[11] *In re Union Carbide Corp Gas Plant Disaster at Bhopal, India in December*, 1984, 634 F Supp 842 (SDNY 1986); *Aguinda v Texaco Inc* 303 F 3d 470 (2d Cir 2002).

[12] Regulation (EU) No 1215/2012 of the European Parliament and of the Council on jurisdiction and the recognition and enforcement of judgments in civil and commercial matters [2012] OJ L351/1.

[13] *Vedanta Resources PLC v Lungowe* [2019] UKSC 20, [2020] AC 1045.

[14] *Okpabi v Royal Dutch Shell Plc* [2021] UKSC 3, [2021] 1 WLR 1294.

deficiencies in the host country's judicial system, and it points to a new path for overcoming the FNC barrier.

iv. Rules in Japan (Rejection Based on Special Circumstances)

In Japan, the rules on international jurisdiction were codified in the amended Civil Procedure Act, which came into effect in 2012.[15] In principle, jurisdiction is recognised at the defendant's domicile (Article 3-2) or the place of the tort (Article 3-3(8)), but Article 3-9 of the same law provides that a claim may be dismissed if 'special circumstances' exist. This provision is similar to FNC and applies when conducting proceedings in Japan would 'harm the fairness between the parties or hinder the proper and prompt conduct of proceedings.'

Thus, the battle over international jurisdiction serves as the first hurdle determining whether transnational human rights litigation can proceed to the merits.

C. Two 'Gaps' in the Context of Business and Human Rights

When applying these jurisdictional principles to the global activities of corporations, two significant 'gaps' emerge, forming fundamental barriers to the access to effective remedies sought by the UNGPs.[16] These are the central challenges that this chapter seeks to overcome.

i. Normative Application Gap

This refers to a situation where the legal norms that would hold a company accountable for human rights violations are absent because the domestic law of the country where the violations occurred (the host country) is ineffective or the law of the country where the company is headquartered (the home country) does not apply across borders. Many human rights abuses are illegal under the domestic laws of the host country. However, there are countless cases where the law is not effectively enforced due to the weakness of the host country's judicial system, widespread corruption, or the strong influence of the company over the government.[17]

A symbol of this gap is the 1984 Bhopal chemical plant accident in India, which resulted in thousands of deaths.[18] The victims sought to hold the US parent company Union Carbide (now Dow) accountable in the US, but the US courts applied the 'forum non conveniens' doctrine, ruling that India was a more appropriate venue for the lawsuit. As a result, victim compensation was limited to inadequate settlements within India, and the parent company's responsibility could not be fully addressed. Similarly, in the 2013 Rana Plaza building collapse in Bangladesh, which claimed the lives of over 1,100 people, European and American brands that had outsourced production to local garment factories that had neglected building safety faced extreme difficulties in pursuing direct legal liability under their home laws for the actions of their suppliers.[19] These cases demonstrate the reality that multinational corporations are exploiting complex corporate

[15] Civil Procedure Act (Japan), Act No 109 of 1996, as amended by Act No 54 of 2011.

[16] S Deva and D Bilchitz (eds), *Human Rights Obligations of Business: Beyond the Corporate Responsibility to Respect?* (Cambridge, Cambridge University Press, 2013).

[17] JA Zerk, *Multinationals and Corporate Social Responsibility: Limitations and Opportunities in International Law* (Cambridge, Cambridge University Press, 2006).

[18] U Baxi, 'Writing about Impunity and Environment: The "Silver Jubilee" of the Bhopal Catastrophe' (2010) 1 *Journal of Human Rights and the Environment* 23.

[19] N Sinkovics et al, 'Rana Plaza Collapse Aftermath: Are CSR Compliance and Auditing Pressures Effective?' (2016) 37 *Accounting, Auditing & Accountability Journal* 617.

structures (corporate veil) to dilute the legal connection between local subsidiaries and headquarters, thereby creating 'lawless zones' beyond the reach of the home country's laws.

ii. Enforcement Gap

This refers to a situation where, even if victims secure a favourable judgment in the home country's court, they are unable to enforce the judgment in practice. Enforcement jurisdiction is strictly based on territoriality, meaning that the enforcement power of the country that issued the judgment typically extends only within its own territory.[20] If the defendant company's primary assets are located in a country other than the judgment country, seizing those assets requires going through the process of recognising and enforcing the foreign judgment in the court of the asset-holding country, which creates an additional barrier.

A classic example of this is the environmental pollution lawsuit filed by indigenous peoples in Ecuador against oil giant Chevron.[21] They secured a judgment in an Ecuadorian court ordering Chevron to pay approximately $9.5 billion in damages, but Chevron had virtually no assets in Ecuador. Chevron argued that the Ecuadorian judgment was obtained through fraudulent means and launched a global legal battle to block its enforcement in countries such as the United States, where its headquarters are located, and Canada, Brazil, and Argentina, where it holds assets. Ultimately, for example, the Canadian Supreme Court ruled that 'Chevron Canada does not operate in Ecuador and is a separate legal entity from Chevron Corporation, which was the subject of the judgment,' and refused to enforce the judgment.[22] In this way, companies can use their global network of legal entities to disperse their assets and avoid the actual enforcement of judicial decisions, even if they are found liable.

In the following sections, we will examine the three main legal tools that the international community has sought to fill these two serious gaps: (1) universal jurisdiction, (2) extraterritorial application of law, and (3) targeted sanctions.

III. Universal Jurisdiction: An Exceptional Tool to Combat Impunity

One of the most ambitious attempts to bridge the 'normative application gap' is universal jurisdiction. This is an exceptional principle that allows any country's domestic courts to exercise criminal jurisdiction based on the gravity of the crime itself, regardless of traditional connecting factors such as the location where the crime was committed or the nationality of the suspect or victim.[23]

A. Historical Origins and Theoretical Basis

The historical origins of universal jurisdiction can be traced back to the prosecution of pirates, who were regarded as 'enemies of all humanity' under customary international law.[24] Pirates

[20] FA Mann, 'The Doctrine of Jurisdiction in International Law' (1964) 111 *Recueil des Cours* 1.

[21] *Chevron Corp v Donziger* 833 F 3d 74 (2d Cir 2016).

[22] *Chevron Corp v Yaiguaje* [2015] SCC 42, [2015] 3 SCR 69.

[23] L Reydams, *Universal Jurisdiction: International and Municipal Legal Perspectives* (Oxford, Oxford University Press, 2003).

[24] AP Rubin, *The Law of Piracy*, 2nd edn (Irvington-on-Hudson, Transnational Publishers, 1998).

operating on the high seas, which belong to no state, and beyond the jurisdiction of any particular state, posed a threat to the commerce and security of all nations. From this practical necessity, the principle that any state has the right to try pirates captured on the high seas in its own courts was established.

This principle underwent a decisive transformation after World War II, when the Nuremberg Trials and the Tokyo Trials expanded its scope beyond specific maritime crimes to crimes against humanity.[25] Although these trials were, strictly speaking, ex post facto trials conducted by the victorious powers, they established the new category of 'crimes against humanity' in international law and made it clear that even national leaders could be held accountable under international law for atrocities committed in the name of sovereignty. This marked a paradigm shift in international law, whereby large-scale human rights violations by states were no longer considered purely domestic issues.

A symbolic example of a single country applying this new norm was Israel's trial of Adolf Eichmann in 1961.[26] Israel asserted universal jurisdiction and tried Eichmann on charges of involvement in the Holocaust. Furthermore, the 'Pinochet case,' in which former Chilean dictator Augusto Pinochet was arrested in London based on a warrant issued by a Spanish judge in 1998, established the 'Pinochet precedent,' which holds that even former heads of state cannot claim sovereign immunity for international crimes such as torture.[27] This case played a decisive role in the transition of universal jurisdiction from theory to practice.

In modern times, this exceptional jurisdiction is theoretically supported by two fundamental concepts of international law. One is *jus cogens* (peremptory norms), which refers to fundamental norms of international law that cannot be derogated from, such as the prohibition of genocide and torture.[28] The other is *erga omnes* (obligations erga omnes), which refers to obligations owed not to individual states but to the international community as a whole.[29] Crimes subject to universal jurisdiction violate *jus cogens*, and their prosecution is considered the fulfillment of an *erga omnes* obligation. In other words, when a state exercises universal jurisdiction, it is understood to be fulfilling its duty to end impunity (the state of not being punished) not only for its own interests but also as a representative of the international community as a whole.

B. Scope under Customary International Law and Treaties

Today, it is widely recognised under customary international law that 'core international crimes,' such as genocide, crimes against humanity, war crimes, and torture, are subject to universal jurisdiction.[30] These crimes are considered to undermine the fundamental interests and values of the international community as a whole due to their extremely serious nature.

This customary law principle has been codified and further strengthened by numerous international treaties. The most important example is the 1949 Geneva Conventions.[31] These four treaties regulate inhumane acts in armed conflicts and impose on signatory states the obligation to either prosecute suspects in their own courts or hand them over to other signatory

[25] R Cryer et al, *An Introduction to International Criminal Law and Procedure*, 4th edn (Cambridge, Cambridge University Press, 2019).

[26] *Attorney-General of the Government of Israel v Eichmann* (1961) 36 ILR 5 (District Court of Jerusalem).

[27] *R v Bow Street Metropolitan Stipendiary Magistrate, ex p Pinochet Ugarte (No 3)* [2000] 1 AC 147 (HL).

[28] A Orakhelashvili, *Peremptory Norms in International Law* (Oxford, Oxford University Press, 2006).

[29] *Barcelona Traction, Light and Power Company, Limited (Belgium v Spain)* [1970] ICJ Rep 3.

[30] A Cassese, *International Criminal Law*, 3rd edn (Oxford, Oxford University Press, 2013).

[31] Geneva Convention for the Amelioration of the Condition of the Wounded and Sick in Armed Forces in the Field (Geneva, 12 August 1949) 75 UNTS 31.

states that request prosecution for particularly serious 'grave breaches' (such as the intentional killing or torture of prisoners of war and indiscriminate attacks on non-military targets). This is known as the principle of '*aut dedere aut judicare*,' or 'extradite or prosecute.' Since nearly all countries have ratified the Geneva Conventions, this obligation has extremely universal legal binding force.

A similar obligation is explicitly stipulated in the 1984 Convention Against Torture.[32] This treaty requires signatory states to prosecute or extradite suspects of torture who are present within their territory, regardless of where the crime was committed or the nationality of the suspect or victim. Furthermore, a series of treaties adopted in the 1970s to address the proliferation of aircraft hijackings (such as the Hague Conventions and the Montreal Convention) also adopt the principle of 'extradite or prosecute' as a core obligation.[33] Through the accumulation of these treaties, the exercise of universal jurisdiction has been elevated from a mere discretionary 'right' of states to an international legal 'obligation' under specific circumstances, significantly strengthening the international legal framework to combat impunity.

C. Modern Application Models and Corporate Responsibility

In recent years, the practice of universal jurisdiction has transcended its former Western-centric focus and is expanding globally. Its scope of application is also suggested to potentially extend beyond state officials to multinational corporations.

i. Prosecution of State Officials (Germany)

Germany's 'Koblenz Trial' is a landmark case in the modern application of universal jurisdiction.[34] The country's International Criminal Code (VStGB) Article 1 grants jurisdiction over genocide, crimes against humanity, and war crimes, regardless of the location of the crime or the nationality of the perpetrator or victim. Based on this provision, German prosecuting authorities indicted Anwar R, a former Syrian intelligence officer residing in Germany, under Section 7 of the VStGB for crimes against humanity for his alleged involvement in torture during the Syrian civil war. The success of this trial was supported by an innovative approach known as 'structural investigation,' which involved systematically collecting testimony from refugees and others and preserving evidence even before the suspect was present in the country. In 2022, the Koblenz Higher Regional Court sentenced Anwar R to life imprisonment, marking the first guilty verdict issued by a court worldwide for state-sponsored torture in Syria.[35]

ii. Corporate Complicity (France)

In France, the case of cement giant Lafarge opened a new path for the prosecution of corporate criminal responsibility.[36] The company was the first corporation in the world to be charged with 'complicity in crimes against humanity' for providing funds to armed groups such as ISIS to

[32] Convention against Torture and Other Cruel, Inhuman or Degrading Treatment or Punishment (New York, 10 December 1984) 1465 UNTS 85.

[33] Convention for the Suppression of Unlawful Seizure of Aircraft (The Hague, 16 December 1970) 860 UNTS 105.

[34] W Kaleck and P Kroker, 'Syrian Torture Investigations in Europe: Breathing Life into Universal Jurisdiction' (2018) 16 *Journal of International Criminal Justice* 165.

[35] Oberlandesgericht Koblenz, Judgment of 13 January 2022, Case No 1 StE 9/21.

[36] Cour de cassation, Judgment of 7 September 2021, No 20-82.676; Cour de cassation, Judgment of 28 February 2024, No 23-81.394.

maintain factory operations during the Syrian civil war. The French Supreme Court upheld the indictment in rulings in 2021 and 2024, issuing a groundbreaking judgment that 'the fact alone of providing millions of euros in funding to an organization while being aware of its criminal activities is sufficient to consider the establishment of conspiracy.'[37] This is a historic precedent clarifying that universal jurisdiction may apply when corporate economic activities contribute to international crimes.

iii. Practices by Non-Western Countries (Senegal, Gambia, Argentina)

In response to criticism that universal jurisdiction is a 'tool of neo-colonialism,' practices by non-Western countries have provided a powerful counterargument.[38] Senegal, based on an agreement with the African Union (AU), established the Extraordinary African Chambers (EAC) and tried former Chadian dictator Hissène Habré for crimes against humanity, sentencing him to life imprisonment (2016).[39] Additionally, regarding allegations of genocide against the Rohingya in Myanmar, Gambia filed a lawsuit against Myanmar at the International Court of Justice (ICJ) based on the erga omnes partes obligation under the Genocide Convention, while Argentina's courts are pursuing criminal responsibility of individual Myanmar military leaders based on the 'pure' universal jurisdiction recognised by its constitution.[40] These developments demonstrate that universal jurisdiction is evolving into a truly global legal principle.

D. Challenges: Sovereignty, Immunity, and Conflict with Politics

While the exercise of universal jurisdiction is powerful in theory, it faces many practical challenges. The first is the conflict with sovereign immunity. Universal jurisdiction conflicts with the principle of sovereign immunity, which grants states and their officials immunity from the jurisdiction of other states.[41] In particular, the International Court of Justice (ICJ) ruled in the Arrest Warrant Case (2002) that sitting heads of state and ministers of foreign affairs enjoy absolute immunity (personal immunity) from the criminal jurisdiction of other states while in office.[42] Second, there is political criticism. In particular, the African Union (AU) has strongly criticised universal jurisdiction as 'imperialism of law' or neo-colonialism, arguing that it is selectively applied by European countries against African leaders.[43] Third, there are practical obstacles. These include the difficulty of collecting evidence abroad, issues related to the protection of victims and witnesses and their access to justice, and the constraints on the vast judicial resources required to prosecute international crimes.[44]

[37] Cour de cassation, Judgment of 28 February 2024, No 23-81.394, para 15.

[38] D Tladi, 'The African Union and Universal Jurisdiction: A Tension of Norms or a Clash of Interests?' (2009) 1 *African Journal of Legal Studies* 5.

[39] Extraordinary African Chambers, *The Prosecutor v Hissène Habré*, Judgment of 30 May 2016, Case No 001/2017.

[40] *The Gambia v Myanmar* [2019] ICJ (Application instituting proceedings); *Querellantes v Aye Ne Win and others*, Case No 4591/2019 (Juzgado Central de Instrucción No 5, Madrid).

[41] H Fox, *The Law of State Immunity*, 3rd edn (Oxford, Oxford University Press, 2013).

[42] Arrest Warrant of 11 April 2000 (*Democratic Republic of the Congo v Belgium*) [2002] ICJ Rep 3.

[43] African Union, 'Decision on the Report of the Commission on the Abuse of the Principle of Universal Jurisdiction' Assembly/AU/Dec.199(XI) (2008).

[44] M Langer, 'The Diplomacy of Universal Jurisdiction: The Political Branches and the Transnational Prosecution of International Crimes' (2011) 105 *American Journal of International Law* 1.

IV. Extraterritorial Application of Law: Questioning the Responsibility of Corporations and States

A more general attempt to fill the 'normative application gap' is the 'extraterritorial application' of domestic law. This approach, primarily taken by the home countries of corporations, seeks to impose discipline on their global activities, and its scope is beginning to extend beyond corporations to include the omissions of states.

A. Legal Basis and Historical Development

Extraterritorial application of law refers to the extension of a state's domestic law beyond its own territory, constituting an important exception to the traditional principle of territoriality. Its theoretical foundations and practical application have evolved significantly over time.

The classical starting point in international law is the 1927 Permanent Court of International Justice ruling in the *Lotus* case.[45] This decision established the so-called 'Lotus principle,' which holds that, in the absence of explicit prohibitions under international law, states possess broad discretion to determine the scope of their domestic laws. This principle laid the foundation for a flexible interpretation that permits states to extend their legislative jurisdiction over extraterritorial acts in order to protect their nationals or economic interests.

The principle has had the greatest practical impact in the field of US antitrust law (monopoly prohibition law). Initially, strict territorialism was applied, but in the landmark 1945 *Alcoa* case, the 'effects doctrine' was established, which holds that US law may be applied to conduct occurring abroad if it has an 'anti-competitive effect' on the US market.[46] This theory was interpreted as an extension of objective territorialism (recognising jurisdiction when the results of an act occur within the country) and became a powerful tool for regulating cross-border economic activities such as international cartels.

However, unilateral extraterritorial application, such as the US Helms-Burton Act (Cuba sanctions), which imposed sanctions even on third-country companies legally trading with Cuba, was strongly opposed by European countries and others as infringing on the sovereignty of other countries and violating international comity.[47] In response, the EU enacted counter-sanctions laws (blocking regulations) to protect its own companies from the extraterritorial application of US laws, causing serious diplomatic friction. The UN General Assembly has repeatedly adopted resolutions stating that such unilateral measures violate international law, and the legitimacy of extraterritorial application is always accompanied by tension with national sovereignty.

B. Vertical Application: Direct Liability of Parent Companies

This approach focuses on capital relationships within corporate groups and seeks to hold parent companies liable for the actions of their overseas subsidiaries by piercing the 'corporate veil.' Under traditional corporate law, parent companies and subsidiaries are separate legal entities,

[45] *SS Lotus (France v Turkey)* [1927] PCIJ Rep Series A No 10.
[46] *United States v Aluminum Co of America* 148 F 2d 416 (2d Cir 1945).
[47] Cuban Liberty and Democratic Solidarity (LIBERTAD) Act of 1996, Pub L No 104-114, 110 Stat 785.

and parent companies are generally not liable for the debts or torts of their subsidiaries.[48] Overcoming this 'corporate veil' has traditionally required reliance on the highly exceptional doctrine of 'piercing the corporate veil,' which has posed significant legal hurdles.

However, recent judicial decisions in common law countries, particularly the United Kingdom, are significantly changing this situation. The UK Supreme Court established a new legal principle in the *Vedanta* case (2019) and the *Okpabi v Shell* case (2021) that a parent company may be directly liable for damages caused by the business activities of its overseas subsidiaries based on a 'duty of care.'[49] This does not deny the legal personality of the subsidiary but holds the parent company liable for its own negligence, namely, the failure to properly supervise and manage the subsidiary's business activities. The court emphasises whether the parent company established and disclosed group-wide safety and environmental policies and supervised their compliance, as well as the extent to which it substantively intervened in the subsidiary's management. This approach is consistent with the global business practices of companies and provides a more realistic avenue for victims to directly sue parent companies in their home countries.

C. Horizontal Application: Discipline Across the Entire Supply Chain

This approach focuses on the flow of products and services, using market access as a lever to impose human rights standards across the entire supply chain. Its two main forms are the legislation of mandatory human rights due diligence (mHRDD) and regulation through trade measures.

Representative examples of the former include France's 'Corporate Vigilance Law' and Germany's 'Supply Chain Act,' as well as the EU's 'Corporate Sustainability Due Diligence Directive (CS3D),' which is emerging as a new global standard.[50] These laws impose legal obligations on companies to identify, prevent, and remedy human rights and environmental risks throughout their supply chains. These laws symbolise a shift from soft law, which relied on voluntary corporate initiatives, to hard law with legal binding force and penalties.

The US Uyghur Forced Labor Prevention Act (UFLPA) is an example of the latter, serving as a powerful tool to exclude forced labour products from the market by presuming that products produced in specific regions are 'made with forced labour' and shifting the burden of proof to importers to demonstrate otherwise.[51] The EU has introduced similar forced labour product regulations, and there is a growing trend toward utilising trade policy as a means of protecting human rights.

D. New Frontier: States' Duty of Care Regarding Climate Change

The concept of extraterritorial application of law is expanding into a new area that questions the responsibility of states for their inaction, not just that of companies. A groundbreaking example of this is the Urgenda Foundation case in the Netherlands.[52] This lawsuit established a completely

[48] PT Muchlinski, *Multinational Enterprises and the Law*, 3rd edn (Oxford, Oxford University Press, 2021).

[49] *Vedanta Resources PLC v Lungowe* [2019] UKSC 20, [2020] AC 1045; *Okpabi v Royal Dutch Shell Plc* [2021] UKSC 3, [2021] 1 WLR 1294.

[50] Loi n° 2017-399 du 27 mars 2017 relative au devoir de vigilance des sociétés mères et des entreprises donneuses d'ordre; Lieferkettensorgfaltspflichtengesetz vom 16 Juli 2021 (BGBl I S 2959).

[51] Uyghur Forced Labor Prevention Act, Pub L No 117-78, 135 Stat 1525 (2021).

[52] *Urgenda Foundation v State of the Netherlands* [2015] HAZA C/09/00456689 (Hague District Court); [2018] GHDHA 200.178.245/01 (Hague Court of Appeal); [2019] ECLI:NL:HR:2019:2007 (Supreme Court).

new model for how the judiciary can enforce the duty of care that sovereign states owe to their citizens in response to the global threat of climate change, which affects multiple generations.

The key to the success of this lawsuit was the court's adoption of the scientific reports of the Intergovernmental Panel on Climate Change (IPCC) as de facto legal standards.[53] The court recognised as undisputed fact the IPCC's scientific consensus that, to prevent dangerous climate change (a temperature rise exceeding 2°C), developed countries must reduce greenhouse gas emissions by 25–40 per cent below 1990 levels by 2020. This scientific benchmark served as the 'yardstick' for determining whether the Dutch government's climate change measures were legally sufficient.

The Dutch Supreme Court concluded that the government's measures did not meet this scientific standard, thereby violating the unwritten duty of care under the Dutch Civil Code and infringing on the right to life (Article 2) and the right to respect for private life (Article 8) guaranteed by the European Convention on Human Rights (ECHR).[54] The court determined that climate change constitutes a 'real and imminent threat' to Dutch citizens and that the state has a positive obligation to take appropriate measures to protect its citizens from this threat. This is a classic example of the 'living instrument' theory, which interprets human rights treaties dynamically to address new threats faced by modern society, rather than merely protecting against direct oppression by the state.

The ruling rejected the government's arguments based on the principle of 'separation of powers' (claiming that climate policy falls within the discretion of the political branch) and the 'drop in the ocean' argument (claiming that reductions by the Netherlands alone are meaningless), and legally ordered the government to achieve more ambitious emission reduction targets (a 25 per cent reduction from 1990 levels by 2020). The victory in the *Urgenda* case served as a catalyst for a global wave of climate change litigation, resonating deeply with lawsuits holding corporations accountable for climate change and the CS3D's requirement that companies develop 'climate transition plans.'

V. Judicial Remedies and Private International Law

The role of private international law in ensuring the availability and effectiveness of judicial remedies is crucial in addressing the 'enforcement gap.'

A. ATS (Alien Tort Statute): A Representative Example of Extraterritorial Civil Litigation Models

The ATS is a representative example of an extraterritorial civil litigation model, established as part of the Judiciary Act of 1789, granting US federal courts jurisdiction over torts committed by foreigners in violation of international law.[55] Following the landmark 1980 *Filártiga v Peña-Irala* decision, this law, which had been largely unused for nearly 200 years, was revived as an important civil remedy for human rights violations committed outside the United States.[56]

[53] Intergovernmental Panel on Climate Change, 'Climate Change 2014: Synthesis Report' (2014).
[54] Convention for the Protection of Human Rights and Fundamental Freedoms (Rome, 4 November 1950) ETS 5.
[55] Alien Tort Statute, 28 USC § 1350 (1789).
[56] *Filártiga v Peña-Irala* 630 F 2d 876 (2d Cir 1980).

However, its golden age came to an end with a series of decisions by the US Supreme Court. In the 2013 *Kiobel* decision, the court applied the 'presumption against extraterritorial application of US law' to the ATS in a case where Nigerian residents sued Dutch and British oil companies.[57] This required that the lawsuit have 'sufficient force and effect within the United States,' rendering the mere presence of a foreign company insufficient, thereby significantly limiting the ability to bring lawsuits regarding human rights violations committed abroad.

The 2018 *Jesner* decision, in a case where victims of terrorist attacks in the Middle East sued a Jordanian bank, ruled that foreign corporations cannot be defendants in ATS-based lawsuits, citing considerations of diplomatic relations and the separation of powers, thereby closing the door to lawsuits against corporations.[58] Furthermore, the 2021 *Nestlé USA* ruling, in a case involving child slave labour on cocoa plantations in Côte d'Ivoire, set an extremely high bar by requiring plaintiffs to prove that the 'related conduct' forming the basis of the claim was carried out within the United States, even if the defendant was a US company, rather than relying solely on 'general business decisions' made within the United States.[59]

ATS holds the advantage of having broad applicability to general violations of international law and the potential to award punitive damages, given its historical context. However, these rulings have severely restricted its application. What was once seen as a beacon of hope now reveals its limitations, and evaluations of its role within the United States remain divided.

B. New Strategies Post-ATS: Lessons from the *Chiquita* Case

As the door to ATS narrows, victims are exploring new litigation strategies. A symbol of this is the lawsuit against Chiquita Brands, a major banana company.[60] The company was sued in a US court by the families of victims who alleged that it had provided financial support to the AUC (United Self-Defense Forces of Colombia), a right-wing paramilitary organisation in Colombia, and aided and abetted serious human rights violations, including murder.

As claims based on the original ATS became increasingly difficult due to the Supreme Court's rulings, the plaintiffs shifted their strategy. They now seek to establish US jurisdiction while applying Colombian law – the law of the place where the wrongful acts occurred – to hold the company liable. This approach assumes that US courts have jurisdiction over the defendant, a US-based company, while seeking to have the wrongful acts themselves adjudicated under the law of another country.

In June 2024, a jury in a federal district court in Florida found that Chiquita knew about the AUC's atrocities and intentionally provided substantial funding for its own benefit.[61] The court ordered the company to pay $38.3 million in damages to the victims' families under Colombian law, marking a historic verdict. This marked a groundbreaking case in which a US multinational corporation was held legally liable by a US jury for its complicity in human rights abuses overseas. The lessons from the *Chiquita* case clearly demonstrate that even after the limitations of the ATS have been recognised, victims can still creatively utilise the framework of private international law to establish the domestic law of the place where the wrongful

[57] *Kiobel v Royal Dutch Petroleum Co* 569 US 108 (2013).
[58] *Jesner v Arab Bank*, PLC 584 US ___ (2018).
[59] *Nestlé USA Inc v Doe* 593 US ___ (2021).
[60] *Doe v Chiquita Brands International Inc*, Case No 08-cv-01916 (SD Fla filed 2008).
[61] *Roe v Chiquita Brands International Inc*, Case No 23-cv-21603 (SD Fla 2024).

act occurred as the applicable law, thereby opening a new avenue for civil remedies in the home country.

C. Private International Law: Domestic Legal Safeguards for Human Rights Protection

Private international law (or conflict of laws) governs two core issues: which country's law should apply to cross-border legal relationships (choice of law) and whether foreign court judgments should be recognised and enforced domestically (recognition and enforcement of foreign judgments).[62] While this may appear to be a technical legal field, it plays a critically important role as a domestic legal 'safety valve' to protect universal values such as human rights in cases of human rights violations that transcend national borders.

First, there is the issue of choice of law. The law applicable to torts has traditionally been the 'law of the place where the tort was committed.' However, when the law of the host country where the human rights violation occurred does not provide adequate protection for the victim, mechanically applying this principle cannot fill the 'gap in the application of norms.' To address this, modern private international law has developed more flexible rules.

i. Rules Aimed at Protecting Victims

The EU's Rome II Regulation is a representative example.[63] The Regulation recognises the right of victims to choose the law of the place where the tort was committed, the law of the place where the damage occurred, or (under certain conditions) the law of their habitual residence in cases of torts related to business activities, such as environmental damage (Article 7) and product liability (Article 5). This enables victims to choose the legal system most favourable to them, thereby increasing the likelihood of effective redress.

ii. Overriding Mandatory Provisions

These are domestic legal provisions that apply regardless of whether foreign law is designated as the applicable law under private international law rules.[64] Examples include fundamental norms regarding human rights protection in the forum state (the state where the court is located) and laws protecting consumers and workers. Corporate human rights due diligence obligations may be interpreted as having the nature of overriding mandatory provisions, in which case, even if human rights violations occur overseas and local laws should apply, it would be possible to hold companies liable under the due diligence laws of the forum state.

Second, there is the issue of the recognition and enforcement of foreign judgments. Even if the victim obtains a favourable judgment in the host country's court, if the defendant company's assets are located in its home country, the recognition and enforcement of the judgment in the home country is essential to fill the 'enforcement gap.' In such cases, the principle of 'public policy' serves as the last line of defence.

[62] SC Symeonides, *Private International Law at the End of the 20th Century: Progress or Regress?* (The Hague, Kluwer Law International, 2000).

[63] Regulation (EC) No 864/2007 of the European Parliament and of the Council on the law applicable to non-contractual obligations (Rome II) [2007] OJ L199/40.

[64] *Dicey, Morris & Collins on the Conflict of Laws*, 15th edn (London, Sweet & Maxwell, 2012).

iii. Refusal of Enforcement Based on Public Policy

Article 118(3) of Japan's Civil Procedure Act provides that recognition of a foreign judgment may be refused if its content or procedure violates Japan's 'public order or good morals.'[65] This serves as a safeguard to prevent foreign judgments that fundamentally deny human rights (eg, judgments that tolerate discrimination based on race or gender, or judgments rendered without proper judicial procedures) from taking effect within Japan. Conversely, there may be cases where a company argues that a high-value compensation judgment obtained by the plaintiff is contrary to public policy in Japan, but the court will carefully assess such claims.

iv. Guarantee of Due Process

In connection with public policy, for a foreign judgment to be recognised, it is a prerequisite that the defendant who lost the case was given an adequate opportunity to defend themselves (due process). This indirectly reviews whether the foreign judicial system meets international standards and is an important requirement from the perspective of human rights protection.

In this way, private international law is not merely a technical rule for selecting applicable law, but a mechanism that embodies substantive value judgments, enabling access to more human rights-protective legal norms through the selection of applicable law and blocking the influence of legal systems that violate human rights within the country through the principle of public policy.

VI. Non-judicial Remedies and Complementary Enforcement Tools

UNGP Pillar 3 emphasises the importance of diverse remedial mechanisms that complement judicial procedures.

A. Non-judicial Remedial Mechanisms: From the Bangladesh Accord to NCPs and CSR

Non-judicial mechanisms are important means of supplementing or replacing time-consuming and costly judicial routes. They interact with each other to form a multi-layered 'remedial ecosystem.' Their forms vary widely, ranging from the corporate level to the industry level and the national level, each with different characteristics and functions.

i. Industry-level Binding Agreements (Accord Model)

The most advanced example of this is the Bangladesh Accord on Fire and Building Safety, which was established in 2013 in response to the Rana Plaza building collapse.[66] The groundbreaking feature of this model is the legally binding arbitration clause agreed upon by the

[65] Civil Procedure Act (Japan), Act No 109 of 1996, art 118(3).
[66] Accord on Fire and Building Safety in Bangladesh (2013).

signatory global companies and labour unions. This mechanism ensures that independent inspection agencies conduct safety inspections of factories, develop improvement plans, and that brand companies guarantee the necessary funding for their implementation. Building on this success, the Accord has evolved into the 'International Accord' and expanded its scope to other countries such as Pakistan.[67] This represents a powerful non-judicial mechanism that goes beyond voluntary corporate initiatives to achieve substantive safety and redress through the use of contract law.

ii. National-level Dialogue Promotion Mechanisms (NCP Model)

The National Contact Points (NCPs) established by each country to monitor the implementation of the OECD Guidelines for Multinational Enterprises are representative examples of state-based non-judicial mechanisms.[68] NCPs are not courts, but rather platforms that promote dialogue and mediation between parties from a neutral standpoint. While they offer the advantages of being free and easily accessible, their recommendations are not legally binding, and resolution depends on the voluntary agreement of the parties involved. As a result, the effectiveness of NCPs varies greatly depending on how they are operated in each country, and there are persistent criticisms that they are 'toothless tigers.' To address these issues, the 2023 revision of the guidelines strengthened procedures to enhance the transparency and effectiveness of NCPs.[69]

iii. Corporate-level Grievance Mechanisms

The UNGPs require companies to establish or participate in effective grievance mechanisms for stakeholders affected by their business activities.[70] To ensure their effectiveness, Article 31 of the UNGPs sets forth eight criteria, including legitimacy, accessibility, predictability, impartiality, transparency, compatibility with rights, and a source of continuous learning. Nippon Steel and Toyota Motor Corporation are among the companies that have established consultation and reporting channels that are also available to their suppliers' employees in an effort to respond to this request.[71] However, many corporate mechanisms face a serious challenge known as the 'grievance mechanism gap,' in which vulnerable workers, especially those at the bottom of the supply chain, are unaware of their existence or are unable to use them for fear of retaliation.

By complementing each other's weaknesses and functioning in coordination, these mechanisms at the corporate, industry, and national levels enable victims to choose the most appropriate remedy based on their circumstances. Strengthening this multi-layered ecosystem as a whole is essential for achieving more accessible remedies.

B. Sanctions as Administrative Enforcement Tools

Targeted sanctions are emerging as swift and powerful administrative measures to complement judicial procedures and address the 'enforcement gap.' Unlike comprehensive economic sanctions

[67] International Accord for Health and Safety in the Textile and Garment Industry (2021).
[68] OECD, 'OECD Guidelines for Multinational Enterprises on Responsible Business Conduct' (2023).
[69] ibid.
[70] United Nations, 'Guiding Principles on Business and Human Rights' (2011) UN Doc A/HRC/17/31, Principle 31.
[71] Nippon Steel Corporation, 'Human Rights Policy' (2022); Toyota Motor Corporation, 'Human Rights Policy' (2021).

that used to target entire countries, these sanctions are designed to precisely target individuals and organisations directly involved in serious human rights abuses or corruption.[72] Specific measures include asset freezes and travel bans to sanctioning countries.

i. The Global Magnitsky Act and the Formation of a 'Sanctions Coalition'

Leading this trend is the US Global Magnitsky Human Rights Accountability Act.[73] This law was enacted in response to the death in prison of Russian tax lawyer Sergei Magnitsky, who had exposed massive corruption by Russian government officials. Initially limited to Russia, the law was later expanded to cover the entire world, enabling sanctions to be imposed on individuals of any nationality who commit human rights abuses or acts of corruption.

This 'behaviour-based' approach was groundbreaking, and the EU, the UK, Canada, Australia, and others have since introduced similar systems (so-called 'Magnitsky-style sanctions'), effectively forming a de facto 'sanctions alliance.'[74] As a result, those subject to sanctions are excluded from major international financial systems and their activities are significantly restricted.

ii. Different Dynamics in Asia

In contrast, sanctions imposed by Asian countries differ from the norm-driven approach of the West. Sanctions imposed by Japan under its Foreign Exchange and Foreign Trade Control Law are primarily based on the implementation of UN Security Council resolutions, and a cautious 'dual-track' approach is taken when it comes to imposing independent sanctions solely on the grounds of human rights violations.[75] South Korea's sanctions are mainly focused on its policy toward North Korea, while Taiwan's sanctions are strongly characterised as a geopolitical tool to demonstrate solidarity with the democratic camp. In these countries, national interests and security concerns tend to outweigh universal values such as human rights in determining sanctions.

iii. Serious Challenges: Due Process and Political Legitimacy

While targeted sanctions are flexible and powerful, they also pose serious challenges. First is the guarantee of due process. Sanctions are imposed by executive authority without judicial review, which means that those targeted may not be given sufficient opportunity to defend themselves and may be listed based on inaccurate information.[76] In the 'Kadi case,' the European Court of Justice ruled that even sanctions based on UN Security Council decisions must be subject to judicial review, clarifying that those targeted have the right to a fair hearing and effective judicial protection under EU law.[77] Second, there is political criticism of 'double standards.' Criticism that

[72] C Portela, 'Targeted Sanctions against Individuals on Grounds of Grave Human Rights Violations: Impact, Trends and Prospects at the EU Level' (2016) Study for the DROI Committee, European Parliament.

[73] Global Magnitsky Human Rights Accountability Act, Pub L No 114-328, 130 Stat 2000 (2016).

[74] Council Regulation (EU) 2020/1998 concerning restrictive measures against serious human rights violations and abuses [2020] OJ L410I/13.

[75] Foreign Exchange and Foreign Trade Act (Japan), Act No 228 of 1949.

[76] Cameron, I, The European Convention on Human Rights, Due Process and United Nations Security Council Counter-Terrorism Sanctions (Uppsala, Iustus Förlag, 2006).

[77] Kadi v Council of the European Union [2008] ECR I-6351 (ECJ).

sanctions are lenient toward allies and selectively applied to geopolitical rivals is deeply rooted and could undermine the legitimacy of sanctions themselves. These challenges raise fundamental issues that must be overcome for targeted sanctions to remain an effective tool for pursuing accountability.

VII. Implementation Gaps in Asia and Future Prospects: Diversifying Remedy Models

The various tools outlined in this chapter are not entirely absent from the institutional framework in the Asian region. However, Asia, which is a key hub of the global supply chain, is also a site of human rights abuses, and faces serious challenges in ensuring access to effective remedies as required by UNGP Pillar 3.

The responses of major Asian countries are not uniform and can be classified into several 'remedial models' that reflect the political and economic contexts of each country. Furthermore, geopolitical changes and drastic shifts in the regulatory environment after 2024 will bring new complexities to these models.

A. Japan Model: 'Policy-driven Non-judicial Dialogue'

Japan's approach is characterised by its focus on government policy support and voluntary corporate initiatives (soft law), rather than the legal obligation of human rights due diligence (hard law) as seen in the EU.[78] This reflects Japan's traditional social norms that prioritise dialogue and consensus-building among stakeholders over adversarial litigation.

At the core of this model is the 'Guidelines for Respecting Human Rights in Responsible Supply Chains,' formulated in 2022 by the Ministry of Economy, Trade and Industry and the Ministry of Foreign Affairs.[79] Based on the UNGPs, these guidelines expect all companies to practice human rights due diligence. Although they are not legally binding, they have had a significant impact in promoting awareness and concrete initiatives among corporate management.

A practical platform that embodies this soft law approach is the non-judicial remedy mechanism known as the 'Business and Human Rights Dialogue and Remedy Mechanism' (JaCER).[80] JaCER is a multi-stakeholder initiative involving companies, industry associations, lawyers, and NGOs, and serves as an advanced point of contact for receiving complaints regarding human rights issues related to member companies both domestically and internationally, and promoting dialogue between the parties involved.

However, this Japanese model faces several challenges. First, JaCER's process is non-public, and its effectiveness depends heavily on the voluntary cooperation of companies willing to engage in dialogue. Additionally, the number of member companies remains limited, and there is a 'grievance mechanism gap' where relief does not reach those actually affected at the end of the supply chain. Second, the emphasis on non-judicial remedies suggests difficulties

[78] Ministry of Economy, Trade and Industry and Ministry of Foreign Affairs (Japan), 'Guidelines for Respecting Human Rights in Responsible Supply Chains' (2022).

[79] ibid.

[80] Japan CSR Consortium, 'Business and Human Rights Dialogue and Remedy Mechanism (JaCER)' (2020).

in accessing judicial remedies. In Japanese courts, the threshold for holding parent companies legally responsible for the actions of their overseas subsidiaries (piercing the corporate veil) remains high, and no groundbreaking precedents such as the UK's *Vedanta* case have emerged.

Thus, while the Japanese model prioritises amicable resolution through dialogue, significant barriers remain to access judicial remedies backed by state coercive power. However, as overseas legal regulations requiring human rights due diligence from business partners, such as the EU's CS3D, are strengthened, Japanese companies are increasingly unable to respond solely through their traditional voluntary efforts, and discussions on the legalisation of human rights due diligence are gaining momentum through a bipartisan parliamentary league.[81] How this model will evolve in the future is a key question.

B. South Korean Model: 'Selective Deterrence Through Punitive "Hard Law"'

The South Korean approach is characterised by the introduction of 'hard law' with strong legal enforcement power for specific issues. The Special Act on Punishment of Serious Accidents (SAPA), enacted in response to strong public demand, imposes severe criminal penalties on business owners and individual managers, functioning as a powerful deterrent mechanism against labour safety and health issues in the country.[82] Actual prison sentences have been handed down to top executives. On the other hand, the 'International Criminal Court Jurisdiction Crimes Punishment Act' has been scarcely utilised in the context of business and human rights, exhibiting a selective enforcement approach where the scope of remedies is limited to specific domestic issues.

In South Korea, following the adoption of the EU's Corporate Sustainability Due Diligence Directive (CS3D), efforts to enact Asia's first mandatory human rights and environmental due diligence law have begun to take shape. On 1 September 2023, the opposition Democratic Party submitted the 'Bill on Human Rights and Environmental Protection for Sustainable Business Operations' to the National Assembly.[83]

If this bill is enacted as currently drafted, Japanese companies that meet the criteria for applicable entities would also be required to conduct human rights due diligence, potentially having significant international implications. However, it has been revealed that two-thirds (65 per cent) of South Korean companies scored 0 (ie, no measures implemented) on the most basic human rights due diligence measures, indicating an extremely low current implementation rate.[84]

Furthermore, the political turmoil caused by the declaration of martial law in December 2024 and the detention of the president in January 2025 is likely to have a significant impact on the advancement of new legislation, including the legalisation of human rights due diligence.

This duality creates a powerful but narrow channel for redress, highlighting the reality that victims of human rights abuses in overseas supply chains are denied equal access to redress.

[81] Parliamentary League for the Promotion of Business and Human Rights (Japan), 'Proposal for the Enactment of Human Rights Due Diligence Legislation' (2023).

[82] Special Act on Punishment of Serious Accidents (South Korea), Act No 17905 of 8 January 2021.

[83] National Assembly of the Republic of Korea, 'Bill on Human Rights and Environmental Protection for Sustainable Business Operations' (2023).

[84] Korea Chamber of Commerce and Industry, 'Survey on Corporate Human Rights Due Diligence Implementation Status' (2023).

C. The Chinese Model: 'State-led Control and Countering External Sanctions'

China's approach differs fundamentally from that of other Asian countries. Despite facing international criticism over serious human rights abuses in Xinjiang, Tibet, and Hong Kong, the Chinese government has developed its own 'Chinese model of human rights' and rejected Western human rights standards.[85]

At the corporate level, the Personal Information Protection Law, which came into effect on 1 November 2021, marked an important turning point.[86] This law focuses on protecting individual rights and carries the risk of heavy fines of up to 50 million yuan or 5 per cent of the previous year's sales for violations. However, its primary purpose is to ensure data sovereignty and national security rather than human rights protection.

A distinctive aspect of China is its organised countermeasures against international human rights sanctions. In response to sanctions imposed by the US and the EU on human rights grounds, China has enacted the 'Anti-Foreign Sanctions Law' and the 'Unreliable Entity List,' establishing a 'counter-sanctions' system to punish Chinese companies and individuals who cooperate with foreign sanctions.[87] This has placed global companies in a serious dilemma, caught between Western human rights sanctions and China's counter-sanctions.

Furthermore, China is accused of using new propaganda campaigns to conceal its human rights abuses against Tibetans and Uyghurs, positioning human rights issues as part of an international information war.[88] This approach clearly prioritises national sovereignty and regime maintenance over coordination with international human rights norms.

D. The Indian Model: 'Prioritising Economic Growth and Selective Regulatory Tightening'

With a population of over 1.4 billion and estimated to have surpassed China in 2023 to become the world's most populous country, India has adopted a model of 'selective regulatory tightening,' prioritising rapid economic growth and foreign investment while introducing strict regulations in specific areas.[89]

In terms of economic policy, the Modi administration is promoting the 'Make in India' and 'Self-Reliant India' policies to actively attract foreign direct investment.[90] However, from a national security perspective, amendments to the law in 2020 introduced regulations requiring entities from countries that share a land border with India or where the actual owners of investments in India are located or are nationals of such countries to obtain government approval for investments, regardless of the industry. This measure effectively targets Chinese companies, and many Chinese firms have sought prior government approval for foreign direct investment in India. However, in many cases, the Indian government has denied such approval.

Regarding corporate social responsibility, the Indian Companies Act has established a unique system requiring all companies that meet any of the following criteria in the most recent fiscal

[85] State Council Information Office of the People's Republic of China, 'Human Rights in China' (2021).
[86] Personal Information Protection Law of the People's Republic of China (2021).
[87] Anti-Foreign Sanctions Law of the People's Republic of China (2021); Provisions on the Unreliable Entity List (2020).
[88] Congressional-Executive Commission on China, 'Annual Report 2023' (2023).
[89] United Nations Department of Economic and Social Affairs, 'World Population Prospects 2022' (2022).
[90] Government of India, 'Make in India' initiative (2014); 'Atmanirbhar Bharat' initiative (2020).

year to establish a CSR committee: (i) net assets of 5 billion rupees or more, (ii) revenue of 10 billion rupees or more, or (iii) net profit of 50 million rupees or more.[91] This is a rare system worldwide that legally mandates companies to allocate a certain percentage of their profits to social contribution activities.

However, India has maintained a cautious stance on the legalisation of international human rights due diligence. This is believed to reflect concerns about imposing additional regulatory burdens on companies amid rapid industrialisation and efforts to attract foreign investment.

E. Singapore Model: 'Adjustment of Judicial Jurisdiction with an Emphasis on Security'

Singapore's approach strongly reflects its geographical and economic national interests. As one of the world's leading shipping hubs, ensuring the safety of the Malacca-Singapore Strait is a top priority.[92] According to statistics from the Regional Cooperation Agreement on Combating Piracy and Armed Robbery against Ships in Asia (ReCAAP), most incidents in this area are not 'piracy' on the high seas, but rather 'armed robbery' occurring within the territorial waters of coastal states. This creates a 'jurisdictional maze' where such incidents fall outside the scope of universal jurisdiction and are beyond Singapore's judicial authority.

Singapore's response prioritises ensuring the safety of maritime traffic across the region through information sharing and coordinated security measures with neighbouring countries, rather than prosecuting individual perpetrators. The 'relief' provided here is aimed at protecting the collective interest of stabilising the business environment rather than restoring individual justice, resulting in a significant gap from a victim-centred perspective.

F. Taiwan Model: 'Democratic Solidarity' and a Tool for Geopolitical Defence

Taiwan's sanctions regime strongly reflects its unique international status and geopolitical environment.[93]

For Taiwan, sanctions are an important diplomatic and defence tool for demonstrating solidarity with the democratic camp and deterring pressure from China. The legal basis for this system primarily relies on administrative measures such as trade laws and the Terrorist Financing Prevention Act. A recent example of its implementation is the strict management of exports to Russia of 57 strategic high-tech goods, including semiconductors, in response to Russia's invasion of Ukraine.

This was a strategic move to clearly demonstrate solidarity with the democratic camp while facing the threat of authoritarianism. Additionally, China has imposed sanctions on US companies that sold weapons to Taiwan by applying its own 'Anti-Foreign Sanctions

[91] Companies Act 2013 (India), s 135.

[92] Regional Cooperation Agreement on Combating Piracy and Armed Robbery against Ships in Asia, 'Annual Report 2023' (2024).

[93] Mainland Affairs Council (Taiwan), 'Cross-Strait Relations and Taiwan's Position' (2023).

Law,' escalating the tit-for-tat sanctions and counter-sanctions surrounding the Taiwan Strait.[94]

G. ASEAN Coordination: The Principle of Non-Interference in Internal Affairs and the 'Five Consensus'

ASEAN adopted the ASEAN Human Rights Declaration (AHRD) in 2012 and established the ASEAN Intergovernmental Commission on Human Rights (AICHR), institutionalising regional human rights mechanisms.[95] However, these frameworks have not become effective due to their structural weaknesses.

The 'ASEAN Way' – based on the principle of non-interference in internal affairs enshrined in the ASEAN Charter and decision-making by consensus – remains the greatest obstacle to any collective action, including sanctions, on the grounds of human rights violations.[96]

This limitation was exposed in ASEAN's response to the military coup in Myanmar. ASEAN agreed on the 'Five-Point Consensus,' which called for the cessation of violence, but the military refused to comply, and ASEAN took only symbolic measures such as excluding military leaders from the summit meeting.[97]

Furthermore, a survey of ASEAN experts showed that while the United States was the preferred choice in 2023, with 60 per cent of respondents choosing the United States over China, this trend reversed in 2024, with China taking the lead.[98] This shift reflects the deepening US-China rivalry, which is undermining ASEAN's unity and centrality.

H. New Developments: Trends and Challenges in Legalisation in the Asian Region

i. Pressure for Legalisation of Human Rights Due Diligence

On July 25, 2024, the EU's Corporate Sustainability Due Diligence Directive (CSDDD) came into effect, imposing obligations on companies to prevent and address negative impacts on human rights and the environment resulting from their business activities, thereby indirectly affecting Asian companies as well.[99]

In particular, Asian companies with close business ties to the EU are now required to implement human rights due diligence across their entire supply chains.

In response, discussions on the legalisation of human rights due diligence have accelerated in Japan, led by a cross-party parliamentary league, and South Korea submitted the 'Bill on Human Rights and Environmental Protection for Sustainable Business Operations' to the National Assembly in September 2023, among other developments, indicating that efforts toward legalisation are gaining momentum across the Asian region.

[94] Ministry of Commerce of the People's Republic of China, 'Announcement on Sanctions against US Companies' (2023).
[95] ASEAN Human Rights Declaration (2012); ASEAN Charter (2007).
[96] H Katsumata, 'Reconstruction of Diplomatic Norms in Southeast Asia: The Case for Strict Adherence to the "ASEAN Way"' (2003) 25 *Contemporary Southeast Asia* 104.
[97] ASEAN, 'Chairman's Statement on the ASEAN Leaders' Meeting' (2021).
[98] ASEAN Studies Centre, 'The State of Southeast Asia: 2024 Survey Report' (2024).
[99] European Union, 'Directive (EU) 2024/1760 of the European Parliament and of the Council on Corporate Sustainability Due Diligence' [2024] OJ L 2024/1760.

ii. Issues with the Technical Intern Training Programme and Labour Mobility within Asia

The US Department of State's 2021 Trafficking in Persons Report highlighted issues with the technical intern training programme, revealing that over 70 per cent of companies employing foreign technical interns were found to be in violation of labour standards laws.[100] This issue has drawn international attention as a structural human rights violation in labour mobility within Asia.

iii. Technological Advances in Supply Chain Transparency

Japanese companies are being urged to enhance the visibility of their supply chains, with ensuring transparency in the value chain and utilising data emerging as key challenges for the future.[101] Advances in AI and blockchain technology are making it technically feasible to trace supply chains to their end points – a task that was previously difficult – which could contribute to enhancing the effectiveness of human rights due diligence.

I. Diversification and Convergence of Remedial Models in Asia

The 'remedial models' of Asian countries vary greatly, reflecting their political and economic systems, stages of development, and geopolitical positions.

Japan's 'dialogue-oriented model,' South Korea's 'punitive selection model,' China's 'regulatory countermeasure model,' India's 'growth-priority model,' Singapore's 'security-centric model,' Taiwan's 'collective defence model,' and ASEAN's 'cooperative constraint model' are each products of different values and practical constraints.

However, international legalisation pressures, such as the EU's CS3D, changes in the private sector, where approximately 70 per cent of major companies now conduct human rights due diligence, and heightened consumer awareness stemming from global boycotts triggered by issues such as child labour and prolonged working hours in poor conditions at factories in Southeast Asian countries since the late 1990s, are beginning to show signs of convergence among these diverse models.[102]

The future development of 'access to remedy' in the Asian region will depend on how these diverse models align with the universal standards sought by the UNGPs. To ensure effective remedies for cross-border human rights abuses while maintaining each country's institutional characteristics, it will be essential to creatively combine the multi-layered tools analysed in this chapter and establish new cooperative frameworks at the regional level.

VIII. Conclusion: A Multi-Layered Approach and Bridge to the Next Chapter

Ensuring accountability for human rights abuses committed by transnational corporations requires a multi-layered approach that combines various tools, such as the universal jurisdiction,

[100] US Department of State, 'Trafficking in Persons Report 2021' (2021).
[101] Japan Business Federation, 'Proposal for Enhancing Supply Chain Transparency' (2023).
[102] Business & Human Rights Resource Centre, 'Corporate Human Rights Benchmark 2023' (2023).

extraterritorial application, targeted sanctions, and private law safeguards analysed in this chapter, rather than a single silver bullet.[103] This complex accountability ecosystem as a whole is key to realising the 'access to effective remedy' sought by UNGP Pillar 3.

The analysis in this chapter shows that remedies for transnational human rights abuses can no longer be achieved by a single state or institution. Under a globalised economy and complex corporate structures, only a multilayered, multi-stakeholder, and multi-institutional approach can provide truly effective remedies.

However, this complexity also creates new challenges. We must address the difficulties inherent in a multi-layered approach, such as overlapping and conflicting institutions, conflicts of jurisdiction, and the risk of political exploitation.

To overcome these challenges and build a truly victim-centred remedy system, it is necessary to continue improving and integrating the tools analysed in this chapter, and above all, to maintain the international community's unwavering commitment to the universal value of human rights.

How will the theoretical and institutional frameworks presented in this chapter function in practice, or where might they fail? In Part II of this volume, which follows in the next chapter, we will apply this framework to specific case studies in Asian countries to examine its actual implementation.

[103] Ruggie, JG, Just Business: Multinational Corporations and Human Rights (New York, WW Norton & Company, 2013).

4

The UN Guiding Principles – A Significant Step but not yet Delivering the Promised Corporate Respect for Human Rights

EBONY BIRCHALL

I. Introduction

The United Nations Guiding Principles on Business and Human Rights (UNGPs),[1] endorsed by the UN Human Rights Council in 2011, represent the leading international initiative for regulating the human rights impacts of multi-national corporations. The UNGPs are a significant milestone in a long history of regulatory efforts in the field of business and human rights (BHR).

Prior to the adoption of the UNGPs, the United Nations and other international organisations for decades debated how to regulate multi-national corporations and other business enterprises. Different stakeholder groups advocated for competing regulatory approaches. Professor John Ruggie, the expert appointed by the UN Human Rights Council to advance BHR regulation navigated the contested terrain using a 'principled form of pragmatism'.[2]

Ruggie used his mandate to develop the UNGPs. The UNGPs deliberately avoid imposing binding legal obligations on business enterprises to secure buy-in from both states and the private sector. The UNGPs articulate a normative framework built on three interrelated pillars:

1. The state *duty* to protect human rights;
2. The corporate responsibility to *respect* human rights; and
3. The need to ensure access to effective *remedy* for rights-holders adversely affected by business activity.

The UNGPs have had considerable normative and policy influence. Nonetheless, widespread corporate human rights abuses persist and the aspiration of embedding respect for human rights into global business practice remains unrealised. Accordingly, while the 15-year anniversary of the UNGPs is a moment for reflection, it is not a time for complacency. Regulatory initiatives to govern multi-nationals have continued to evolve since the UNGPs, though similar debates and tensions continue to persist.

[1] Human Rights Council, 'Guiding Principles on Business and Human Rights: Implementing the United Nations "Protect, Respect and Remedy" Framework', UN Doc A/HRC/17/31 (21 March 2011).

[2] Interim Report of the Special Representative of the Secretary-General on the Issue of Human Rights and Transnational Corporations and Other Business Enterprises, E/CN.4/2006/97, 2006, para 81.

The chapter examines the genesis of the UNGPs and the regulatory debates that shaped their formulation. Understanding the development of the UNGPs helps explain key features of the instrument and provides essential context for ongoing debates about corporate responsibility, which remain salient 15 years after their endorsement. The chapter begins by outlining the origins of the UNGPs, offering a snapshot of the corporate practice dilemmas and regulatory challenges that preceded Ruggie's mandate. Section III analyses the process by which Ruggie developed the UNGPs. Section IV explores the key features of the UNGPs framework. Sections V and VI consider the post-UNGPs landscape, analysing both the successes and the critiques of the regime. The chapter concludes by offering reflections on 15 years of the UNGPs.

II. Prior to Ruggie's Mandate

In the decades leading to Ruggie's mandate, the BHR landscape was fraught with challenges. Globalisation had led to the rapid expansion of multi-national corporations into Global South countries. The rapid rise of globalisation brought serious concerns about the impact of multinationals on local communities and workers, including in relation to workplace health and safety, child labour, modern slavery, land displacement and environmental pollution.

Several high profile human rights abuses put a spotlight on the risks raised by corporate activities. As a prominent example, the Nike 'sweatshop' controversy attracted significant attention. In the 1990s, Nike faced allegations of poor working conditions, low wages, and child labour in their overseas factories particularly in Southeast Asia. For decades, Nike denied responsibility on the basis that the complaints raised occurred in factories they didn't own and therefore investigating conduct in supplier factories was 'beyond their scope'. This was a widely held industry view at this time in history.[3] After facing intense public pressure and boycotts, the company eventually acknowledged their responsibility and implemented positive changes to promote supply chain transparency.[4] Other prominent examples of BHR abuses in this period included Union Carbide's negligently managed factory causing thousands of deaths and ongoing health issues as a result of leaked toxic gas in Bhopal, India;[5] Unocal's alleged complicity in forced labour, displacement and rape during the construction of a pipeline in Myanmar;[6] and allegations of child labour in Gap's supply chain particularly in Cambodia.[7]

Meanwhile, regulation of multi-nationals had not kept pace with the changing BHR landscape. As Ruggie highlighted, from 1991 to 2001, almost all (94 per cent) of state based regulatory

[3] DJ Doorey, 'The Transparent Supply Chain: From Resistance to Implementation at Nike and Levi-Strauss' (2011) 103 *Journal of Business Ethics* 587, 591.

[4] ibid 587.

[5] B Desai, 'The Bhopal Gas Leak Disaster Litigation: An Overview' in KS Sik, MCW Pinto and JJG Syatauw (eds), *Asian Yearbook of International Law, Volume 3 (1993)* (Leiden, Brill, 1994) www.jstor.org/stable/10.1163/j.ctv2gjwtmd.10; H Ellis-Petersen, '"Bhopal's Tragedy Has Not Stopped": The Urban Disaster Still Claiming Lives 35 Years On' *The Guardian* (8 December 2019) www.theguardian.com/cities/2019/dec/08/bhopals-tragedy-has-not-stopped-the-urban-disaster-still-claiming-lives-35-years-on.

[6] 'Doe v. Unocal' (*EarthRights International*) earthrights.org/case/doe-v-unocal/; BBC News, 'Unocal Pays out on Burma "Abuses"' *BBC News* (22 March 2005) news.bbc.co.uk/2/hi/asia-pacific/4371995.stm.

[7] P Kenyon, 'Gap and Nike: No Sweat?' (*BBC News*, 15 October 2000) news.bbc.co.uk/2/hi/programmes/panorama/970385.stm.

development on foreign investment aimed to facilitate rather than to regulate or limit.[8] The discussion below highlights the key regulatory initiatives that existed prior to Ruggie's appointment in 2005.[9]

Regulation surrounding BHR has gone through several movements throughout history. Deva explained the first phase of regulatory history from 1973–1992 highlighted tensions between 'rights and responsibilities', with Global South countries wanting binding obligations placed on multi-nationals, while Global North countries were more concerned with rights of multinationals to operate in host states. The phase concluded with the suspension of negotiations on the failed regulatory initiative, the 1990 UN draft Code.[10]

The OECD Guidelines were established as part of this first phase of regulation, in 1976.[11] However as of 2005, the OECD Guidelines had only 38 adhering states and so they could not be considered universal authority on standards for BHR.[12] Moreover, the OECD Guidelines lacked a dedicated chapter on human rights until the influence of the UNGPs in 2011.

The ILO Tripartite Declaration of Principles[13] were also part of the first phase, being adopted in 1977. This instrument had broader reach given the near universal membership of the ILO. However, this instrument focused on labour-related aspects of BHR only. Neither the OECD Guidelines nor the ILO Tripartite Declaration of Principles provided the clarity required by all stakeholders in BHR.

The UN Global Compact (UNGC) was introduced in 2000 and aims to support the private sector to voluntarily align with ten principles from international instruments relating to human rights, labour rights, environment and anticorruption.[14] The UNGC's first principle is that business should support and respect internationally proclaimed human rights and the second being that business should ensure they are not complicit in human rights abuse.[15] More recently, the UNGC has also introduced a focus on advancing broader social goals, such as the Sustainable Development Goals (SDGs).[16] While these principles were an important starting point, the UNGC does not provide specificity around which human rights are relevant, directions on how businesses should implement the principles, or any form of monitoring mechanism to enforce implementation.

[8] UNCTAD, World Investment Report 2002 (Geneva 2002), 7 as cited in JG Ruggie, 'The Social Construction of the UN Guiding Principles on Business and Human Rights' in *Research Handbook on Human Rights and Business* (Cheltenham, Edward Elgar, 2020).

[9] The initiatives mentioned here were key in the BHR field at this time, however, this is not a complete list. The UN High Commissioner on Human Rights provided an annexure to a report in 2005 to list and analyse the various standards or initiatives in BHR: Report of the United Nations High Commissioner on Human Rights on the responsibilities of transnational corporations and related business enterprises with regard to human rights, UN Doc E/CN.4/2005/91 [Annex II and III].

[10] S Deva, 'The UN Guiding Principles on Business and Human Rights and Its Predecessors: Progress at a Snail's Pace?' in I Bantekas and MA Stein (eds), *The Cambridge Companion to Business and Human Rights Law* (Cambridge, Cambridge University Press, 2021) 148, www.cambridge.org/core/books/cambridge-companion-to-business-and-human-rights-law/un-guiding-principles-on-business-and-human-rights-and-its-predecessors/077964CAC0B1765D955F8CF7B20FE020.

[11] Current version: Organisation for Economic Co-operation and Development (OECD), 'OECD Guidelines for Multinational Enterprises on Responsible Business Conduct' (OECD, 2023).

[12] Report of the United Nations High Commissioner on Human Rights on the responsibilities of transnational corporations and related business enterprises with regard to human rights, UN Doc E/CN.4/2005/91, para 13.

[13] Current version: International Labour Organization, 'Tripartite Declaration of Principles concerning Multinational Enterprises and Social Policy', 5th edn (International Labour Office, 2017).

[14] 'What Is the UN Global Compact | UN Global Compact', unglobalcompact.org/what-is-gc.

[15] 'The Ten Principles | UN Global Compact', unglobalcompact.org/what-is-gc/mission/principles.

[16] 'Our Mission | UN Global Compact', unglobalcompact.org/what-is-gc/mission.

Then, in 2003, the UN had a failed attempt to create binding norms for business, known as 'the draft Norms'.[17] The draft Norms were a set of guidelines developed and adopted by the UN Sub-Commission on the Promotion and Protection of Human Rights. However, the UN Commission on Human Rights (the predecessor to the UN Human Rights Council (UNHRC)) declined to adopt the draft Norms due to opposition from business and some states.

The draft Norms proposed to introduce obligations on corporations. The first paragraph of the draft Norms titled 'General obligations' stated:

> Within their respective spheres of activity and influence, transnational corporations and other business enterprises **have the obligation** to promote, secure the fulfilment of, respect, ensure respect of and protect human rights recognized in international as well as national law, including the rights and interests of indigenous peoples and other vulnerable groups.[18] (Emphasis added).

The obligations contained in the draft Norms were to be implemented via several means, including 'periodic monitoring by the United Nations, other international and national mechanisms' and through self-evaluation of 'the impact of their own activities on human rights'.[19] Moreover, business were to provide reparations to those 'adversely affected by failures to comply with these Norms'.[20]

Discussions amongst stakeholders on the draft Norms were polarised in large part due to the prospect of binding guidelines on BHR. Civil society welcomed the promise of binding obligations and implementation mechanisms. Key arguments for the adoption of the draft Norms included: the initiative was comprehensive and clear, it provided a common set of human rights standards for business, and it addressed mistrust amongst civil society of voluntary initiatives which fail to consistently address human rights risks.[21]

Business on the other hand resisted binding obligations, and, as Ruggie noted, states tend to side with business.[22] Key arguments against the draft Norms included: the shift from voluntary adherence to binding obligations was significant and unjustified, the tone of the document was unduly negative and failed to acknowledge the positive influence of business on human rights, and imposing obligations on business is a misstatement of international law (as some argue only states can be subject to international law).[23]

In the wake of the failed draft Norms, the UN High Commissioner for Human Rights consulted stakeholders and reported on the BHR landscape. The 2005 report highlighted the importance of clarifying the gaps in understanding the responsibilities of business in relation to human rights, identified several issues requiring further study (including the need to clarify emerging concepts in BHR and the need to more effectively include the views of states and stakeholders from developing countries), and called for continued dialogue and consultation amongst stakeholders.[24] Five months after this report, Professor John Ruggie was appointed as Special Representative on the issue of human rights and transnational corporations and other business enterprises. The history outlined in this section, particularly the failure of the draft Norms, provides important

[17] Norms on the Responsibilities of Transnational Corporations and Other Business Enterprises with regard to Human Rights 2003, UN Doc. E/CN.4/Sub.2/2003/12/Rev.2.

[18] ibid para 1.

[19] ibid para 16.

[20] ibid para 18.

[21] Report of the United Nations High Commissioner on Human Rights on the responsibilities of transnational corporations and related business enterprises with regard to human rights, UN Doc E/CN.4/2005/91, para 21.

[22] JG Ruggie, 'Business and Human Rights: The Evolving International Agenda' (2007) 101 *American Journal of International Law* 819, 822.

[23] Report of the United Nations High Commissioner on Human Rights on the responsibilities of transnational corporations and related business enterprises with regard to human rights, UN Doc E/CN.4/2005/91, para 20.

[24] ibid para 52.

context to understanding Ruggie's approach. The next section continues by discussing Ruggie's mandate and his development of the UNGPs.

III. Ruggie's Mandate and the Development of the UNGPs

Ruggie's initial mandate began in 2005. He was tasked to 'identify and clarify standards of corporate responsibility and accountability for transnational corporations and other business enterprises with regard to human rights'.[25] He initially produced a 2008 report outlining the 'Protect, Respect and Remedy' framework.[26] The UNHRC welcomed this approach and subsequently asked Ruggie to serve a further term with the purpose of operationalising the three pillar framework. Ruggie then developed the UNGPs over the following three years, and the UNHRC endorsed the UNGPs in 2011.[27]

Throughout his mandate, Ruggie faced the challenging task of finding solutions to a 'divisive' and 'deadlocked' issue.[28] Ruggie contributed a list of written works and interviews recording decisions he made to build the consensus amongst stakeholders that ultimately secured the endorsement of the UNGPs.[29] He reported using several strategies to build support for the UNGPs. First, he explained in his interim report that he approached the task with a *principled form of pragmatism*: 'an unflinching commitment to the principle of strengthening the promotion and protection of human rights as it relates to business, coupled with a pragmatic attachment to what works best in creating change where it matters most – in the daily lives of people'.[30] While he was guided by the desire to protect human rights, he knew that he also had to prioritise aligning stakeholders and gaining support of states and business, otherwise the initiative would fail like the earlier UN draft Norms.

Second, Ruggie sought to achieve *process legitimacy* during the development of the UNGPs to bring all stakeholders together and to gain broad support for the initiative. He aimed to achieve process legitimacy through four tactics:[31]

1. Establishing a common factual baseline on BHR issues including by mapping patterns of human rights abuse, identifying standards and best practices and analysing the business case for promoting human rights.
2. Convening nearly 50 international multistakeholder consultations across the globe, which explored a diverse range of industries, operating environments, jurisdictions and responses to human rights challenges.

[25] Commission on Human Rights, 'Human Rights and Transnational Corporations and Other Business Enterprises: Human Rights Council Resolution 2005/69', E/CN.4/2005/L.10/Add.17 (20 April 2005), para. 1(a).

[26] UN Special Representative of the Secretary-General, Rep. of the Human Rights Council, Protect, Respect and Remedy: A Framework for Business and Human Rights, UN Doc. A/HRC/8/5 (7 April 2008).

[27] UN Special Representative of the Secretary-General, Rep. of the Human Rights Council, Guiding Principles on Business and Human Rights: Implementing the United Nations 'Protect, Respect and Remedy' Framework, UN Doc. A/HRC/17/31 (21 March 2011).

[28] C López, 'The "Ruggie Process": From Legal Obligations to Corporate Social Responsibility?' in D Bilchitz and S Deva (eds), *Human Rights Obligations of Business: Beyond the Corporate Responsibility to Respect?* (Cambridge, Cambridge University Press, 2013) 62, www.cambridge.org/core/books/human-rights-obligations-of-business/ruggie-process-from-legal-obligations-to-corporate-social-responsibility/09F962173BC73F2198B56D7D213C3919.

[29] See, eg, Ruggie (n 22); JG Ruggie, *Just Business: Multinational Corporations and Human Rights*, 1st edn (New York, WW Norton & Company, 2013); Ruggie (n 8); JG Ruggie, C Rees and R Davis, 'Ten Years After: From UN Guiding Principles to Multi-Fiduciary Obligations' (2021) 6 *Business and Human Rights Journal* 179.

[30] Commission on Human Rights, 'Interim Report of the Special Representative of the Secretary General on the Issue of Human Rights and Transnational Corporations and Other Business Enterprises', UN Doc E/CN.4/2006/97 (22 February 2006), para 81.

[31] Ruggie (n 29) Ch 4; Ruggie (n 8) 17.

3. Conducting sight visits to companies in a range of sectors and jurisdictions, and meeting with community leaders and workers representatives to get the input from people on the ground.
4. Conducting pilot projects in a range of sectors and jurisdictions to inform principles contained in the UNGPs in relation to human rights due diligence and grievance mechanisms.

Third, Ruggie framed the UNGPs as 'nothing new'. He used a narrative that the UNGPs did not create new obligations, but instead elaborated on existing standards for states and business within a single coherent document.[32] Ruggie avoided the much debated question of whether corporations can be subjected to international law by imposing a social expectation that corporations will respect human rights, rather than a legal obligation.[33] This 'nothing new' narrative helped to generate the necessary support from business and states.[34]

Ruggie reported that he perceived the UNGPs enjoyed strong support from government and business, and while major human rights groups did generally support the UNGPs, they were less enthusiastic than other stakeholders as the UNGPs had not achieved their desire for legal binding regulation.[35] Even though the UNGPs did ultimately receive the support required to be adopted by the UNHRC, the processes adopted by Ruggie, and the end product of the UNGPs, are not entirely free from criticism, as discussed below.

IV. An Outline of the UN Guiding Principles

The UNGPs operationalise the three pillar 'Respect, Protect, Remedy' framework. The UNGPs contain 31 principles that are divided under these three pillars, and each principle contains a commentary. The introduction to the UNGPs provides that the principles apply to all states and all business enterprises, 'regardless of their size, sector, location, ownership and structure'.[36] Further, the principles should be implemented in a non-discriminatory manner, recognising that certain groups, populations and genders face heightened or different risks.[37]

Ruggie explained the reasoning behind the three-part framework. He said that corporate conduct at the global level is shaped by three governance systems: traditional law and governance at the domestic and international levels driven by states; civil governance such as advocacy, law suits and other forms of pressure; and corporate governance which internalises within corporations elements of the other two systems.[38] Through the UNGPs, he aimed to generate a normative platform to better align the three governance systems, so that each could compensate for the shortcomings of the others and play mutually reinforcing roles to bring about cumulative change

[32] UN Special Representative of the Secretary-General, Rep. of the Human Rights Council, Guiding Principles on Business and Human Rights: Implementing the United Nations 'Protect, Respect and Remedy' Framework, UN Doc. A/HRC/17/31 (21 March 2011), para 14.

[33] On the debate on whether business can be subject to international law, see, eg, N Bernaz, 'Business, International Human Rights Law and International Criminal Law: Shifting Boundaries The Universal Declaration of Human Rights and the Development' in *Business and Human Rights* (Abingdon, Routledge, 2017) 104.

[34] Deva (n 10) 159.

[35] Ruggie (n 8) 17.

[36] UNHRC, 'Guiding Principles on Business and Human Rights: Implementing the United Nations "Protect, Respect and Remedy" Framework' (2011) UN Doc A/HRC/17/31, para 1.

[37] ibid para 1.

[38] Ruggie (n 8) 12.

over time.[39] The role of states is to *protect* through legal governance, the role of business (beyond compliance with law) is to *respect* human rights which requires due diligence to avoid infringing on the rights of others and to remedy harm when it occurs, and the rationale of civil society and rightsholders is to realise rights through meaningful engagement with business and access to remedy.[40] The discussion below summarises the principles organised under the three-part framework.

A. State Duty to Protect (Pillar I: Principles 1–10)

States must protect against human rights abuse within their territory as a foundational principle (principle 1), which requires taking steps to prevent, investigate, punish and redress abuse. States should set out the expectation that all business operations in their territory respect human rights (principle 2). States should perform regulatory and policy functions by enforcing laws requiring business to respect human rights, ensuring laws and policies do not constrain but enable business to respect human rights, providing effective guidance to business on how to respect human rights, and encouraging business to communicate their human rights impacts (principle 3). States should take additional steps to protect human rights in cases where a business is owned, controlled or receives substantial support from the state (principle 4). States should exercise oversight to meet their international human rights obligations when contracting with or legislating on business operations to provide services that may impact human rights (principle 5). When conducting commercial transactions with business, states should promote respect for human rights (principle 6).

Principle 7 recognises that the risk of gross human rights abuse is heightened in conflict-affected areas. Therefore, states should engage with business at the earliest state possible to help them identify, precent and mitigate risk of human rights abuse (principle 7(a)). States should assist business to assess and address the heightened risk of abuse, with particular attention on gender-based and sexual violence (principle 7(b)). States should deny access to support and services to business involved with gross abuses and that refuse to cooperate to address the situation (principle 7(c)). States should ensure their policy, legislation, regulation and enforcement are effective in addressing the risk of corporate human rights abuse (principle 7(d)).

States should ensure policy coherence throughout governmental departments, agencies and other state-based institutions (principle 8). Economic agreements made by states can limit domestic policy space and may constrain states from fully implementing human rights obligations. Therefore, states should maintain adequate policy space to meet their obligations (principle 9). When acting as members of multilateral institutions dealing with business-related issues, states should encourage such institutions to promote business respect for human rights and draw from the UNGPs to promote shared understanding and cooperation (principle 10).

B. Business Responsibility to Respect (Pillar II: Principles 11–24)

Business should respect human rights as a foundational principle by avoiding infringement of human rights and addressing adverse human rights impacts when they occur (principle 11). The

[39] ibid.
[40] ibid.

relevant human rights principles referred to in principle 11 include at a minimum the International Bill of Human Rights and the fundamental rights in the ILO's Declaration on Fundamental Principles and Rights at Work (principle 12). Respecting human rights requires business to avoid causing or contributing to adverse human rights impacts, to address impacts when they occur, and to seek to prevent or mitigate impacts that are directly linked to their operations and their relationships, even when they have not contributed to such impacts (principle 13). All business enterprises regardless of their size, sector, operational context, ownership and structure have a responsibility to respect, and the means through which business meet such responsibility will vary according to factors including the size of the business (principle 14).

The UNGPs do not merely state that business should respect human rights, but they also provide guidance on how this should occur. Principle 15 states business should have in place policy and processes appropriate to their size and circumstances, including policy commitment to meet their responsibility to respect, a human rights due diligence process (HRDD) to identify, prevent, mitigate and account for impacts on human rights, and processes to enable remediation in cases of adverse human rights impacts. Ruggie explained, '[t]he logic is straightforward: in order for an enterprise to demonstrate to itself, let alone anyone else, that it respects human rights it must have systems in place whereby it can *know and show* that it does (italics added).'[41] Ruggie's concept of HRDD and that businesses need to 'know and show'[42] their respect for human rights have been significant contributions in the BHR landscape, which will be explored in the section below on successes of the UNGPs.

Principles 16–24 elaborate on this practical guidance for business on how respect for human rights should occur. Business should express their commitment to respect human rights in a policy which is: approved at the most senior level, informed by relevant expertise, clear on expectations of personnel and partners linked to its operations, publicly available and communicated to staff and business partners, and embedded in policy and procedure throughout business operations (principle 16). The process of HRDD should: cover adverse impacts caused or contributed to through business operations or through business relationships, vary in complexity in relation to the size, risks, nature and context of the business, and be ongoing in recognition that human rights risks change over time as the business and its operating context evolves (principle 17).

The initial step in conducting HRDD is to identify and assess adverse human rights risks by drawing on human rights expertise and through meaningful consultation with potentially affected groups and other stakeholders (principle 18). To prevent and mitigate human rights impacts, business should effectively integrate findings from assessments by: ensuring that responsibility for addressing impacts is assigned to the appropriate level and function within the business, and that internal decision-making, budget allocations and oversight enables effective response to adverse impacts (principle 19a). Business should take appropriate action to prevent and mitigate adverse human rights impacts, and the action required will vary according to its involvement in the impact: where a business causes or contributes to an adverse impact it should take steps to cease or prevent the impact, and where a business is not the cause but is directly linked to an impact via a business relationship, it should use any leverage it has to prevent or mitigate the impact or consider ending the relationship (principle 19b). Business should track the effectiveness of their responses to adverse impacts and tracking should be based on qualitative and quantitative indicators and draw from feedback from various sources including affected stakeholders (principle 20).

[41] ibid 14.

[42] The 'know and show' phrase is stated in the commentary to principle 15 of the UNGPs.

Business should communicate externally to stakeholders on human rights impacts in a form or frequency that reflects its human rights impacts, and which is accessible, and include sufficient information to evaluate responses to adverse impacts, however such communication should not pose risks to stakeholders, staff or commercial confidentiality (principle 21).

The UNGPs acknowledge that even when business implements human rights policies and practices, it still may cause or contribute adverse human rights impacts. In cases of adverse impacts, business should provide remedy or cooperate in legitimate remediation processes (principle 22). This principle is elaborated on further in pillar three on access to remedy, discussed below.

The UNGPs acknowledge that local contexts and state laws may affect the human rights risks of business operations. Business should comply with all applicable laws and respect internationally recognised human rights, seek ways to honour internationally recognised human rights when faced with conflicting requirements and treat the risk of causing or contributing to human rights abuses as a legal compliance issue in whichever context they operate within (principle 23). In situations where it is not possible to address all adverse human rights impacts simultaneously, business should first prevent or mitigate impacts that are most severe or where a delayed response would make the impact irremediable (principle 24).

C. Access to Remedy (Pillar III: Principles 25–31)

States must take steps to ensure rightsholders impacted by corporate human rights abuses have access to effective remedy as a foundational principle (principle 25). States should take steps to ensure the effectiveness of domestic judicial mechanisms in relation to corporate human rights abuses, including by reducing any barriers that may exist (principle 26). States should also provide effective non-judicial grievance mechanisms for the remedy of corporate human rights abuses (principle 27). States should facilitate access to effective non-state-based grievance mechanisms to enhance access to remedy for corporate human rights abuses (principle 28). Business should establish or participate in effective operational-level grievance mechanisms to facilitate early and direct remediation of corporate human rights abuses (principle 29). Industry or other multi-stakeholder initiatives should also ensure effective grievance mechanisms are available (principle 30).

Principle 31 sets out effectiveness criteria for non-judicial grievance mechanisms. Such mechanisms should be legitimate, accessible, predictable, equitable, transparent, rights-compatible and a source of continuous learning. Operational-level grievance mechanisms should also be based on engagement and dialogue with stakeholder groups.

V. Successes of the UNGPs

The UNGPs have been transformative in terms of cementing in international norms that business must respect human rights. Unlike the UN Global Compact, which provides a list of principles that business can elect to adopt, the UNGPs provide a normative statement outlining corporate responsibility. The UNGPs radically shifted discourse in international law from a focus on the sovereign state, to better reflect a globalised economic context that has brought shifts in power amongst state, business and society.[43]

[43] K McPhail and CA Adams, 'Corporate Respect for Human Rights: Meaning, Scope, and the Shifting Order of Discourse' (2016) 29 *Accounting, Auditing & Accountability Journal* 650, 657–58.

The UNGPs have also provided a strong foundation upon which future progress can be built. Ruggie intended for the UNGPs to be viewed as reflexive and dynamic, with the hope that they would trigger an iterative process of interaction between states, business and civil society that would produce cumulative change over time.[44] The UNGPs have achieved this intention for the UNGPs to trigger further developments, as demonstrated in the examples below.

The UNGPs have influenced the development of other international instruments. For example, the UNGPs also impacted the development of ISO26000, a guidance on social responsibility developed by the International Organization for Standardization. The development of this guidance occurred simultaneously with Ruggie's mandate to develop the UNGPs, and he reported the teams involved ensured that the human rights provisions were closely aligned.[45]

The OECD Guidelines have also incorporated the UNGPs, including the insertion of a dedicated chapter on human rights, and the requirement for business to conduct human rights due diligence.[46] The OECD Guidelines are particularly noteworthy in having a complaints mechanism, whereby adhering states to the OECD Guidelines must establish an agency called National Contact Point (NCP) to hear complaints relating to breaches by multi-nationals. This mechanism has resulted in meaningful outcomes towards access to remedy, including for rightsholders in Asia. For example, 681 Cambodian families filed an NCP complaint alleging ANZ Banking Group were responsible for non-compliance with OECD Guidelines as the bank financed a sugar plantation project that displaced them from their land.[47] In 2020, ANZ agreed to financially compensate the families, providing an amount equivalent to its gross profits from the loan. ANZ also committed to enhancing its policies and grievance mechanisms to prevent future involvement in projects associated with human rights abuses.[48]

The UNGPs have influenced regional and state-based policy. As an early example from 2011, the EU not only endorsed the UNGPs, but the European Commission aligned its definition of CSR to fit the UNGPs and implemented a strategy recommending that all member states develop National Action Plans (NAPs).[49] Soon after, the UNWG reiterated the call for states to develop NAPs to implement the UNGPs.[50] The first handful of states launched their NAPs in 2013 and 2014; around ten years later, 34 states had launched NAPs and a further four states had NAPs on human rights with dedicated chapters on business and human rights.[51] Several Asian states have launched NAPs in recent years: Indonesia (2023), Japan (2020), Nepal (2023), Thailand (2019) and Vietnam (2023).

Ruggie's introduction of the corporate responsibility to undertake HRDD has been evolutionary as it gained immediate and ongoing traction. As Ruggie pointed out in a 2011 interview, '[b]efore 2008, no one had ever used the term "human rights due diligence". It was introduced in

[44] Ruggie (n 8) 15.

[45] ibid 18.

[46] ibid.

[47] Australian National Contact Point, *Specific Instance Submitted by Equitable Cambodia and Inclusive Development International on Behalf of 681 Cambodian Families* (Final Statement, 27 June 2018); Australian National Contact Point, *Regarding Complaint Submitted by Equitable Cambodia and Inclusive Development International on Behalf of Cambodian Families* (Follow Up Statement, 27 February 2020).

[48] ibid.

[49] Communication from the Commission to the European Parliament, the Council, the European Economic and Social Committee and the Committee of the Regions (2011), A renewed EU strategy 2011-14 for Corporate Social Responsibility, available at eur-lex.europa.eu/legal-content/EN/TXT/?uri=celex%3A52011DC0681; Ruggie (n 8) 18.

[50] Report of the Working Group on the issue of human rights and transnational corporations and other business enterprises A/HRC/23/32 (14 March 2013) 21.

[51] 'National Action Plans on Business and Human Rights' (*OHCHR*) www.ohchr.org/en/special-procedures/wg-business/national-action-plans-business-and-human-rights.

my 2008 report. It is now everywhere.'[52] Ruggie explained that in only three years the HRDD had already spread to a variety of international and domestic policy.

Fifteen years after the UNGPs, HRDD provisions have now sparked hard law in some regions. Most notably, the EU's Corporate Sustainability Due Diligence Directive (CSDDD) passed in July 2024.[53] HRDD principles have also inspired laws such as conflict mineral regulation in the US and the EU, modern slavery legislation in the UK and Australia, as well as the French Duty of Vigilance laws.[54]

HRDD uptake is relatively nascent in Asia. On 13 June 2025, the Corporate Human Rights and Environmental Due Diligence Act was reintroduced to the National Assembly of the Republic of Korea. The bill was first introduced in September 2023 but since expired.[55] Research from 2023 reports that while HRDD is a relatively new concept to Asia, the influence of overseas trends has led some multi-nationals in the seafood and palm oil industry to begin implementing HRDD in their operations.[56]

VI. Critiques of the UNGPs

While it is undeniable that the UNGPs brought sweeping changes to the BHR landscape, this does not mean they have been able to solve the complex challenges related to the human rights impacts of corporate conduct. This section highlights several critiques or limitations of the UNGPs and Ruggie's process.

The first critique concerns the limited participation of affected individuals and communities during Ruggie's process. Even though Ruggie reported conducting site visits at businesses to speak to workers and conducting meetings with community leaders,[57] critics have argued that not enough effort was made to facilitate participation of rightsholders.[58] For example, advocates had requested that Ruggie pay country visits to investigate specific instances of abuse. They reasoned that visits would provide an accountability mechanism, and moreover, lessons learned by Ruggie on these visits could inform his mandate. Ruggie denied this request on the basis that such investigation would derail the focus of the mandate to develop standards and guidance.[59]

Second, the normative basis of the UNGPs has been said to be weak for several reasons. Civil society groups were critical of the UNGPs because they failed to impose binding obligations on business. Relatedly, Lopez argued that the failure of the UNGPs to incorporate any form of accountability mechanism has rendered them weak in terms of their normative force.[60] Deva

[52] Interview with Michael Connor and John Ruggie, 'Business and Human Rights: Interview with John Ruggie' (30 October 2011) business-ethics.com/2011/10/30/8127-un-principles-on-business-and-human-rights-interview-with-john-ruggie/.

[53] See T Nakamura, 'The EU Corporate Sustainability Due Diligence Directive – Challenges and Potentials in The ASEAN Context' ch 6 of this volume.

[54] Ruggie (n 8) 18.

[55] J Tae-ho et al, '[Press Release] Asia's First Corporate Human Rights and Environmental Due Diligence Bill Reintroduced in South Korea' (13 June 2025) ktncwatch.org/news/press-release-asias-first-corporate-human-rights-and-environmental-due-diligence/.

[56] Oxfam, 'Policy Paper on Human Rights Due Diligence' (2023) oi-files-cng-v2-prod.s3.eu-west-2.amazonaws.com/asia.oxfam.org/s3fs-public/Policy%20Briefing%20HRDD_revised%20160924.pdf?VersionId=px0lx2A8RBEphFTsP3inMtTMqG4BwSdk.

[57] Ruggie (n 29) Ch 4; Ruggie (n 8) 17.

[58] López (n 28) 69–70; Surya Deva, 'Human Rights and Humanizing Business' in *Humanizing Business* (Cham, Springer International Publishing, 2022) 132; Deva (n 10) 164.

[59] López (n 28) 70.

[60] ibid 72.

argued the UNGPs provide a weak normative basis because Ruggie grounded business responsibility to respect human rights on 'social expectations', and this poses concerns for the promotion of human rights, including because there is a lack of clarity around what relation this social expectation has with the International Bill of Rights.[61]

Third, the terminology of the UNGPs has been criticised on a few points. The UNGPs deviate from the 'respect, protect and fulfil' framework in the International Bill of Rights. In the UNGPs, neither states nor business is expected to complete the full three part framework of 'respect, protect and fulfil', leaving gaps in human rights responsibilities in relation to corporate conduct.[62] The UNGPs also deviate from the use of human rights terminology when referring to abuses of human rights, by using the business-friendly terms 'adverse impact' and 'risk assessment'.[63] It has been argued that as a result of the UNGPs risk management perspective, business has focused on risk to business instead of focusing on risks to human rights.[64]

These limitations of the UNGPs can be understood as a product of Ruggie's 'principled pragmatism' approach. Ruggie aimed to develop an initiative that would be acceptable to business and states because otherwise it would fail as had happened with the draft Norms. Further, he repeatedly mentioned the importance of achieving buy-in from business, because he believed without business uptake any initiative developed would not be implemented. Due to this pragmatism, Ruggie prioritised the acceptance and interests of business over that of individuals and communities impacted by corporate conduct. While this pragmatism may have been necessary at the time of Ruggie's mandate to push the regulatory landscape forward, these shortcomings must be addressed to realise the promised corporate respect for human rights.

VII. Developments Since the UNGPs

The UNHRC has continued focused work on BHR since the endorsement of the UNGPs in 2011. The Working Group on Business and Human Rights (BHR Working Group)[65] was established in 2011 to promote the dissemination and implementation of the UNGPs.[66] The BHR Working Group consists of five experts in the field of BHR, one from each of the five UN recognised regions. They undertake country visits, write annual reports, and produce communications as part of the UN Special Procedures.[67] They also chair the annual UN Forum on BHR, which has become the world's largest platform for dialogue between the range of stakeholders in BHR.

In 2014, the UNHRC adopted a resolution to form an intergovernmental working group to elaborate a possible international legally binding instrument on business and human rights (LBI Working Group).[68] The LBI Working Group has been constituted for over a decade and consensus does not seem likely in the near future. Negotiations have encountered significant disagreements,

[61] Deva (n 10) 165; Deva (n 58) 132.

[62] Deva (n 10) 165.

[63] ibid.

[64] B Fasterling, 'Human Rights Due Diligence as Risk Management: Social Risk Versus Human Rights Risk' (2017) 2 *Business and Human Rights Journal* 225.

[65] Also known as: Working Group on the issue of human rights and transnational corporations and other business enterprises.

[66] UN Human Rights Council Resolution A/HRC/RES/17/4 (6 July 2011).

[67] The Working Group on Business and Human Rights provides information and publications on their website: 'Working Group on Business and Human Rights' (*OHCHR*) www.ohchr.org/en/special-procedures/wg-business.

[68] UN Human Rights Council, Elaboration of an international legally binding instrument on transnational corporations and other business enterprises with respect to human rights, A/HRC/RES/26/9 (14 July 2014).

primarily reflecting geopolitical, ideological, and practical tensions. The next chapter of this book analyses the work of the LBI Working Group in detail; however, it is useful to summarise several of the core disagreements below.[69]

First, there is division over the scope of the proposed legally binding instrument. Many participating Global South countries argue the treaty should specifically target transnational corporations, reflecting concerns about corporate abuses often involving foreign investors. Conversely, several participating Global North countries argue for a broader scope covering all businesses – not just transnational corporations – emphasising universal applicability and fairness.

Second, enforcement mechanisms and accountability remain contentious. Civil society and many Global South countries demand robust accountability provisions such as strong extraterritorial jurisdiction, rightsholder remedy mechanisms, and direct corporate liability. Whereas states with powerful corporate sectors, mainly in the Global North, resist binding extraterritorial obligations due to fears of litigation risks and impacts on competitiveness.

Third, there are disagreements about the practicality and political feasibility of the proposed binding instrument. Some stakeholders argue that attempting a comprehensive binding instrument is overly ambitious and could undermine ongoing incremental progress under other frameworks, primarily the UNGPs. Others counter that only binding obligations can effectively close existing accountability gaps.

Lastly, there is tension regarding compatibility and complementarity with existing soft-law instruments and domestic regulatory frameworks. Critics express concern that a binding instrument may duplicate or undermine existing norms such as the UNGPs, or national laws like mandatory due diligence initiatives, whereas others argue a binding instrument would complement and strengthen existing measures. These fundamental disagreements have slowed negotiations, illustrating the complexity inherent in establishing global consensus on legally binding human rights standards for businesses.

VIII. Reflections on Fifteen Years of UNGPs

The history outlined in this chapter explains the context that informed the approach taken by Ruggie in developing the UNGPs. The chapter explained Ruggie's pragmatic approach, and the principles contained within the UNGPs. It then analysed the successes and limitations of Ruggie's approach and briefly outlined the status of the proposed legally binding instrument. The chapter concludes by providing two reflections at this 15-year anniversary of the UNGPs.

First, there is still work to be done. The introduction of the UNGPs was a significant step and spurred momentum for increased regulation of multi-nationals. However, as Ruggie himself acknowledged, the UNGPs marked merely 'the end of the beginning'.[70] Much work remains to ensure that the regulation of corporate conduct is grounded in a robust normative framework shaped by the experiences of affected individuals and communities.

Statistics demonstrate that current regulation in BHR is not yet delivering the promised business respect for human rights. The World Benchmarking Alliance published its first social

[69] For comprehensive analysis, see A Crockett, A Tang and JH Sendut, 'A Decade of UN Business and Human Rights Treaty Negotiations – Something to See Here?' ch 5 of this volume.

[70] Presentation of Report to United Nations Human Rights Council, Professor John G Ruggie, Special Representative of the Secretary-General for Business and Human Rights, Geneva (30 May 2011), www.ohchr.org/Documents/Issues/TransCorporations/HRC%202011_Remarks_Final_JR. pdf.

benchmark in July 2024, to assess the world's 2,000 most influential corporations in three areas: respect for human rights, provision of decent work, and ethical actions. Ninety per cent of the assessed corporations failed the assessment, scoring less than half the available points.[71] The benchmark results showed assessment of corporations against criteria required under the UNGPs, including that only 20 per cent of the assessed corporations conduct some steps of HRDD, and only nine per cent show how they consult workers or communities impacted by their operations.[72]

Secondly, the relative lack of meaningful progress toward a binding instrument on BHR over the past decade underscores the prudence of John Ruggie's pragmatic and incremental approach embodied in the UNGPs. Since their endorsement in 2011, the UNGPs have become the authoritative normative framework within the field, successfully shaping corporate human rights policies, influencing domestic regulation, and becoming a foundational reference point in advocacy and accountability efforts globally. While they are not legally binding, their widespread adoption demonstrates the strategic value of starting from an achievable consensus rather than ambitious but contentious legal mandates.

In contrast, efforts towards the legally binding instrument have repeatedly stalled due to significant political divisions, procedural disagreements, and resistance from influential states and corporate stakeholders. Over the past ten years, the negotiations have highlighted stark geopolitical and economic interests, illustrating the complexity and inherent difficulties in achieving comprehensive global legal instruments within the business and human rights sphere. These persistent obstacles have validated Ruggie's cautious and pragmatic decision to initially pursue voluntary standards and broad-based consensus rather than immediate legally enforceable obligations.

Although incrementalism inherently faces criticism for not fully addressing the pressing accountability gap, the UNGPs have undeniably driven substantial positive change. They have prompted a cascade of regulatory initiatives, with a broad uptake in the development of national action plans on BHR, and with some governments event adopting mandatory HRDD laws. In Asia, Europe, and elsewhere, tangible regulatory and business practices inspired by UNGP principles have emerged, embedding human rights considerations more deeply into corporate governance and operations than might otherwise have been possible.

Despite valid critiques of the UNGPs, they have provided essential foundations for subsequent regulatory developments and a transformative shift in corporate culture. In the face of continuing international deadlock over the legally binding instrument, the incremental yet tangible achievements of the UNGPs demonstrate that pragmatic, consensus-driven approaches, though imperfect, may be more effective at moving the dial forward.

[71] World Benchmark Alliance, '90% of World's 2,000 Most Influential Companies Failing to Ensure Human Rights, Decent Work and Ethical Conduct' (*World Benchmarking Alliance*, 2 July 2024) www.worldbenchmarkingalliance.org/news/social-benchmark-press-release-2024/.

[72] ibid.

5

A Decade of UN Business and Human Rights Treaty Negotiations – Something to See Here?*

ANTONY CROCKETT, AARON TANG AND JEFFERI HAMZAH SENDUT

Over a decade has passed since the Open-Ended Intergovernmental Working Group on Transnational Corporations and Other Business Enterprises with Respect to Business and Human Rights (the Working Group) was established in 2014 by UN Human Rights Council (UNHRC) Resolution 26/9.[1] Tasked with elaborating a legally binding instrument on business and human rights (LBI),[2] the Working Group's annual sessions have been marked by significant divisions between participating States on the scope and content of the proposed LBI, as well as its relationship with the UN Guiding Principles on Business and Human Rights (UNGPs).[3]

The slow progress in the LBI negotiations has not been lost on participants. Ecuador, which has chaired the Working Group since its inception, has responded in more recent years by pursuing a renewed strategy aimed at facilitating refocused and productive negotiations.

In light of these circumstances, this chapter takes stock following just over ten years since the start of Working Group negotiations in 2015, with a focus on recent initiatives pursued by Ecuador as well as other developments which have collectively created a tentative route towards a workable compromise on an LBI.

The chapter begins by providing an overview of the Working Group negotiations and the most recent draft of the LBI (the 2023 Draft),[4] along with the core disagreements which have marked the process (Section I).

The chapter goes on to consider how Ecuador as Working Group chair has attempted to facilitate progress towards a concluded LBI, through (i) the circulation of proposed draft LBI language intended to promote compromise, (ii) the establishment of the 'Friends of the Chair' grouping of States, and (iii) backing the UNHRC's adoption of Decision 56/116[5] in July 2024

* The views expressed in this chapter are those of the authors alone and do not necessarily reflect those of Herbert Smith Freehills Kramer or any of its clients. The authors would like to thank their colleagues who provided assistance in connection with this chapter.

[1] United Nations Human Rights Council Resolution 26/9 (11 July 2014) UN Doc A/HRC/RES/26/9 (Resolution 26/9).

[2] In full, 'an international legally binding instrument to regulate, in international human rights law, the activities of transnational corporations and other business enterprises'.

[3] UNHRC 'Report of the Special Representative of the Secretary-General on the issue of human rights and transnational corporations and other business enterprises – Guiding Principles on Business and Human Rights: Implementing the United Nations "Protect, Respect and Remedy" Framework' (2011) UN Doc A/HRC/17/31.

[4] Updated Draft Legally Binding Instrument to Regulate, in International Human Rights Law, the Activities of Transnational Corporations and Other Business Enterprises (July 2023) (2023 Draft).

[5] UNHRC Decision 56/116 (12 July 2024) UN Doc A/HRC/DEC/56/116 (Decision).

mandating the Working Group to hold intersessional consultations assisted by legal experts (Section II).

The chapter then examines some of the significant uncertainties which remain for the Working Group process, which call into question whether consensus can yet be reached. It considers (i) how Working Group participants might continue to respond to the process established by Decision 56/116, in view of the diverse positions a concluded LBI would need to account for, (ii) the role of the EU and USA in the coming years, and (iii) the potential ramifications of the UN's financial challenges (Section III).

Finally, the chapter concludes with a reflection on wider parallel trends concerning business respect for human rights (Section IV).

I. An Overview of the Working Group Negotiations and the 2023 Draft

A. Background to the Working Group

The establishment of the Working Group in 2014 represented the start of a new 'phase' in UN standard setting on business and human rights.[6] The start of the Working Group's activities followed earlier and ultimately aborted efforts to create a Code of Conduct on Transnational Corporations, as well as the UN Sub-Commission for the Promotion and Protection of Human Rights' approval in 2003 of Norms on the Responsibilities of Transnational Corporations and Other Business Enterprises with regard to Human Rights.[7]

These early initiatives were eclipsed by the UNHRC's unanimous endorsement of the UNGPs in 2011. As detailed further in Section I(C) below, the UNGPs' universally applicable but non-binding 'Protect, Respect and Remedy' framework set the stage for the contestation which surrounded the establishment of the Working Group three years later, through UNHRC Resolution 26/9.

Following an initiative led by Ecuador and South Africa,[8] Resolution 26/9 established the Working Group with a mandate 'to elaborate an international legally binding instrument to regulate, in international human rights law, the activities of transnational corporations and other business enterprises'.[9] Resolution 26/9 was adopted on 26 July 2014, with 20 votes in favour, 14 against, and 13 abstentions,[10] and the Working Group's first session was held a year later in July 2015.[11] In an arrangement which has continued to the time of writing, the Working Group's first session saw Ecuador's representative elected as Chair-Rapporteur.[12]

[6] S Deva, 'From business or human rights to business and human rights: what next?' in S Deva and D Birchall (eds), *Research Handbook on Human Rights and Business* (Cheltenham, Edward Elgar, 2020) 3–4.

[7] ibid 4.

[8] And additionally co-sponsored by Bolivia, Cuba and Venezuela. See JG Ruggie, 'The Past as Prologue? A Moment of Truth for the UN Business and Human Rights Treaty' (Harvard Kennedy School, 7 July 2014) 2; O De Schutter, 'Towards a New Treaty on Business and Human Rights' (2015) 1 *BHRJ* 41.

[9] Resolution 26/9 (n 1) Clause 1.

[10] ibid 3.

[11] UNHRC 'Report on the first session of the open-ended intergovernmental working group on transnational corporations and other business enterprises with respect to human rights, with the mandate of elaborating an international legally binding instrument' (5 February 2016) UN Doc A/HRC/31/50.

[12] ibid 4.

B. The 2023 Draft

Following initial deliberations during the Working Group's first to third sessions (2015–2017), the first full 'zero draft' LBI (the Zero Draft) was circulated by the Chair-Rapporteur in the run up to the Working Group's fourth session in 2018.[13] The Zero Draft was followed by a revised draft circulated in each of the subsequent three years, as well as most recently by the 2023 Draft, which served as the basis for negotiations during the ninth, tenth and eleventh Working Group sessions in 2023, 2024 and 2025 respectively.

The scope of the 2023 Draft is set out in its Article 3. The 2023 Draft would apply 'to all business activities, including business activities of a transnational character'.[14] A business activity has a 'transnational character' where it is 'undertaken in more than one jurisdiction or State', has a significant element of its planning, direction, distribution or other processes taking place 'through any business relationship in another State or jurisdiction', or 'has a significant effect in another State or jurisdiction'.[15] The 2023 Draft would cover 'all internationally recognized human rights and fundamental freedoms binding on the [LBI's] States Parties'.[16]

Under Article 6.1 on prevention, States Parties would be required to 'regulate effectively the activities of all business enterprises within their territory, jurisdiction, or otherwise under their control'. States Parties would also have a specific obligation under Article 6.2 to 'adopt appropriate legislative, regulatory, and other measures' to, amongst other things, 'prevent the involvement of business enterprises in human rights abuse' and 'ensure respect by business enterprises for internationally recognized human rights and fundamental freedoms'.[17] Article 6.4 specifies that these appropriate measures 'shall include legally enforceable requirements for business enterprises to undertake human rights due diligence'.[18]

The term 'human rights due diligence' would be defined as 'the processes by which business enterprises identify, prevent, mitigate and account for how they address their adverse human rights impacts'.[19] Such processes 'will in every case' comprise: (a) the evaluation of any adverse human rights impacts which the business may be involved with 'through its own activities or as a result of its business relationships', (b) taking 'appropriate' prevention and mitigation measures, (c) monitoring the effectiveness of these measures, and (d) regularly and accessibly communicating steps taken to stakeholders.[20]

The obligation on States Parties under Article 6.2 to adopt appropriate preventative measures would additionally cover, as per Article 6.4, the adoption of supplementary 'supporting or ancillary measures as may be needed' to ensure that business' human rights due diligence processes are accompanied by related steps reinforcing respect for human rights. These steps encompass businesses: (a) publishing 'regular' human rights impact assessments 'prior and throughout their operations', (b) integrating 'a gender and age perspective', (c) particularly accounting for 'the needs of those who may be at heightened risks of vulnerability or marginalization', (d) meaningfully consulting 'with potentially affected groups and other relevant stakeholders', (e) protecting

[13] Draft Legally Binding Instrument to Regulate, in International Human Rights Law, the Activities of Transnational Corporations and Other Business Enterprises (16 July 2018) (Zero Draft).
[14] 2023 Draft (n 4) Article 3.1.
[15] ibid Article 1.5.
[16] ibid Article 3.3.
[17] ibid Articles 6.2(a)–(b).
[18] ibid Article 6.4.
[19] ibid Article 1.8.
[20] ibid Article 1.8(a)–(d).

those such as human rights defenders, and (f) 'insofar as engagement with indigenous peoples takes place', doing so 'in accordance with the internationally recognized standards of free, prior, and informed consent'.

Article 6.5 envisages States Parties taking necessary measures 'to ensure that business enterprises take appropriate steps to prevent human rights abuse by third parties' which they control, manage or supervise, 'including through the imposition of a legal duty to prevent such abuse in appropriate cases'.[21]

Furthermore, the 2023 Draft provides under Article 8 that States Parties 'shall adopt such measures as may be necessary to establish a comprehensive and adequate system of legal liability' for legal and natural persons conducting business activities.[22] Article 8.1 specifies that such legal liability would attach in relation to 'human rights abuses' which 'may arise' from a person's business activities or relationships.[23]

Specific provision would be made under Article 8.3 for each State Party, subject to its own 'legal principles', to establish liability for 'conspiring to commit human rights abuse' and 'aiding, abetting, facilitating, and counselling the commission of human rights abuse'.[24] States Parties would also be required to adopt measures 'consistent with [their] domestic legal and administrative systems' to ensure such liability is proportionate and victim-responsive, and that barriers to access to justice, including in relation to burdens of proof, are addressed appropriately.[25]

The 2023 Draft also includes provisions dealing with a range of other issues, including the rights and protection of victims, access to remedy, States Parties' jurisdiction over business-related human rights abuses, limitation periods in domestic law, applicable law in domestic judicial proceedings, mutual legal assistance, international cooperation, and consistency with wider international law.[26]

C. The Core Disagreements Marking the Working Group Negotiations

In the period immediately prior to the Working Group's inception, Ecuador had characterised the proposed LBI as a step towards changing an 'unfair world order', through 'a legal framework that holds transnational corporations accountable for their human rights violations'.[27] This framing proved highly contentious. Ecuador and its co-sponsors of Resolution 26/9 were sharply criticised by the USA, along with the EU and its Member States, which all declared that they would not participate in the Working Group if established.[28]

[21] ibid Article 6.5.

[22] ibid Article 8.1.

[23] ibid.

[24] ibid Article 8.3.

[25] ibid Articles 8.2, 8.4–8.5.

[26] ibid Articles 4, 5, 7, 9, 10, 11, 12, 13, 14. See generally I Bantekas, 'Towards a UN Business and Human Rights Treaty' in I Bantekas and MA Stein (eds), *The Cambridge Companion to Business and Human Rights Law* (Cambridge, Cambridge University Press, 2021) 587–610.

[27] R Patino, 'Ecuador's FM wants transnational corporations held accountable' (*Al Jazeera*, 1 November 2014) www.aljazeera.com/opinions/2014/11/1/ecuadors-fm-wants-transnational-corporations-held-accountable. See also D Bilchitz, 'The Necessity for a Business and Human Rights Treaty' (2016) 1(2) *BHRJ* 203.

[28] J Martens and K Seitz, 'The Struggle for a UN Treaty: Towards global regulation on human rights and business' (Global Policy Forum and Rosa Luxemburg Stiftung, 2016) 21–22, rosalux.nyc/wp-content/uploads/2020/11/RLS-NYC_struggle_for_a_un_treaty_EN.pdf. See also Bantekas (n 26) 583.

The USA labelled the proposed LBI a 'competing initiative' to the UNGPs, representing 'a threat to the [UNGPs] themselves'.[29] The USA adopted the position that 'a one-size-fits-all instrument is not the right approach to handling the complex fabric that is regulation of business',[30] an objection echoed in the years since. Similarly, the EU and its Member States were 'puzzled' by Ecuador and South Africa's push for the Working Group, a move which was said to have 'disregarded more appropriate and effective options'. Calling the vote on Resolution 26/9 a 'critical juncture', the EU and its Member States warned that the Working Group would 'divide the [UNHRC] not only on the vote, but in the years to come'.[31]

Moreover, while the UNHRC's unanimous endorsement of the UNGPs included that of its 13 Asia-Pacific Member States,[32] Resolution 26/9 only saw affirmative votes from seven Asia-Pacific States, with two voting against, and four abstaining.[33] Even among those Asia-Pacific States which supported the Working Group's establishment, notable nuances are evident. For example, while India welcomed Resolution 26/9 as providing an 'acceptable roadmap' to 'seek justice' for victims of human rights violations, China's affirmative vote was tempered by a statement highlighting that developing an LBI would be a 'complex issue', requiring 'detailed and in-depth research', and a 'gradual, inclusive and open' process.[34]

As foreshadowed by the diverse positions described above, the adoption of Resolution 26/9 has indeed been followed by intense debates on the form and substance of the proposed LBI. The chief points of disagreement which have dominated Working Group negotiations have been thoroughly analysed by commentators. While this chapter does not comprehensively rehearse these points, they have concerned, at a high level, the scope of the LBI, the nature and prescriptiveness of its obligations, and perceived ambiguities in its drafting.[35]

It has been particularly difficult for the Working Group to progress towards a compromise on whether the LBI's scope should be limited to covering 'transnational corporations and other business enterprises of a transnational character', or instead should cover the activities of all

[29] USA, 'Explanation of Vote: A/HRC/26/L.22/Rev.1 on BHR Legally-Binding Instrument' (26 June 2014) geneva.usmission.gov/2014/06/26/proposed-working-group-would-undermine-efforts-to-implement-guiding-principles-on-business-and-human-rights/.

[30] ibid.

[31] EU, '"Elaboration of an international legally binding instrument on Transnational Corporations and Other Business Enterprises with respect to human rights": EU Explanation of Vote' (2014) archive.globalpolicy.org/images/pdfs/GPFEurope/HRC_resolution_Explanation_of_vote_EU.pdf.

[32] The Asia-Pacific States which were members of the UN Human Rights Council on 16 June 2011 were Bahrain, Bangladesh, China, Japan, Jordan, Kyrgyzstan, Malaysia, Maldives, Pakistan, Qatar, Republic of Korea, Saudi Arabia, and Thailand. See 'Membership of the Human Rights Council 19 June 2010–18 June 2011 by regional groups' (*UNHRC*) www.ohchr.org/en/hr-bodies/hrc/group20102011.

[33] In favour: China, India, Indonesia, Kazakhstan, Pakistan, Philippines, Vietnam; against: Japan, Republic of Korea; abstaining: Kuwait, Maldives, Saudi Arabia, United Arab Emirates. See Treaty Alliance, 'Resolution on binding human rights standards passes in Human Rights Council' (*Global Policy Forum*, 27 June 2014) archive.globalpolicy.org/component/content/article/221-transnational-corporations/52651-treaty-alliance-press-release-on-resolution-on-binding-human-rights-standards.html.

[34] India, 'Consideration of Draft Resolution A/HRC/26/L.22/Rev 1. Elaboration of an international legally binding instrument on transnational corporations and business enterprises with respect to human rights: Explanation of Vote by India' (Permanent Mission of India Geneva, June 2014) archive.globalpolicy.org/images/pdfs/GPFEurope/HRC_resolution_Explanation_of_vote_-_India.pdf; Ruggie (n 8) 2; C Si, 'Towards a Business and Human Rights Treaty' (Master's Thesis, Norwegian Centre for Human Rights, 2015) 45.

[35] See also R Subasinghe, 'A Neatly Engineered Stalemate: A Review of the Sixth Session of Negotiations on a Treaty on Business and Human Rights' (2021) 6(2) *BHRJ* 384, 386: '[t]hese concerns can broadly be summarized as follows: non-alignment with the UN Guiding Principles on Business and Human Rights … extraterritorial jurisdiction and impedance on state sovereignty; overly broad definitions of "victim" and human rights "abuse"; focus on punitive legal liability and accountability mechanisms; lack of clarity on the scope of human and environmental rights covered; and differences in opinion on the "objective" of the Treaty coupled with concerns about the political and diplomatic viability of the instrument'.

businesses.[36] This has proven to be the single most persistent divide in the Working Group's negotiations.[37] Broadly speaking, many participating Global South States have insisted on an exclusively transnational focus, while participating Global North States (as well as some Global South States) have advocated that the LBI should apply to all business activity, whether transnational or not.[38]

The root of this divide lies in the text of Resolution 26/9. Although Resolution 26/9 conferred on the Working Group a mandate to elaborate an LBI to regulate 'the activities of transnational corporations *and other business enterprises*',[39] a footnote to a preambulatory clause states that the term 'other business enterprises' shall denote 'all business enterprises that have a transnational character in their operational activities, and does not apply to local businesses registered in terms of relevant domestic law'.[40]

While Ecuador did express 'a certain degree of openness' on the issue in early Working Group negotiations,[41] positioning which would become important in later years,[42] several other States emphasised the importance of maintaining a strict focus on transnational businesses.

For example, South Africa used its general statement at the Working Group's second session in 2016 to declare that Resolution 26/9 'clearly outlined' that an LBI's 'primary purpose' would be to regulate the activities of transnational corporations and other business enterprises 'that have a transnational character'.[43] Adopting a policy argument mirrored by other States advocating for a focus on transnational business activities, South Africa has referred to transnational corporations as operating within 'current gaps in international law' which would be filled in its view by an LBI.[44]

[36] States have sometimes drawn a distinction between the proposed LBI focusing on 'transnational corporations and other business enterprises', versus a focus on 'business activities of a transnational character'. See Updated Draft Legally Binding Instrument to Regulate, in International Human Rights Law, the Activities of Transnational Corporations and Other Business Enterprises (with textual proposals submitted by States during the ninth and tenth sessions of the Working Group) (2025) (2023 Draft with Textual Proposals) 24–25.

[37] See S Deva, 'Scope of the Proposed Business and Human Rights Treaty: Navigating through Normativity, Law and Politics' in S Deva and D Bilchitz (eds), *Building a Treaty on Business and Human Rights: Context and Contours* (Cambridge, Cambridge University Press, 2017) 154. Commentators have also debated whether an LBI could impose international legal obligations directly on corporations – see, eg, L McConnell, 'Assessing the Feasibility of a Business and Human Rights Treaty' (2017) 66 *ICLQ* 143, 146–51; LC Backer, 'Principled Pragmatism in the Elaboration of a Comprehensive Treaty on Business and Human Rights' in Deva and Bilchitz (ibid) 112–13; C Macchi, 'A Treaty on Business and Human Rights: Problems and Prospects' in JL Černič and N Carrillo-Santarelli (eds), *The Future of Business and Human Rights: Theoretical and Practical Considerations for a UN Treaty* (Cambridge, Intersentia, 2018) 71–76; AF López Latorre, 'In Defence of Direct Obligations for Businesses Under International Human Rights Law' (2020) 5 *BHRJ* 56; Bantekas (n 26) 584–85; Bilchitz (n 27) 207. However, per R McCorquodale, *Business and Human Rights* (Oxford, Oxford University Press, 2024) 193: 'all the later drafts [of the proposed LBI], while focusing on the regulation of business activity in relation to human rights impacts, do so through the prism of state obligations to put these regulations in place'.

[38] C Sudhoff, 'Scope of a UN treaty on business and human rights' (Global Policy Forum and Rosa Luxemburg Stiftung, 2024) 2–3, www.globalpolicy.org/sites/default/files/download/Scope%20of%20UN%20Treaty%20Business%20%26%20Human%20Rights.pdf.

[39] Resolution 26/9 (n 1) Clause 1 (emphasis added).

[40] See C Lopez and B Shea, 'Negotiating a Treaty on Business and Human Rights: A Review of the First Intergovernmental Session' (2015) 1 *BHRJ* 111, 113; Bilchitz (n 27) 220; Deva (n 37) 167–68; Backer (n 37) 115; Macchi (n 37) 68–69; McCorquodale (n 37) 193–94.

[41] Macchi (n 37) 69.

[42] See Section II below.

[43] South Africa, 'General statement delivered by South Africa (on behalf of the African Group)' (24 October 2016) 2, www.ohchr.org/sites/default/files/Documents/HRBodies/HRCouncil/WGTransCorp/Session2/SouthAfricaGeneral.docx.

[44] South Africa, 'General statement delivered by South Africa' (23 October 2017) 2, www.ohchr.org/sites/default/files/Documents/HRBodies/HRCouncil/WGTransCorp/Session3/OralInterventions/SouthAfrica.pdf.

Similarly, Indonesia affirmed at the Working Group's third session that '[e]xtending the scope of the instrument to all business enterprises … would not only go beyond the mandate given by Resolution 26/9 but would mean to open a long negotiating process with uncertain outcomes'.[45] Indonesia also referred to a 'gap in the international legal system', which Indonesia asserts has been exploited by transnational corporations through 'complex corporate structure[s]' enabling them to 'avoid their responsibilities for human rights violations', unlike domestic businesses already 'regulated by national laws'.[46]

On the other hand, the EU and its participating Member States have steadfastly opposed limiting the proposed LBI's scope to transnational business activities.[47] The written contribution submitted by the EU for the Working Group's first session in 2015 emphasised that a 'focus on solely transnational corporations … neglects the fact that many abuses are committed by enterprises at the domestic level', thereby undercutting a 'fundamental element' of the universally applicable UNGPs.[48] The EU's opening statement at the Working Group's fourth session raised the further objection that '[c]overing all companies is important to ensure non-discrimination and a level playing field', while expressing a willingness to consider distinctions based on 'size and other characteristics'.[49]

The EU's advocacy for a widened scope was joined by the USA during its first participation in substantive negotiations at the Working Group's eighth session in 2022, which followed the initial US appearance at the Working Group a year earlier.[50] The USA noted 'a general concern that limiting application of provisions of the LBI to business activities of a transnational character would, in some cases, be unduly narrow and inconsistent with the UNGPs'.[51]

It is against the background of this and other deep divisions between Working Group participants that Ecuador's successive Chair-Rapporteurs have in recent years pursued a renewed approach in pursuit of compromise.

II. A Renewed Approach and the Emergence of a Tentative Route to Compromise

At the start of the Working Group's tenth session in December 2024, Chair-Rapporteur Marcelo Vázquez Bermúdez was keen to highlight that the Working Group was 'under very

[45] Indonesia, 'Statement of the Delegation of Indonesia: 3rd Open-Ended Working Group on Transnational Corporations and Other Business Enterprise with Respect to Human Rights' (October 2017) 1, www.ohchr.org/sites/default/files/Documents/HRBodies/HRCouncil/WGTransCorp/Session3/OralInterventions/Indonesia-Subject2.Scopeofapplication.pdf.

[46] ibid.

[47] JL Černič, 'European Perspectives on the Business and Human Rights Treaty Initiative' in Černič and Carrillo-Santarelli (n 37) 242–43; I Zamfir, 'Towards a binding treaty on business and human rights' (European Parliamentary Research Service 2022) 11, www.europarl.europa.eu/RegData/etudes/BRIE/2022/729435/EPRS_BRI(2022)729435_EN.pdf.

[48] EU, 'Inter-Governmental Working Group (IGWG) on the elaboration of an international legally-binding instrument on transnational corporations and other business enterprises with respect to human rights: Submission of the European Union' (July 2015) 1, www.ohchr.org/sites/default/files/Documents/HRBodies/HRCouncil/WGTransCorp/Session1/EuropeanUnion.doc.

[49] EU, 'Open-ended intergovernmental working group on transnational corporations and other business enterprises with respect to human rights (4th session): Opening remarks by the European Union' (15 October 2018) 3, www.ohchr.org/sites/default/files/Documents/HRBodies/HRCouncil/WGTransCorp/Session4/EuropeanUnion.docx.

[50] D Palombo, 'The US at the Margins of Business and Human Rights' (2023) 25 *ICLR* 247, 250.

[51] 'Compilation of statements delivered by States during the State-led negotiations of the eighth session' (24-28 October 2022) (Compilation of statements in the eighth session negotiations) 8, www.ohchr.org/sites/default/files/documents/hrbodies/hrcouncil/wgtranscorp/session8/igwg-8th-compilation-state-statements.pdf.

different circumstances' as compared with its inception in 2014, and that a 'number of essential factors have changed the situation'.[52] This was so much so that his opening address hailed the arrival of a 'historic opportunity' for States to 'breathe renewed vigour into the substantive negotiations'.

Amongst other things cited as a basis for optimism, Chair-Rapporteur Vázquez Bermúdez referred to the 'growing number of participating States', as well as how the Working Group is 'now equipped with an important range of tools' which 'can and should be used … to speed up the negotiating process'. These changes are attributable, at least in part, to initiatives pursued by Ecuador in its capacity as Working Group chair, the results of which have become particularly prominent in recent years.

A. Substantive Compromises

The stage for Chair-Rapporteurs' most recent initiatives was set by what has amounted to a significant shift in Ecuador's positioning on the proposed LBI. Broadly speaking, Ecuador had led the push for Resolution 26/9 with an initial focus on transnational corporations, as well as an international system portrayed as structurally biased in their favour. Ecuador has since adapted its approach to align more closely with those States which had originally trenchantly opposed the establishment of the Working Group.

This shift has occurred in the context of changes in Ecuador's domestic politics.[53] May 2017 saw the administration of President Lenín Moreno take over from that of Rafael Correa. The impact of the transition was immediately evident in the prelude to the Working Group's third session in October 2017, which saw Ecuador's planned circulation of proposed elements for a draft LBI delayed until just three weeks prior to the session's start.[54]

The start of the Moreno Administration also saw María Fernanda Espinosa, who had served as Ecuador's nominated Chair-Rapporteur during the Working Group's first two sessions (2015-2016), take up the position of Foreign Minister.[55] Espinosa was replaced as Chair-Rapporteur by Guillaume Long, who then resigned after the Working Group's third session and was in turn replaced in February 2018 by Luis Gallegos.[56]

The Moreno Administration would have a further Chair-Rapporteur in Emilio Rafael Izquierdo Miño (for the Working Group's fifth and sixth sessions) (2019–2020), before being succeeded by the administration of President Guillermo Lasso in May 2021. This saw Izquierdo Miño remain in place as Chair-Rapporteur until the appointment of Cristian Espinosa Cañizares to the post for the Working Group's ninth session (2023).

The Lasso Administration was in turn succeeded by that of President Daniel Noboa in November 2023. Chair-Rapporteur Vázquez Bermúdez was appointed by the Noboa Administration shortly before the Working Group's tenth session. Following 13 April 2025 runoff elections, President Noboa was declared the winner of a fresh presidential term.[57]

[52] Chair-Rapporteur, '1st Meeting, 10th Session of Open-ended Intergovernmental Working Group on Transnational Corporations', webtv.un.org/en/asset/k17/k17af2y62z (opening address available from 39:55) (interpretation).

[53] D Cassel, 'The Third Session of the UN Intergovernmental Working Group on a Business and Human Rights Treaty' (2018) 3(2) *BHRJ* 277, 279.

[54] ibid.

[55] ibid 277.

[56] ibid 283.

[57] K Robertson, 'Daniel Noboa Wins Reelection in Ecuador' (*Americas Society/Council of the Americas*, 14 April 2025) www.as-coa.org/articles/daniel-noboa-wins-reelection-ecuador.

Substantively, Ecuador's shifting position has been demonstrated by the way that the successive iterations of the draft LBI circulated by Ecuador as chair have dealt with the vexed question of its scope. Ecuador's proposed elements for a draft LBI envisaged a scope covering 'the activities of TNCs [(Transnational Corporations)] and OBEs [(Other Business Enterprises)] that have a transnational character',[58] while the subsequent Zero Draft referred to 'any business activities of a transnational character'.[59] The adoption of this focus on regulating 'transnational' activities represented an initial compromise, but was unsuccessful in placating proponents of an exclusive focus on 'Transnational Corporations and Other Business Enterprises', as well as those in the opposite camp advocating for a general scope of application covering all business activities.[60]

The Zero Draft was followed by a revised 2019 draft LBI (the 2019 Draft), which applied 'except as stated otherwise, to all business activities, including particularly but not limited to those of a transnational character'.[61] Significantly, this was the first time a draft of the proposed LBI caught all business activities, albeit still with a particular focus on transnational activities.[62] This formulation was diluted further in the 2020 draft LBI (the 2020 Draft), which applied 'to all business enterprises, including but not limited to transnational corporations and other business enterprises that undertake business activities of a transnational character'.[63]

The 2021 draft LBI (the 2021 Draft) removed reference to 'transnational corporations' altogether from its scope provision, providing instead that the instrument would apply to 'all business activities, including business activities of a transnational character',[64] a formulation maintained in the current 2023 Draft which formed the basis of negotiations at the Working Group's ninth, tenth and eleventh sessions.[65]

Ecuador has articulated four main reasons to justify this change, namely that 'the nature of a company is irrelevant to its victims', 'wholly domestic companies can be responsible for serious human rights harms', 'there are major risks of transnational companies structuring themselves in a way to avoid falling within the scope of the instrument', and 'international standards on business and human rights apply to all business enterprises'.[66]

This shift has been noted with satisfaction by a number of the proposed LBI's original opponents. For example, the general statement of the EU at the Working Group's fifth session in 2019 specifically referenced how the 2019 Draft appeared 'to address a key EU concern about the scope of the Instrument, given that the scope is no longer limited to transnational corporations and activities', while still calling for 'greater clarification'.[67]

[58] Elements for the Draft Legally Binding Instrument on Transnational Corporations and Other Business Enterprises with Respect to Human Rights (29 September 2017) Article 2.

[59] Zero Draft (n 13) Article 3(1).

[60] Cassel (n 53) 280.

[61] Revised Draft Legally Binding Instrument to Regulate, in International Human Rights Law, the Activities of Transnational Corporations and Other Business Enterprises (16 July 2019) Article 3(1).

[62] C Methven O'Brien, 'Confronting the Constraints of the Medium: The Fifth Session of the UN Intergovernmental Working Group on a Business and Human Rights Treaty' (2020) 5 *BHRJ* 150, 152.

[63] Second Revised Draft Legally Binding Instrument to Regulate, in International Human Rights Law, the Activities of Transnational Corporations and Other Business Enterprises (6 August 2020) Article 3(1). See Bantekas (n 26) 607–608.

[64] Third Revised Draft Legally Binding Instrument to Regulate, in International Human Rights Law, the Activities of Transnational Corporations and Other Business Enterprises (17 August 2021) (2021 Draft) Article 3(1). See McCorquodale (n 37) 194.

[65] 2023 Draft (n 4) Article 3.1.

[66] Chair-Rapporteur, 'IGWG TNCs/OBEs: Guidelines for intersessional work ahead of 9th session' (23 March 2023) 2–3, www.ohchr.org/sites/default/files/documents/hrbodies/hrcouncil/igwg/session9/igwg-9th-guidelines-intersession-mar-2023.pdf. See Sudhoff (n 38) 3.

[67] 'Annex to the report on the fifth session of the open-ended intergovernmental working group on transnational corporations and other business enterprises with respect to human rights (A/HRC/43/45)' (2019) 20, www.ohchr.org/sites/default/files/Documents/HRBodies/HRCouncil/WGTransCorp/Session5/Annex_CompilationStatements_5th_session.pdf.

While the evolution of the draft LBI as a result of the negotiations conducted at the Working Group's sessions is to be expected, the willingness of Ecuador in its capacity as chair to gradually expand the scope of the draft LBI has been notable. The move represents a meaningful adjustment of its positioning on a highly vexed question.

This is brought into sharp relief when considered against the reactions to the change which have been put forward by several States which were early backers of the Working Group process.[68] While Ecuador's position is that a proposed LBI applying to all business activities would be 'consistent with' Resolution 26/9's mandate, 'in particular because a footnote in a preambular paragraph does not impose legal limits' on the Working Group's work,[69] China had already affirmed the opposite view at the Working Group's fifth session, a stance it repeated the following year.[70]

At the Working Group's eighth session in 2022, India reiterated 'its position that this instrument should focus only on business activities of a transnational nature and not to national enterprises as we already have domestic laws to regulate them',[71] while Pakistan stressed at its ninth session that the impact of transnational corporations 'is the gap in international law that this Working Group [is] mandated to bridge'.[72]

Similarly, Indonesia stated at the Working Group's ninth session that 'the text has been shifted away from the core spirit of … Resolution 26/9 … which we supported', and that the draft LBI's definitions and scope 'must be well-crafted in such a way that serve the main purpose [reflected] when this instrument was initiated in the first place'.[73] Indonesia's position has been mirrored by the Philippines, a fellow member of the Association of Southeast Asian Nations, which has expressed its concern 'that the heart of the mandate of [Resolution 26/9] which expressly limits the scope of the LBI to the activities of TNCs and OBEs, remains unaddressed', reiterating a call 'to revert or limit the scope of the LBI'.[74]

[68] Sudhoff (n 38) 2.

[69] Chair-Rapporteur (n 66) 3.

[70] China, '对序言、第1条、第2条的评论' (2019) 3, www.ohchr.org/sites/default/files/Documents/HRBodies/HRCouncil/WGTransCorp/Session5/PanelPreambleArt1/China_PreambleAndArticle1_2.docx; 'Annex to the report on the sixth session of the open-ended intergovernmental working group on transnational corporations and other business enterprises with respect to human rights (A/HRC/46/73)' (2020) 36 www.ohchr.org/sites/default/files/Documents/HRBodies/HRCouncil/WGTransCorp/Session6/igwg-6th-statement-compilation-annex.pdf.

[71] India, 'General Statement by India under Agenda Item 4 at the Eighth Session of the Open-Ended Intergovernmental Working Group for the elaboration of an International Legally Binding Instrument on Transnational Corporations and other Business Enterprises with respect to Human Rights' (24 October 2022) para 11, www.ohchr.org/sites/default/files/documents/issues/transcorporations/session8/submissions/2022-10-25/stm-IGWG-session8-state-india.pdf. India reiterated this position at the Working Group's tenth session – see India, '1st Meeting, 10th Session of Open-ended Intergovernmental Working Group on Transnational Corporations', webtv.un.org/en/asset/k17/k17af2y62z (statement available at 1:16:55).

[72] 'Compilation of general statements from States and non-State stakeholders made during the ninth session of the open-ended intergovernmental working group on transnational corporations and other business enterprises with respect to human rights' (2023) (Compilation of ninth session general statements) 15 www.ohchr.org/sites/default/files/documents/hrbodies/hrcouncil/igwg-transcorp/session9/igwg-9th-compilation-general-statements.pdf. Pakistan reiterated this position at the Working Group's tenth session – see Pakistan, '1st Meeting, 10th Session of Open-ended Intergovernmental Working Group on Transnational Corporations' webtv.un.org/en/asset/k17/k17af2y62z (statement available at 1:44:45).

[73] Compilation of ninth session general statements (n 72) 11. Indonesia reiterated this position at the Working Group's tenth session – Indonesia, '1st Meeting, 10th Session of Open-ended Intergovernmental Working Group on Transnational Corporations' webtv.un.org/en/asset/k17/k17af2y62z (statement available at 1:23:45).

[74] 'Annex to the report on the seventh session of the open-ended intergovernmental working group on transnational corporations and other business enterprises with respect to human rights (A/HRC/49/65)' (2021) (annex to seventh session report) 17, www.ohchr.org/sites/default/files/documents/issues/business/2022-09-13/igwg-7th-annex-general-statements.pdf.

More broadly, Ecuador also used its prerogative as chair to circulate informal 'Chair Proposals' for discussion during the eighth Working Group session in 2022, which provided suggested drafting for consideration in relation to certain key definitions for the proposed LBI, as well as a range of substantive provisions.[75] These included the draft LBI's provisions on prevention, access to remedy, legal liability, and jurisdiction.

The Chair Proposals were circulated by then Chair-Rapporteur Izquierdo Miño and were accompanied by explanatory commentary. Amongst other things, this expressly described the Chair Proposals as intended to 'streamline the text', 'clarify the linkages between different Articles, with clearer cross-referencing and more consistent use of terminology', and 'ensure an appropriate level of flexibility for State implementation … but without in any way undermining or diminishing' the proposed LBI's effectiveness.[76]

These aspects of the Chair Proposals can be seen as a response to criticism from a range of States, which have characterised provisions of the draft LBI as being unworkably prescriptive, ambiguously worded, or a combination of the two. This perspective is well illustrated by the USA's remarks at its first appearance at the Working Group, during its seventh session in 2021. There, the USA emphasised its concerns with aspects of the draft LBI, including what the USA considered the 'creation of wide-ranging liability for an overly broad, ill-defined range of human rights abuses'.[77]

The Chair-Rapporteur's approach to these issues was exemplified by the suggested Chair Proposals seeking to simplify and introduce flexibility into Article 6 of the draft LBI on prevention. The description of human rights due diligence in Article 6 was moved into a freestanding definition, and drafting was added emphasising that due diligence processes 'will vary in complexity with the size of a business enterprise, the risk of severe adverse human rights impacts, and the nature and context of the operations of that business enterprise'.[78] These changes were eventually incorporated into the 2023 Draft.[79]

Other Chair Proposals proved less enduring. For instance, the Chair Proposal on Article 7 of the draft LBI regarding access to remedy would have significantly reduced its granularity. Instead of obliging States Parties to confer the 'necessary competence' on their courts and non-judicial mechanisms 'to enable victims' access to adequate, timely and effective remedy' as contemplated in the 2021 Draft,[80] the Chair Proposals would have obliged States Parties to 'promote' access to justice, 'progressively reduce' obstacles to effective remedies, and ensure that State agencies 'can either deliver, or contribute to the delivery of' effective remedies. This change was not adopted in the 2023 Draft, which substantially maintained the 2021 Draft's formulation.[81]

More broadly, the Chair-Rapporteur's introduction of the Chair Proposals was not without controversy, with certain States regarding them as an illegitimate diversion from the

[75] Chair-Rapporteur, 'Suggested Chair proposals for select articles of the LBI' (6 October 2022) UN Doc A/HRC/WG.16/8/CRP.1 (Chair Proposals).

[76] Chair-Rapporteur, 'Suggested Chair proposals for select articles of the LBI' (2022) www.ohchr.org/sites/default/files/documents/hrbodies/hrcouncil/igwg/session8/2022-11-24/igwg-8th-suggested-chair-proposals-commentary.pdf.

[77] Annex to seventh session report (n 74) 24.

[78] Chair Proposals (n 75) 2.

[79] 2023 Draft (n 4) Article 1(ii).

[80] 2021 Draft (n 64) Article 7.1.

[81] Chair Proposals (n 75) 4; 2023 Draft (n 4), Article 7.1. See A Crockett and J Hamzah Sendut, 'UN business and human rights treaty negotiations continue: one step forward, two steps back?' (*Herbert Smith Freehills*, 8 November 2022) www.herbertsmithfreehills.com/insights/2022-11/un-business-and-human-rights-treaty-negotiations-continue-one-step-forward-two-steps.

negotiated text of the 2021 Draft.[82] As recorded in the official report on the Working Group's eighth session, '[s]ome delegations and many non-governmental organizations considered that the [Chair Proposals] could undermine the convergence developed over the past seven sessions'.[83]

The Chair-Rapporteur was forced to clarify that the text of the draft LBI itself remained the 'formal basis for negotiations'.[84] Ecuador subsequently issued a letter on behalf of the Chair-Rapporteur after the Working Group's eighth session had concluded, which somewhat defensively noted that 'chairs making proposals for text to be considered alongside other drafts during negotiations of human rights instruments is a fairly common practice'.[85]

Notwithstanding, the Chair Proposals served as an important means for Ecuador to signal to stakeholders, and in particular original detractors of the Working Group, that it was avoiding a rigid approach to the draft LBI. It is therefore not surprising that the USA referred to the Chair Proposals as 'a promising step in the right direction',[86] while the EU said they included 'important changes'.[87]

B. Friends of the Chair

While floating the Chair Proposals, Chair-Rapporteur Izquierdo Miño also communicated the names of the States who would make up a newly constituted group of 'Friends of the Chair' in September 2022, namely Azerbaijan, France, Indonesia, Portugal, and Uruguay.[88]

The Friends of the Chair initiative had been announced by the Chair-Rapporteur during the preceding year, with the aim of supporting 'consultations with a view to facilitating and advancing work on the [draft LBI] during the intersessional period, aiming at ensuring the broadest possible cross-regional support'.[89] Although the Chair-Rapporteur had initially been unable to secure the participation of an African State, the Working Group's eighth session in 2022 saw Cameroon join the group.[90]

[82] Crockett and Hamzah Sendut (n 81). See also K Seitz, 'No more sideshow' (Global Policy Forum and Rosa Luxemburg Stiftung 2022) 2, www.globalpolicy.org/sites/default/files/download/Briefing_8th%20session_UN-Treaty.pdf.

[83] UNHRC 'Report on the eighth session of the open-ended intergovernmental working group on transnational corporations and other business enterprises with respect to human rights' (30 December 2022) UN Doc A/HRC/52/41, 6.

[84] ibid 8.

[85] A Dávalos, 'Letter on behalf of the Chair-Rapporteur' (24 November 2022) www.ohchr.org/sites/default/files/documents/hrbodies/hrcouncil/igwg/session8/2022-11-24/igwg-8th-letter-chair-rapporteur-nov-2022.pdf.

[86] 'Compilation of general statements from States and non-State stakeholders made during the eighth session' (2022) (compilation of eighth session general statements) 19, www.ohchr.org/sites/default/files/documents/hrbodies/hrcouncil/wgtranscorp/session8/igwg-8th-compilation-general-statements.pdf.

[87] ibid 20.

[88] Chair-Rapporteur, Letter on the Friends of the Chair (7 September 2022) 2, www.ohchr.org/sites/default/files/documents/issues/business/2022-09-13/igwg-8th-letter-chair-rapporteur.pdf.

[89] 'Report on the seventh session of the open-ended intergovernmental working group on transnational corporations and other business enterprises with respect to human rights' (29 December 2021) 6, documents.un.org/doc/undoc/gen/g21/397/55/pdf/g2139755.pdf. See D Cassel, 'Friends of the Chair: New Impetus for the UN Business & Human Rights Treaty Process?' (*Business & Human Rights Resource Centre*, 26 September 2022) www.business-humanrights.org/en/blog/friends-of-the-chair-new-impetus-for-the-un-business-human-treaty-process/.

[90] S Luthango and M Schulze, 'The EU and the Negotiations for a Binding Treaty on Business and Human Rights' (German Institute for International and Security Affairs, 16 March 2023) 3, www.swp-berlin.org/publications/products/comments/2023C16_BindingTreatyBHR.pdf; E Aba, 'Reflections on a week of negotiations on a legally binding instrument on business & human rights' (*Business & Human Rights Resource Centre*, 1 November 2022) www.business-humanrights.org/en/blog/reflections-on-a-week-of-negotiations-on-a-legally-binding-instrument-on-business-human-rights/.

Between the eighth and ninth Working Group sessions, intersessional regional consultations were organised by the Friends of the Chair to progress the development of the draft LBI.[91] The Chair-Rapporteur used feedback from these consultations, as well as the input received from participants at the Working Group's eighth session, to produce the 2023 Draft which formed the basis of negotiations at the most recent ninth, tenth and eleventh sessions.[92]

C. UNHRC Decision 56/116

The inclusion of France and Portugal as Friends of the Chair set the stage for the most important of the recent initiatives pushed by Ecuador, the UNHRC's 11 July 2024 Decision 56/116 on '[e]nhancing the support capabilities' of the Working Group (the Decision).[93]

The Decision formally established a process of accelerated work on the draft LBI from 2025-2027, providing for the Working Group to convene up to 10 intersessional thematic consultations each year. These ongoing consultations are mandated to focus on 'clusters of articles'[94] of the draft LBI, with the assistance as necessary of legal experts selected by the Chair Rapporteur.[95] The Decision also requested that the UN High Commissioner for Human Rights enhance the support capabilities provided by his office to the Working Group.

Importantly, the Decision received wide ranging backing and was adopted by the UNHRC without a vote. During consideration of the Decision, Ecuador expressed 'a very special thanks' to its co-sponsors,[96] which included three EU Member States – the two Western European Friends of the Chair, France and Portugal, along with Luxembourg. France welcomed the 'strong transnational momentum' behind the Decision and reaffirmed that it would 'continue to be active and involved in the group of the Friends of the Chair'.[97]

Similarly, Belgium delivered a statement agreed by the EU which praised the 'constructive and transparent' approach to negotiations on the Decision, as well as the Chair-Rapporteur's commitment to 'constructive initiatives' to 'achieve tangible progress' towards a concluded LBI.[98] Voicing support for the involvement of legal experts in the Working Group's processes, Belgium described the Decision as representative of a 'new impetus', which 'should allow for the emergence of an instrument which is legally sound and implementable, in line with the UN Guiding Principles, and which can gather broad, cross-regional support'.

[91] 'Compilation of the outcomes of the friends of the Chair intersessional consultations, in line with the note verbale of 2 March 2023' (2023) www.ohchr.org/sites/default/files/documents/hrbodies/hrcouncil/igwg-transcorp/session9/igwg-9th-compilation-outcomes-friends-chair-intersessional-consultations.pdf. No consultation for the African group was convened within the timeframe set by the Chair-Rapporteur – see UNHRC 'Report on the ninth session of the open-ended intergovernmental working group on transnational corporations and other business enterprises with respect to human rights' (26 December 2023) UN Doc A/HRC/55/59 (ninth session report), 4.

[92] Ninth session report (n 91) 3.

[93] Decision (n 5). See J Bellion-Jourdan, 'Ten years on, talks for a business and human rights treaty get new impetus' (*Geneva Solutions*, 11 August 2024) genevasolutions.news/human-rights/ten-years-on-talks-for-a-business-and-human-rights-treaty-get-new-impetus.

[94] Decision (n 5) Clause 1.

[95] 'Selected legal experts for the open-ended intergovernmental working group on transnational corporations and other business enterprises with respect to human rights' (July 2024) www.ohchr.org/sites/default/files/documents/hrbodies/hrcouncil/igwg-transcorp/session10/igwg-10th-legal-experts.pdf.

[96] Ecuador, '35th Meeting – 56th Regular Session of Human Rights Council' (11 July 2024) webtv.un.org/en/asset/k1f/k1fyg973ay (statement available at 14:50) (interpretation).

[97] ibid (statement available at 19:51) (interpretation).

[98] ibid (statement available at 16:03).

The warm reception given by EU Member States to the Decision is a far cry from the initial opposition to the fundamental concept of an LBI demonstrated just over a decade ago. This contrast was further underlined at the Working Group's tenth session later in 2024, where the EU reaffirmed that it 'completely support[s] the efforts to adopt an international legal framework promoting the respect of human rights by business'.[99] The EU expressed that a 'well designed and broadly supported [LBI] has the potential to enhance global protection against business-related human rights abuses and create a global level playing field for all companies worldwide'.[100]

A number of other participants at the Working Group's tenth session characterised the Decision as a step forward. Portugal regarded negotiations as having moved to 'a new stage', with 'more time, resources and technical support for meaningful discussions'.[101] While continuing to refer to the 2023 Draft as having 'fundamental issues', Japan expressed an openness to begin participating 'more proactively', given the Working Group was entering 'into a new phase'.[102] Australia, which has also taken a sceptical approach to the proposed LBI, expressed its hope that 'the future intersessional work and the assistance of the legal experts will enable a more fulsome consideration of and progress on' its issues of concern.[103]

III. Remaining Uncertainties and Enduring Complexities

Despite the optimism engendered by the Decision, the Working Group's future negotiations will still need to contend with a range of significant challenges. This Section focuses on three other key areas of uncertainty, which, depending on how they are resolved, could prevent consensus. These are (i) the extent to which the accelerated process prescribed by the Decision will be sufficient to bridge the gaps which remain between participants, (ii) the role of the EU and USA going forward, and (iii) resource constraints.

A. Remaining Gaps between Working Group Participants

By way of illustration, a review of the negotiations at the Working Group's ninth and tenth sessions reveals that consensus on numerous substantive points in the 2023 Draft remains some distance away. Even leaving aside the problem of the proposed LBI's scope, discussed earlier in this chapter, Working Group participants continue to suggest detailed and nuanced amendments to other important provisions in the 2023 Draft.

For example, the USA proposed amending Articles 6.1 and 6.2 of the 2023 Draft to modify mandatory language directing States Parties to adopt preventative measures to ensure business respect for human rights (from 'shall' to 'should'), and the UK expressed reservations to the

[99] EU, '1st Meeting, 10th Session of Open-ended Intergovernmental Working Group on Transnational Corporations' (16 December 2024) webtv.un.org/en/asset/k17/k17af2y62z (statement available at 1:05:01).

[100] ibid.

[101] Portugal, '1st Meeting, 10th Session of Open-ended Intergovernmental Working Group on Transnational Corporations' (16 December 2024) webtv.un.org/en/asset/k17/k17af2y62z (statement available at 1:13:21).

[102] Japan, '1st Meeting, 10th Session of Open-ended Intergovernmental Working Group on Transnational Corporations' (16 December 2024) webtv.un.org/en/asset/k17/k17af2y62z (statement available at 1:30:21) (interpretation).

[103] Australia, '1st Meeting, 10th Session of Open-ended Intergovernmental Working Group on Transnational Corporations' (16 December 2024) webtv.un.org/en/asset/k17/k17af2y62z (statement available at 1:39:11).

Article 6.4 provision envisaging 'legally enforceable' human rights due diligence requirements on businesses.[104]

Meanwhile, Brazil and Honduras sought to add express reference to financial sector businesses to the Article 6(c) provision which would oblige States Parties to adopt measures to 'ensure the practice of human rights due diligence'.[105] Honduras alongside Mexico, Colombia and Ghana proposed that States Parties should introduce measures to ensure businesses undertake environmental and health impact assessments, in addition to the human rights impact assessments already envisaged by Article 6.4(a).[106]

States also made an eclectic mix of proposals in respect of other provisions of the 2023 Draft, including those on access to remedy, legal liability, and jurisdiction. These provisions have been considered controversial by a number of States due to their potentially complex implications for domestic legal systems.

The USA has continued to stress that the text 'retains overly broad jurisdictional provisions, unclear liability provisions, inconsistencies with international law, and potential criminalization of an ill-defined range of activity'.[107] In a related vein, China has emphasised that 'all countries' legal sovereignty must be recognised' and compatibility between the 2023 Draft and 'national legal systems' should be strengthened.[108]

Notwithstanding, other Working Group participants have conversely sought to expand the reach of the 2023 Draft's provisions. For instance, Palestine, Ghana and South Africa proposed specific new provisions in Article 8 of the 2023 Draft on legal liability. These proposed provisions would seek to establish the joint and several responsibility of businesses, envisage criminal liability for acts causing, contributing or linked to human rights abuses or violations, and contemplate disapplying the 'rule on exhaustion of local remedies' in certain circumstances.[109]

Accommodating the diverse views on offer in the Working Group negotiations while still making appropriate headway will continue to be a challenge for the intersessional consultations and legal experts selected pursuant to the Decision. The legal experts' continued ability to meaningfully assist negotiations may be further complicated depending on how States respond to their input.

As envisaged by the Chair-Rapporteur, the role of the legal experts during the intersessional consultations is to assist the Chair-Rapporteur in preparing 'non-papers' for discussion, along with 'proposals or possible solutions addressing identified divergences'.[110] For example, the first of the intersessional consultations were held from 15–16 April 2025, and saw the Chair-Rapporteur introduce a non-paper on Articles 4, 5 and 7 of the 2023 Draft.[111]

[104] 2023 Draft with Textual Proposals (n 36) 38, 41.

[105] ibid 39. See C Sudhoff, 'Surprising advances' (Global Policy Forum and Brot für die Welt 2025) 4, www.globalpolicy.org/sites/default/files/download/Briefing_0325_UN-Treaty_10_e_0.pdf.

[106] 2023 Draft with Textual Proposals (n 36) 42. See Sudhoff (n 105) 4–5.

[107] USA, 'General Statement of the United States of America' (16 December 2024) 4, www.ohchr.org/sites/default/files/documents/hrbodies/hrcouncil/igwg-transcorp/session10/1-general-statements/member-and-observer-states/igwg-10th-general-statement-usa.pdf.

[108] China, '1st Meeting, 10th Session of Open-ended Intergovernmental Working Group on Transnational Corporations' (16 December 2024) webtv.un.org/en/asset/k17/k17af2y62z (statement available at 1:57:10) (interpretation).

[109] 2023 Draft with Textual Proposals (n 36) 61.

[110] UNHRC 'Report on the tenth session of the open-ended intergovernmental working group on transnational corporations and other business enterprises with respect to human rights' (20 December 2024) UN Doc A/HRC/58/XX (tenth session report) 7.

[111] 'Proposed programme of work for the first intersessional thematic consultation towards the 11th session of the Open-ended Intergovernmental Working Group on transnational corporations and other business enterprises with respect to human rights, focused on articles 4 (rights of victims), 5 (protection of victims) and 7 (access to remedy) of the updated draft legally binding instrument' (15–16 April 2025) www.ohchr.org/sites/default/files/documents/

This comes against the background of several Working Group participants having emphasised that the involvement of the legal experts should not detract from the intergovernmental nature of the negotiations.[112] These stances disclose a degree of caution among participating States, well illustrated by the UK expressly stating that 'it does not regard the interpretations of the draft treaty by the legal experts as authoritative for the purposes of treaty interpretation'.[113]

B. The Role of the EU and USA

The positions of the EU and USA over the coming years represents another source of uncertainty for the Working Group process. Along with Ecuador's aforementioned efforts, it is likely that the EU's gradual warming to the proposed LBI was at least partially influenced by its adoption of the Corporate Sustainability Due Diligence Directive (CS3D),[114] which entered into force on 25 July 2024. Amongst other things, the CS3D established a requirement on in-scope businesses to conduct risk-based human rights and environmental due diligence.

A detailed examination of the CS3D is beyond the scope of this chapter, but its influence on the EU's participation in the Working Group was evident from the EU's general statement at the tenth session. The EU noted that the CS3D provided 'the basis for EU engagement, especially with respect to human rights due diligence and related provisions'.[115]

Nevertheless, it will be important to continue monitoring whether the European Commission, which has been representing the EU to date in the Working Group, is granted in the near term a formal negotiating mandate from the EU Council.[116] This remains pending at the time of writing. Such a mandate would allow for the EU's substantive participation in line-by-line negotiations. The lack of a mandate forced the EU to preface its contributions in more recent Working Group discussions with the disclaimer that they did not constitute a negotiating position on behalf of the EU.[117]

During the tenth session, the EU referenced the new membership of the European Commission which took office following European parliamentary elections in June 2024, and stated that a decision 'on a possible EU negotiation mandate' was forthcoming.[118] The European Parliament had already adopted a resolution in January 2024 calling on the EU Council to accord the European Commission 'an ambitious mandate for [the Working Group] negotiations as soon as possible', entailing an EU position aiming 'for strong provisions in terms of enforcement and monitoring mechanisms, as well as in relation to access to justice'.[119]

hrbodies/hrcouncil/igwg-transcorp/session11/pow-OEIGWG-1st-intersessional-consultation-15-and-16-April-PdN-Room-XVII.pdf; 'Non-paper Article 4, 5 and 7 of the Updated Draft Legally Binding Instrument' (2025) www.ohchr.org/sites/default/files/documents/hrbodies/hrcouncil/igwg-transcorp/session11/OEIGWG_Non-paper_on_Articles_4%2C_5_and_7_for_2025.pdf.

112 Tenth session report (n 110) 7–8.

113 UK, '8th Meeting, 10th Session of Open-ended Intergovernmental Working Group on Transnational Corporations' (19 December 2024) webtv.un.org/en/asset/k13/k13w8sloeg (statement available at 2:12:18).

114 See McCorquodale (n 37) 195; N Bueno et al, 'The EU Directive on Corporate Sustainability Due Diligence (CSDDD): The Final Political Compromise' (2024) 9(2) *BHRJ* 294, 299.

115 EU (n 99).

116 Bellion-Jourdan (n 93).

117 See, eg, compilation of statements in the eighth session negotiations (n 51) 10. See also Zamfir (n 47) 11.

118 EU (n 99).

119 European Parliament, 'Resolution on Shaping the EU's Position on the UN Binding Instrument on Business and Human Rights, in Particular on Access to Remedy and the Protection of Victims' (18 January 2024) P9_TA(2024)0042, para 13.

The European Parliament's resolution declared support for an LBI which, among other things, provides for a 'compulsory framework', including an obligation on States Parties to adopt measures 'to ensure the practice of environmental due diligence and respect of human rights by all business enterprises'.[120] It additionally recognised the need for the LBI to deal proportionately with small and medium-sized enterprises, and to allow States Parties 'the flexibility to adapt their preventative frameworks to their own legal systems, while preserving the primary of human rights'.[121]

It is possible that the development of a substantive EU negotiating position has been complicated by the need to delineate between those elements of the proposed LBI falling within EU competence, and those falling within the competence of EU Member States, as a matter of EU law.[122] Furthermore, given the difficult negotiations which preceded the adoption of the CS3D, it cannot be taken for granted that sufficient consensus will be reached for the European Commission to be given the 'ambitious' mandate sought by the European Parliament. This is particularly in light of the additional uncertainty introduced by the European Commission's introduction in 2025 of its Sustainability Omnibus Package, aimed at simplifying EU sustainability rules.[123]

Moreover, even if a substantive negotiating mandate based on the CS3D is granted, there are several ways in which the CS3D diverges from the current 2023 Draft.[124] While the CS3D's use of a size threshold to identify in-scope businesses could conceivably be adapted for use in the proposed LBI as a compromise solution to the 'transnational' versus 'all business activities' debate,[125] a similar suggestion was already made by the EU to no avail as far back as the Working Group's fourth session in 2018.[126] In any event, given that the 2023 Draft's scope provision now aligns with the EU's position favouring an inclusive scope, it is unclear whether the EU would be willing to offer up an alternative approach.

With regards to the USA, the start of the second Trump Administration in 2025 makes the exact US role in the years ahead difficult to predict.[127] Perhaps the most distinctive aspect of the former Biden Administration's approach to the proposed LBI was the USA's push to move the proposed LBI towards a framework agreement model. The USA raised a framework agreement in 2021 as an example of an 'alternative' model for exploration, presented as better aligned with the UNGPs and more likely to command broad support.[128]

The USA's general statement at the Working Group's eighth session in 2022 more forthrightly advocated for 'a less prescriptive approach, more akin to a framework agreement',

[120] ibid para 22.

[121] ibid paras 18, 22.

[122] Luthango and Schulze (n 90) 5–6.

[123] 'The EU Omnibus Package – What do we know so far?' (*Herbert Smith Freehills*, 3 March 2025) www.herbertsmithfreehills.com/notes/esg/2025-posts/The-EU-Omnibus-Package-%E2%80%93-What-do-we-know-so-far-.

[124] See N Bernaz et al, 'The UN Legally Binding Instrument and the EU proposal for a Corporate Sustainability Due Diligence Directive: Competences, comparison and complementarity' (Friends of the Earth 2022) friendsoftheearth.eu/wp-content/uploads/2022/10/Complementarity-study-on-EU-CSDDD-and-UN-LBI-October-2022.pdf; K Mohamadieh et al, 'Complementarity of the Legally Binding Instrument on Business and Human Rights and the EU Corporate Sustainability Due Diligence Directive' (Coopération Internationale pour le Développement et la Solidarité 2025) www.cidse.org/2025/03/20/complementarity-of-un-and-eu-instruments-on-business-and-human-rights/.

[125] Bernaz et al (n 124) 12–13; Mohamadieh et al (n 124) 2.

[126] EU (n 49) 3.

[127] cf Palombo (n 50).

[128] Annex to seventh session report (n 74) 25. See also, J Batura, 'Framing Business & Human Rights?: Introducing the Symposium on a Framework Agreement as an Alternative Regulatory Proposal' (*Volerrechtsblog*, 20 June 2022) voelkerrechtsblog.org/framing-business-human-rights/.

combined with optional protocols.[129] The proposal was noted with interest by Germany, Japan, and the UK.[130] Moves by the second Trump Administration impacting the proposed LBI and the UN system more widely will again be an issue to watch.

C. Resource Constraints

Finally, it is worthwhile to recall that the UN system currently faces what UN Secretary-General António Guterres described in January 2024 as a 'full-blown liquidity crisis', which required the UN to implement 'aggressive cash conservation measures'.[131]

The situation has had an impact on the Working Group. For instance, the switch from Chair-Rapporteur Espinosa Cañizares to Vázquez Bermúdez led to the postponement of the Working Group's tenth session from October to December 2024. In announcing the change of dates, Ecuador noted that the administrative difficulties were compounded by the 'UN Secretariat liquidity challenges', amongst other things.[132]

The potential ramifications of the UN liquidity crisis for the process established for the Working Group by the Decision were further emphasised during the Working Group's tenth session. Chair-Rapporteur Vázquez Bermúdez invited the Office of the High Commissioner for Human Rights' Chief Financial Officer to brief the Working Group on budgetary matters, including potential cuts to the resources available for the Decision's implementation.[133]

Concerns of this kind have since been borne out. To take just one example, the Chair-Rapporteur's updated 2025 Roadmap for the implementation of the Decision noted that it was 'subject to the resources approved by the [UN General Assembly], of the PBI (Programme budget implications) linked to HRC Decision 56/116 for 2025 and allotment of resources … for implementation for both staff and activities'.[134]

For all the complexities of the Working Group negotiations, it is clear therefore that the possible consequences of a simple lack of resources should not be underestimated.

IV. Conclusion

The past ten years have seen the Working Group engaged in difficult negotiations on the proposed LBI. Their divisive nature can be attributed to the project's scale and ambition. Unlike the soft law UNGPs, the need for concretised, legally binding obligations in the proposed LBI has meant that Working Group participants have had to grapple with complex issues at the heart of national regulatory approaches to business. Some of the divergent positions adopted during the

[129] Compilation of eighth session general statements (n 86) 19.

[130] Compilation of eighth session general statements (n 86) 8, 12; Crockett and Hamzah Sendut (n 81).

[131] A Guterres, Letter from UN Secretary-General to all Permanent Representatives of UN Member States (25 January 2024) www.un.org/pga/wp-content/uploads/sites/108/2024/01/SG-Letter-on-Liquidity-Crisis.pdf.

[132] Ecuador, Letter Regarding the Working Group's Tenth Session (19 September 2024) www.ohchr.org/sites/default/files/documents/hrbodies/hrcouncil/igwg-transcorp/session10/nv-ecuador-dates-10th.pdf.

[133] Tenth session report (n 110) 7.

[134] 'OEIGWG Chair-Rapporteur updated 2025 Roadmap for the implementation of HRC Decision 56/116, including the intersessional thematic consultations towards the 11th session of the Open-ended Intergovernmental Working Group (OEIGWG) on transnational corporations and other business enterprises with respect to human rights' (2025) 1, www.ohchr.org/sites/default/files/documents/hrbodies/hrcouncil/igwg-transcorp/session10/igwg-10th-chair-rapporteur-updated-2025-roadmap.pdf.

negotiations have been rooted in fundamentally contrasting perspectives on the global economy and the role of business, engaging matters not easily reduced to a single, coherent legal text.[135]

However, even though consensus on a range of issues remains elusive, Ecuador's leadership of the Working Group process has in recent years produced results, helping bring on side some of the proposed LBI's most trenchant sceptics. The process established by the Decision is slated to run until 2027, and its introduction of legal experts may engender a technocratic approach more conducive to a workable compromise, but much remains uncertain.

Of course, developments in the Working Group have not happened in isolation. The endorsement of the UNGPs by the UNHRC in 2011 was the starting point for parallel trends which have continued to gain momentum. Responsible business conduct has risen steadily on the agendas of both policymakers and boardrooms. Associated stakeholder expectations, regulatory pressure and legislative action have, and will continue to, impact business operations worldwide, and have already affected the negotiations on the proposed LBI.

This chapter touched briefly on the influence of the EU's CS3D which is likely, in one form or another, to have some impact on business not only in the EU but around the world. More widely, the prevalence of national mandatory human rights due diligence laws continues to increase, and a broader group of States have continued to introduce and build upon National Action Plans aimed at implementing the UNGPs. While mandatory human rights due diligence has not yet been introduced by any Asian State at the time of writing, the impact of these global trends continues to be salient, especially on Asian businesses with an international footprint.

In summary, while progress on the proposed LBI has been slow, the broader business and human rights landscape, including in connection with global policy priorities such as climate change, has continued to mature. For businesses, the importance of adopting responsible policies and practices, with effective human rights due diligence at their centre, cannot be ignored, regardless of the eventual outcome of the negotiations for the LBI.

[135] D Birchall, 'Between Apology and Utopia: The Indeterminacies of the Zero Draft Treaty on Business and Human Rights' (2019) 42 *STLR* 289, 292; cf M Koskenniemi, 'The Politics of International Law' (1994) 1 *EJIL* 4, 31.

6

The EU Corporate Sustainability Due Diligence Directive – Challenges and Potentials in the ASEAN Context

TAMIO NAKAMURA

I. Introduction

The EU adopted the Corporate Sustainability Due Diligence Directive (CSDDD, or the Directive hereafter)[1] in May 2024, which took effect on 26 July 2024.[2] Prior to its adoption, some EU Member States including France,[3] the Netherlands[4] and Germany[5] had legislated national mandatory measures that require companies to pay due diligence to human rights and environmental adverse impacts throughout their supply chains. However, these national measures differed in scope, nature of obligations and enforcement mechanisms.[6] The Directive was adopted, first, to avoid such fragmentation of national rules on supply chains applicable to companies operating in the EU,[7] second, to take a lead in effective implementation of the relevant international norms, especially the United Nations' Guiding Principles on Business and Human Rights adopted in 2011

[1] Directive (EU) 2024/1760, [2024] OJ L 5.7.2024.

[2] For major primary documents that show important developments in the legislative process of CSDDD, see the Commission's original proposal on 23 February 2022 (COM (2022)71), the European Parliament's original negotiation position on 1 June 2023 (A9-0184/2023), the Council document for starting trilogue on 6 June 2023 (2022/0051(COD), No. 10267/23), and the Council document indicating its final position after trilogue on 15 March 2024 (2022/0051 (COD), No. 6145/24).

[3] Loi n° 2017-399 relative au devoir de vigilance des sociétés mères et des entreprises donneuses [Law on the Duty of Vigilance of Parent Companies and Donor Companies] (inserting Arts L 225-102-4 and 225-102-5 into Commercial Code 1807) See generally A Nissen, *The European Union, Emerging Global Business and Human Rights* (Cambridge, Cambridge University Press, 2023) 155–86.

[4] Wet zorgplicht kinderarbeid 2019 [Child Labour Care Act 2019] See generally Nissen (n 3) 187–210.

[5] Lieferkettensorgfaltspflichtengesetz (LkSG) [Supply Chain Due Diligence Act] 2021 See generally R Grabosch (Hrsg [ed]), *Das Neue Lieferkettensorgfaltspflichtengesetz* [*The New Supply Chain Due Diligence Act*] (Baden-Baden, Nomos, 2021); M Rothermel, *LkSG – Lieferkettensorgfaltspflichtengesetz: Kommentar* [*The New Supply Chain Due Diligence Act: Commentary*] (Frankfurt am Main, Fachmedien Recht und Wirtschaft, 2022); H Fleischer and P Mankowski, *LkSG: Lieferkettensorgfaltspflichtengesetz: Kommentar* [*The New Supply Chain Due Diligence Act: Commentary*] (München, CH Beck, 2023).

[6] For a comparative discussion on the relevant national laws, see, eg, H-J De Kluiver, 'Towards a Framework for Effective Regulatory Supervision of Sustainability Governance in Accordance with the EU CSDD Directive: A Comparative Study' (2023) 20 *European Company and Financial Law Review* 203.

[7] CSDDD recital 31.

(UNGP hereafter)[8] by transforming those principles into legally binding rules,[9] and third, to require companies to contribute to achieving the EU climate-neutral goal in 2050 through due diligence actions.[10]

The Directive applies to both European and non-European companies, with slightly different thresholds.[11] It applies to those companies established in the EU (EU companies) which have a net worldwide annual turnover of more than 450 million euros for each of the last two consecutive financial years[12] and have more than 1,000 employees.[13] It also applies to those companies formed in third countries (non-EU companies) which have a net annual turnover of more than 450 million euros in the EU for each of the last two consecutive financial years.[14] No employee threshold is set for non-EU companies. The companies above are subdivided into three categories; the largest,[15] the next largest[16] and the rest, for the purpose of different dates of application of national measures that implement the Directive. The Member States must adopt and publish necessary legal measures to comply with the Directive by 26 July 2026 and start applying the measures to the relevant companies according to their size, the largest from 26 July 2027, the next largest from 26 July 2028, and the rest from 26 July 2029.[17]

The Directive is a significant legal attempt to fill a 'global human rights governance gap':[18] international human rights and environmental treaties typically provide state obligations, leaving private parties' rights and obligations to national implementing measures. However, as national legal measures in many countries allow private law relations wide freedom, including freedom of contract under the principle of private autonomy, explicit public law mandatory intervention in private legal relations remains limited, especially in relation to human rights protection. Thus, a governance gap emerges. The same is true of transnational private law relations such as global supply chains. The parties to transnational contract will choose an applicable national law according to their agreement, and the governance gap will appear in that national law of their choice. In this respect, the EU, a macro-regional transnational entity, is an exception. It can either regulate directly transnational private relations by a 'Regulation' which is directly applicable to all relevant parties, or indirectly by a 'Directive' which requires the Member States to implement the same rights and obligations stipulated in the Directive through their appropriate national measures. The CSDDD is one of those Directives, which explicitly deals with public law issues of human rights and environmental protection as well as climate change mitigation in private law relations.

[8] For an explanation of the underlying idea of the UNGP by the leading drafter, see J Ruggie, 'Protect, respect and remedy: a framework for business and human rights: report of the Special Representative of the Secretary-General on the Issue of Human Rights and Transnational Corporations and Other Business Enterprises' (2008) digitallibrary.un.org/record/625292?v=pdf.

[9] CSDDD recitals 4–6.

[10] CSDDD recitals 10–13.

[11] The thresholds are calculated in general on an individual company basis, although a group of companies are evaluated on a consolidated basis (Art 2 and recital 27). The thresholds could be amended in the future (Art 36 (2)).

[12] CSDDD Art 2(1) and (5).

[13] The term 'employee' used in the Directive is taken to mean workers in non-standard form of employment if they fulfil the EU law criteria of worker status established by the Court of Justice of the EU (recital 39).

[14] CSDDD Art 2(2) and (5).

[15] EU companies with 5,000 employees and more than 1.5 billion euros worldwide turnover, and non-EU companies with more than 1.5 billion euros net annual turnover generated in the EU.

[16] EU companies with 3,000 employees and more than 900 million euros worldwide turnover; non-EU companies with more than 900 million euros net annual turnover generated in the EU.

[17] CSDDD Art 37.

[18] E George, *Incorporating Rights: Strategies to Advance Corporate Accountability* (Oxford, Oxford University Press, 2021) 17. See also, O Martin-Ortega, 'Human Rights Due Diligence for Corporations: From Voluntary Standards to Hard Law at Last?' (2014) 32 *Netherlands Quarterly of Human Rights* 44.

The CSDDD has attracted practical attention outside the EU as well, since the Directive applies to EU and non-EU companies, and many of those have their supply chains in Asian countries where there are serious concerns in relation to human rights and environmental protection. The collapse of Rana Plaza in Dhaka, Bangladesh in 2013 epitomised the lack of protection of human rights of workers in garment factories, who are often forced to experience unsafe and unfair working conditions. Over 1,100 people lost their lives, and about 2,500 were injured in the incident.[19] Since the factories in the building formed a part of supply chains of well-known fast fashion brands (both EU and non-EU), the brand owner companies as well as the factory owners and the public authority received criticism for their lack of care for workers' safety and rights.[20] Eleven years after the collapse, although factory safety has been distinctively improved, issues of ensuring the basic rights of workers in Bangladesh remain problematic. Clean Clothes Campaign, for example, claims that many fashion brands 'remain passive while their supplier factories keep workers and union organisers under threat of arrest',[21] and the International Labour Organisation (ILO hereafter) also points out 'persistent issues concerning trade union registration, anti-union discrimination, unfair labour practices and violence' in Bangladesh.[22]

In this chapter, we are going to discuss challenges and potentials of the Directive applied in the ASEAN context to assess the extent to which the Directive would contribute to its objective of preventing and remedying serious human rights violations and environmental damages in the ASEAN region. In the next section, we will discuss the main features of the due diligence system that the Directive aims to establish, making comparison with the UNGP where necessary. In the following two sections, we explore some challenges and potentials of the Directive's due diligence system in the ASEAN context, and finally, we will conclude with general observations based on the preceding discussion.

II. The CSDDD

A. Human Rights and Environmental Due Diligence Obligations

The Directive generally follows the UNGP's risk-based approach to the problem of human rights abuse: to prevent or minimise the most severe impacts first.[23] The severity should be assessed by factors such as scale (nature and manner of abuse, etc), scope (number of victims, etc) and irremediability of impacts,[24] and the priority should be based on the severity and likelihood of the adverse impacts.[25]

[19] International Accord, '10 Years Since the Rana Plaza Collapse in Bangladesh' (24 April 2023), internationalaccord.org/10-years-rana-plaza-bangladesh-accord/.

[20] For example, Clean Clothes Campaign, founded in the Netherlands in 1989, has been one of the vocal civil organisations on the point since the disaster occurred. See, eg, 'Rana Plaza: Demands to brands' (28 May 2013) cleanclothes.org/news/2013/05/02/rana-plaza-demands-to-brands.

[21] Clean Clothes Campaign, '11 years since the Rana Plaza collapse factories are safer but the root causes of tragedy persist' cleanclothes.org/news/2024/11-years-since-the-rana-plaza-collapse-factories-are-safer-but-the-root-causes-of-tragedy-persist.

[22] ILO, 'The Rana Plaza disaster ten years on: What has changed?' webapps.ilo.org/infostories/en-GB/Stories/Country-Focus/rana-plaza#intro.

[23] CSDDD Arts 8(4), 9. As to the UNGP, see, E Bon Tai Soon et al (ed), *Business and Human Rights in Southeast Asia: A Practitioner's GuideKit for SMEs on Human Rights Compliance regarding the Environment and Labour* (Kuala Lumpur, Malaysia, AmerBON, Advocates, 2022) 42.

[24] CSDDD Art 3(1)(l)(v).

[25] CSDDD Art 9(2).

The Directive also reflects the UNGP's foundational and operational principles of due diligence for companies, although the Directive makes those principles into legally binding and enforceable rules. Article 5 of the Directive sketches out stages of the due diligence process for a company similar to those in the UNGP, followed by articles that provide for specific obligations for each stage. Thus, a company is required to integrate due diligence into its policies and risk management systems. This includes adopting a 'code of conduct' describing rules and principles to prevent and cease adverse impacts on human rights and environmental concerns that are listed in the Annex of the Directive (Art 7). Next, the company is to identify and assess actual and potential adverse impacts (Arts 8 and 9), and to prevent and mitigate potential adverse impacts (Art 10). Then the company is required to bring to an end actual adverse impact, and, if it is impossible, at least minimise them (Art 11), and to provide remediation from actual adverse impacts (Art 12). The company is also required to establish and maintain a complaints procedure in the company that should be available without hindrance and harassment (Art 14), to monitor the effectiveness of its due diligence policy and measures (Art 15), and to communicate publicly on due diligence (Art 16).

In addition to these obligations, the Directive provides a cross-cutting obligation, which the UNGP has mentioned less prominently: the obligation for a company to carry out meaningful engagement with stakeholders (Art 13). Although the UNGP refers to stakeholder engagement at critical stages of the due diligence process,[26] the Directive has extended this to almost all stages of the due diligence process: stages of identification and assessment, prevention and mitigation, termination or suspension of a business relationship with business partners, remediation, and monitoring.[27] Moreover, companies are required to provide 'relevant and comprehensive' information to the stakeholder in a timely manner to make the engagement effective and meaningful.[28]

The above due diligence obligations extend beyond a company's own operations to cover the operations of its subsidiaries and its business partners in its chain of activities. The chain of activities includes upstream business related to 'the production of goods or the provision of services' of a company, and downstream business related to 'the distribution, transport and storage of a product' of a company.[29] It should be noted that the provision of services is categorically excluded from the downstream scope.[30] Thus, the recital 26 explains that regulated financial undertakings, for instance, are under due diligence obligations only in the upstream part of their chain of activities. Such limitations contrast with the unqualified scope of business relationships with 'business partners, entities in its value chain' in the UNGP.[31]

The substantive scope of due diligence under the CSDD Directive is wider than the UNGP, since the former extends to environmental obligations (Annex Part II) as well as human rights obligations (Annex Part I). As to human rights obligations, the substantive coverage of the Directive is as comprehensive as the UNGP. However, the Directive prioritises certain human rights specifically listed up in Annex Part I section 1. To name a few; the right to life, the prohibition of the worst forms of child labour, the right to organise and the right to hold collective bargaining. Section 1 rights are the rights a company has to pay special attention to in the due diligence process, in the sense that due diligence obligations towards those rights arise irrespective of foreseeability of the inherent risk of the rights' infringement of a company's chain of

[26] *See*, UNGP Principles 18 (identifying and assessing stage), 20 (mitigation stage: verifying effectiveness), 21 (communication stage), 29 and 31 (grievance mechanism).

[27] CSDDD Art 13 (3).

[28] CSDDD Art 13 (2).

[29] CSDDD Art 3 (1)(g).

[30] CSDDD recital 26.

[31] UNGP Commentaries to Principles 13 and 17.

activities, whereas section 2 rights (those not listed in Section 1) attract due diligence obligations only when a company's abuse has directly impaired the right and the company could have reasonably foreseen the risk to the rights.[32] The Directive explains this prioritisation only in broad terms such that the distinction is made 'in order to achieve a meaningful contribution to the sustainability transition'.[33] Presumably the distinction is made on the basis of the risk-based approach, weighing up both empirical evidence of past events and prospective compliance costs to be borne by companies.

To provide support to companies and stakeholders, the Commission intends to issue guidelines in relation to due diligence obligations: for companies, guidelines including guidance and best practices on how to conduct due diligence, which are to be issued by 26 January 2027, and for stakeholders, guidelines including information on how to engage throughout the due diligence process, which are to be made available by 26 July 2027.[34]

B. Climate Obligations

Unlike the UNGP, the CSDDD imposes on a company another separate obligation to take action against climate change. This reflects the current European Green Deal policy announced in 2019.[35] One of its main targets is to achieve net-zero emissions of greenhouse gases by 2050.[36] Companies are required to adopt, implement and update annually their transitional plans for climate change mitigation (including absolute emission reduction targets of scope 1, 2 and 3 greenhouse gases in five-year steps beginning from 2030 up until 2050), thus aiming to ensure through their best efforts that their business model and strategy are compatible with the transition to a sustainable economy, and that global warming is limited to 1.5℃ in line with the Paris Agreement and the EU's 2050 climate neutrality targets.[37] However, since this requirement is 'an obligation of means and not of results',[38] companies may be excused for not reaching their planned targets if they have good reasons, and, in turn, the supervisory authorities in the Member States are required 'at least' to 'supervise the adoption and design' of the plan and its updates,[39] which implies that they may not be required to supervise the *implementation* of the plan, unless the Member States' law commands otherwise.

C. Enforcement

In contrast with the UNGP's non-legally binding soft law approach, the CSDDD generally takes a hard law approach. Thus, the Directive stipulates legally binding obligations, accompanied by serious legal consequences of public and private law liabilities for non-compliance.

The Directive lays out two enforcement mechanisms. The first is a traditional public enforcement mechanism. It directs the Member States to designate one or more public supervisory authorities, that are independent, impartial and transparent, to supervise compliance with the

[32] CSDDD Art. 3(1)(c) and recital 32.
[33] CSDDD recital 32.
[34] CSDDD Art 19 (1)(2)(3).
[35] Commission Communication on the European Green Deal, COM/2019/640 final.
[36] Regulation (EU) 2021/1119 (European Climate Law), [2021] OJ L 243/1.
[37] CSDDD Art 22.
[38] CSDDD recital 73.
[39] CSDDD recital 73.

human rights and environmental due diligence obligations as well as climate obligations (Art 24). Those authorities must be equipped with adequate powers and resources to investigate and inspect the company in question, and to make necessary orders including interim measures, and to impose penalties on the company when necessary (Art 25). The Member States must lay down effective, proportionate and dissuasive penalties of pecuniary and non-pecuniary nature: (a) when they set a maximum limit of pecuniary penalties, that should be high enough and 'shall be not less than 5% of the net worldwide turnover of the company', and if this penalty fails to achieve the result, (b) a public statement of a company's infringement (so-called 'name and shame' sanction) (Art 27).

The second mechanism is civil litigation, based on civil liability under the Member States' tort law of negligence (Art 29). This mechanism only deals with human rights and environmental due diligence obligations, not climate obligations. When a company fails to prevent, cease or minimise adverse impacts, in contravention of Arts 10 or 11 of the Directive, and that failure causes damage to victims' legal interests protected under the Member States' law, then the company is held liable for full compensation of the damage, but any type of over-compensation such as punitive damages is excluded. Although the human rights and environmental due diligence obligations under the Directive extend to a company's business partners in its chains of activities, the civil liability of a company does not arise if the damage was caused solely by its business partners in its chain of activities,[40] otherwise joint liability would arise.

In order to ensure an effective remedy,[41] the Directive makes some provisions to require the Member States to address practical and procedural barriers that victims would typically face in civil litigations. Thus, the Member States must ensure in their national law that there should be no restrictive limitation periods nor prohibitively expensive cost of proceedings, that claimants should be able to seek injunctions, to bring representative (group) actions and to have a discovery of evidence under the control of defendants by a court order.[42]

The Directive also provides that the Member States must ensure that the rules in Article 29 concerning the civil litigation (including procedural matters) must be 'of overriding mandatory application' even when the applicable law to the case is a third country law.[43] For example, when adverse impacts would arise in a third country which would be caused by a company and its business partners based in that country, and the third country law is chosen as the law of the case in accordance with international private law, the rules in Article 29 should nevertheless override the third country law to the extent that the Article 29 rules are engaged.

D. Private Enforcement System of Public Rights and Standards for Global Supply Chains

The CSDDD is most significant in that it attempts to establish a private enforcement system of public law rights and standards of human rights and environmental protection throughout a company's global supply chain. The UNGP has indicated a similar idea but remained voluntary and flexible. Thus, the UNGP Principle 19 mentions only that a company 'should' take 'appropriate action' on its own as well as exercise its 'leverage', to the greatest extent possible, towards

[40] CSDDD Art 29(1).
[41] CSDDD recital 82.
[42] CSDDD Art 29(3).
[43] CSDDD Art 29(7).

its business partners in order to prevent or cease the adverse impacts that they may cause. The Directive transforms this into binding legal rules with a view to introducing a more standardised system of private regulation of public law rights and standards.

In this respect, particular attention should be paid to the combined effect of Articles 10, 11, 27 and 29 of the Directive. According to these articles, a company is not just required to take necessary action for its own operation for prevention and cessation of the adverse impacts, such as implementing its prevention/corrective action plan, and modifying its purchase and distribution practices. When it is appropriate to share the responsibilities of adverse impacts between a company and its business partners, the company is also required to 'seek' contractual assurances to comply with its code of conduct and prevention/corrective action plan from its direct business partners (tier 1), and, if necessary, 'may seek' contractual assurances from its indirect business partners (tiers 2 and further up/down the chain of activities) via chain of contracts between tiers 1 and 2 and between tiers 2 and 3 and so on, if these are at all possible, in which every contracting party pledges to comply with the same code of conduct and prevention/corrective action plan.[44] When such assurances are obtained, the company must verify their compliance. For that purpose, it can use independent third-party verification including industry or multi-stakeholder initiatives.[45] A company is also required to provide 'targeted and proportionate support' to its micro, small or medium-sized undertakings (SME) partners, such as providing access to capacity-building, or, if compliance with the code of conduct or prevention/corrective action plan would cause actual or imminent bankruptcy of the SME, targeted and proportionate financial support.[46] Similarly, but optionally, a company may engage with its (non-SME) business partners and provide them with guidance and support, including access to capacity-building, loans and financing.[47] These supports may be needed when a company has some prospect of success in persuading its business partners but feels a need to increase its leverage which is otherwise insufficient to change the partners' adverse behaviour concerning human rights and the environment.

The private governance system described above, if successfully set up, might function as a private enforcement system of public law rights and standards listed in the Annex of the Directive. Those rights and standards are incorporated into a 'code of conduct'[48] by reference, which forms a part of private contracts between a company and its business partner. The effective compliance with the code of conduct is to be monitored through private verification process, and to be enforced ultimately by civil litigation based on negligence liability (Art 29), as well as formal public law enforcements by the supervising authorities of the Member States (Art 27).

It must be pointed out, however, that this desired system is based on some strong assumptions which may not be forthcoming in practice. In a supplier-side monopoly, for example, a company's supplier (business partner) has a stronger negotiating position, and the company may have hardly any 'leverage' over the other.[49] Or in some cases, a company may not expect a long enough relationship with its business partners to have them implement its prevention/corrective action plan and enhanced action plans. Or business partners may not be willing to give contractual

[44] CSDDD Art 10 (2)(4) and recital 46; Art 11(3)(5) and recital 53.
[45] CSDDD Art 10 (5) and Art 11(6).
[46] CSDDD Art 10(2)(e) and recital 46; Art 11(3)(f) and recital 54.
[47] CSDDD Art 10(3) and Art 11(4).
[48] CSDDD Art 7(2)(b).
[49] See, Commentary to the UNGP Principle 19.

assurances without any reservations. The same doubts can be greater in relations between tiers 1 and 2, or tiers 2 and 3 business partners. These are all just theoretical questions, but more significantly, in practice, is it realistic to expect a legal system that is effective in Europe to function equally effectively outside Europe?

It is true that the Directive, foreseeing possible difficulties in managing the contractual due diligence system, stipulates that, when contractual engagement fails to achieve the desired result, a company is required to refrain from making new or extending existing relations, in order to either (a) take an enhanced prevention action plan and temporary suspension of the business relationship when it still has reasonable expectation of success, or (b) as a last resort, terminate the relationship when it has no reasonable expectation of success.[50] At the same time, it also stipulates that if the termination would exacerbate the adverse situation, the company would not be required to terminate the relation but would need to justify its decision and continue its engagement with the business partner by taking appropriate action for improvement.[51]

However, whether those final measures would be sufficient or appropriate to compensate unfulfilled assumptions is not clear. More broadly, it is worthwhile considering whether the private governance system that the CSDD Directive attempts to build would be feasible outside of Europe. As many EU and non-EU companies' global supply chains involve operations in the ASEAN region, where natural resources, raw materials and labour are available in abundance, due diligence obligations under the Directive would inevitably become relevant to them. Therefore, it is pertinent to ask, in the context of the ASEAN region, whether the Directive's private scheme would work and contribute to achieving the basic goal of preventing and terminating the most serious adverse impacts on human rights and the environment. To this question we now turn.

III. The CSDDD in ASEAN Context

A. ASEAN Social Context

A typical example of human rights concerns that companies may have operating in this region would be regarding child labour.[52] The concern relates to the right of the child to be protected from economic exploitation, the prohibition of the employment of a child under the age at which compulsory schooling is completed, and the prohibition of the worst forms of child labour.[53] Although all ASEAN states have ratified the UN Convention on the Rights of the Child (UNCRC hereafter) and they reaffirmed at ASEAN level their commitments to fully implement UNCRC in 2019,[54] their national situations of implementation seem to remain problematic, judging from the documents that appear regularly in the process of periodic verification by the Committee on the Rights of the Child at the United Nations. In its concluding observations in 2022, for

[50] CSDDD Art 10(6) and Art 11(7).

[51] CSDDD Art 10(6) and Art 11(7).

[52] For other concerns, see, eg, AB Wahab, 'Business and human rights in ASEAN: lessons from the palm oil sector in Malaysia' (2019) 7 *Journal of ASEAN Studies* 73–85; D Lim and G Mukherjee, 'Business and human rights challenges in ASEAN: the role and modalities of the State' in M Mohan and C Morel (eds), *Business and Human Rights in Southeast Asia: Risk and the Regulatory Turn* (London, Routledge, 2015) 30.

[53] CSDDD Annex Part I section 1 points 8, 9 and 10.

[54] Joint Statement on Reaffirmation of Commitment to Advancing the Rights of the Child in ASEAN (on 2 November 2019 at Bangkok, Thailand) sean.org/joint-statement-on-reaffirmation-of-commitment-to-advancing-the-rights-of-the-child-in-asean/.

example, the Committee expressed deep concern to Cambodia 'about the large number of children involved in child labour, including in hazardous work, in domestic work under slavery-like conditions and in so-called "debt bondage", such as in the construction, brickmaking, agricultural and textiles industries.'[55] Similar concerns have been repeatedly expressed to Indonesia,[56] Malaysia,[57] the Philippines,[58] Thailand[59] and Viet Nam.[60] As for Laos, its national law was found to be unclear regarding the minimum age of employment.[61] The current situation in Myanmar is unclear because its periodic review documents have been unavailable since the last review in 2012.

From these concluding observations, one can perceive certain problems in common across the region, with Singapore being the exception. It is not just the newer ASEAN states such as Cambodia and Laos, but also some of the older ones that have received similar criticisms about their national laws being either unclear, insufficient, substandard compared to widely accepted international standards, or uncoordinated and inconsistent between national and local levels.[62] They have also been criticised for their weak law enforcement due to lack of knowledge among local officials and stakeholders, lack of well-trained enforcement officers, or corruption.[63]

In some cases, the causes of the adverse impacts (for the present purpose, child labour) seem to be rooted in a particular social and economic structure, as in Myanmar, where the state owns or controls most companies in the extractive and large-scale energy-related sectors, and laws applicable to them to prevent human rights and environmental adverse impacts are absent.[64] Or, in the case of Indonesia, according to the Committee of the Rights of the Child, Indonesia's implementation of the National Plan of Action for the Elimination of the Worst Forms of Child Labour was hampered by a general perception of work as being part of the education process, and a service to parents, and a perception of the child as being a 'family asset'.[65]

In short, relevant laws relating to child labour regulation are insufficient and/or uncertain and/or under-enforced in many parts of the ASEAN. This worsens the human rights and environmental governance gap.

[55] The Committee on the Rights of the Child, Concluding observations on the combined fourth to sixth periodic reports of Cambodia, CRC/C/KHM/CO/4-6 (2022), para 45.

[56] The Committee on the Rights of the Child, Concluding observations to Indonesia 1994 para 16, 2004 para 84, 2014, para 71.

[57] The Committee on the Rights of the Child, Concluding observations to Malaysia 2007 paras 90, 91 and 93.

[58] The Committee on the Rights of the Child, Concluding observations to the Philippines 2005 para 79, 2009 para 72, 2022 para 38.

[59] The Committee on the Rights of the Child, Concluding observations to Thailand 1998 para 29, 2006 para 70, 2012 paras 29, 74.

[60] The Committee on the Rights of the Child, Concluding observations to Viet Nam 1993 para 6, 2003 para 51, 2012 para 69, 2022 para 47.

[61] The Committee on the Rights of the Child, Concluding observations to Laos 2018 para 41.

[62] The Committee on the Rights of the Child, Concluding observations to Brunei Darussalam 2016 para 66; Cambodia 2022 paras 6, 46; Indonesia 2014 para 71; Laos 2011 paras 63-64; Malaysia 2007 para 90; Myanmar 2012 paras 7, 21; Thailand 2012 paras 29-30, 74-75; Viet Nam 2022 para 48.

[63] The Committee on the Rights of the Child, Concluding observations to Brunei Darussalam 2016 para 66; Cambodia 2022 para 46; Indonesia 2014 paras 71, 73; Laos 2018 para 41 and 2011 para 8; Malaysia 2007 para 92; the Philippines 2022 para 38; Viet Nam 2022 para 48. For more extensive empirical study that finds the same effect, *see*, Human Rights Resource Centre, *Business and Human Rights in ASEAN: A Baseline Study* (Depok, Human Rights Resource Centre, 2013).

[64] The Committee on the Rights of the Child, Concluding observations to Myanmar 2012 para 21.

[65] The Committee on the Rights of the Child, Concluding observations to Indonesia 2014 para 71.

B. ASEAN Way of Human Rights Commitments

The situation of child labour focused on above, however, should be considered as part of a broader picture, because there seems to exist a contradictory long-term trend of increasing usage of law at ASEAN level. ASEAN is an intergovernmental organisation that has no legislative power on its own, independent of its Member States. However, since the 1990s, the ASEAN states have gradually increased use of legal instruments, such as international treaties among themselves, or more often, measures drafted in a legal form but not given a binding force, such as non-binding declarations on certain legal issues. The recent broad picture, however, on closer inspection, ironically confirms the traditional legal characteristic of ASEAN. The newly emerged semi-legal technique is being employed in a particular way (the so-called 'ASEAN way'), which generally aims to secure every ASEAN state and its executive government an autonomous and wide discretion at national level.

Take, for instance, the ASEAN Charter[66] adopted in 2007 to illustrate the point. It is a legally binding constitutional document of ASEAN, which, first, establishes a legal personality and capacity to act as ASEAN, second, codifies the traditional state practices among the Member States regarding its organisational structure and its operational rules, including decision-making rules, and thirdly, clarifies its purposes and principles.[67] The purposes include promotion and protection of human rights and fundamental freedoms,[68] and the principles include the principle of respect for fundamental freedoms, the promotion and protection of human rights, and the promotion of social justice.[69] However, the purposes and principles are balanced with such qualification phrases as 'with due regard to the rights and responsibilities of the Member States of ASEAN',[70] or another principle of 'non-interference in the internal affairs of ASEAN Member States'.[71] In this way the ASEAN states have embedded the ASEAN way of state-discretionary human rights commitments in their constitutional document.

The same point can be made for later developments. As the Charter mentioned an ASEAN human rights body to be established,[72] the ASEAN Intergovernmental Commission on Human Rights was inaugurated in 2009,[73] as a consultative body, primarily to advise ASEAN sectoral bodies and the Member States on human rights matters.[74] Based on this Commission's draft, the ASEAN Human Rights Declaration was adopted in 2012,[75] which is drafted in a legal form but not given a legally binding force. For example, its Article 27 paragraph three stipulates:

> (3) No child or any young person shall be subjected to economic and social exploitation. Those who employ children and young people in work harmful to their morals or health, dangerous to life, or likely to hamper their normal development, including their education, should be punished by law. ASEAN Member States should also set age limits below which the paid employment of child labour should be prohibited and punished by law.

[66] asean.org/wp-content/uploads/images/archive/publications/ASEAN-Charter.pdf.

[67] See generally, W Woon, *The ASEAN Charter: A Commentary* (Singapore, NUS Press, 2015).

[68] ASEAN Charter Art 1(7).

[69] ASEAN Charter Art 2(2)(i).

[70] ASEAN Charter Art 1(7).

[71] ASEAN Charter Art 2(2)(e).

[72] ASEAN Charter Art 14.

[73] Cha-Am Hua Hin Declaration on the Intergovernmental Commission on Human Rights on 23 October 2009. asean.org/wp-content/uploads/2021/09/Declaration-AICHR.pdf.

[74] ASEAN Intergovernmental Commission on Human Rights (Terms of Reference) (2009) points 3 and 4. aichr.org/wp-content/uploads/2020/02/TOR-of-AICHR.pdf.

[75] asean.org/asean-human-rights-declaration/.

The provision generally follows Article 32 of UNCRC,[76] but does not refer to the state obligation to regulate working hours and conditions, nor define 'child' or 'young person' by age (note that this definition point is separate from the issue of setting a minimum age for an employable child). In contrast, UNCRC defines a child as every human being below the age of 18 years unless majority is attained earlier under the law applicable to the child.[77] It is fair to say, however, the lack of definition for 'child' has been compensated in part by ratifying International Labour Organization (ILO) Conventions and adjusting national laws accordingly in relation to the minimum age of child employment. The ILO Minimum Age Convention No. 138, which sets out the minimum age for work to be at least 15 years old, is ratified by all ASEAN states,[78] while Cambodia, Laos and Myanmar set the minimum to 14 years old, making use of the exception clause in the Convention for developing countries.[79] Similarly, the ILO Worst Forms of Child Labour Convention No. 182, which prohibits all forms of slavery or similar practices, child prostitution, using a child for illicit activities, and any work likely to harm the health, safety or morals of children, is also ratified by all ASEAN states.[80] Nevertheless, the basic point remains true that ASEAN states retain a wide discretion in how and to what extent they regulate working conditions for children and young persons. In this way, ASEAN states uphold the rights of the child while enjoying a wide margin for regulating non-illegal child labour in their jurisdictions. This example of the ASEAN way of state-discretionary human rights commitment indicates that legal certainty, an essential component of the rule of law, tends to be insufficient. The lack of legal certainty undoubtedly does not contribute to robust enforcement either.

The picture becomes even more problematic when it comes to collective rights of workers.[81] Here the same ASEAN way of commitment appears in the ASEAN Human Rights Declaration Article 27 paragraph two:

> (2) Every person has the right to form trade unions and join the trade union of his or her choice *for the protection of his or her interests*, in accordance with national laws and regulations. (italics added)

It should be noted that this provision leaves the right to collective bargaining and collective action unmentioned, at most by implication in the italicised part above. Behind the italicised vague wording remain differences among ASEAN states in recognising collective rights of workers. Some states have ratified both ILO Conventions Nos. 87 and 98, which relate to the right to organise and join trade unions and the right to take collective bargaining.[82] Others have ratified neither of them,[83] and the rest have ratified only one of them.[84] This is another example of lack of legal certainty, and a source of public under-enforcement.

[76] UNCRC Article 32 provides: '1. States Parties recognize the right of the child to be protected from economic exploitation and from performing any work that is likely to be hazardous or to interfere with the child's education, or to be harmful to the child's health or physical, mental, spiritual, moral or social development. 2. … States Parties shall in particular: (a) Provide for a minimum age or minimum ages for admission to employment; (b) Provide for appropriate regulation of the hours and conditions of employment; (c) Provide for appropriate penalties or other sanctions to ensure the effective enforcement of the present article.'

[77] UNCRC Art 1.

[78] normlex.ilo.org/dyn/normlex/en/f?p=NORMLEXPUB:11300:0::NO:11300:P11300_INSTRUMENT_ID:312283:NO.

[79] See, Article 2 (1)(3) and (4) of the Convention.

[80] normlex.ilo.org/dyn/normlex/en/f?p=NORMLEXPUB:11300:0::NO:11300:P11300_INSTRUMENT_ID:312327:NO.

[81] CSDDD Annex Part I, section 1, point 13.

[82] Cambodia, Indonesia, and the Philippines.

[83] Brunei Darussalam, Laos, and Thailand.

[84] Malaysia (No. 98 only), Myanmar (No 87 only), Singapore (No. 98 only), and Viet Nam (No. 98 only).

Companies that are subject to the CSDD Directive may face these human rights concerns and the legal and social context in carrying out their due diligence obligations throughout their direct or indirect operations in the ASEAN region.

C. The ASEAN Way of Environmental Commitments

Similarly, the ASEAN way of commitments appears in the field of environmental protection. It has not contributed to improving effective implementation and enforcement of relevant regulatory laws. A case in point is transboundary haze pollution in this region. Typically, fires originating in the forests and peatlands of the Indonesian island of Sumatra and Kalimantan (the Indonesian part of the island of Borneo) have repeatedly polluted surrounding ASEAN states with haze since the 1970s. The most critical cases so far happened in 1997–98, and in 2013–15 when El Niño related drought exacerbated the situation.[85] The factors which recently contributed to causing the fires were logging rain forests for timber (mainly in the 1960s and 1970s) and clearing forests for large-scale agricultural uses including pulp wood and palm oil plantations (mainly from the 1990s).[86] Repeated haze pollution prompted ASEAN states to adopt the ASEAN Agreement on Transboundary Haze Pollution (the Haze Agreement hereafter) in 2002 to prevent and monitor transboundary haze pollution in the spirit of solidarity and partnership.[87] The Haze Agreement directs each contracting state to establish an appropriate legal framework to prevent, monitor, and minimise forest and land fires,[88] and provides that a state experiencing forest fire 'may' request a joint emergency response through the provision of assistance from the other states.[89] While most ASEAN states ratified the Haze Agreement promptly, Indonesia did not ratify it until October 2014, after a month earlier Singapore legislated its Transboundary Haze Pollution Act 2014[90] to make it possible for persons in Singapore to sue for civil and criminal liabilities against persons outside Singapore who cause haze pollution in Singapore.[91] After that the Indonesian government started to strengthen national regulations and enforcements, resulting in, for example, an Indonesian Supreme Court judgment of *Kementerian Lingkungan Hidup Dan Kehutanan RI v PT. National Sago Prima* (*Ministry of Environment and Forestry of the Republic of Indonesia v PT National Sago Prima*) in 2018, ordering a plantation company which caused forest fires to pay around 319 billion Rupiah (circa 185 million euros) in damages.[92] Nevertheless, national enforcements seem to remain inadequate, and haze pollution is recurring in the region.[93]

[85] S Seah and H Varkkey, 'Breaking the Vicious Cycle of Haze and Climate Change in Southeast Asia' (published online on 11 October 2023) fulcrum.sg/breaking-the-vicious-cycle-of-haze-and-climate-change-in-southeast-asia/.

[86] D Glover and T Jessup (eds), *Indonesia's Fires ad Haze: The Cost of Catastrophe* (Singapore, Institute of Southeast Asian Studies, 1999) 5–6. Individual farmers living near forests, using the slash-and burn method of agriculture, also contributed to the 1997 fire. ibid 6–7.

[87] Haze Agreement Art 3.

[88] Haze Agreement Art 4.

[89] Haze Agreement Art 12.

[90] sso.agc.gov.sg/Act/THPA2014. See also M Mohan, 'A Domestic Solution for Transboundary Harm: Singapore's Haze Pollution Law' (2017) 2 *Business and Human Rights Journal* 325.

[91] Transboundary Haze Pollution Act 2014 Arts 4, 5 and 6.

[92] Putusan Mahkamah Agung Nomor (Supreme Court Decision No.) 3067 K/Pdt/2018. putusan3.mahkamahagung.go.id/direktori/putusan/376742557caf719d498418c8b6b39b78.html.

[93] For the meteorological data, see asmc.asean.org/home/; for visual dataset for the tree loss and forest fires in the ASEAN region, see sasawijayantii.users.earthengine.app/view/peatland-apn-project.

IV. Challenges and Potentials of the CSDDD in the ASEAN Context

A. How Far is a Company Able to, and How Far should a Company Complement 'Publicness' Privately?

The above discussion suggests that in the ASEAN region, official perception and application of human rights and environmental protection generally tend to retain a wide margin of discretion for each government in balancing individual rights and interests with public interest. In other words, a fundamental challenge remains in this region to align states' performance of their duty to guarantee human rights and environmental protection with relevant international norms including the UNGP Principle 1 and other non-binding or binding agreements, many of which the ASEAN states have subscribed to. In this respect the ASEAN Intergovernmental Commission on Human Rights could play an important role, although its power is limited to recommendation at present.[94]

Given the CSDDD was made in the EU, where the rule of law, human rights protection and liberal democracy[95] are deemed to be 'common values', the Directive, when applied in a non-EU context which does not necessarily share all of these elements, would work on a strong assumption that all non-European states are equally willing to carry out their duty to protect human rights as advised in UNGP Principle 1, and would ask companies to establish a private system of human rights and environmental due diligence to fill a global human rights governance gap.

That assumption invites a fundamental challenge for EU or non-EU companies operating in the ASEAN region, especially in operating indirectly through their supply chains there. When a relevant government in the region constantly fails to guarantee specific human rights listed in the Annex Part I section 1 of the Directive due to the uncertainty of its national law or its chronic under-enforcement, how effectively would those companies be able to exercise their due diligence in relation to their local business partners? Do the partners take human rights seriously, even if the partners should ever agree to make assurances to comply with the companies' codes of conduct? Are those companies 'required' to offer 'capacity-building' (including human rights education) to the local business partners, even if that offer might work against their business interests? A most likely general answer would be to do what a reasonable company would do in that situation, since non-compliance with the due diligence obligations would result in civil liability based on negligence. But that answer would only make the normative question dependent on complex factual circumstances. This would not guide nor encourage any company which is struggling to find its proper role in preventing or mitigating human rights and environmental adverse impacts, especially when a host state's public enforcement on the matter is severely limited. In actuality, finding this practical normative standard for a private company to carry out public purpose obligations in competition with local public authorities would be the most sensitive and fundamental challenge for the CSDDD scheme to achieve its objectives in the ASEAN

[94] ASEAN Intergovernmental Commission on Human Rights (Terms of Reference) (2009) point 4.

[95] See recital 1 of the Directive referring to Article 2 TEU and EU Charter of Fundamental Rights. See also Opinion 2/13 (EU Accession to the European Convention on Human Rights) ECLI:EU:C:2014:2454, paras 167–168 (emphasising that the existence of mutual trust between the Member States so that the set of common values stated in Article 2 TEU will be recognised and that the law of the EU that implements them will be respected).

region. It is hoped that the EU Commission guidelines as scheduled to be announced in 2027[96] will help clarify the points.

B. Enhancement of Remedial Process by the Judiciary?

From the perspective of potential victims, there is another challenge. That is how far the Directive could help to enhance judicial protection of victims against adverse impacts. Relevant to this point is Article 29 of the Directive.

As mentioned earlier, paragraph 7 of Article 29 provides that the rules stipulated in that Article are of overriding mandatory application. The purpose of this provision seems to be to ensure that victims could pursue their claims in any EU Member State's court to get compensation under the harmonised essential overriding rules of Article 29, even when the court chooses to apply a third country's law to the case.[97]

However, the provision may not always achieve the desired results, especially when the adverse impacts are caused in a non-EU country (eg, an ASEAN state), jointly by a non-EU company and its business partner, both having their seats in non-EU countries (eg, a Japanese company and its Indonesian business partner in its supply chain). In this situation, (a) if a court of an EU Member State would somehow seize the jurisdiction of the case under the Brussels I Recast Regulation[98] and select the third country law as applicable law to the case under the Rome II Regulation,[99] it can apply Article 29 to override the law of the third country, as necessary. Nevertheless, even in this case, enforcing that judgment in the third country might prove difficult because the third country court might not recognise such a European judgment on various grounds, including being contrary to public policy of that country.[100] (b) If, on the other hand, a third country court would seize the jurisdiction of the case in accordance with its international private law, that court might treat Article 29 as a mere fact, rather than an applicable law of the case, to apply the third country law regardless of Article 29. Thus, overriding application of Article 29 may not always take effect in practice in litigations against non-EU parties.[101]

Nevertheless, Article 29, if it is taken as a model, may well inform non-EU courts and/or legislators in reforming their substantive and procedural rules to ensure effective remedies for victims of human rights abuses and environmental adverse impacts. Indeed, some significant developments have already been made in ASEAN, although limited to environmental cases, that would resolve some of the procedural concerns listed in paragraph three of Article 29. That paragraph mentions several procedural concerns that victims would face in their civil liability litigation relating to due diligence obligations.

The Philippine Supreme Court in *Oposa v Factoran*[102] in 1993 granted all minor petitioners represented by their parents the standing (*locus standi*) of a class action for 'their generation as

[96] CSDDD Art 19.
[97] CSDDD recital 90.
[98] Regulation (EU) No. 1215/2012 (Brussels I Recast), [2012] OJ L 351/1.
[99] Regulation (EC) No 864/2007 (Rome II), [2007] OJ L 199/40.
[100] S Schmid and C Thomale, 'Private Enforcement in the EU Corporate Sustainability Due Diligence Directive – A critical comparative law and economic analysis of the Final Compromise' Faculty of Law Blogs/University of Oxford posted on 22 May 2024. blogs.law.ox.ac.uk/oblb/blog-post/2024/05/private-enforcement-eu-corporate-sustainability-due-diligence-directive.
[101] For further discussion, see, eg, N Perrone, 'Perspectives of Extraterritorial Jurisdiction for Environmental Damage in the Proposal of the European Directive on Corporate Sustainability Due Diligence' (2023) 3 *Italian Review of International and Comparative Law* 389.
[102] G.R. No. 101083 (1993, Philippine Supreme Court).

well as generations yet unborn'. In that case the petitioners sought for cancellation of all existing and future timber licence agreements concluded by the government to prevent further deforestation. The Court also granted the relief sought. In doing so, the Court applied precautionary principle and intergenerational justice to lighten the petitioners' burden of *prima facie* proof of cause of action, especially in relation to the causation between the timber licences and the environmental damages (water shortages, salinization of water, etc). The court in conclusion found the timber licence agreements were violating the petitioners' constitutional right to a balanced and healthful ecology and the right to health.

After this landmark decision, procedural rules reforms followed in the Philippines, and the Rules of Procedure on Environmental Cases[103] was promulgated by the Supreme Court in 2010 to ensure effective access to justice and remedy for the victims of environmental damage.[104] The new rules set out several innovations, including a special expedited procedure to dispose of a strategic lawsuit against public participation (SLAPP),[105] the special civil actions relating to the writ of *kalikasan* and the writ of continuing mandamus. The latter is a continuing court order upon a losing party to act as ordered by the judgment till the party accomplishes it.[106] The former is an injunctive relief against violation or threatening violation of a persons' constitutional right to a balanced and healthful ecology by a public official or employee or a private individual or entity's act or omission that involve environmental damage of such magnitude as to prejudice the life, health or property of inhabitants in two or more cities or provinces.[107] Under this writ of *kalikasan* procedure, moreover, the petitioners are exempt from docket fee,[108] and the procedure includes discovery of evidence by 'ocular inspection' order and 'production or inspection of documents or things' order,[109] which would help the petitioners to substantiate their claims.

Another development of similar kind is the Singaporean legislation of Transboundary Haze Pollution Act 2014 on transboundary haze pollution liability, as mentioned earlier.[110] All these developments address the concerns listed in Article 29 of the Directive. It would, therefore, be reasonable to expect that, encouraged by and taking inspiration from Article 29, judiciaries and/or legislatures in some ASEAN states would spontaneously develop their case-law and/or procedural rules in relation to not just environmental cases but also to cases of adverse human rights impact.[111] This might happen especially when the national constitution recognises the relevant

[103] Rules of Procedure on Environmental Cases (A.M. No. 09-6-8-SC) adopted and took effect in 2010. lawphil.net/courts/supreme/am/am_09-6-8-sc_2010.html.

[104] For further detail of the reform and its consequences in the 2010s, see B Sta. Maria, 'Rule-making for rights protection in the Philippines: The judiciary's new powers for environmental regulation and access to remedy for business-related rights abuses' in M Mohan and C Morel (eds), *Business and Human Rights in Southeast Asia: Risk and the Regulatory Turn* (London, Routledge, 2015) 225.

[105] Rules of Procedure on Environmental Cases, Rule 6.

[106] Rules of Procedure on Environmental Cases, Rule 8. As a judicial precedent prior to the Rule 8, see *Metro Manila Development Authority v Concerned Residents of Manila Bay*, G.R. Nos. 171947-48 (2008, Philippine Supreme Court).

[107] Rules of Procedure on Environmental Cases, Rule 7.

[108] Rules of Procedure on Environmental Cases, Rule 7, section 4.

[109] Rules of Procedure on Environmental Cases, Rule 7, section 12.

[110] See section 2.3.

[111] See, eg, In Thailand, a special division for complex environmental cases was established in the Court of Appeal and the Supreme Court respectively. See N Kiettikunwong, 'The Green Bench: Can an Environmental Court Protect Natural Resources in Thailand?' (2019) 21 *Environment, Development and Sustainability* 385–404. See also UNDP, *Evolving Justice: ASEAN Judges Conference* 5–6 October 2023, Bangkok, Thailand, Conference Report (Bangkok, UNDP, 2023) 42 (A Thai Supreme Court Judge presenting a Draft of Environmental Procedure Act in Thailand) www.undp.org/sites/g/files/zskgke326/files/2023-12/Report%20of%20the%20JIN%20ASEAN%20Judges%20Conference%202023.pdf.

rights,[112] and the judiciary has the procedural rule-making power and the power of judicial review on legislative and executive actions under the Constitution, as in the case of the Philippines.

Since environmental NGOs have played a vital role in pursuing human rights and environmental litigations, it is essential to analyse further how the CSDDD would enhance the role of stakeholders, including civil society as well as companies themselves, in preventing and ceasing human rights and environmental adversities in the ASEAN context.

C. Engagement in the Due Diligence Process

The Directive provides for two types of engagement for a company under the Directive. The first is engaging with a company's business partners. In preventing and ceasing human rights and environmental adverse impacts, the company 'may' engage with its business partner about the company's expectations for preventing and ceasing these impacts, and could provide or enable access to capacity-building, guidance, and administrative and financial support.[113] When a company's business partner is an SME, engagement in the form of 'targeted and proportionate support' is required where necessary.[114] The Directive also recommends that even when prevention and cessation obligations are not fulfilled, companies should prioritise engagement with their business partners over terminating the business relationship, so as to ensure that the prevention and cessation measures are effective.[115] Those explicit provisions, however, form only part of the first type of engagement. Implicitly the Directive expects engagement with business partners to be carried out at all stages of the due diligence process. For example, in adopting 'appropriate' measures to prevent and cease potential and real adverse impacts, due account should be taken of the company's ability to 'influence' the business partner that may (jointly) cause or have caused the adverse impacts.[116] Recitals 45 and 53, for example, explain that the company's influence includes its ability to 'persuade' the relevant business partner.[117] The recital 54 also mentions that 'by sharing the value along the chain of activities' a company can pursue its responsible purchasing or distribution practices. This first type of engagement is essentially a process of persuasion and nurturing mutual trust, within a long-term business relationship, to fulfil the due diligence obligations as the first party.

In the ASEAN context, this type of engagement will become particularly crucial. As discussed earlier,[118] many ASEAN states' commitments to human rights and environmental protection have significant limitations, and social perception of human rights may vary greatly within the region. In this situation a company may not be able to establish a contractual system of due diligence with its standardised code of conduct at the outset. If a company requires a long-term business relationship in its operation, it might have to start with providing its business partners guidance and information on relevant human rights and environmental risks in their operation, offering support for prevention where necessary, before it tries to persuade them to comply with its standardised code of conduct on a trial basis, and subsequently verifying their compliance.

[112] See, eg, As to the right to healthy environment, the Constitutions of Indonesia (Art 28H(1)), the Philippines (Art II section 16) and Viet Nam (Art 43).

[113] CSDDD Arts 10(3) and 11(4).

[114] CSDDD Arts 10(2)(e) and 11(3)(f).

[115] CSDDD recital 50 in relation to Art 10(6) and recital 57 in relation to Art 11(7).

[116] CSDDD Art 10(1)(c) and Art 11(1)(c).

[117] See also recitals 50 and 57 which state that collaborations with another company in a similar position may be necessary in some cases to prevent and cease adverse impacts at the level of indirect business relationships.

[118] See sections 2.1 to 2.3.

Generally, in a long-term business relationship, it is essential to have not just formal contractual legal force, but also flexible force in the form of practical reason based on mutual trust. When the mutual trust grows in the relationship, the company will find it easier to persuade its business partner to sign up to its code of conduct formally, making it a part of their contract. At that point, the company might also introduce an independent third-party verification if the risk, once materialised, would be significant and serious.

The second type of engagement is the one with its stakeholders.[119] This is to realise a participatory process of dialogue and collaboration between the company and its potential victims, to keep the due diligence process effective and enable all parties involved to act proactively at any stage of the process. The Directive provides that stakeholder consultation should take place at every critical stage of the due diligence process so that the process is meaningful. The stages consist of (a) gathering risk information, (b) developing prevention and corrective action plans and enhanced action plans, (c) suspension and termination of a business relationship, (d) adopting remedial measures, and (e) developing monitoring indicators.[120] In addition, a company's employees and their representatives should be consulted when the company is developing its due diligence policy, including code of conduct[121] – this is a stage between (a) and (b). To ensure effective engagement, the Directive also imposes an obligation on companies to identify and address barriers to stakeholder engagement, especially by protecting participants from retaliation or retribution by maintaining confidentiality or anonymity.[122]

Closely related to this participatory engagement is the notification mechanism and complaint procedure required to be established under Article 14 of the Directive. It directs the Member States to ensure that companies are required under their law to establish 'a fair, publicly available, accessible, predictable and transparent' complaints procedure which ensures the confidentiality of complainants to prevent retaliation.[123] Entitled complainants include those who are potential or affected victims and their legitimate representatives, including civil society organisations and human rights defenders, trade unions and other workers' representatives, and civil society organisations that are active and experienced in related areas when the complaint is about adverse environmental impacts.[124] The innovative aspect of the Directive is that it goes a step further than the UNGP to provide for the right to have effective feedback.[125] Thus, non-anonymous complainants are entitled to request timely and appropriate follow-up from the company, to meet with the company's representative of an appropriate level to discuss the impacts, and to be provided with the reasons why their complaint was considered founded or unfounded.[126]

In the ASEAN context, stakeholder engagement will likely be indispensable, especially in consulting employees of a company and its business partners. However, for instance, in the case of environmental risks that will affect the critical human rights listed in the Annex Part I section 1 (eg, the prohibition of causing any measurable environmental degradation, and the right of individuals, groupings and communities to lands and resources), significant barriers may remain

[119] CSDDD Art 13. The stakeholders are defined broadly to include employees, trade unions and workers' representatives of the company, its subsidiaries and its business partners, consumers of their products and services, national human rights and environmental institutions, civil society organisations whose purposes include the protection of the environment, and the legitimate representatives of those individuals, groupings, communities or entities (Art 3(1)(n)).
[120] CSDDD Art 13(3).
[121] CSDDD Art 7(2).
[122] CSDDD Art 13(5) and recital 65.
[123] CSDDD Art 14(3).
[124] CSDDD Art 14(2).
[125] cf The UNGP Principle 29, Principle 31 and its commentary (e) do not touch upon the right to have effective feed-backs.
[126] CSDDD Art 14(4).

in realising participation of potential or actual victims and their civil society representatives in the due diligence process. This is partly because a company's interests may conflict with those of stakeholders, and partly because national public law that guarantees stakeholder participation in environmental assessment and/or access to environmental information may be insufficient or ineffective to support and complement the private due diligence system. Since the issue of stakeholder participation is, by its nature, going beyond a private contractual relationship, a public law intervention is essential to ensure the effective participation of stakeholders, regardless of a company's willingness to engage.

However, in the general context of ASEAN, serious challenges seem to remain before stakeholders' participatory rights by public law can be guaranteed, judging from the current drafting process of an ASEAN declaration on environmental rights. The ASEAN Intergovernmental Commission on Human Rights established a Working Group for drafting the instrument in 2023,[127] and the Working Group made public its 'draft ASEAN declaration on environmental rights' (the March draft[128] hereafter) for comments in March 2024.[129] One of the objectives stated in the March draft was 'promoting the full and effective implementation of the rights of access to environmental information, public participation in environmental decision-making' and access to justice and effective remedies (point 1 (3)). When the Working Group published a revised draft in May (the May draft[130] hereafter), after taking account of the comments made, the whole paragraph about participation and access had been bracketed off, suggesting its deletion or substantial amendments in the subsequent consultation process. Correspondingly, the March draft's general provision point 3 (every person's right to protect the environment) and the specific provisions relating to every person's right to access to environmental information (point 13) and the right to participate in decision-making in environmental matters (point 15) have been bracketed off in the May draft. Most tellingly, the March draft's point 18 is also now in brackets in the May draft, which is as follows:

> [Human rights and environmental due diligence and risk assessment for decisions or activities that are likely to have a significant impact on the environment or human rights should be incorporated by AMS [ASEAN Member States] into both public and private sector decision-making.]

On a different but related note, the March draft contained a separate provision to address another barrier to civil society participation. Point 22 of the March draft provided that the ASEAN member states should, firstly, take adequate and effective measures to recognise and protect those who promote and strive for environmental rights, secondly, ensure they are free from threat and retaliation in any form, and thirdly, take appropriate, effective, and timely measures to prevent, investigate, deter, and punish threats or intimidation against those who promote and strive for environmental rights. Point 22 is now also bracketed off entirely in the May draft.

In July 2024, the Working Group referred the May draft to the ASEAN Intergovernmental Commission on Human Rights, which will in turn consult relevant ASEAN Sectoral Bodies (particularly the meetings of senior officials as well as ministers on the environment) before submitting it for adoption by ASEAN leaders.[131] As the general rule of decision-making at

[127] aichr.org/news/press-release-36th-meeting-of-aichr-28-february-3-march-2023-asean-secretariat/.
[128] The March draft is available at www.environmental-rights.net/. No information is available on the comments made on the March draft. The present author used information available at the Asian Research Institute for Environmental Law's website, since only limited information on the activities of the Working Group is available at the ASEAN Intergovernmental Commission on Human Rights official web page.
[129] asean.org/the-3rd-asean-environmental-rights-working-group-meeting/.
[130] May draft is available at www.environmental-rights.net/.
[131] www.environmental-rights.net/.

ASEAN meetings is by consensus,[132] the future of these draft provisions do not look promising. In any event, the point is that national legislation will be necessary to support and complement the second type of private engagement obligation under the Directive, if that engagement is to be effective in practice.

V. Conclusion

Some general observations can be made from the preceding discussion. Firstly, the Directive is based on the EU's normative assumption on the rule of law, including sufficiently clear and adequate public regulatory law and its robust enforcement, and the general acceptance and standardised understanding of human rights in society.[133] Not only are these conditions not fulfilled in many parts of ASEAN, but the current situation is also unlikely to change rapidly. Hence, it is highly likely that companies with their business partners in the region will face significant challenges in carrying out due diligence obligations essentially by themselves, with limited expectation of public law enforcement by public authorities in relation to human rights and environmental protection. In that situation the most effective response for a company may be first and foremost to engage with their business partners and stakeholders, rather than seeking for contractual assurances. Having a 'code of conduct', not as a formal part of the contract with business partners, but as an indicator of good practice, may still be useful since it would serve as a basis for a company to persuade its business partners to respect human rights and environmental standards in their operations. Active engagement with business partners and stakeholders in their specific circumstances would bring more focused and practical responses to actual or potential adverse impacts. Once the engagement becomes regular, mutual cooperative spirit could pave the way for a formal contractual relation as regards human rights and environmental protection.

Second, companies in this situation may wish to participate in an industry-wide initiative or a multi-stakeholder initiative, if those are available in their own industry, in order to strengthen their leverage or persuasive power. The Directive does allow this course of action in fulfilling the due diligence obligations in general,[134] or specifically in relation to an independent third-party verification.[135] However, relevant requirements and operational principles that such initiatives must satisfy are indicated neither adequately nor clearly in the Directive. Further details are entrusted to the Commission's future 'guidance' which will be made in collaboration with Member States sometime in the unspecified future.[136]

Third, this guidance, however, will also become a real practical and theoretical challenge for the Commission and Member States. The practical challenge for them is to study and compare successful versus unsuccessful industry-wide initiatives and/or multi-stakeholder initiatives in order to identify necessary conditions for success.[137] The theoretical challenge is that they will need to find a new balance and combination of public law requirements and private law freedom, because the initiatives, however constructed in a form of private law scheme, will be employed

[132] ASEAN Charter Art 20(1).
[133] See n 95.
[134] CSDDD Art 20(4).
[135] CSDDD Arts 10(5), 11 (6), and 20(5).
[136] CSDDD Art 20(4) and (5).
[137] In particular, the experience and practice in negotiating and implementing the 'Bangladesh Accord' and later the 'International Accord' after the Rana Plaza disaster may be informative. Due to space limitations, no further details will be discussed here. See generally, J Salminen, 'The Accord on Fire and Building Safety in Bangladesh: A New Paradigm for Limiting Buyers' Liability in Global Supply Chains?' (2018) 66 *American Journal of Comparative Law* 411.

by companies as a functional alternative or supplement to a public system of ensuring human rights and environmental standards. Thus, on the one hand, the initiatives must satisfy such requirements as are expected in public regulation, including equal treatment of the participants, a fair and transparent process of decision-making, and keeping the initiative accountable to the participants.[138] On the other hand, the initiative must retain adequate flexibility, as private law would generally allow, to respond spontaneously and proactively to potential or actual critical risks. The CSDDD does not stipulate adequate requirements in this respect. It does refer to some requirements in relation to independent third-party verification, including requirements to act 'with objectivity and complete independence from the company', to be 'free from any conflicts of interest' and 'free from external influence', and to take no 'action incompatible with their independence'.[139] However, some of those requirements are repetitive and, in any case, seem to be insufficiently comprehensive, because, for example, the principle of equal treatment of participants is missing: if verification is to be done by an industry-wide initiative, it should be done in an equal manner to all the participants.

Lastly, some elements of the Directive may work as a model for ASEAN states' law reform as well as business partners and stakeholders' new goals. Even if the Directive's central idea of a contractual compliance system may not materialise nor work effectively in the ASEAN context in the short term, some points made in the Directive, particularly Article 29 paragraph 3, regarding procedural hardships and possible legal solutions, may inform the ASEAN states' legislature and judiciary as well as civil society organisations that work for human rights and environmental protection. This aspect of the Directive may encourage other ASEAN states to follow the example of the Philippines' Supreme Court's innovation of procedural rules on environmental cases.

[138] In this regard, the points made by the scholars of 'Global Administrative Law' may be informative. See B Kingsbury, N Krisch and RB Stewart, 'The Emergence of Global Administrative Law' (2005) 68 *Law and Contemporary Problems* 15–61; B Kingsbury, 'Frontiers of Global Administrative Law in the 2020s' in JNE Varuhas and S Wilson Stark (eds), *The Frontiers of Public Law* (Oxford, Hart Publishing, 2019) 41.

[139] CSDDD Art 20(5).

PART II

Asian Case Studies of the Use of Civil Human Rights Litigation against Corporations

7

Japan[1]

KENNETH TSUI, MATTHEW WONG AND JASON HO CHING CHEUNG

I. Introduction: Japanese Constitutional Commitments and the Business-Human Rights Nexus

Japan's constitution, similar to those of other Asian-Pacific jurisdictions, emphasises the protection of individual rights, with Chapter III of the Constitution of Japan (the 'Constitution') enshrining a broad range of civil liberties. Among these, Article 13 of the Constitution ('Article 13') plays a fundamental role as it is the overarching article highlighting that 'all of the people shall be respected as individuals' and that the right to life, liberty, and the pursuit of happiness shall be the 'supreme consideration in legislation and other governmental affairs'.

Article 13 governs state-civilian relations. Nonetheless, Japan's effort in protecting human rights and civil liberties has extended to private law as the government has, in recent years, introduced policies which aim at holding private corporations to account for and respect human rights. While Article 13 is not 'directly applicable' in disputes between private parties, the court has accepted that human rights enshrined in the Constitution and international treaties could be 'indirectly applied' and could be taken into account when adjudicating disputes. Therefore, it is possible for private parties to be held accountable for infringement of human rights. This chapter argues that such an extension is affected by international instruments, including the UN Guiding Principles on Business and Human Rights (the 'UNGPs')[2] and the OECD Guidelines for Multinational Enterprises,[3] which have prompted jurisdictions, including Japan, to promote human rights initiatives among private entities. In Japan, this shift has produced a patchwork of policy, soft law instruments, and incremental legal reforms that aim to reconcile international expectations with domestic legal and cultural traditions.

Section II of this chapter situates Japan within the broader international movement to protect human rights and hold businesses accountable for human rights impacts. It begins by outlining the constitutional and treaty-based foundations of Japan's human rights framework, highlighting how courts have cautiously applied international norms in private disputes. It then examines the role of international and soft law instruments in shaping Japan's evolving approach. These

[1] The authors would like to thank Dr Kazuaki Nishioka for his tremendous support and assistance in the preparation and writing of this chapter. It would not have been completed without the insight and comments Dr Nishioka shared.

[2] For details, see ch 2 by K Matsuki and A Burke, 'Litigations Against Corporations: Why Enforce Human Rights Against Multinationals?'.

[3] Available at www.oecd.org/en/publications/2023/06/oecd-guidelines-for-multinational-enterprises-on-responsible-business-conduct_a0b49990.html.

instruments, while non-binding, have spurred the government to adopt policy initiatives such as the National Action Plan on Business and Human Rights,[4] signalling an incremental but meaningful alignment with global standards.

Section III turns to domestic developments. Here, it analyses the 2024 amendment to the Act for Eliminating Discrimination against Persons with Disabilities, which strengthened the obligation of companies to provide reasonable accommodation. It also reviews the implementation of the National Action Plan and the Ministry of Economy, Trade and Industry ('METI')'s guidelines on human rights due diligence in supply chains, including the publication of good practice guides. A comparative perspective with recent European Union legislation, particularly the Corporate Sustainability Due Diligence Directive, is also provided, underscoring the differences between Japan's industry-driven, voluntary framework and the EU's binding, regulatory approach.

Beyond these policy initiatives, Section IV critically assesses the gaps and structural challenges in Japan's human rights protection. These include judicial conservatism in applying international law, reliance on soft law rather than binding obligations, and cultural and institutional barriers to substantive equality in areas such as gender and LGBTQ+ rights. Illustrative cases, including those concerning racial discrimination, same-sex marriage, and women's rights, reveal both the potential and the limitations of Japan's legal system in advancing human rights.

Finally, Section V discusses the resolution of human rights-related disputes in Japan. It highlights the recent landmark decision invalidating the Eugenics Protection Law as a further progress in recognition of human rights, while also considering the prospects of Japanese corporations facing litigation for their subsidiaries' human rights abuses abroad and the private international law rules in this regard.[5]

Taken together, these discussions attempt to provide a comprehensive overview of Japan's gradual yet significant steps toward embedding human rights norms into its legal and corporate governance frameworks. The discussion also reveals deeper tensions between constitutional ideals, international expectations, and domestic practices, an issue that continues to shape Japan's cautious and incremental steps forward in the field of human rights.

II. International and Soft Law Frameworks

Japan has ratified key United Nations human rights treaties, including the International Covenant on Social, Economic and Cultural Rights ('ICSECR'), International Covenant on Civil and Political Rights ('ICCPR'),[6] the Convention on the Rights of the Child, the International Convention on the Elimination of All Forms of Racial Discrimination ('CERD') and the Convention on the Rights of Persons with Disabilities ('CRPD').[7] These ratified international treaties form part of the Japanese domestic law once promulgated in the *kampō* and have to be faithfully implemented under the constitution.[8]

[4] Available at www.mofa.go.jp/fp/hr_ha/page23e_000551.html.

[5] For detailed discussion on private international law issues, see ch 3 by D Ishii, 'International Jurisdiction, Universal Jurisdiction, Extraterritoriality and the Enforcement of Human Rights Across Borders'. This chapter mainly aims to give an overview of current accounts in Japan on business and human rights from a substantive law standpoint.

[6] Except the ICCPR Optional Protocol which allows individuals to submit complaints about human rights violations to the UN Human Rights Committee.

[7] For information on Japan's ratification of international human rights law, see U. Minn. Hum. Rts. Libr., 'Ratification of Human Rights Treaties – Japan', www1.umn.edu/humanrts/research/ratification-japan.html.

[8] Y Iwasawa, 'Effectuation of International Law in the Municipal Legal Order of Japan' in Ko Swan Sik, M Christopher W Pinto, and JJG Syatauw (eds), *Asian Yearbook of International Law* (London, Kluwer, 1994) 143, 148; Article 98(2) of the Constitution of Japan, Promulgated on 3 November 1946.

Since the 1990s, international human rights treaties have been applied by the Japanese courts in certain areas, whereas the legislature has refrained from interpreting and codifying the treaties.[9] On the flipside, the Japanese courts have since borne the task of adapting to, adopting and propagating the international norms enshrined in international human rights treaties. Although this demonstrates that Japan is generally willing and open to adapting the global norms embodied in the international treaties, it is observed that the Japanese courts tend to place domestic law and precedents over international human rights law.[10]

The effect of these international treaties differs. Since the ratification of these international treaties, only some of them were said to be directly applicable in Japan. For instance, based on the interpretation of Article 2 of the ICSECR, the Japanese Supreme Court, in the *Shiomi* case ruled that the ICSECR does not provide for a concrete right to be granted to individuals immediately and is therefore not directly applicable.[11] This reading adopted by the Supreme Court in *Shiomi* is contested for it does not sit well with the wording of Article 2 of ICSECR requiring contracted states to 'undertake to take steps' to progressively realise the rights recognised in the ICSECR.[12]

On the contrary, the ICCPR has generally been accepted as directly applicable,[13] and the Japanese courts have now accepted that the ICCPR 'possesses self-executing and immediately executable character'.[14] Although ICCPR has the force of law and was said to be accorded supremacy over domestic law,[15] it does not necessarily trump domestic law when they contradict each other.[16] Instead, as Professor Saitō observes,[17] the Japanese courts handle claims involving ICCPR in six ways: (1) to rule based on the relevant constitutional law or statute without paying due regard to the claimant's emphasis on certain ICCPR rights; (2) to rule that the ICCPR is not violated without providing reasons as to whether the treaty is engaged in the case; (3) to rule with reference to the language used by the ICCPR without providing reasons as to whether the treaty is engaged in the case; (4) to rule on the substance of the ICCPR; (5) to rule that the ICCPR is not self-executing; and (6) to acknowledge the ICCPR is self-executing and rule based on the ICCPR.

[9] T Webster, 'International Human Rights Law in Japan: The View at Thirty' (2010) 23(2) *Columbia Journal of Asian Law* 241–67 at 242.

[10] YK Tyagi, 'Influence of the ICCPR in Asia' in D Moeckli, H Keller and C Heri (eds), *The Human Rights Covenants at 50: Their Past, Present, and Future* (Oxford, Oxford University Press, 2018; online edn, Oxford Academic, 23 August 2018) Part I(3).

[11] Y Iwasawa, 'Chapter 2 Concept of Direct Applicability: The International Approach' in Y Iwasawa, *Domestic Application of International Law* (Leiden, Brill, 2022) 22.

[12] See for instance, Iwasawa (n 8) 23–24; see also the Dutch reading in Judgment of 20 April 1990, Supreme Court, 22 *Neth YB International Law* 376, 378, (1991) 96 *ILR* 389 (Netherlands).

[13] H Floretta and T Öhlinger, *Die Menschenrechte der Vereinten Nationen* (Manz, 1978) 54–57; J Velu, *L'effets directs des instruments internationaux en matière de droits de l'homme* (1981) 33–53; Y Iwasawa, *International Law, Human Rights, and Japanese Law: The Impact of International Law on Japanese Law* (Oxford, Clarendon Press, 1998) 49–56; D Weissbrodt, 'United States Ratification of the Human Rights Covenants' (1978) 63 *Minn. L. Rev.* 35, 71.

[14] Judgment of 28 October 1994, Osaka High Ct., in 1513 *Hanrei jihō* 71, 86, 38 j.a.i.l. 118 (1995) (Japan); Judgment of 15 March 1996, Tokushima Dist. Ct., in 1597 *Hanrei jihō* 115, 123, 40 j.a.i.l. 118 (1997) (Japan); Judgment of 3 February 1993, Tokyo High Ct., reproduced in part in *Gaikokujin Hanzai Saibanreishu* 55 (1994) (Japan); Judgment of 27 March 1997, Sapporo Dist. Ct., in 1598 *Hanrei jihō* 33, 41 j.a.i.l. 92 (1998), 127 ilr 173 (Japan).; Seven Koreans v. Japan (Osaka H. Ct., 27 October 2005).

[15] M Dean, *Japanese Legal System*, 2nd edn (Abingdon, Routledge-Cavendish, 2002) 166; HRC, 'Fourth Periodic Report of Japan, Addendum' (1 October 1997) UN Doc CCPR/C/115/Add.3, para 11.

[16] See for instance, *Chon v Minister of Justice*, 41 *Gyōsai Reishū* 404 (Tokyo District Court, 13 March 1990).

[17] *Saitō Yoshitaka, Kokusai Jinken Kiyaku B Kiyaku no Wagakuni Saibansho ni okeru Tekiyō* [Applications of the International Covenant on Civil and Political Rights by Japanese Courts] in *Gendai Kokusai Shakai To Jinken No Shosō: Miyazaki Shigeki Sensei Koki Kinen* [Aspects of Contemporary International Society and Human Rights: To Commemorate the 70th Birthday of Professor Miyazaki Shigeki] (Sumiyoshi Yoshihito ed, 1996) 55, 66–75.

Traditionally, international treaties are more readily applied against a state's act as compared to complaints targeted at private entities.[18] However, in recent years, the Japanese courts have welcomed the approach of applying international treaties in private disputes that involve infringement of international treaties. This is particularly significant in cases related to racial discrimination. In at least three cases,[19] the Japanese courts have coined the tort of racial discrimination, based on their assessment of international norms and international treaties, to fill the lacuna of the domestic law, which does not provide for a remedy against racial discrimination in its Criminal or Civil Code. These cases also seem to suggest that the court is slow in ruling that a government's omission in legislating to combat racial discrimination constitute a contravention of international human right principles, albeit at the same time, finding that private conduct that violates or risks violating other's basic rights could potentially infringe ICCPR and CERD.[20]

This gradual extension of international standards to private conduct parallels a broader global shift toward recognising that non-state actors – especially corporations – have responsibilities under international human rights frameworks. In Japan, this shift has been reinforced through the adoption and promotion of soft law instruments, which, while not legally binding, have considerable normative influence.

The UNGPs provide the most influential framework in this regard. They articulate three interrelated pillars: (1) the State's duty to protect against human rights abuses by third parties, including businesses; (2) the corporate responsibility to respect human rights; and (3) the need for access to an effective remedy for victims. Japan has formally endorsed the UNGPs and incorporated their principles into domestic policy initiatives, such as the formulation of its National Action Plan on Business and Human Rights (2020–2025). This plan outlines expectations for Japanese companies, particularly those operating abroad, to conduct human rights due diligence and to prevent, mitigate, and remediate adverse impacts.

Alongside the UNGPs, the OECD Guidelines for Multinational Enterprises have played a key role in shaping Japan's corporate conduct standards. Although also non-binding, the Guidelines have been integrated into Japan's economic diplomacy and investment policy, with the Japanese National Contact Point (NCP) serving as a mediation and advisory mechanism for disputes and compliance concerns. The Guidelines address a broad range of issues, including human rights, labour relations, environmental protection, and anti-corruption measures, and are particularly relevant given Japan's status as a major exporter of capital and technology.

Japan's embrace of these frameworks reflects a broader governance preference for persuasive guidance over prescriptive regulation. This 'soft law' orientation aligns with Japan's administrative style, which often relies on informal guidance to shape behaviour without imposing binding legal obligations. The flexibility of this approach enables gradual alignment with international standards while avoiding politically contentious legislative reforms. However, it also raises concerns about effectiveness, particularly where compliance depends on voluntary corporate action and where enforcement mechanisms are weak or absent.

[18] T Webster, 'International Human Rights Law in Japan: The View at Thirty' (2010) 23(2) *Columbia Journal of Asian Law* 241–67 at 242; *Pe v Kitaura* 1468 *HANREI JIHŌ* 122, 130 (Osaka D. Ct., 18 June 1993), partially translated in 37 *JAPANESE ANN. INT'L L.* 152 (1994) at 153.

[19] See for instance, T Webster, 'Arudou v. Earth Cure: Judgment of November 11, 2002, Sapporo District Court' (2007) 9 *Asian-Pacific Law & Policy Journal* 297–321; T Webster, 'Bortz. v. Suzuki (translation and commentary)' (2007) 16 *Pacific Rim Law and Policy Journal* 631–69; T Webster, 'McGowan v Narita, case note and commentary' (2007) 9(2) *Australian Journal of Asian Law* 346–64.

[20] See for instance, *Arudou v Earth Cure*, 1150 *HANREI TAIMUZU* 185 (Sapporo D. Ct., 11 November 2002) at 193; A Bortz, 1045 *Hanrei Taimuzu* 231.

In sum, while Japanese courts have cautiously expanded the domestic reach of international human rights treaties, especially in the private law context, the more substantial transformation in corporate human rights responsibilities has come through Japan's engagement with soft law instruments such as the UNGPs and OECD Guidelines. Together, these frameworks signal Japan's willingness to adapt to global norms, but their practical impact will ultimately depend on the robustness of implementation and the development of stronger mechanisms to hold both state and corporate actors accountable.

III. Domestic Implementation and Recent Developments

Japan, in recent years, has also called for legislative and policy measures, showing commitment towards the protection of human rights, especially focusing on binding businesses via legislative methods and policies.

This part of the chapter will aim to describe the latest progress of amendments and initiatives to eliminate discrimination by providing reasonable accommodation, conducting human rights due diligence and a national roadmap for aligning with international standards.

A. The Act for Eliminating Discrimination against Persons with Disabilities

The Act Partially Amending the Act for Eliminating Discrimination against Persons with Disabilities was enforced in April 2024, stipulating the obligation of companies to provide reasonable accommodation ('Amendment'). The original act, the Act for Eliminating Discrimination against Persons with Disabilities ('Act') was established in June 2013[21] and aimed 'to promote the elimination of discrimination on the basis of disability'.[22] This section will aim to describe both the key provisions of the original act and the progress of the new amendment.

i. Timeline and Key Provisions

The original act had aimed to cover a wide range of responsibilities and measures, mostly focusing on discrimination within companies and administrative organs. One key provision would be Chapter 2 Article 6, stipulating the formation of a basic policy by the government on the elimination of discrimination on the basis of disability.[23] In fact, this basic policy eventually led to the enforcement of the Act in June 2016.

Before the Amendment, companies were only required to 'endeavour' to provide accommodation for persons with disabilities.[24] During the review stipulated by Article 7 of the Supplementary Provisions of the Act, the national government has decided to obligate companies to ensure reasonable accommodation.[25] The key difference is that if the burden associated with a request for accommodation by a disabled person is not disproportionate, 'administrative organs,

[21] Cabinet Office Japan, 'FY2023 Annual Report on Government Measures for Persons with Disabilities' (Cabinet Office Japan, 2024) 2.
[22] Article 1 of the Act for Eliminating Discrimination Against Persons with Disabilities (Amended 2024).
[23] ibid Article 2.
[24] Article 7 of the Act for Eliminating Discrimination Against Persons with Disabilities (Before Amendment).
[25] Article 7 of the Act for Eliminating Discrimination Against Persons with Disabilities (Amended 2024).

etc. and companies, in conducting their administrative affairs or business, must provide reasonable accommodation.'[26]

From the government reports, the idea was based on the 'social model' of disability, that persons with disabilities do not just suffer from their physical or mental disabilities but by 'barriers they face in the society.'[27] Thus, the provision of reasonable accommodation could help to eliminate their disabilities, for example, by providing an 'elevator' instead of 'stairs', disability could be eliminated.[28]

ii. Progress of the Act

The government focused on four aspects when examining the progress of the Act; namely (i) revision of manuals for government officials and employees of local public entities; (ii) revision of handling guidelines at related ministries and agencies; (iii) a consultation system, (iv) other initiatives.[29]

The Act's Article 9 and 10 have created great progress for the Amendment, as they require directions in the form of manuals to be provided.[30] Progress in providing manuals can be seen as positive. According to the Annual Report,'[a]s of April 1, 2023, all of the prefectures and designated cities had formulated the Handling Directions for Employees of Local Public Entities, while 99% of core cities, 90% of general cities and 66% of towns and villages had also formulated the handling directions, and the percentage of general cities and towns and villages is trending upwards.'[31] This demonstrates an impressive effect in educating the public about the Act.

As required by Article 11, paragraph (1) of the Act,[32] necessary guidelines should be provided by the competent minister. Each minister will decide on guidelines that contain examples of 'disparate and unfair discriminatory treatment and provision of reasonable accommodation', which will then be sorted and introduced in The White Paper on Persons with Disabilities 2024.[33] However, as accurately pointed out in the Annual Report, the severity and symptoms of disabilities are diverse, leading to a requirement of flexible rather than strict and uniform responses that blindly follow the provided examples. The progress and effects of this guideline are still uncertain.

The Cabinet Office has also decided to conduct consultation initiatives, with the pilot consultation point project 'Intermediary Desk', implemented in October 2023 being the prominent measure. It performs the role of legal explanation and connecting inquirers to appropriate consultation points.[34] The Intermediary Desk has provided assistance for persons with disabilities who had unfair treatment or unanswered requests, and has also provided instructions to companies on what to do after the enactment of the Act. From 16 October 2023 to 31 March 2024, a total number of 1,163 cases were dealt with, with most consultations coming from persons with disabilities or from companies, and the number of requests has been showing an increasing trend.[35]

As for other initiatives, the Cabinet Office has also attempted to raise awareness by holding explanatory meetings and seminars for companies, advertisements both online and offline. More

[26] Cabinet Office Japan, 'FY2023 Annual Report' (n 21) 2.
[27] ibid 3.
[28] ibid.
[29] ibid 4–8.
[30] Articles 9 and 10 of the Act for Eliminating Discrimination Against Persons with Disabilities (Amended 2024).
[31] Cabinet Office Japan, 'FY2023 Annual Report' (n 21) 4.
[32] Article 11(1) of the Act for Eliminating Discrimination Against Persons with Disabilities (Amended 2024).
[33] Cabinet Office Japan, 'FY2023 Annual Report' (n 21) 5.
[34] ibid 7.
[35] ibid.

importantly, Regional Support Councils for Eliminating Discrimination against Persons with Disabilities were established, and 1 April 2023 all of the prefectures and designated cities, as well as 88 per cent of the core cities. Establishment by other general as well as towns and villages have also been seeing an upward trend.[36]

B. National Action Plan on Businesses and Human Rights

Under the trend of recognising the importance and impact of businesses on human rights, and the increasing attention given to respecting human rights in business activities, the 'Protect, Respect and Remedy' Framework ('UN Framework') was presented at the 8th session of the Human Rights Council (HRC).[37] The UN Framework categorises the relations between enterprises and human rights into three categories: (1) the State duty to protect against human rights abuses by third parties, including business; (2) the corporate responsibility to respect human rights; and (3) access to remedy. These three pillars form the backbone and framework of this National Action Plan ('NAP'), which covers a period of five years between FY2020 and FY2025.[38]

The Japanese government has implemented various legislative measures and policies contributing to the protection of human rights,[39] and the Japanese government aims to further promote shared recognition and understanding among the relevant ministries and agencies, to enhance cooperation among the relevant ministries and agencies, and to ensure interministerial policy coherence through the publication of the NAP.[40]

The NAP further aims to: (1) protect and promote human rights for society as a whole, including international society; (2) ensure policy coherence and clarify relevant laws, regulations, policies, and future measures in relation to business and human rights to promote inter-ministerial cooperation; (3) ensure and enhance international competitiveness and sustainability of Japanese business enterprises; (4) contribute to achieving SDGs.[41]

The Japanese government, in formulating the NAP, had carried out a baseline study to assess the current Japanese legislation and policies, followed by ten consultation meetings with leading organisations.[42] It is notable that the Japanese government has made specific efforts to ensure the participation of SMEs in the formulation process, as SMEs account for 70 per cent of all employment in Japanese society.[43] An Inter-Ministerial Committee was then established along with an Advisory Committee and a Working Group.[44] Seminars and public comments were invited in the process of formulating the NAP, and overseas experts were also able to exchange views on the NAP.[45]

The NAP sets out the existing framework and measures taken to reach different sustainability goals between businesses and human rights. It also sets out future measures planned by the Japanese government to further protect human rights, promote corporate responsibility to

[36] ibid 8.
[37] Ministry of Foreign Affairs of Japan, 'National Action Plan on Businesses and Human Rights' (Ministry of Foreign Affairs of Japan, 2020) 2.
[38] ibid 31.
[39] ibid 4.
[40] ibid.
[41] ibid 6–7.
[42] ibid 7.
[43] ibid.
[44] ibid.
[45] ibid.

respect human rights and improve access to remedies.[46] The NAP focuses largely on enforcement of existing laws, refining and amending existing legislation, and promoting human rights values and human rights due diligence based on the UNGP.

C. Guidelines

After the launch of the NAP, in November 2021, as part of a follow up on the National Action Plan, results from questionnaires on human rights in supply chains were published.[47] This led to the METI to form the Study Group on Guidelines for Respecting Human Rights in Supply Chains, and eventually formulating and publishing the guidelines.[48] The guidelines call for (i) a human rights policy; (ii) human rights due diligence; (iii) remedies. However, it is important to emphasise that the guidelines are not legally binding and merely encourage that business enterprises in Japan 'should strive in efforts to respect human rights'.[49]

The guidelines firstly call for an establishment of a human rights policy in enterprises, to 'express their commitment to meet their responsibility to respect human rights'[50] and that it should fulfil five requirements, '(i) It is approved at the most senior level of the business enterprise; (ii) it is informed by relevant internal and/or external expertise; (iii) It stipulates the business enterprise's human rights expectations of personnel, business partners and other parties directly linked to its operations, products, or services; (iv) it is publicly available and communicated internally and externally to all personnel, business partners and other relevant parties; (v) it is reflected in the operational policies and procedures necessary to embed it throughout the business enterprise.'[51]

Next, the enterprises should carry out human rights due diligence ('HRDD'), which are acts undertaken by business enterprises to identify, prevent, and mitigate adverse impacts on human rights.[52] The guidelines provide instructions to (i) identification and assessment; (ii) prevention or mitigation; (iii) tracking of effectiveness; (iv) communication and information disclosure. These instructions are detailed, with examples and factors to be assessed, for example, during identification and assessment, the enterprises could consider a 'criteria of severity',[53] in order for proper prioritisation of responses.

Lastly, the guidelines divide remedies into two kinds: (i) non-state entities' responses and (ii) state entity responses. Companies should provide a grievance mechanism to meet several requirements and the government has also established grievance mechanisms. Namely, trials in courts for judicial processes and other non-judicial government organisation remedies such as dispute resolution systems or the Japanese National Contact Point.[54]

In April 2023, the METI released a collection of HRDD case studies (Reference Material on Practical Approaches for Business Enterprises to Respect Human Rights in Responsible Supply

[46] ibid 9.
[47] The Inter-Ministerial Committee on Policy Promotion for the Implementation of Japan's National Action Plan on Business and Human Rights, 'Guidelines on Respecting Human Rights in Responsible Supply Chains' (Ministry of Economy, Trade and Industry of Japan, September 2022) 3.
[48] ibid.
[49] ibid 7.
[50] ibid 8.
[51] ibid 15.
[52] ibid 8.
[53] ibid 23.
[54] ibid 35.

Chains) for companies. METI will 'strive to advance activities for raising companies' awareness of the Reference Material.'[55] The effectiveness of the guidelines remains unknown.

To further support the promotion and implementation of the HRDD goals, in 2024, the Japan External Trade Organisation and the International Labour Organisation ('ILO') published a guide titled 'Responsible Business Conduct and Human Rights Due Diligence: Good Practices of Japanese Companies'[56] (the 'Good Practices Guide') to support HRDD through providing corporation with advice and guidance and promote cooperation between the public and private sector in addressing the structural challenges in conducting HRDD. The Good Practices Guide provided detailed mechanisms and policies, ranging from the formulation of policies to post-implementation evaluation, which could be adopted by corporations to comply with HRDD missions advocated by the UNGPs, ILO Tripartite Declaration of Principles concerning Multinational Enterprises and Social Policy ('MNE Declaration') and the OECD Guidelines.[57]

D. Development and Progress – Comparison between EU and Japan

HRDD legislation mandating companies to prevent and mitigate rights violations in their global operation is becoming more common in Europe. The European Union has implemented a Corporate Sustainability Due Diligence Directive (the 'CSDDD) in July 2024.[58] The Directive was introduced to address urgent environmental and social challenges by embedding sustainability and human rights considerations into corporate governance and operations, particularly for large companies operating in the EU. It obliges companies to implement rigorous monitoring, reporting, and remediation mechanisms, which can increase operational costs and complexity but also drives innovation, efficiency, and competitiveness.

Further, the Directive has significant extraterritorial effect, applying not only to large EU companies but also to non-EU companies with substantial business activities in the EU market. It requires covered companies to conduct due diligence across their entire global operations and value chains – both upstream and downstream – to identify, prevent, and mitigate adverse human rights and environmental impacts regardless of where these occur. This broad scope means that companies worldwide must comply with the directive's obligations if they, although not physically present in EU, meet a turnover threshold. Therefore, the Directive effectively extends EU sustainability standards beyond its borders, leveraging the EU market to promote responsible corporate behaviour globally.

The implementation of the Directive shows that a policy-driven approach is adopted in EU countries, whereas the Japanese effort is relatively industry-driven. This can be seen in the adoption of only soft law in Japan primarily because companies are said to be voluntarily making progress. As reflected in the Nippon Keidanren's survey in 2024, 76 per cent of the surveyed Japanese corporations reported that initiatives related to the UNGPs are currently in force,

[55] Business and Human Rights Policy Office, Minister's Secretariat of Japan, 'Reference Material on Practical Approaches for Business Enterprises to Respect Human Rights in Responsible Supply Chains Released' (Ministry of Economy, Trade and Industry of Japan, 4 April 2023, www.meti.go.jp/english/press/2023/0404_004.html).

[56] Japan External Trade Organisation and the International Labour Organisation 'Responsible Business Conduct and Human Rights Due Diligence: Good Practices of Japanese Companies' (International Labour Organization and Japan External Trade Organization 2024, www.jetro.go.jp/ext_images/world/scm_hrm/JETRO_RBC_HRDD2024en.pdf) 3.

[57] ibid 8.

[58] Directive of the European Parliament and of the Council of 13 June 2024 on corporate sustainability due diligence and amending Directive (EU) 2019/1937 and Regulation (EU) 2023/2859, [2024] OJ L, 2024/1760. For details, see ch 6 by T Nakamura, 'The EU Corporate Sustainability Due Diligence Directive: Challenges and Potentials in the ASEAN Context'.

recording an improvement as compared to the last survey.[59] Similarly, in 2022, the Business and Human Rights Resources Centre ('BHRRC') reported that 79 per cent Japanese companies publicly commit to respecting human rights, and 40 per cent pledge to uphold the labour rights specified by the International Labour Organisation. However, the same report suggests that there is a significant gap between these commitments and concrete actions such as HRDD and stakeholder engagement. Nearly 64 per cent of the companies scored zero on all three HRDD indicators, and 85 per cent scored zero on stakeholder engagement, a key element for effective HRDD. Only nine companies, including Asahi Group, Fast Retailing, and NEC, which are large enterprises, achieved full points on HRDD indicators, showing that strong HRDD is possible and could inform future legislation in Japan.[60] Whereas, small and medium sized enterprises have often been less involved.[61] Japanese companies' average human rights scores are comparable to other G7 countries overall, but lag behind those in France and the UK. BHRRC asserts that the gap presents Japan with an opportunity to lead by developing policy measures that raise corporate human rights performance.[62] Despite the statistics being gathered before the publication of the guidelines, it reveals the critical issue that HRDD and corporate responsibilities to promote human rights ultimately require voluntary corporate adoption – the lack of engagement might potentially turn the Action Plan and corporations' vows to lip service.

With different forms of guidance being provided, especially with the Good Practice Guides, the Japanese government is obviously endeavouring to assist the corporations by providing methodological recommendations on how they could protect and respect human rights during their courses of business. These guidelines have been welcomed by both the BHRRC and the United Nations Development Programme.[63] Nonetheless, the effectiveness could only be evaluated in due course and the legislature's effort might ultimately be required to provide Japanese corporations a better foundation for human rights implementation.[64]

IV. Gaps and Challenges in Human Right Protection

Despite notable progress, the Japanese approach continues to face structural limitations: the absence of binding legal obligations might connote less deterrence for non-compliance.

Japanese courts can apply international human rights law through two mechanisms. The first one is a direct application, meaning that courts directly invoke treaty provisions in their judgments. The other is indirect application, where courts interpret the Constitution and domestic laws in accordance with international human rights standards. While direct applications are available on paper, Japanese courts have traditionally been reluctant to invoke international law directly.[65] Instead, they prefer to interpret constitutional provisions in accordance with

[59] Keidanren Action and Policy, '持続可能な社会の実現に向けた企業の取り組み状況' [Corporate Initiatives to Realize a Sustainable Society], www.keidanren.or.jp/journal/times/2024/0201_04.html.

[60] Business and Human Rights Resources Centre, *Evidence from Japanese Companies Assessment on Human Rights Due Diligence* (2022) 2.

[61] J Polakiewicz, 'Corporate Responsibility to Respect Human Rights: Challenges and Opportunities for Europe and Japan' (2012) CALE Discussion Paper No.9 (October 2012) 54.

[62] ibid 3–4.

[63] ibid 4; and see United Nations Development Programme, 'Due diligence of companies in the field of human rights: how the experience of state regulations in the EU and Japan can be useful for Kyrgyzstan' (UNDP Kyrgyzstan, 16 January 2024, www.undp.org/kyrgyzstan/stories/due-diligence-companies-field-human-rights-how-experience-state-regulations-eu-and-japan-can-be-useful-kyrgyzstan).

[64] ibid 4.

[65] See Section II above.

international human rights obligations, using treaties as only supplementary material to reinforce domestic constitutional protections.[66] Justice of the Supreme Court from 1989 to 1999, Justice Sonobe, recognised that applying international law directly in Japanese courts is the 'last resort' – only when there is no applicable domestic law.[67] However, the Ministry of Foreign Affairs has emphasised that the Constitution constitutes the supreme law of Japan, taking precedence over the International Covenant on Civil and Political Rights in its domestic application. Moreover, the Constitution can be interpreted as encompassing a scope of human rights equivalent to that of the Covenant. Consequently, no conflict is likely to arise between the two. In light of the Japanese courts' broad interpretative authority regarding the Constitution, it is therefore doubtful that a situation would ever emerge in which domestic law would be inapplicable and international law would instead govern.

The difficulty in implementing international human rights law in Japan is exemplified by the case concerning the right of government officials to strike. This case demonstrates that Japanese courts have often interpreted the law in ways that align more closely with political or policy considerations, rather than focusing on the true meaning or legislative intent behind the law.

Specifically, Article 8(1)(d) of the ICSECR provides for 'the right to strike, provided that it is exercised in conformity with the laws of the particular country.' Meanwhile, Article 8(2) explicitly allows for 'lawful restrictions on the exercise of these rights by members of the armed forces or of the police or of the administration of the State.'

However, in the *Zen-norin Case* (All Agriculture and Forestry Union dispute), decided by the Supreme Court Grand Bench on 25 April 1973, the court emphasised the public service character of government officials. The court held that public officials are 'servants of the whole community,' whose duties are inherently public in nature. Unlike private sector employees, government officials serve the entire populace rather than pursuing profit-driven objectives. Therefore, the court ruled that strikes by public officials did not violate the Constitution.[68] Despite the decision of *Zen-norin* Case is based on the right to strike under the Constitution and does not engage the ICSECR,[69] given the similarity of the rights provided for, the outcome will likely be similar if the Japanese courts are tasked to decide on a case concerning the 'right to strike' under Article 8(2) of the ICSECR.

The Japanese government has also addressed this issue in relation to Article 8 of the ICSECR, noting that Article 8(2) of the ICSECR permits lawful restrictions on these rights for 'civil servants,' recognising that no agreement would be possible if Japanese laws and ordinances regarding civil servants were overridden by the Covenant. Accordingly, Japan reserves the right not to be bound by the provisions of Article 8(1)(d) of the ICSECR in this respect.[70]

This illustrates that Japan's restrictive interpretation of the law poses challenges to the effective implementation of human rights legislation, particularly in cases where maintaining governmental structure and public order is prioritised over the protection of human rights.

[66] Ministry of Foreign Affairs in Japan, 'I. General Comments.' (Ministry of Foreign Affairs in Japan, www.mofa.go.jp/policy/human/civil_rep4/general.html).

[67] I Sonobe, 'Nihon no Saikō Saibansyo ni okeru Kokusai Jinken Hō no Saikin no Tekiyō Jyōkyō' in K Serita, T Muesue, K Yakushiji and S Sakamoto (eds), *Kokusai Jinken Hō to Kenpō* (International Human Rights and Constitution, 2006) 17–24.

[68] Sup. Ct. Japan, Case No. 1968 (A) 2780, 25 April 1973.

[69] As ICSECR only came into force after the *Zen-Norin* Case.

[70] Government of Japan, 'Mid-term Report on the Progress Made in the Implementation of the Recommendations Issued at the Second Cycle of the Universal Periodic Review' (Government of Japan, January 2017, upr-info.org/sites/default/files/documents/2017-03/japan_mid-term_2nd_cycle_2017.pdf).

Despite possessing the power of constitutional review under Article 81 of the 1946 Constitution, the Japanese Supreme Court has only invalidated 13 laws in its history.[71] One key reason is the Court's frequent reliance on the doctrine of non-justiciable 'political questions,' which effectively removes entire categories of governmental action from judicial scrutiny.

A notable example is the Tokyo District Court decision of 1 July 2014,[72] in which plaintiffs challenged the Japanese Cabinet's decision to reinterpret the Constitution so as to permit the exercise of collective self-defence, which was previously prohibited under constitutional interpretation. Subsequent legislation and actions, including the dispatch of Self-Defence Force units, prompted the plaintiffs to allege violations of Article 96(1) of the Constitution. They further claimed infringements of rights such as the 'right to live in peace' and *jinkakuken* (personality rights), seeking compensation for mental distress.

The Tokyo District Court denied all allegations and dismissed the claims, simply stating that the plaintiffs' 'legally protected rights were not infringed'. The judgment illustrates the constraints of Japan's 'private rights model' of judicial power – it focuses on providing *post facto*[73] relief through dispute resolution and limits constitutional examination to situations involving infringement of individual rights.

This conservative and restrictive judicial practice has thwarted individuals' ability to pursue human rights claims through the local courts. In situations where local legislation potentially conflicts with international human rights laws, citizens face substantial challenges in obtaining judicial remedies. As a result, the courts' role in supervising administrative action and safeguarding fundamental rights has been significantly weakened.

In recent years, Japanese courts and policymakers have faced growing pressure to address human rights issues relating to LGBTQ+ persons. However, the absence of a coherent legal framework has resulted in fragmented constitutional interpretations and inconsistent outcomes on socially sensitive issues. While there is no binding international treaty specifically governing LGBTQ+ rights, Japan remains the only G7 nation without comprehensive anti-discrimination legislation or recognition of same-sex marriage.

In June 2023, Japan enacted its first national legislation on LGBTQ+ matters – the Promotion of Public Understanding of Diversity in Sexual Orientation and Gender Identity Bill. Yet, the law is mostly symbolic, merely calling for 'promoting understanding' rather than prohibiting discrimination, and providing no enforceable legal mechanism to secure rights for LGBTQ+ individuals. Furthermore, the government ultimately adopted a significantly watered-down version of the bill. For example, the original draft's categorical statement that 'discrimination is not tolerated' was replaced with 'unfair discrimination is not tolerated,' suggesting that certain forms of discrimination could still be permissible. Such diluted and ambiguous wording leaves room for interpretation that may favour the conservative policy stance of the government.

The fragmented nature of Japan's approach is further reflected in the ongoing nationwide litigation over same-sex marriage, initiated in 2019. Six district courts have issued divergent rulings on whether the legal ban on same-sex marriage is compatible with the Constitution. The Nagoya District Court held that the ban violates Articles 14 and 24, affirming the principle of equality and rejecting gender-based marriage restrictions.[74] The Tokyo[75] and Fukuoka[76] District

[71] H Miwa, 'Assessing the Conservative Nature of the Supreme Court of Japan via Ideal Point Estimation of Justices' (2025) 22 *J Empir Leg Stud* 186–215, doi-10.1111/jels.12411.

[72] Sup. Ct. Japan, Case No. 2016 (wa) 13525.

[73] A legal or administrative remedy that is granted *after* an event, action, or violation has already taken place.

[74] Nagoya District Court, Japan, Case No. 平成31(ワ)597.

[75] Tokyo District Court, Japan, Case No. 平成31(ワ)3465.

[76] Fukuoka District Court, Japan, Case No. 令和1(ワ)2827.

Courts stopped short of declaring the ban unconstitutional but found that the absence of any legal framework for same-sex couples to form families violates the Constitution. In contrast, more conservative rulings have emerged elsewhere. The Osaka District Court concluded that the Constitution protects marriage only between a man and a woman, interpreting Article 24 – which states that marriage is 'based on the mutual consent of both sexes' – as implicitly tied to the purpose of reproduction, which same-sex couples cannot fulfil.[77]

The divergences among the courts are substantial. Some have relied exclusively on Article 14 of the Constitution, emphasising equality before the law, while others have focused primarily on Article 24, which governs marriage and family relations. Even among those courts that have found constitutional violations, there is disagreement over the appropriate remedy – some have called for immediate legislative action, while others have deferred to the political process. Until now, no national initiative has been undertaken to harmonise these judgments through statutory reform or concrete policy measures. As a result, the legal landscape remains fragmented and lacks universal application, leaving the rights of LGBTQ+ individuals in Japan only partially protected. Given the amount of cases, it is expected that the issue will eventually be heard before the appellate court in due course.

Although over 538 municipalities and 33 prefectures[78] have independently established 'partnership oath systems' for same-sex couples, the 'partner' cannot become a legal heir as a spouse, petition for adult guardianship, jointly hold parental authority over a child, or receive tax and social security benefits. However, because different municipalities have established varying rules and scopes of benefits for same-sex partnerships, couples in certain areas may enjoy significantly fewer rights and protections than those in others. This disparity is particularly evident when comparing municipalities with more progressive jurisdictions, such as Tokyo, with more conservative ones like Osaka, where recognition frameworks are narrower in scope and offer fewer practical benefits.

All these challenges present a more deep-rooted issue: the pervasive nihonjinron ideology, which constructs Japan as a culturally unique, homogeneous society characterised by group loyalty, harmony, and hierarchy. This discourse, propagated by political, intellectual, and business elites and embedded in education and official rhetoric, functions as a political ideology that legitimises resistance or delay in fully implementing international human rights standards. It fosters cultural essentialism, portraying Japanese individuals as defined by culture rather than as autonomous rights holders, thereby creating a barrier to rights-based social change. Furthermore, the Japanese legal system, influenced by European civil law and traditional values, incorporates a broad 'public welfare' clause in the Constitution that could be used to justify limitations on individual rights, often favouring social harmony and majority interests over individual freedoms. This judicial conservatism, combined with institutional and bureaucratic control, restricts effective remedies and judicial activism in human rights enforcement.

Social attitudes in Japan, particularly those surrounding traditional gender roles, significantly impede the achievement of substantive equality for women, even though formal legal protections exist. While Japan has ratified major international human rights treaties such as Committee on the Elimination of Discrimination against Women ('CEDAW') and enacted laws like the Equal Employment Opportunity Law ('EEOL') and the Basic Law for a Gender-Equal Society, deep-rooted social expectations continue to shape women's lives and limit the practical impact of these legal reforms. For example, women are still widely expected to prioritise family responsibilities

[77] Osaka District Court, Japan, Case No 平成31(ワ)1258.

[78] Marriage for All Japan, 'パートナーシップ制度導入自治体' [Local governments that have introduced a partnership system] (Marriage for All Japan, 2025, www.marriageforall.jp/database/partnership/).

over professional ambitions, leading to social pressure to leave the workforce after marriage or childbirth. This is reinforced by persistent stereotypes that define women primarily as wives and mothers, and by workplace cultures that often marginalise women who pursue careers, resulting in a gender pay gap and underrepresentation in leadership positions. Even when legal remedies for discrimination exist, women may be reluctant to assert their rights due to fears of social ostracism or being labelled as disruptors of group harmony – a value highly prised in Japanese society. Furthermore, discriminatory clauses remain in the Civil Code, such as different minimum marriage ages for men and women and restrictions on women's remarriage after divorce, reflecting the endurance of patriarchal norms. Political and business elites, as well as some segments of the media, have at times reinforced these attitudes by invoking cultural narratives like nihonjinron, which emphasise group harmony and traditional roles as uniquely Japanese values. As a result, the gap between formal legal equality and substantive, lived equality persists, with social attitudes acting as a powerful brake on the realisation of women's rights and broader gender equality in Japan. This demonstrates that legal change alone is insufficient without corresponding shifts in societal norms and expectations, and that the struggle for substantive equality is as much about transforming culture as it is about reforming laws.

V. Dispute Resolution

A. Domestic Litigation and Access to Remedies

Japanese courts have historically taken a restrained role in human rights disputes, particularly where corporate conduct is involved. However, recent years have seen a modest uptick in rights-based litigation.

The Supreme Court's ruling on the Eugenics Protection Law ('EPL') in 2024 marks a pivotal moment in the country's human rights landscape. This landmark decision invalidated a law that had enabled the forced sterilisation of nearly 25,000 individuals from 1948 to 1996, primarily targeting persons with disabilities. The court's handling of the case reflects a significant shift in both judicial attitude and the legal framework surrounding human rights in Japan.

First, the Supreme Court ruled that the EPL was unconstitutional as it violates personal dignity as enshrined in the Constitution. The Supreme Court of Japan found the Eugenics Protection Law (EPL) unconstitutional for violating Article 13 and Article 14 of the Constitution. Article 13 emphasises the inviolability of personal dignity and the right to pursue happiness and Article 14 guarantees equality under the law and prohibits discrimination. The court determined that the EPL fundamentally undermined the principles reflected by these provisions as forced sterilisations inflicted deep psychological and physical harm on individuals, particularly those with disabilities. By the same reason, it violated human dignity, being a core human right. Further, the EPL disproportionately targeted individuals with disabilities, particularly women, perpetuating systemic discrimination and marginalisation. By institutionalising eugenic practices that aimed to control the reproductive rights of these individuals, the law reinforced societal prejudices against them, violating their right to equal protection and respect under the law.

Second, the Supreme Court ruled that the 20-year statutory limitations for human rights violations based on unconstitutional laws is inapplicable in this case. This allows victims to seek redress despite the lapse of time since the repeal of the law. On one hand, the judgment shows the court's willingness, including to create exceptions to rescue out-of-time applications, to address historical injustices, on the other, it signifies a broader recognition of individual rights and the judiciary's role in correcting legislative failures.

Third, the Supreme Court's ruling could be read as an alignment with global human rights principle. Recommendations from UN human rights bodies, including the UN Human Rights Committee and the Committee on the Elimination of Discrimination against Women, had repeatedly urged Japan to provide remedies for victims of forced sterilisations. Ruling against the EPL, the judgment coincides with and sparks the Japanese government's commitments under various international treaties, including the Convention on the Rights of Persons with Disabilities. For instance, the ruling has prompted the Japanese government to create an Action Plan Against Ableism, highlighting the growing recognition of disability rights within the legal framework. Therefore, this ruling is significant not only for its immediate impact on survivors but also for its broader implications for human rights in Japan. The Supreme Court's ruling signals a transformative moment for human rights in Japan, suggesting a newfound commitment to addressing historical injustices and ensuring access to remedies for victims of discrimination. It reflects a growing awareness of the need for legal mechanisms that empower marginalised communities. Moving forward, this decision may inspire further litigation related to human rights abuses and foster a gradual development of human rights.

While no major cases on corporate human rights due diligence have yet reached final judgment, legal academics and practitioners are increasingly exploring the potential for strategic litigation, particularly in areas like labour exploitation, supply chain abuses, and environmental harm.

B. Extraterritorial Litigation and Private International Law

In the increasingly globalised world, multinational corporations headquartered in one jurisdiction can face lawsuits based on their subsidiaries' conduct in another jurisdiction. A landmark European case in the field of business and human rights is the UK Supreme Court's decision in *Vedanta Resources PLC and Another v Lungowe and Others*.[79] In this case, more than 1,800 Zambian villagers sued Vedanta Resources Plc, a UK-domiciled parent company, and its Zambian subsidiary Konkola Copper Mines (KCM), alleging environmental damage, personal injury, and loss of livelihood caused by mining operations in Zambia.

The UK Supreme Court addressed four key issues. First, it rejected the argument that bringing claims against Vedanta in England amounted to an abuse of EU law, holding that there was a genuine claim to be tried. Second, it confirmed that parent companies may owe a duty of care to third parties if they actively intervene in their subsidiaries' operations or assume responsibility through group-wide policies. Third, while Zambia was thought to be the natural forum as it is the location where the injury is incurred and the evidence is recorded, the UK Supreme Court nevertheless accepted jurisdiction in England. Finally, the Court ruled that access to justice considerations, including the lack of funding and legal capacity in Zambia, justified hearing the case in England. The case of *Vedanta* affirms both the potential liability of parent companies for foreign operations and the role of home state courts in providing remedies when host state forums are inadequate.

Similar litigation has yet to take place in Japan. However, given the scale of Japan's economy and its corporations, the multinational corporations headquartered in Japan are similarly

[79] *Vedanta Resources PLC and Another v Lungowe and Others* [2019] UKSC 20.

exposed to liability risks incurred by their subsidiaries abroad. Therefore, it is foreseeable that possible litigation akin to *Vedanta* could sooner or later arise.

The Japanese Code of Civil Procedure helpfully provides detailed jurisdictional rules. Firstly, the Japanese courts are allowed to assume jurisdiction in a case involving a Japanese parent corporation based on its domicile.[80] Second, jurisdiction could be exercised over the foreign subsidiaries by way of joinder of parties.[81] However, it must be noted that the Japanese courts may refuse to exercise jurisdiction under the special circumstances rule in Article 3-9 if fairness or due administration of justice requires.[82]

After accepting jurisdiction, the Japanese courts will have to decide on the applicable law. As the victim and the Japanese parent corporation will unlikely be in a contractual relationship,[83] the former will, in principle, have to rely on a tortious action. If such an analysis is correct, *lex loci damni*, that is, the law of the place where the result of the wrongful act occurred, will be the law applicable to such claims.[84] However, it has been argued that as the double actionability principle remains in Japan, Japanese law, being the law of the Japanese parent company's place of incorporation, will also be applicable, and will inevitably add an extra hurdle for the victim to surmount.[85]

VI. Conclusion

Japan's engagement with human rights in the business context is best described as cautious yet steadily evolving. Recent reforms, including disability discrimination amendments, the National Action Plan on Business and Human Rights, and government-led guidelines on supply chain due diligence, indicate that Japan has begun to internalise international standards and promote corporate accountability. Judicial practice, while traditionally restrained, has also shown signs of greater willingness to address past injustices, as seen in the landmark ruling against the Eugenics Protection Law. Apart from local developments, Japan has been seen on the international stage, assisting other countries in developing human rights and HRDD initiatives.[86]

Nevertheless, significant challenges remain. Japan's reliance on soft law and voluntary corporate compliance limits the effectiveness of its framework, particularly when compared with binding developments in Europe. Courts remain conservative in applying international treaties directly, and the fragmented legal treatment of socially sensitive issues – such as LGBTQ+ rights and gender equality – reveals structural and cultural barriers to full human rights realisation. Extraterritorial liability for multinational corporations, a pressing issue in other jurisdictions, has yet to be tested in Japan, but it looms as a likely frontier.

[80] Code of Civil Procedure, Articles 3–2(3).

[81] ibid Articles 3–6(2).

[82] ibid Articles 3–9.

[83] Act on General Rules for Application of Laws 2006, Article 7ff.

[84] ibid Article 17.

[85] Y Nishitani, 'Corporate Due Diligence and Conflict of Laws: "Business and Human Rights"' Asia' (2022) 28(1) *Korea Private International Law Journal* 829; D Yokomiz, 'Business to Jinken ni kansurn Shido Gensoku to Teishokuho' ['Guiding Principles on Business and Human Rights' and Conflict of Laws]. Ronkyu Jurist [Quarterly Jurist] 1560, at 39–43; 41–43.

[86] United Nations Development Programme, 'Japan and UNDP Launched Two Joint Projects in Kazakhstan to Promote Corporate Human Rights Due Diligence and Tackle Climate Change' (UNDP Kazakhstan, 9 September 2022, www.undp.org/kazakhstan/news/japan-and-undp-launched-two-joint-projects-kazakhstan-promote-corporate-human-rights-due-diligence-and-tackle-climate-change).

Looking forward, Japan's human rights trajectory will depend on its ability to bridge the gap between formal commitments and practical enforcement. Stronger legislative mandates, more consistent judicial engagement, and the continued mobilisation of civil society will be necessary to transform principles into practice. If these steps are taken, Japan has the potential to move from a patchwork of voluntary initiatives to a more coherent and binding system that both protects individuals and positions Japanese corporations as credible global leaders in responsible business conduct.

8

South Korea

JONG HYEOK LEE AND YOUNGSU SUH

I. Introduction

The Republic of Korea (Korea) has emerged as one of the world's leading trading nations, with its annual trade volume consistently surpassing USD 1 trillion in recent years. This economic prominence is supported by the global operations of numerous multi-national corporations (MNCs) headquartered in Korea, spanning sectors such as technology, manufacturing, and finance. These MNCs are embedded in complex global supply chains, positioning Korea as a key jurisdiction for addressing cross-border legal issues concerning corporate social responsibility (CSR) and environmental, social, and governance (ESG) standards. In this context, the interaction between domestic substantive law, private international law, and international legal frameworks constitutes the basis of Korea's evolving legal landscape. This chapter explores the domestic legislation addressing ESG concerns and, from the perspective of private international law, examines issues of jurisdictional immunity, international jurisdiction, governing law, and the recognition and enforcement of foreign judgments in cross-border lawsuits against MNCs, underscoring their relevance to the global discourse on corporate accountability.

II. Substantive Law

A. Commercial Law

i. The Korean Reality: Governance Beyond Legal Personality

A distinctive feature of Korean corporate groups is that core functions, such as management, human resources, and finance, are coordinated not by individual companies but by a central figure, the group leader (*chong-su*), or by a central coordinating body acting on the group leader's behalf. As a result, major business decisions are made at the group level. However, this coordinating entity, often referred to as the 'group headquarters,' lacks legal personality under Korean law. Despite its considerable influence, it remains difficult to impose legal duties or liabilities on it.

The Korean Commercial Code (KCC) regulates companies on an individual-entity basis rather than as corporate groups, creating challenges in addressing management practices that operate across multiple affiliated entities and complicating the enforcement of ESG standards. This section first examines the legal duties and potential liabilities of directors within group-affiliated companies. It then explores the mechanisms available under the KCC for attributing liability to those who exercise control over affiliates, such as parent companies and controlling shareholders, including the liability of quasi-directors under Article 401-2 and the application of the doctrine of piercing the corporate veil.

ii. Director's Duties and Liabilities

a. Director's Duties in General

According to Article 382(2), directors stand in a relationship of mandate with the company and are required to perform their duties with the duty of care prescribed in Article 681 of the Korean Civil Code. Article 382-3 additionally imposes a duty of loyalty. Although academic debate continues as to whether these provisions reflect the Anglo-American concept of fiduciary duty, the prevailing view is that Korean law does not draw a meaningful distinction between the duty of care and the duty of loyalty. In practice, the Supreme Court of Korea (SCK) rarely differentiates between the two.[1] Directors are also subject to specific statutory duties in conflict-of-interest situations, including prohibitions on engaging in competing business (Article 397), misappropriation of corporate opportunities (Article 397-2), and self-dealing transactions (Article 398).

Although not expressly stated in the KCC, duty to monitor has been recognised as part of the duty of care owed by directors. The SCK has held that non-executive directors are responsible not only for voting on board agenda items but also for supervising the actions of representative and executive directors in the management of the company's affairs. If they fail to discharge this duty despite having sufficient grounds to suspect illegality, they may be held liable for any resulting damage to the company.[2] The SCK has further clarified that the scope of the duty to monitor depends on factors such as the company's size, internal structure, industry characteristics, applicable regulatory framework, and financial condition. Even in large and highly specialised companies where distinct functions are allocated to co-representative and executive directors under an internal division of roles, such an arrangement does not relieve other directors of their duty to monitor overall business affairs. Each board member remains responsible for ensuring that internal control and reporting systems are properly established and operate effectively.[3] The SCK has recently emphasised that outside directors, even if not involved in daily operations, may breach their duty to monitor if they (i) fail to push for the establishment of an internal control system where none exists, or (ii) neglect to act despite having reason to suspect that an existing system is not functioning properly.[4]

In 2025, the opposition Democratic Party proposed an amendment to Article 382-3 to clarify that directors owe a duty of loyalty not only to the company but also to all shareholders. The amendment further required directors to actively protect the interests of all shareholders and to treat them fairly and without discrimination in the performance of their duties. However, the acting president vetoed the bill on 1 April, and it subsequently failed to pass. Following the impeachment of President Yoon Suk-yeol on 4 April, the opposition's leading presidential

[1] The SCK, as exemplified by its ruling of 14 June 2002 (Docket No. 2001Da52407), generally does not distinguish between the duty of care and the duty of loyalty. It often characterises a director's misconduct simply as a violation of the 'duty of care or loyalty' and does not apply different legal standards to the two. However, in exceptional cases, such the SCK's ruling on 28 January 2016, Docket No. 2014Da11888 and the SCK's ruling on 24 August 2016, Docket No. 2016Da222453, the Court explicitly referred to a breach of the 'duty of loyalty.'

[2] The SCK's ruling on 25 June 1985, Docket No. 84DaKa1954; the ruling on 10 December 2004, Docket Nos. 2002Da60467 and 2002Da60474; the ruling on 6 July 2006, Docket No. 2004Da8272; the ruling on 20 September 2007, Docket No. 2007Da25865; and the ruling on 13 December 2007, Docket No. 2007Da60080.

[3] The SCK's ruling on 11 September 2008, Docket No. 2006Da68636.

[4] The SCK's ruling on 12 May 2022, Docket No. 2021Da279347.

candidate pledged to reintroduce the amendment, making the scope of duties imposed on directors a matter of ongoing attention.

b. Director's Duty of Care in Corporate Groups

Each company within a corporate group is a separate legal entity, and its directors are required to act solely in the best interests of that company. The SCK reaffirmed this principle in its decision of 30 March 2023 (Docket No. 2019Da280481), holding both the CEO and the chairperson of the board of the parent company liable for damage resulting from a high-risk derivative transaction undertaken to defend a subsidiary against a hostile takeover. The Court found that they had failed to conduct an adequate risk assessment, thereby breaching their duty of care. It further held that even within a corporate group, directors must base their decisions on benefits to their own company. General group-wide interests are insufficient to justify a director's conduct under the business judgment rule. This decision reflects a judicial trend towards narrowing the scope of that rule and imposing stricter standards of oversight.

In line with this jurisprudence, directors of a controlled company owe duties exclusively to that company, and any conduct that causes harm to the subsidiary for the benefit of the parent company or the group constitutes a breach of duty. However, the KCC does not expressly address whether directors of a controlling company owe duties in relation to the management of its subsidiaries. Although the SCK has yet to decide this question, a lower court has held that, under the principle of separate corporate personality, directors of a parent company are not responsible for supervising the directors of its subsidiary (Seoul Southern District Court, 10 September 2003, Docket No. 2003Gahap1749). Nonetheless, many scholars argue that, in order to safeguard the interests of the controlling company's shareholders, its directors should exercise oversight over the conduct of the subsidiary's directors, and failure to do so may constitute a breach of duty.[5] Even if such an oversight duty is recognised, however, its precise scope remains undefined, and the conditions under which liability may be imposed are still unsettled.[6]

c. Director's Liability and the Business Judgment Rule

Under Article 399, directors are liable to the company for damages resulting from intentional or negligent violations of law, the articles of incorporation, or their duties. Korean courts generally characterise this liability as contractual in nature, arising from the mandate relationship between the directors and the company. Violations of law or the articles of incorporation, such as engaging in bribery or unfair trade practices, are deemed breaches of duty, to which the business judgment rule does not apply.

By contrast, when assessing compliance with more general duties, Korean courts apply the business judgment rule. In its decision of 2003Da69638, the SCK held that directors satisfy the duty of care if they collect and review the necessary information and reach a decision that is substantially reasonable and in the best interests of the company. In its decision of 2001Da52407, the SCK further held that both the duty of care and the duty of loyalty are fulfilled if directors act in good faith, following appropriate procedures and relying on adequate information.

[5] KS Kim, HJ Rho and KH Chun, *Hoesabeop* (*Company Law*), 8th edn (Parkyoungsa, 2024) 445.

[6] Notably, the KCC does not impose any obligation to establish internal control systems at the corporate group level. This stands in contrast to the Act on the Supervision of Financial Conglomerates, which, under Article 9, requires financial conglomerates to implement group-wide internal control systems.

d. Director's Liability to Third Parties

A distinctive feature of the KCC is Article 401, which permits third parties to claim damages directly from directors. Under Article 401(1), where directors breach their duties intentionally or through gross negligence, thereby causing harm to third parties, they are jointly and severally liable. While directors ordinarily owe duties only to the company by virtue of the mandate relationship, Article 401 provides an exceptional statutory basis for third-party claims arising from breaches of such duties. In its decision of 14 February 2008 (Docket No. 2006Da82601), the SCK recognised this provision as a special category of liability intended to safeguard the interests of third parties.

Article 401 serves as a complement to the doctrine of veil-piercing by offering a more direct and accessible route for holding directors liable to third parties. To succeed under Article 401, a plaintiff must establish a breach of duty, intentional or grossly negligent misconduct, and resulting damage. Korean courts have applied this provision in a range of contexts, including: (i) cases where a company enters into a contract or receives payment despite knowing, or having reason to know, that it is unable to perform due to financial distress; (ii) instances of reckless or unlawful management that severely impair the company's financial or operational condition and result in losses to creditors or shareholders; (iii) failures by directors to fulfil their duty to monitor, resulting in harm to third parties; (iv) misleading statements in publicly issued documents, such as securities filings, periodic business reports, or material event disclosures, that cause financial loss to third parties; and (v) tortious conduct by the company where the director knowingly participates in or oversees the wrongful acts. In particular, where directors are aware of and involved in the company's tortious conduct, the likelihood of liability under Article 401 is especially high.

iii. Quasi-Director's Liability

Where a controlling shareholder (such as a parent company), a director of the controlling company, or a group leader instructs directors of a controlled company to act against that company's interests, for example by prioritising the interests of the group or the controlling company, or by engaging in conduct that results in human rights violations, questions arise as to whether minority shareholders or third parties can hold them liable. Article 401-2 provides a statutory basis for imposing liability equivalent to that of directors on those who effectively direct or manage a company's business without formal appointment as directors. Article 401-2(1) recognises three categories of quasi-directors: (i) shadow directors, who direct the actions of formally appointed directors by exercising influence over the company; (ii) *de facto* directors, who, by using the title of director, manage the company's business on the basis of their influence over it; and (iii) apparent directors, who exercise executive authority under a title that suggests official status and authority, despite lacking formal appointment as directors.

Quasi-directors may incur liability equivalent to that under Articles 399 and 401, either to the company or to third parties. Among the three categories collectively referred to as quasi-directors, shadow directors are of particular concern, especially in cases where a parent company, as a controlling shareholder, gives instructions to the directors of a subsidiary, thereby interfering with its business operations. Korean courts have interpreted the concept of shadow directors to include not only natural persons but also corporate entities, such as parent companies.[7] This interpretation opens the possibility of holding a parent company liable as a shadow director.

[7] The SCK's ruling on 25 August 2006, Docket No. 2004Da26119.

Accordingly, where a subsidiary engages in human rights violations or infringes the rights of minority shareholders under instructions from its parent company, affected parties may seek damages directly from the parent company. While a parent company's influence over its subsidiary is often presumed, specific instructions are difficult to prove, particularly when they are informal or implied. In light of these evidentiary challenges, some scholars argue that courts should either presume the existence of such instructions in certain circumstances or adopt a lower evidentiary threshold to ensure effective enforcement.[8]

iv. Piercing the Corporate Veil

The doctrine of piercing the corporate veil is a key aspect of corporate accountability in Korea and has long been recognised in Korean case law. In exceptional circumstances, it permits courts to disregard the legal separation between a company and its shareholders to prevent manifest injustice. This allows courts to hold the shareholder or controlling entity behind the company liable where the company's separate legal personality has been misused. The SCK first recognised this doctrine in 1988, and since then, Korean jurisprudence has developed two principal categories of application: (i) claims against controlling shareholders or parent companies, and (ii) cases involving newly created companies formed to evade existing debts.

In the first category, Korean courts distinguish between (a) the hollowing out of corporate personality and (b) the abuse of corporate personality. A hollow corporate entity exists where the company functions essentially as an extension of the shareholder's personal business, whereas abuse refers to the use of the corporate structure to pursue unjust or unlawful ends. To determine whether corporate personality has been hollowed out, Korean courts consider various factors, including: (i) the commingling of finances and operations between the company and its shareholder; (ii) the failure to observe corporate formalities, such as convening shareholders' or board meetings as required by law or the articles of incorporation; (iii) undercapitalisation disproportionate to the scale of the business; (iv) overlapping directorships across affiliated companies; and (v) the shared use of assets or premises without proper accounting separation, particularly where such arrangements prejudice the interests of creditors.

In cases involving abuse of corporate personality, the SCK has required not only objective indicators but also subjective intent, such as an intention to evade legal obligations. In particular, in parent–subsidiary relationships or in cases involving special purpose companies, the SCK has made clear that a showing of subjective purpose or intent is necessary to invoke the doctrine of abuse.[9] In such cases, the Court has held that veil-piercing requires both (a) effective control by the parent company and (b) improper use of the subsidiary's legal personality, such as employing it to shield the parent from liability. However, it remains unsettled whether the same requirement of subjective intent applies to claims based solely on the hollowing out of corporate personality.

Although Korean courts have thus far applied veil-piercing only in cases involving contractual liability, the prevailing academic view supports its extension to tort claims.[10] Accordingly, if a subsidiary commits wrongful acts, such as human rights violations, under the

[8] Kim et al (n 5) 515.

[9] In its decision of 25 August 2006 (Docket No. 2004Da26119), the SCK held that even where a parent company holds 100% of a subsidiary's shares and exercises strong control over it, such facts alone are insufficient to establish abuse of corporate personality. The Court required both (i) objective indicators, such as commingling of assets, business operations, and external transactions, and (ii) a subjective intent to misuse the corporate personality to evade legal obligations or achieve unlawful ends, such as avoiding debts.

[10] Kim et al (n 5) 67.

effective control of its parent company, affected third parties may seek to pierce the corporate veil and pursue liability directly against the parent company.

B. Special Laws

i. ESG Framework Laws in Individual Domains

As of April 2025, Korea does not have a comprehensive legal framework dedicated to ESG matters, but instead addresses relevant concerns through a range of sector-specific statutes. The Framework Act on Sustainable Development sets out fundamental principles and defines the respective responsibilities of the state, local governments, citizens, and businesses.[11] Complementing this, the Framework Act on Carbon Neutrality and Green Growth to Cope with the Climate Crisis enshrines the national target of achieving carbon neutrality by 2050[12] and outlines policies on emissions reduction, climate adaptation, just transition, and green growth.

In addition to these overarching frameworks, socially responsible business practices are encouraged through legislation targeting specific sectors and actors. The Social Enterprise Promotion Act supports certified social enterprises through measures such as assistance with management, training, and facility costs; preferential treatment in public procurement; tax benefits and social insurance subsidies; and financial support.[13] The Act on the Promotion of Small and Medium Enterprises encourages SMEs to operate with due regard for their social responsibilities toward employees, business partners, consumers, and local communities, and authorises the state and local governments to support such efforts.[14] Moreover, the Government Procurement Act empowers the Administrator of the Public Procurement Service to incorporate social and environmental values, such as environmental protection, human rights, labour standards, fair trade, and consumer protection, into public procurement procedures, thereby promoting corporate accountability in the public sector.[15]

ii. Environmental Disclosure and Greenwashing Regulations

The Financial Investment Services and Capital Markets Act, as complemented by the Financial Services Commission's Regulation on Issuance and Disclosure of Securities, requires listed companies to submit business reports containing information on greenhouse gas emissions, green technology certifications, and workforce composition.[16] Additional environmental disclosure obligations arise under the Act on the Promotion of Environmental Technology and Environmental Industry, which mandates certain large listed companies to disclose their environmental management plans and performance, including emission levels and reduction targets.[17]

In response to the growing problem of greenwashing, the Fair Trade Commission revised its Guidelines for Reviewing Environmental Claims and Advertising in 2023. The revision aims

[11] Articles 3–5 of the Act.
[12] Articles 7 of the Act.
[13] Articles 10–14 of the Act.
[14] Article 62-7 of the Act.
[15] Article 6 of the Act.
[16] Article 159(4) of the Act and Article 4-3(1) of the Regulation.
[17] Articles 16-2, 16-8 and 16-9 of the Act.

to enhance predictability and consistency in enforcement by clarifying the standards applicable to environmental claims and advertisements made by businesses. Key changes include: (i) the separation of the 'clarity of expression' requirement from the previously combined 'truthfulness principle,' establishing it as an independent standard; (ii) the introduction of a new 'completeness principle,' which requires full disclosure of information that may materially influence consumer decisions; and (iii) the elaboration of the 'life cycle principle,' which obligates companies to consider a product's entire life span when making environmental representations. The amended Guidelines also classify misleading environmental claims and advertisements into four categories – false or exaggerated, deceptive, unfair comparative, and defamatory – and provide detailed criteria for evaluating each type.

iii. Environmental Damage Relief Act

In general, under tort law, the burden of proving causation between a wrongful act and the resulting harm lies with the plaintiff. However, in environmental tort claims under the Korean Civil Code, establishing causation is often particularly difficult due to the scientific complexity of pollution mechanisms, the presence of multiple contributing factors, and victims' constrained access to technical or financial resources. Recognising these challenges, the SCK has, since 1984, relaxed the burden of proof in environmental litigation. The Court has cautioned that requiring strict scientific proof of actual causation may deny victims judicial relief for environmental harm. Under this jurisprudence, plaintiffs need only show that: (i) the defendant's facility emitted pollutants; (ii) some of those pollutants reached the affected area; and (iii) harm subsequently occurred. The burden then shifts to the defendant to rebut causation by proving either: (i) that the emitted substances did not include a causative agent; or (ii) that the concentration of such agents remained within a safe range.[18]

Against this backdrop, the Act on Liability for Environmental Pollution Damage and Relief therefrom was enacted on 31 December 2014 and entered into force on 1 January 2016. Aimed at clarifying the liability of business operators, easing the evidentiary burden on victims, and ensuring prompt and fair redress,[19] the Act introduces a statutory presumption of causation in Article 9. The SCK has emphasised that this provision does not merely codify existing case law but significantly strengthens victim protection by further lowering the burden of proof.[20]

Under Article 9(1), where there is a substantial probability that a facility caused environmental damage, causation is presumed. Article 9(2) sets out relevant factors for determining such substantial probability, including the facility's operation, the nature of its equipment, the types and concentrations of causative substances involved, the meteorological conditions, the timing and location of the damage, and the overall pattern of harm. This presumption may be rebutted under Article 9(3) if the operator proves either: (i) that the harm was caused by another independent source, or (ii) that the operator fully complied with applicable environmental regulations and took appropriate preventive measures under Article 4(3). Importantly, consistent with prior SCK jurisprudence, 'another source' must be construed as an entirely unrelated cause; the mere existence of multiple contributing factors does not sever the causal link. This interpretation

[18] The SCK's ruling on 12 June 1984, Docket No. 81Da558; the ruling on 12 January 2012, Docket Nos. 2009Da84608, 84615, 84622, 84639.

[19] Article 1 of the Act.

[20] The SCK's ruling on 28 December 2023, Docket No. 2019Da300866.

aligns with Article 10, which imposes joint and several liability where the precise cause of damage cannot be identified.

The SCK applied Article 9 for the first time in its decision of 28 December 2023 (Docket No. 2019Da300866), which concerned a hydrofluoric acid leak from a chemical facility. The Court found a substantial probability that the acid had dispersed into the air and settled at ground level, thereby causing the harm. It upheld compensation awards of KRW 7 million to each of the 19 plaintiffs. The Court held that once a victim demonstrates the factors listed in Article 9(2), causation is presumed, and there is no need to prove direct contact between the pollutant and the injury. This decision marks a significant step toward enhancing judicial access for victims of environmental harm, confirming that indirect evidence may suffice to establish liability under the Act.

In proceedings concerning the extraterritorial torts of MNCs, it should be noted that the statutory presumption of causation under the Act applies only where Korean law is designated as the governing law of torts. Accordingly, even if foreign victims bring claims before Korean courts, the presumption under Article 9 may be invoked only if Korean law is applicable to the tortious conduct.

iv. Serious Accidents Punishment Act

The Serious Accidents Punishment Act (SAPA), which entered into force on 27 January 2022, was enacted to strengthen the accountability of business owners and senior management personnel for the prevention of serious industrial and public accidents. According to Article 1, the purpose of the Act is to protect the lives and physical safety of workers and the public by penalising violations of safety and health obligations. A distinctive feature of the Act is that it imposes direct obligations on 'responsible management personnel,' including not only CEOs but also group chairpersons, who may be held personally liable for accidents occurring under their effective control.

The Act applies not only to employees under employment contracts with the company but also to workers providing labour through subcontracting or outsourcing arrangements, and in the case of public accidents, to members of the general public. Under Articles 2(2) and 2(3), 'serious accidents' include incidents involving death, long-term injury, or illness resulting from workplace hazards or defects in materials, products, or public-use facilities. Business owners and responsible management personnel are required to establish and implement safety and health management systems, conduct inspections, prepare recurrence prevention plans, comply with government orders, and ensure legal compliance across all business operations, including those outsourced.[21]

Where a serious accident resulting in death occurs due to a breach of these duties, criminal penalties may include imprisonment of at least one year or fines of up to KRW 1 billion for individuals, and up to KRW 5 billion for corporate entities.[22] In addition, Article 15 allows courts to award up to five times the amount of actual damages where the violation is attributable to intentional or grossly negligent misconduct. In determining the amount, courts must consider factors such as the degree of fault, the nature and severity of the harm, the extent of unjust enrichment obtained, and any remedial measures taken following the violation.

[21] Articles 4, 5, and 9 of the Act.
[22] Articles 6, 7, 10, and 11 of the Act.

C. Proposed and Emerging ESG Initiatives

i. Legislative Initiative for ESG Due Diligence

In 2023, a bill entitled the Act on Human Rights and Environmental Protection for Sustainable Corporate Management was proposed to introduce mandatory due diligence obligations concerning human rights and environmental risks throughout corporate operations and supply chains. The bill applied to large enterprises employing at least 500 workers or generating annual revenue of more than KRW 200 billion. Covered companies would be required to establish due diligence systems, publish annual reports, operate grievance mechanisms, and provide effective remedies for harm. Where a plausible link exists between harm and a company's business or supply chain, liability would be presumed unless the company proves legal compliance or absence of causation. Senior management personnel could be held jointly liable for failure to fulfil their oversight duties.

The bill expired with the term of the 21st National Assembly of Korea (2020–2024) but was reintroduced in June 2025 with certain amendments. If eventually enacted and classified as overriding mandatory rules, it could serve as a legal basis for foreign victims to bring claims before Korean courts against Korean companies for human rights violations or environmental harm.

ii. Proposals for a Comprehensive ESG Framework

Two bills were introduced to establish a comprehensive legal framework for ESG standards. One proposed the creation of a national ESG policy system, including a ten-year basic plan, the integration of ESG principles into public procurement and financial regulation, and the imposition of mandatory disclosure obligations on businesses. The other called for five-year ESG promotion plans by government authorities, compulsory ESG disclosures for large companies, and the introduction of third-party ESG assessment mechanisms. Although both proposals were discarded at the end of the legislative session, discussions on comprehensive ESG legislation remain ongoing. While no overarching ESG framework law has yet been reintroduced, provisions on ESG standards have been incorporated into the Korea Housing Finance Corporation Act, which calls for the application of ESG standards to the operation of the Housing Finance Credit Guarantee Fund in order to promote long-term returns and social responsibility.

iii. ESG Disclosure under the KSDS

In April 2024, the Financial Services Commission (FSC), through the Sustainability Standards Board of the Korea Accounting Standards Board, announced the forthcoming release of the Korean Sustainability Disclosure Standards (KSDS). The draft KSDS aligns with the ISSB framework and aims to ensure both international interoperability and domestic applicability. It comprises: (i) general requirements for sustainability-related financial disclosures, based on IFRS S1; (ii) climate-related disclosures addressing governance, strategy, risk management, and performance metrics, based on IFRS S2; and (iii) optional supplementary disclosures reflecting domestic policy priorities.

The KSDS is intended to reduce the reporting burden on Korean companies subject to international ESG regulations, such as the EU's Corporate Sustainability Reporting Directive (CSRD), while taking into account the practical capacities of local firms. Although the FSC initially planned to begin phased implementation in 2025, the timeline has been deferred to 2026 or later due to delays in international standard-setting and calls from industry for more time to prepare.

III. Jurisdictional Immunity

In lawsuits concerning human rights violations brought against MNCs before Korean courts, the issue of jurisdictional immunity derived from the principle of sovereign immunity under public international law may arise. This is particularly relevant where a Korean company is alleged to have acted in concert with a foreign government in the commission of human rights violations abroad. For instance, during the 2017 Rohingya crisis in Myanmar, when the military was responsible for the killing of approximately 10,000 people and the displacement of around 700,000 Rohingya to Bangladesh, UN Special Rapporteur characterised the events as constituting genocide, crimes against humanity, and war crimes. An official UN report also listed several corporations, including Korean companies, as having allegedly donated funds to or engaged in commercial transactions with the Myanmar military.[23]

In such cases, where foreign victims file claims against a Korean company in Korean courts, which recognise the jurisdictional immunity of foreign states only in respect of sovereign (non-commercial) acts, the question may arise whether the company can argue that its conduct should be equated with that of the foreign state and thereby invoke sovereign immunity.

However, Korean courts are unlikely to accept such assertions. In cases brought by Korean victims against Japanese companies that employed them as forced labour with the involvement of the Japanese government during World War II, the SCK, in its decisions of 24 May 2012 (Docket Nos. 2009Da22549 and 2009Da68620), ruled in favour of the victims and ordered the companies to pay damages. Although the issue of jurisdictional immunity was not expressly addressed in those rulings, the SCK has taken the position that such immunity does not extend to private corporate entities. Accordingly, a company that has participated in unlawful acts committed by a foreign state, such as human rights violations, would not be entitled to invoke the sovereign immunity of that state before Korean courts.

IV. International Jurisdiction

Cross-border claims brought against MNCs before Korean courts imply that claims for damages may be brought not only against a foreign subsidiary but also against its Korean parent company. It is evident that Korean courts have general jurisdiction over claims against the Korean parent company. The more complex issue concerns jurisdiction over the foreign subsidiary. In this context, although various questions may arise under the Korean Private International Law Act (KPILA), the following issues are of particular importance: whether Korean courts may exercise jurisdiction over the foreign subsidiary, particularly on the basis of jurisdiction over connected claims or emergency jurisdiction; whether the exercise of jurisdiction may be declined under Article 12 of the KPILA, despite jurisdiction being established, on the ground that Korean courts do not constitute the appropriate forum; and whether, if Korean law introduces statutory duties of

[23] UN Human Rights Council, 'The Economic Interests of the Myanmar Military' (A/HRC/42/CRP.3) (5 August 2019) paras 1 and 143.

care applicable to parent companies in relation to their subsidiaries, such provisions could serve as a basis for establishing jurisdiction over the subsidiary – either by recognising jurisdiction over connected claims or by allowing Korean courts to exercise jurisdiction without resorting to the doctrine of *forum non conveniens*.

A. General Jurisdiction

Article 3(3) of the KPILA provides relatively broad grounds for establishing general jurisdiction over corporate bodies. Under this provision, Korean courts may exercise jurisdiction if a corporate body's (i) actual principal place of business, (ii) statutory domicile, (iii) centre of administration, or (iv) place of incorporation is located in Korea. This reflects the principle of *actor sequitur forum rei*, under which a plaintiff must bring the claim in the defendant's forum. Where general jurisdiction is established pursuant to Article 3(3), Korean courts may hear any case involving the defendant, regardless of subject matter, whether contentious or non-contentious, on the basis of the strong connection between the defendant and the forum.

In transnational tort claims against MNCs brought before Korean courts, a Korean parent company would generally satisfy at least one of the jurisdictional grounds under Article 3(3), thereby establishing general jurisdiction. However, Korean courts may also have general jurisdiction over foreign subsidiaries. While a foreign subsidiary's place of incorporation and statutory domicile are ordinarily located abroad, its actual principal place of business or centre of administration may, in certain circumstances, be deemed to be in Korea. For example, if the foreign subsidiary operates a Korean branch that generates substantial revenue, Korean courts may find that its principal place of business is located in Korea. In addition, if the subsidiary's board meetings are regularly held in Korea, particularly at the offices of the Korean parent company, this may support the conclusion that its centre of administration is situated in Korea. In such cases, especially where the subsidiary is involved in providing products or services linked to human rights violations, Korean courts may have general jurisdiction over the subsidiary without relying on the provisions on special jurisdiction under the KPILA.

B. Jurisdiction over Connected Claims

If legal doctrines or legislation enabling cross-border lawsuits against MNCs become more concrete, it may become a practical reality that MNCs headquartered in Korea are brought before Korean courts as co-defendants in such cases. A defining feature of such lawsuits in Korea is that claims for damages arising from extraterritorial torts committed by foreign subsidiaries are brought not before the courts of the subsidiary's domicile, but rather before the courts of the Korean parent company's domicile. In such instances, the Korean parent company may be included as a co-defendant alongside the foreign subsidiary. However, where claims against both the Korean parent company and the foreign subsidiary are brought jointly before a Korean court, the parent company is likely to argue, pursuant to Article 12 of the KPILA, that the Korean court is an inappropriate forum and that the foreign subsidiary's home jurisdiction constitutes a more appropriate forum.

In this context, Article 6(2) of the KPILA, which governs the joinder of parties, becomes particularly relevant. According to this provision, a Korean court may exercise jurisdiction over multiple defendants in a single action where: (i) the court has general jurisdiction under Article 3 over one of the co-defendants; (ii) the claims against the co-defendants are closely connected;

and (iii) joint adjudication is necessary to avoid the risk of contradictory judgments. With respect to condition (i), at least one of the parent company or the subsidiary must be subject to general jurisdiction in Korea, effectively serving as an anchor defendant and thereby establishing a sufficient connection to the forum. For conditions (ii) and (iii), interpretive guidance may be drawn from Article 25(2) of the Korean Civil Procedure Act (KCPA), which considers the commonality of rights or obligations at issue and the identity of the factual or legal causes underlying the claims.[24]

The issue is whether the criteria set out in the UK Supreme Court's 2019 *Vedanta* decision[25] may inform the interpretation of conditions (ii) and (iii) above, with particular regard to the doctrine of *forum non conveniens*, and, if so, to what extent. In that case, claims were brought jointly against a foreign subsidiary and a UK parent company, based on alleged tortious conduct committed by the subsidiary, with the UK parent company serving as the anchor defendant. The Court held that the UK courts had jurisdiction over the subsidiary, primarily because there was a real issue to be tried in the claim against the parent company, and England was not a clearly inappropriate forum for the consolidated proceedings. The relevant considerations identified by the Court and related case law include the following: (a) whether there is a real issue to be tried between the claimant and the anchor defendant; (b) whether the claim against the anchor defendant is not merely a device to bring the foreign defendant within the jurisdiction; (c) whether the foreign defendant is a necessary and proper party to the claim against the anchor defendant; (d) whether there is a real prospect of success in the claim against the foreign defendant; and (e) whether the UK is the proper forum for the trial of the claims, or, even if another jurisdiction appears more appropriate, whether there is a real risk that substantial justice cannot be obtained in that alternative forum.

In relation to point (d) above, while it is not necessary to reach a concrete conclusion by applying the governing law at the stage of determining international jurisdiction, a preliminary examination of the substantive law invoked as the basis for the plaintiff's claims may be unavoidable. In legal actions against MNCs, plaintiffs are likely to base their damages claims against a parent company on specific statutory duties owed by that company. Accordingly, the statutory basis must be identified at the jurisdictional stage, even though the likelihood of success need not be definitively established. Therefore, the key issue in establishing jurisdiction over the foreign subsidiary is whether the applicable substantive law imposes a duty of care or due diligence on the parent company with respect to the subsidiary's extraterritorial torts. If special legislation imposing such duties on parent companies is introduced into Korean law, this aspect of public interests may be relevant in the analysis under Article 12, particularly in conjunction with Article 6(2).

C. Special Jurisdiction for Torts – Claims against Subsidiaries

Article 44 of the KPILA provides that Korean courts have international jurisdiction over tort claims where the tortious act occurred in Korea, was directed toward Korea, or caused damage in Korea. However, this provision does not apply if the tortfeasor could not have foreseen the resulting harm in Korea. Article 44 thus explicitly recognises both the place of the tortious act and the place of the resulting harm as grounds for establishing international jurisdiction.

[24] Article 25(2) of the KCPA provides that multiple persons may join as co-litigants in a single action if the rights or obligations at issue are common to them, or arise from the same factual or legal grounds.

[25] *Vedanta Resources Plc v Lungowe* [2019] UKSC 20, [2019] 2 WLR 1051.

In cross-border claims brought against MNCs, however, the scope of Article 44 is limited for the following reasons. First, Korean courts already have general jurisdiction over claims brought against a Korean parent company, making special jurisdiction under Article 44 unnecessary.[26]

Second, in cases against both a Korean parent company and a foreign subsidiary, the place of the resulting harm is generally the foreign country in which both the subsidiary and the victims are located. Even in exceptional cases where harm to physical integrity manifests in Korea and Korea may be deemed the place of the resulting harm, the requirement of foreseeability set out in the proviso to Article 44 would likely not be satisfied. Furthermore, with respect to the foreign subsidiary, the place of the tortious act and the place of the resulting harm both coincide in the same foreign country, namely where the subsidiary operates and the victims reside. Thus, in each of the scenarios outlined above, Korean courts cannot assert jurisdiction over the foreign subsidiary pursuant to Article 44.

Third, in cases brought against a Korean parent company, it may be argued that the place of the tortious act is not the foreign country where the subsidiary operates but Korea, where the parent company is located. If Korean law recognises a duty of due diligence on the part of the parent company with respect to human rights violations committed by its domestic or foreign subsidiaries, a failure to discharge that duty could be characterised as an omission. In such circumstances, Korea could be construed as the place of the tortious act, as the location where the duty was to be performed. However, this interpretation presupposes the existence of a specific legal norm imposing a duty of due diligence on the parent company in the particular case. Furthermore, even if Article 44 were found to apply, the special jurisdiction it provides would overlap with the general jurisdiction already established over the Korean parent company, thereby rendering it redundant.

D. Special Jurisdiction for Shareholder Claims against Parent Companies

Article 25 of the KPILA sets out special jurisdiction rules for disputes concerning the internal affairs of corporate bodies. Under this provision, if Korean courts have general jurisdiction over a corporate body, the following disputes may also be brought before Korean courts: (i) actions brought by the corporate body against a current or former member arising from the capacity as a member; (ii) actions brought by a current member against another current or former member arising from the capacity as a member; and (iii) actions brought by a former member against a current member arising from the capacity as a member. In contrast to the KCPA,[27] which provides a broader range of special jurisdiction provisions for disputes involving corporate bodies, the KPILA adopts a more limited approach, focusing exclusively on internal, membership-related disputes. This more restrictive approach serves to prevent

[26] However, if special jurisdiction under Article 44 is recognised for tort claims, it would strengthen the plaintiff's position in asserting jurisdiction before Korean courts. Even if the Korean parent company invokes Article 12 to argue that the courts should decline jurisdiction on the ground that the foreign subsidiary's home country constitutes a more appropriate forum, Korean courts may be less inclined to accept such an argument where special jurisdiction for torts has also been established.

[27] The KCPA sets out special jurisdiction rules for disputes involving corporate bodies and their members. These include: (i) actions brought by a corporate body against a member, or by one member against another (Article 15(1)); (ii) actions brought by a corporate body against its directors, promoters, or auditors (Article 15(2)); (iii) actions brought by the creditors of a corporate body against its members (Article 16); and (iv) actions brought by a corporate body or its creditors against former members, directors, promoters, or auditors, as well as actions brought by a former member against current members (Article 17).

excessive forum shopping by plaintiffs, which could otherwise prejudice the procedural position of minority shareholders.

In exceptional cases where Korean courts have general jurisdiction over a foreign subsidiary, they may also have jurisdiction over claims brought against its Korean parent company under categories (ii) or (iii) above. For example, where a victim who is a current or former shareholder of the foreign subsidiary suffers harm resulting from the subsidiary's extraterritorial torts, the victim may bring a claim in Korean courts against the Korean parent company in its capacity as a co-shareholder of the subsidiary. If the victim is a current shareholder, jurisdiction may be established under category (ii); if a former shareholder, under category (iii). It should be noted, however, that this analysis presupposes the applicability of the foreign subsidiary's personal law pursuant to Article 30 of the KPILA, and that such law recognises the possibility of one shareholder bringing a claim against another in the circumstances described.

In practice, the utility of Article 25 is limited, as Korean courts typically have general jurisdiction over the Korean parent company. Nevertheless, even where such jurisdiction exists, the courts may decline to exercise it under the doctrine of *forum non conveniens*, as set forth in Article 12. In the scenarios described above, however, the likelihood that Korean courts would decline jurisdiction on this basis may be reduced.

If the foreign subsidiary is publicly listed, particularly through depository receipts rather than common shares, further questions may arise as to whether the plaintiff can assert a claim based on shareholder status. Depository receipts represent indirect ownership and may not confer shareholder rights recognised under the subsidiary's personal law. Accordingly, it is necessary to determine whether the plaintiff qualifies as a shareholder under that law and, if so, whether such status provides standing to bring the claim.

E. Doctrine of *Forum Non Conveniens*

Article 12 of the KPILA, introduced by the 2022 amendment, codifies the doctrine of *forum non conveniens*. Under this provision, even when Korean courts have international jurisdiction under the KPILA, they may decline to exercise it in exceptional cases where proceeding in Korea would be manifestly inappropriate. To invoke Article 12, the following six conditions must be satisfied: (i) Korean courts must have international jurisdiction under the KPILA; (ii) there must be a foreign court available to exercise jurisdiction; (iii) in light of all the circumstances, it must be inappropriate for the case to be heard in Korea and more appropriate for it to be heard in the foreign forum; (iv) the existence of such exceptional circumstances must be clearly established; (v) the defendant must raise the objection before the first hearing on the merits; and (vi) the case must not involve a choice of court agreement designating Korean courts.

In practice, the assessment of condition (iii) is particularly significant. Although Article 12 does not enumerate the relevant factors, courts are expected to evaluate all pertinent circumstances on a case-by-case basis. This typically includes private interests considerations, such as the proximity of evidence, the availability of witnesses, and the potential application of a different substantive law in the alternative forum. Public interests factors may also be taken into account, including the appropriateness of applying the law of the forum to a dispute that has a close local connection.

Although the SCK's ruling on 25 March 2021 (Docket No. 2018Da230588) applied the KPILA as it stood prior to the 2022 amendment, the factors identified in that case remain instructive for interpreting Article 12 of the current KPILA. These considerations are particularly relevant in the proceedings concerning the extraterritorial activities of MNCs, where foreign plaintiffs seek redress from Korean parent companies for harm caused by their foreign subsidiaries. In that case, Chinese sellers who had supplied goods under a contract with a Chinese buyer but had not received payment brought a lawsuit in Korea against the Korean parent company of the Chinese buyer, arguing that it should be held jointly liable under Article 63 of the former Chinese Company Law.

While the lower courts dismissed the claim for lack of international jurisdiction, the SCK reversed, noting the following: (i) the defendant's principal place of business was in Korea; (ii) as the sole shareholder of the Chinese buyer, the defendant had reasonable access to evidence necessary for its defence; (iii) the plaintiffs voluntarily chose to litigate in Korea despite geographic and linguistic disadvantages; (iv) the defendant could have reasonably foreseen being sued in Korea if its subsidiary failed to perform contractual obligations; (v) key evidence, such as receipts and confirmations, could be reviewed in Korea and the plaintiffs would bear the risk of insufficient proof; (vi) the defendant's assets subject to enforcement were located in Korea; and (vii) the mere fact that Chinese law applied did not preclude the exercise of jurisdiction by Korean courts. The dispute in that case turned on whether the subsidiary owed the payment and whether its corporate veil could be pierced, both of which were issues that did not necessitate extensive fact-finding or evidence collection in China.

On the contrary, cross-border lawsuits against MNCs involving human rights violations committed by foreign subsidiaries may require extensive local procedures in the foreign jurisdiction, including witness testimony and expert assessments. In such instances, Korean courts may be more inclined to find that Korea is not an appropriate forum. Where crucial evidence or witnesses are located abroad, or where no legal basis exists under Korean or foreign law to hold the Korean parent company liable for the acts of its subsidiary, defendants are likely to invoke the doctrine of *forum non conveniens*, and Korean courts may give active consideration to staying or dismissing the proceedings.

F. Emergency Jurisdiction

Korean courts cannot adjudicate a case if they lack international jurisdiction under the KPILA. However, in exceptional circumstances where no foreign forum is available and a refusal to hear the case would result in a denial of justice, Korean courts may assert jurisdiction as a last resort. This form of supplementary jurisdiction is commonly referred to as *forum necessitatis* or emergency jurisdiction.

Although the KPILA does not explicitly provide for such jurisdiction, it may be recognised in exceptional cases pursuant to Article 2, which sets out the general principle that there must be a substantial connection between the dispute or the parties and the forum. It may be considered whether the criterion articulated in the UK Supreme Court's *Vedanta* judgment – the requirement that the UK must be the proper forum for the consolidated claims, or, even if a foreign jurisdiction appears more appropriate, there must be a significant risk that substantial justice cannot be obtained in that alternative forum – may serve as a useful framework for recognising emergency jurisdiction under Korean law in cross-border claims brought against MNCs. However, this remains a complex issue, as questioning the efficacy of foreign judicial systems may risk being construed as encroaching upon foreign sovereignty.

V. Governing Law

In principle, a claim for damages arising from an extraterritorial tort committed by a foreign subsidiary is governed by the law of the country in which the subsidiary is located, as this generally constitutes both the place of the tortious act (Handlungsort) and the place of the resulting harm (Erfolgsort). MNCs often establish subsidiaries and conduct business in foreign jurisdictions to take advantage of local regulatory environments, which may result in insufficient remedies for victims under the subsidiary's local law. As a result, an increasing number of victims are seeking to bring claims not only against the foreign subsidiary but also against the parent company before the courts of the parent company's home jurisdiction and to invoke the application of that jurisdiction's law. However, under private international law, the legal basis for applying the law of the parent company's location differs depending on whether the claim is directed against the subsidiary or the parent company.

For the law of the parent company's location to govern a claim against a subsidiary, an exception must be made to the general rule that the law of the place where the tort occurred applies. This may be achieved in several ways: by characterising the parent company's personal law as an overriding mandatory rule that applies even when the subsidiary's local law is designated as the governing law; or by invoking the forum's public policy to displace the law of the subsidiary's location and substitute it with the law of the forum. Where the parent company and the subsidiary are considered joint tortfeasors, the place of the tort is generally identified as the place of the subsidiary's conduct. If the application of the law of the parent company's location is also pursued in such case, a consistent legal rationale must be maintained. By contrast, for claims brought directly against the parent company, the law of its location may be applied either by construing the place of the tort as the place where the parent company failed to fulfil its duty of oversight, namely the place where the legal obligation arose, or by applying the parent company's personal law.

A. Tort

i. General Rule: Law of the Place of Tort

Article 52(1) of the KPILA establishes the general rule that the law governing a tort shall be the law of the place where the tort occurred. In cases involving distant torts, where the place of the tortious act and the place of the resulting harm are located in different countries, Article 52(1) recognises both as potential connecting factors but does not specify which should prevail. The SCK addressed this issue in its decision of 24 May 2012 (Docket No. 2009Da22549), which concerned forced labour during the Japanese occupation. The Court held that where the place of the tortious act and the place of the resulting harm are located in different jurisdictions, the victim may choose the more favourable law as the applicable law. In that case, the plaintiffs had previously lost a claim in Japan under Japanese law and were deemed to have implicitly chosen Korean law; accordingly, the Court applied Korean law.

In disputes involving MNCs, where the parent company is not the direct perpetrator of the tort but is alleged to have breached a duty of care in connection with harm caused extraterritorially by its subsidiary, the question arises as to whether the place of the tort should be deemed the location of the subsidiary or that of the parent company. If the parent company's failure to fulfil its duty of care is characterised as an omission occurring at its place of establishment, and if the place of the omission is interpreted as the place where the legal obligation is imposed, then the parent company's location may be treated as the place of the tortious act. In such circumstances, if the subsidiary's location is deemed the place of the resulting harm, the case would constitute a distant tort, and the victim may invoke the law of the parent company's location as the applicable law.

However, Article 21(1) of the KPILA provides a general escape clause allowing the court to apply the law of another country if it is manifestly more appropriate in light of all the circumstances. Whether a victim's selection of the law of the parent company's location in a distant tort case may be displaced under Article 21(1), thereby leading to the application of the law of the subsidiary's location instead, remains an open question.

ii. Exceptions to the General Rule

Articles 52(2), 52(3), and 53 of the KPILA provide exceptions to the general rule set out in Article 52(1) by introducing alternative connecting factors. Article 52(2) applies where, at the time of the tort, both the tortfeasor and the victim shared a common habitual residence in the same country. In such cases, the law of that shared habitual residence governs the tort, even if it differs from the law of the place where the tort occurred. Article 52(3) further provides that where a tort infringes upon a pre-existing legal relationship, the tort claim shall be governed by the law of the country to which the law governing that relationship belongs.

In cross-border tort claims against MNCs, Article 52(3) may be invoked in various scenarios. For example, if a foreign victim brings a tort claim before Korean courts against a foreign subsidiary and its Korean parent company, and there exists a prior legal relationship, such as an employment contract between the victim and the subsidiary, the law governing the tort claim against the subsidiary, but not against the Korean parent company, may be designated as the law of the country to which the law governing that employment contract belongs. In another scenario, if a shareholder of the subsidiary files a tort claim against the Korean parent company in its capacity as a co-shareholder, the applicable law may be connected to the subsidiary's personal law (*lex societatis*) pursuant to Article 30 of the KPILA. Similarly, where a creditor brings a tort claim against the parent company in an attempt to pierce the corporate veil of the subsidiary, the governing law may also be determined with reference to the subsidiary's personal law.

Article 53 recognises party autonomy in determining the governing law for tort claims. However, this autonomy is subject to significant limitations: the agreement must be concluded after the occurrence of the tort, and the parties may choose only Korean law as the applicable law. In tort claims brought against parent companies in relation to extraterritorial torts committed by their subsidiaries, if Korea enacts legislation imposing a duty of care on parent companies for the actions of their subsidiaries, it remains contested whether such legislation could be rendered applicable through the exercise of party autonomy.

iii. Extraterritorial Application of Korean Law?

When a foreign plaintiff brings a claim before Korean courts and Korean law is found to govern conduct committed abroad by either a Korean parent company or its foreign subsidiary, this does not, in itself, amount to the extraterritorial application of Korean law, unless a specific Korean statute provides otherwise. For example, if a serious accident occurs abroad due to the conduct of a foreign subsidiary, and it is found that the accident resulted from intentional or grossly negligent misconduct by responsible management personnel of the Korean parent company who breached their duty to ensure safety and health under the SAPA, a question arises as to whether foreign victims may seek damages of up to five times the actual loss under Article 15 of the SAPA. This issue ultimately concerns the relationship between Article 15 of the SAPA and Articles 52 and 53 of the KPILA.

In principle, tort liability for accidents occurring abroad must be determined in accordance with the general choice-of-law rules set out in the KPILA. Article 15 of the SAPA may apply only if Korean law is designated as the governing law under those rules. If the case does not fall within Articles 52(2), 52(3), or 53 of the KPILA, but the Korean parent company exercises substantive control over the foreign business site, the place of conduct may be deemed to be Korea – even if the harm occurred abroad – provided that the accident was caused by intentional or grossly negligent misconduct by responsible management personnel. It is important to emphasise that Article 15 of the SAPA does not apply merely because the statute governs the criminal punishment aspects of the incident.[28] This analysis may also be extended to situations in which Korea enacts legislation imposing responsibilities on parent companies to identify, prevent, and address adverse human rights impacts arising from the operations of their foreign subsidiaries or affiliates.

B. Personal Law of Corporations

Article 30 of the KPILA establishes that matters concerning a corporate body are governed by the law of the place of its incorporation. In its decision of 1 August 2018 (Docket No. 2017Da246739), the SCK held that the scope of Article 30 encompasses all legal issues relating to a corporate body, including its formation and dissolution, internal organisation and governance, rights and obligations of its organs and members, and its legal capacity. Accordingly, questions concerning whether a member of a corporate body may be held liable to the corporate body's creditors, and, if so, to what extent, must be resolved under the law of the jurisdiction in which the corporate body is incorporated.

This position was reaffirmed by the SCK in a judgment rendered on 3 April 2025 (Docket No. 2022Da288836, 288843), which involved a cross-border dispute concerning a wholly owned Chinese subsidiary and its Korean parent company. The issue was whether a creditor of the Chinese subsidiary could bring a direct payment claim against the Korean parent company based on the Chinese doctrine of lifting the corporate veil. The Court held that where a party seeks to pierce the corporate structure and impose liability on a shareholder or controlling party for the corporate body's debts, the matter concerns whether a member of the corporate body should be liable to its creditor. Therefore, absent exceptional circumstances, the law governing veil-piercing must be the corporate body's personal law, namely the law of the place of its incorporation.

In proceedings concerning the extraterritorial activities of MNCs, the question of whether a parent company may be held liable for the tortious acts of its foreign subsidiary under the doctrine of veil-piercing should, in principle, be determined under the subsidiary's personal law. This is because the issue involves disregarding the subsidiary's separate legal personality

[28] Korean nationals who violate the SAPA while abroad are generally subject to criminal punishment. Article 3 of the Korean Criminal Code adopts the principle that Korean nationals who commit crimes under Korean law outside the territory of Korea shall be punishable. The SAPA contains no provision excluding the application of this principle. Although practical enforcement may be difficult in such cases, the SAPA may apply to accidents that occur at business sites of foreign subsidiaries established under foreign law, where employees affiliated with the Korean parent company are dispatched or seconded to those sites, and where the Korean parent company exercises effective control over their operations. While this may appear to constitute extraterritorial application of the SAPA, such application arises as a consequence of the general principles of Korean Criminal Code.

in order to hold the parent company liable in its capacity as a shareholder. However, with respect to the law governing the parent company's liability for torts committed by its foreign subsidiary more generally, other approaches may be available. The strictest is the cumulative application of both the subsidiary's and the parent company's personal law. A more permissive approach allows for the selective application of either law. In some cases, only the parent company's personal law may apply. The choice of law depends on whether the personal laws of the parent company and/or the subsidiary contain provisions governing liability for such conduct, and if so, who may be held liable, under what conditions liability arises, and what legal consequences may follow.

C. Overriding Mandatory Rules

Article 20 of the KPILA recognises the applicability of Korea's overriding mandatory rules even where the governing law is foreign. A provision qualifies as an overriding mandatory rule if it expressly states its application regardless of the governing law, or if its territorial scope is clearly defined. However, in proceedings concerning the extraterritorial activities of MNCs, it remains uncertain whether Korea's doctrine of piercing the corporate veil meets this threshold. In its judgment of 23 August 2013 (Docket No. 2012Gahap10763), the Seoul Central District Court declined to apply Korea's veil-piercing doctrine to a company incorporated in the British Virgin Islands, holding that the doctrine does not constitute an overriding mandatory rule. The Court emphasised that the doctrine, being uncodified and developed through case law and academic theory, does not warrant application where its non-application would not lead to an outcome manifestly incompatible with Korea's public policy.

However, if Korea were to enact legislation imposing a duty of care on parent companies with explicit application to extraterritorial torts of foreign subsidiaries, such legislation could potentially qualify as an overriding mandatory rule. A related question arises as to whether comparable laws in countries such as France or Germany, which impose a duty of care on parent companies with respect to their subsidiaries, could be treated as overriding mandatory rules of a third country. However, absent exceptional circumstances, it would be difficult for such provisions to be applied as overriding mandatory rules of a third country.

D. Public Policy

Article 23 of the KPILA provides that even where foreign law is designated as the governing law, it will not be applied if its application would lead to a result that is contrary to Korea's public policy (*ordre public*). The determination of what constitutes Korea's public policy under Article 23 requires a case-specific analysis.

In proceedings brought in Korea against MNCs, Article 23 may be invoked where the law of a foreign subsidiary's home jurisdiction or another foreign law is designated as the governing law for claims against either its Korean parent company or the subsidiary itself. If the relevant foreign law provides a reasonably adequate level of protection for victims, such as by recognising a right to compensation or by providing for the award of meaningful damages, it is unlikely to be considered incompatible with Korea's public policy.

Indeed, in a recent case where Chinese plaintiffs sought to hold a Korean parent company liable for the debts of its Chinese subsidiary, the SCK, in its judgment of 3 April 2025 (Docket No. 2022Da288836, 288843), held that the application of Article 63 of the former Chinese Company

Law, which presumes shareholder liability in single-member companies, did not contravene Korea's public policy. This ruling suggests that the application of foreign law will not be precluded merely because it imposes stricter liability than Korean law, so long as it affords meaningful remedies to victims. Furthermore, where the applicable foreign law, unlike Korean law, recognises a duty of care owed by the parent company to its subsidiary, it may be difficult to reject the application of that law on public policy grounds. By contrast, if the foreign law entirely denies the possibility of redress, for example by refusing compensation or by limiting damages to a nominal amount, its application may be deemed incompatible with Korea's public policy and, in such cases, Korean law may be applied in substitution.

VI. Recognition and Enforcement of Foreign Judgments

Article 217(1) of the KCPA provides that a foreign judgment may be recognised in Korea if the following conditions are satisfied: (i) the judgment is final and binding or has equivalent legal effect; (ii) the foreign court exercised international jurisdiction in a manner consistent with the jurisdictional principles recognised under Korean law; (iii) the losing party was duly served and afforded a reasonable opportunity to respond, or otherwise participated in the proceedings; (iv) the judgment does not violate Korea's public policy; and (v) a reciprocity exists between Korea and the foreign jurisdiction, or that jurisdiction applies standards substantially similar to those under Korean law. In proceedings brought against MNCs, particular concerns may arise with respect to the public policy requirement under condition (iv).

First, the recognition of a foreign judgment that imposes liability on a Korean parent company for breaches of a duty of care in connection with torts committed extraterritorially by its foreign subsidiary may give rise to questions under Korea's public policy. This issue becomes particularly sensitive where Korean law does not expressly recognise a parent company's duty of care. However, the mere absence of an equivalent statutory or judicially recognised duty under Korean law does not, in itself, preclude recognition. Rather, a fact-specific assessment is required to determine whether recognition would result in an outcome that is manifestly incompatible with Korea's public policy. The imposition of liability on a parent company is not, by itself, sufficient to justify refusal of recognition. Korean law acknowledges the doctrine of piercing the corporate veil, and the KCC imposes liability on quasi-directors. In addition, legislative efforts are currently underway in Korea to introduce statutory human rights due diligence obligations applicable to parent companies.

Although not in the context of recognising foreign judgments, Korean courts have upheld claims by foreign plaintiffs based on foreign law against Korean parent companies in connection with the conduct of their foreign subsidiaries. For example, in its decision of 3 April 2025 (Docket No. 2022Da288836, 288843), the SCK upheld a lower court ruling that partially granted the claims of Chinese plaintiffs against a Korean parent company. The Court applied Article 63 of the former Chinese Company Law, which shifts the burden of proof in single-member limited liability companies, requiring the shareholder to demonstrate the separation of personal and corporate assets. The Court held that imposing joint and several liability on the Korean parent company for contractual obligations of its Chinese subsidiary did not contravene Korea's public policy.[29]

[29] Similarly, in its decision of 19 January 2021 (Docket No. 2019Na2054956), the Seoul High Court considered a claim brought by Chinese insurance companies seeking to hold a Korean parent company liable for a fire accident involving its

Second, an issue may arise as to whether a foreign judgment awarding non-compensatory damages against a Korean parent company could be refused recognition in Korea on the ground that it violates Korea's public policy. Korean courts have traditionally been reluctant to recognise foreign judgments granting punitive or other non-compensatory damages that grossly exceed the scope permitted under Korean law.[30] However, the SCK's landmark decision of 11 March 2022 (Docket No. 2018Da231550) marked a shift in this approach. The Court upheld the recognition and enforcement of a Hawaii judgment awarding treble damages for unfair competition. It held that a foreign judgment awarding non-compensatory damages may be recognised if the underlying conduct falls within a regulatory domain of Korean law that similarly allows the awarding of damages exceeding actual compensation. In the case at hand, although Korea's Monopoly Regulation and Fair Trade Act does not provide for punitive damages, it does authorise treble damages. Because the defendant's conduct at issue in the Hawaii proceedings fell within the regulatory domain under the Korean statute, and because the amount awarded did not exceed the statutory multiple authorised under that statute, the Court concluded that recognition of the foreign judgment would not contravene Korea's public policy.

In light of Korea's evolving legislative landscape, as reflected in statutes such as the SAPA, the Fair Transactions in Subcontracting Act, and the Product Liability Act, which permit treble or quintuple damages in specific regulatory contexts, the likelihood of recognising and enforcing foreign judgments awarding non-compensatory damages for human rights violations may increase. This is particularly the case where the underlying conduct and the scale of damages correspond to categories of Korean law that similarly allow for substantial awards exceeding compensatory damages.

VII. Conclusion

The legal framework governing ESG issues in Korea remains at a nascent stage, marked by a fragmented set of individual statutes and evolving principles in private international law. While these existing instruments offer a preliminary foundation, they remain insufficient to address the complex challenges posed by cross-border lawsuits against MNCs and the broader demands of corporate accountability. The absence of comprehensive legislation presents substantial obstacles both for victims seeking remedies and for corporations striving to meet evolving compliance expectations.

To reinforce its role as a global leader in sustainable governance, Korea is actively pursuing the development of more coherent and robust ESG legislation. Advancing such reforms would not only bring Korea into closer alignment with international standards but also enhance legal certainty for corporations and improve access to remedies for affected individuals. A unified legal framework would contribute to greater fairness, transparency, and enforceability in the global pursuit of corporate accountability.

Chinese subsidiary. Although the Court rejected liability under Chinese tort law due to insufficient evidence of vicarious liability, it partially upheld the claim on the grounds of abuse of shareholder rights under Chinese corporate law. On appeal, the SCK, in its ruling on 3 July 2025 (Docket No. 2021Da220741), upheld the High Court's finding of liability under Chinese corporate law, while partially overturning the judgment on the grounds of errors in the determination of damages for delay under Chinese law, and remanded the case.

[30] For example, the Seoul Eastern District Court's decision on 10 February 1995, Docket No. 93Gahap19069; the Seoul Southern District Court's decision on 20 October 2000, Docket No. 99Gahap14496; the Busan High Court's decision on 23 July 2009, Docket No. 2009Na3067.

9

The Philippines

RUBY ROSSELLE "ROSS" TUGADE

I. Introduction

In 2016, the European Parliament adopted a non-legislative resolution on the EU-Philippines Framework Agreement on Partnership and Cooperation that encouraged the Philippines, among others, to implement the UN Guiding Principles on Business and Human Rights.[1] The clause pertaining to the application of the Guiding Principles was directly connected to the grant of the Generalised Scheme of Preferences Plus (GSP+) status by the European Union upon the Philippines,[2] a 'special incentive to pursue sustainable development and good governance' relating to trade.[3]

As of 2025, the Philippines is the only country in the Southeast Asian region to enjoy this preferred status as a trade partner, conditioned on the implementation of international conventions on human rights, labour rights, the environment, and good governance.[4] The Philippines' continued enjoyment of this preferential status once came under threat due to massive violations of human rights under the government's anti-illegal drug policy under former President Rodrigo Duterte.[5] With the succeeding administration exerting efforts to recalibrate relations with the EU post-Duterte, the Philippines was able to secure an extension of the GSP+ benefits in 2023 for another four years, or until 2027.[6] While the widespread human rights violations accompanying the so-called 'Drug War' abated after Duterte, a host of human rights issues are still present in the country. A hostile environment for human rights defenders persists, with business entities at times complicit or directly participating in the perpetration of human rights abuses.[7]

Despite the UN's recommendation of the adoption of a concrete National Action Plan on Business and Human Rights (NAP) as a tool to give effect to the Guiding Principles, along with

[1] European Parliament non-legislative resolution of 8 June 2016 on the draft Council decision on the conclusion, on behalf of the Union, of the Framework Agreement on Partnership and Cooperation between the European Union and its Member States, of the one part, and the Republic of the Philippines, of the other part [2016] OJ 86/76.

[2] ibid.

[3] European Commission, 'Generalised Scheme of Preferences Plus (GSP+)' (*Access2Markets*) trade.ec.europa.eu/access-to-markets/en/content/generalised-scheme-preferences-plus-gsp.

[4] ibid.

[5] S Strangio, 'EU Threatens Philippine Trade Perks Over Rights Abuses' *The Diplomat* (21 September 2020) thediplomat.com/2020/09/eu-threatens-philippine-trade-perks-over-rights-abuses/.

[6] A Leah Gonzales, 'DTI: EU Parliament Backs Proposed 4-Yr Extension of EU GSP+' *Philippine News Agency* (22 November 2023) www.pna.gov.ph/articles/1214180.

[7] Global Rights Compliance, 'From Retaliation to Remedy: Violations against Defenders of Business-Related Human Rights Abuses in the Philippines' (Global Rights Compliance, 2023).

the encouragement upon states to produce their respective NAPs, the Philippines has not yet firmed up the process to develop its own.[8] The Philippine legal framework itself is marked by 'key deficiencies' and wide gaps when it comes to business and human rights.[9] Nevertheless, the absence of a NAP or a concrete policy instrument articulating the Philippines' business and human rights framework does not necessarily translate to a lack of legal principles and rules that support remedies against business-related human rights abuses. The government's medium-term economic plans hint at addressing issues that interact with state's human rights obligations. In the Philippine Development Plan for 2023–2028 (PDP 2023–2028), the National Economic and Development Authority (NEDA) emphasised the need for strategies that will ensure macro-economic stability while recovering from the ruinous effects of the COVID-19 pandemic.[10] Integrated in the PDP 2023–2028 are core human rights concerns concerning social, economic, and cultural rights as well as encompassing issues such as environmental protection and climate change.

This chapter presents the aspects of the Philippine legal framework that accommodates the standards contained in the Guiding Principles, including remedies for business-related human right abuses. Three topical issues are taken up as illustrative cases: (1) extractive industries and 'mega' infrastructure projects, (2) platform work and labour rights, and (3) gender equality policies in corporate settings. These examples highlight a fragmented approach to seeking remedies and addressing issues of business-related human rights abuses in the Philippines. The chapter takes stock of the efficacy of such current available remedies, including litigation before courts and human rights inquiries, and considers the prospects of an integrated approach to business-related human rights violations.

II. The Legal Framework for Corporate Accountability and Pathways to Remedies

After 14 years under martial law and the overthrow of the Marcos regime, Filipinos ratified a new constitution in 1987 that featured a strong human rights orientation. This 'post-Marcos project' sought to crystallise human rights ideals into legal instruments with corresponding institutions for the protection of these rights.[11] A distinct feature of the sophisticated human rights legal framework constitutionally propped after the dictatorship was its 'de-ideologised' character that prioritised fixed, procedural, and predictable interpretations.[12] As such, human rights practice in the Philippines took the path of formal legalism in its implementation. This trajectory has inherent limitations owing to the classical formulation of human rights in international law as protections against the state.

Philippine law mirrors the conundrum in international law marked by the absence of 'primary rules in respect to business'[13] in the Business and Human Rights framework for

[8] Asia Centre, 'Business and Human Rights in Southeast Asia: Developing National Action Plans' (2021) 14.

[9] S Jr Madrona, 'Institutionalizing the UN Guiding Principles on Business and Human Rights in the Philippines' (2024) 12 *DLSU Business Notes and Briefings* 2, 4.

[10] National Economic and Development Authority, 'Philippine Development Plan (2023–2028)' (2023).

[11] R Pangalangan, 'Human Rights Discourse in Post-Marcos Philippines' in TWD Davis and B Galligan (eds), *Human Rights in Asia* (Cheltenham, Edward Elgar, 2011) 62.

[12] ibid.

[13] I Cismas and S Macrory, 'The Business and Human Rights Regime under International Law: Remedy without Law?' in J Summers and A Gough (eds), *Non-State Actors and International Obligations: Creation, Evolution and Enforcement* (Leiden, Brill, 2018) 223.

dealing with corporate violations. Actors in the Philippines' human rights space utilise various legal vehicles to seek redress for corporate violations of human rights precisely because of the lacuna in Philippine substantive law and the country's highly formalist formulation of rights. These legal vehicles have not been limited to tort litigation; creative ways of carving accountability pathways have included broader constitutional and public interest litigation as well as public human rights inquiries.

A. Constitutional Principles Related to the Guarantee and Protection of Human Rights

The structure and draftsmanship of the 1987 Constitution immediately signals its explicit human rights bearings. A key constitutional state policy is the value placed on 'the dignity of every human person' and the guarantee and 'full respect for human rights.'[14] Two key articles of the charter are dedicated to human rights: Article III on the Bill of Rights and Article XIII on Social Justice and Human Rights, with the latter section providing for the mandate and powers of an independent Commission on Human Rights.[15] Desierto posits that the human rights principles in the constitution adopts a cosmopolitan and universalist spirit, and therefore carrying a continuity with the state's earlier participation in the development of related international legal norms.[16] The abundant reference to human rights in the Philippines' constitution thus signals both formal and normative congruence with international human rights law.

An ostensible alignment with the traditional formulation of human rights in international law as legal entitlements available to individuals against the state[17] flowed into the natural limits of interpretation and enforcement in the Philippines' domestic sphere. The constitutional standard in the Philippines with respect to the application and interpretation of the protections in the Bill of Rights pertain to the public acts of state actors. This 'public/private distinction' is largely retained in Philippine constitutional law as a function of the 'state action doctrine,' articulated by the framers of the constitution and by the Supreme Court in subsequent cases.[18] *People v Marti* lays down the doctrinal interpretation of the Supreme Court in this regard: 'In the absence of governmental interference, the liberties guaranteed by the Constitution cannot be invoked against the State.'[19] Since the pronouncement in *Marti*, the Court has decided cases that may have seemingly evaded its self-imposed limitation on the application of the Bill of Rights into private matters.[20] Still, the Court has only carved out a narrow qualification to the state action doctrine, in that the Bill of Rights may be applied to private individuals provided that they 'act under the color of a state-related function,' such as the conduct of civilian volunteers for government law enforcement agencies.[21]

[14] 1987 Constitution, Art II, s 11.

[15] 1987 Constitution, Art XIII, s 17.

[16] D Desierto, 'A Universalist History of the 1987 Philippine Constitution (II)' [2010] *Historia Constitucional: Revista Electrónica de Historia Constitucional* 427, 460.

[17] A D'Amato, 'The Concept of Human Rights in International Law' (1982) 82 *Columbia Law Review* 1110, 1110.

[18] RLA Pangalangan, 'The Blurring of the Public/Private Distinction: Obsolescence of the State Action Doctrine' (2016) 90 *Philippine Law Journal* 84, 85–86.

[19] *People v Marti*, G.R. No. 81561, 18 January 1991.

[20] Pangalangan (n 18) 106.

[21] *Miguel y Remegio v People*, G.R. No. 227038, 31 July 2017.

The forecast that the rigid state action doctrine will likely be shaken to its core because of the increasing instances of egregious acts by private entities including corporate actors[22] may find footing in broader Philippine public law. Almost half a century before the ratification of the 1987 Constitution, the Philippine Supreme Court has already articulated a well-developed definition of social justice as a legal standard in *Calalang v Williams*:

> Social is 'neither communism, nor despotism, nor atomism, nor anarchy,' but the humanization of laws and the equalization of social and economic forces by the State so that justice in its rational and objectively secular conception may at least be approximated. Social justice means the promotion of the welfare of all the people, the adoption by the Government of measures calculated to insure economic stability of all the competent elements of society, through the maintenance of a proper economic and social equilibrium in the interrelations of the members of the community, constitutionally, through the adoption of measures legally justifiable, or extra-constitutionally, through the exercise of powers underlying the existence of all governments on the time-honored principle of *salus populi est suprema lex*.[23]

Outside of the Bill of Rights, social justice is a potent principle for the guarantee of legal entitlements, freedoms, and an expansive understanding of human dignity. Moored on the articulation in *Calalang*, the Supreme Court continues to adopt the standard of social justice for cases decided under the 1987 Constitution. Under this rubric of social justice, 'the law bends over backwards' to provide redress to underprivileged members of society.[24] It is explicit from contemporary uses of the social justice legal standard that the Court has not limited itself its application to acts by public actors. Such an application finds support within the 1987 Constitution itself, where social justice principles in Article XIII can be the philosophical and policy basis for finding corporations liable for private wrongs.[25] This is constitutionally tenable for as long as the invocation involves situations impacting human dignity, socio-economic conditions, and the common good.[26] The bifurcated structure of human rights principles in the 1987 Constitution – set out in Article III and Article XIII – may thus allow for the redress of human rights breaches that overcome the limits of the state action doctrine.

Relatedly, issues of interpretation have been arisen before the Supreme Court as to the mandate of the independent Commission on Human Rights (CHR), whose powers and functions were set out in Article XIII. The CHR is the Philippines' national human rights institution in accordance with the Paris Principles.[27] While the Court's tailored understanding in *Simon v Commission on Human Rights* is that the 1987 Constitution limits the CHR to fact-finding activities for violations of civil and political rights,[28] the threshold question in the case only pertains to body's investigative and contempt powers. In principle, *Simon* did not effectively limit the scope of human rights issues that the CHR can publicly espouse in terms of other public activities such as education, advocacy, and national inquiries. In this vein, the CHR is constitutionally equipped to address issues on social, economic, and cultural rights.[29] A liberal and expansive reading of the CHR's mandate is also the interpretive foundation of its own declaration of competence to hear

[22] Pangalangan (n 18) 105.
[23] *Calalang v Williams*, G.R. No. 47800, 02 December 1940.
[24] *Department of Agrarian Reform v Itliong*, G.R. No. 235086, 06 July 2022.
[25] See eg *Ebal v Thenamaris Philippines, Inc.*, G.R. Nos. 241844 & 257584, 29 November 2023.
[26] 1987 Constitution, Art XIII, s 1.
[27] E Palmer, 'The Effectiveness of National Human Rights Institutions' Relationships with Civil Society: The Commission on Human Rights in the Philippines' (2019) 25 *Australian Journal of Human Rights* 299, 300.
[28] *Simon v Commission on Human Rights*, G.R. No. 100150, 05 January 1994.
[29] Palmer (n 27) 304.

public petitions against fossil fuel corporations dubbed as 'carbon majors.'[30] Thus, despite apparent jurisdictional challenges to 'hearing' the climate change petitions, the CHR proceeded with setting up a National Inquiry on Climate Change.[31]

The CHR's National Inquiry on Climate Change Report illustrates the constitutional body's interpretation of how the Philippines' human rights legal framework can accommodate the Guiding Principles on Business and Human Rights. By its own account, the CHR concedes the lack of legal precedent to take cognisance of what essentially are private acts by transnational or multi-national corporations.[32] Responding first to the legal issue that the 1987 Constitution only allows the CHR to investigate civil and political rights, the CHR adopted an evolutive and contextual understanding of its mandate: 'all human rights are interrelated, interdependent, and indivisible; that one cannot consider civil and political rights separately from economic, social and cultural rights.'[33] Further into the report, the CHR asserts that it is not bound by territorial limits in the exercise of its jurisdiction. According to the CHR, it has the power to determine 'how it must perform its constitutional duty,' purportedly on the basis of the principle of *competence de la competence* found in international law. Moreover, the CHR insisted that the performance of its duties is 'neither constrained by nor anchored on the principle of territoriality alone.'[34]

Arguably, the CHR's Report adopts an overextended interpretation of the commission's constitutional mandate. As a consequence, the Report may have strained its own legitimacy due to flaws in the interpretation of principles under general international law and the textual basis of its own mandate and powers. If at all, the significance of the Report lies in the incorporation and formal recognition of the Guiding Principles, for the first time, in any official domestic process. The civil society-led pressure that resulted to the CHR's National Inquiry on Climate Change is also instructive when it comes to implementing the Guiding Principles in a domestic setting. Part of the Guiding Principles' recommendations on business is, after all, to assess the local contexts of their operations to ensure compliance with human rights laws and principles.[35] To acquire sufficient knowledge on this context, the Guiding Principles urge business enterprises to consult independent experts, civil society, and national human rights institutions.[36]

Beyond the limitations of the Report, the CHR has already faced an 'erosion of legitimacy' owing to past political and leadership issues it had confronted.[37] Concentrating all efforts to deepen the integration of the Guiding Principles into one national human rights institution may, in turn, be counterproductive in the long run. This is especially so when the Philippines has an advanced legal infrastructure for public interest litigation and civil society advocacy. The Supreme Court is especially a significant forum, as it has in the past granted ordinary citizens the standing to file suits concerning public matters.[38]

[30] J Peel and HM Osofsky, 'A Rights Turn in Climate Change Litigation?' (2018) 7 *Transnational Environmental Law* 37, 57–58.

[31] ibid 58.

[32] Commission on Human Rights of the Philippines, 'National Inquiry on Climate Change Report' (Commission on Human Rights of the Philippines, 2022) 3.

[33] ibid.

[34] ibid 4.

[35] United Nations Office of the High Commissioner for Human Rights, 'Guiding Principles on Business and Human Rights: Implementing the United Nations "Protect, Respect and Remedy" Framework' (2011) [ST/]HR/PUB/11/4 25.

[36] ibid 26.

[37] Palmer (n 27) 312.

[38] A Bedner and W Berenschot, 'Legal Mobilisation and Civil Society' in E Hansson and ML Weiss, *Routledge Handbook of Civil and Uncivil Society in Southeast Asia*, 1st edn (Abingdon, Routledge, 2023) 84.

B. Rights Litigation before the Supreme Court and the Promulgation of Rules Concerning the Protection of Rights

Part of the corrective legal innovations in the 1987 Constitution to safeguard against abuse and executive encroachment of the judiciary's independence is the 'expanded certiorari jurisdiction' of the Supreme Court.[39] Expanded certiorari jurisdiction accommodates varied ways of invoking standing, including citizens' suits. Ordinarily, citizens must show direct injury before the Court allows the filing of suits. Under the expanded certiorari jurisdiction of the Supreme Court, the mere fact of being a citizen already satisfies the injury requirement 'when the proceeding involves the assertion of a public right.'[40] Moreover, the Supreme Court has adopted the 'transcendental importance' doctrine of legal standing, when 'the issues raised are of paramount importance to the public.'[41] The expansion of judicial review in the 1987 Constitution ushered in a period of 'judicial activism' in the Supreme Court and made way for 'liberal interpretations of constitutional rights protection' in public interest litigation cases.[42] At the heart of the expanded certiorari jurisdiction is a functional remedy for 'grave abuse of discretion, actions or the exercise of a function that violate the Constitution.'[43] Equally important when considering 'transcendental importance' in public interest cases is that it may be a vehicle to allow direct recourse to the Supreme Court by way of exception to the hierarchy of courts. In this manner, allowing the narrow exception 'prevents courts from the paralysis of procedural niceties when clearly faced with the need for substantial protection.'[44]

After a robust period of judicial activism, the Supreme Court later refined and effectively reined in the invocation of expended certiorari jurisdiction most notably in the case of *Gios-Samar, Inc. v Department of Transportation and Communication*.[45] The Supreme Court took note that this expanded certiorari jurisdiction no longer confined judicial power 'to its traditional ambit of settling actual controversies involving rights that were legally demandable and enforceable.'[46] However, the court stressed in the same breath that the presence of a legal question remained an indispensable requirement.[47] The court clubs this basic requirement with other parameters, namely that there must be no questions of fact unless they are essential, and that the usual requisites of judicial review[48] must be met if the case involves a question of constitutionality.[49] In taking pains to clarify the rules on standing in *Gios-Samar*, the Supreme Court operated in part to consider the institutional demands of cases anchored on transcendental importance. The main opinion in *Gios-Samar* stressed that the related procedural rule on hierarchy of courts is a 'constitutional imperative' that allows the Supreme Court to filter cases and, in effect, decongest its clogged dockets.[50]

[39] *Pangilinan v Cayetano*, G.R. Nos. 238875, 239483 & 240954, 16 March 2021.
[40] *Francisco v House of Representatives*, G.R. No. 160261, 10 November 2003.
[41] ibid.
[42] Peel and Osofsky (n 30) 62.
[43] *Association of Medical Clinics for Overseas Filipino Workers, Inc. (AMCOW) v GCC Approved Medical Centers Association, Inc.*, G.R. No. 207132, 06 December 2016.
[44] *The Diocese of Bacolod v Commission on Elections*, G.R. No. 205728, 21 January 2015.
[45] *Gios-Samar, Inc. v Department of Transportation and Communication*, G.R. No. 217158, 12 March 2019.
[46] ibid.
[47] ibid.
[48] In Philippine law, the requisites for judicial review are: (1) actual case or controversy; (2) parties must possess *locus standi*; (3) timeliness of raising constitutional questions; and (4) issues of constitutionality must be the crux or *lis mota* of the case. See *Francisco v House of Representatives* (n 40).
[49] KA Alonzo, 'Procedural Impact of *Gios-Samar, Inc. v Department of Transportation and Communications* on Certiorari in the Traditional and the Expanded Form' (2021) 94 *Philippine Law Journal* 705, 746.
[50] ibid 733.

Notably, the court observed in *Gios-Samar* that cases involving 'social rights' often invoke the extended certiorari jurisdiction principle. In fact, the court specifically mentions what is perhaps the most oft-cited and successful public interest litigation case it has decided under the 1987 Constitution: *Oposa v Factoran*.[51] A careful reading of *Oposa* will reveal that it does not rely on transcendental importance nor does it demonstrate a relaxation of the traditional rules on standing. What it does, however, is to verbalise – as *obiter dictum* – in Philippine jurisprudence the 'twin concepts of "inter-generational responsibility" and "inter-generational justice"' to demand the enforcement of the constitutional rights.[52] Specifically, the petitioners in *Oposa* hinged their cause of action on the government's grant of timber licence agreements to various corporations as a violation of their right to a healthful and balanced ecology. Through *Oposa*, the Supreme Court 'secured its place in history, and the international environmental community heaped praises on it for its decision,' though Gatmaytan criticises this praise as 'largely misplaced.'[53] While the misguided reverence for *Oposa* as a paragon of strategic litigation is due to the wide misunderstanding of its *obiter dictum* as one that confers standing, Gatmaytan submits that the value of the case may lie in its pronouncement that the right to a balanced and healthful ecology is a demandable, actionable right.[54] In any case, *Oposa* is still a historical artefact of how public interest litigation was done before the Supreme Court.

Aside from certiorari, litigants have also used petitions for the issuance of a writ of mandamus to compel the performance of acts enjoined by law. Within the decisions of the Supreme Court, there have been instances that a 'writ of continuing mandamus' was granted to litigants who sought relief from what they identified as ongoing violations of the right to a healthful and balanced ecology. The writ of continuing mandamus commands 'continuing compliance with a final judgment' which will only be satisfied 'upon the final return of the writ when the court deems that the judgment has been fully implemented.'[55] The Supreme Court has, in one instance, granted the writ of continuing mandamus to the resident marine mammals of Tañon Strait, represented by their human stewards.[56]

In *Resident Marine Mammals*, the petitioners – 'toothed whales, dolphins, porpoises, and other cetacean species' inhabiting the strait[57] – alleged violations of the right to a balanced and healthful ecology from the implementation of a service contract for offshore oil drilling conducted by the Japan Petroleum Exploration Co., Ltd (JAPEX). The court directed the impleaded concerned government agencies to ensure that any drilling or extraction activities in the Tañon Strait must comply with the National Integrated Protected Areas System (NIPAS) Act and Presidential Decree No. 1586 (Environmental Impact Statement System). Continuing mandamus is now an available remedy that may be granted by courts through the consolidated Rules of Procedure for Environmental Cases (RPEC).[58] However, continuing mandamus 'is losing support even within the Court's ranks'[59] and the impact of decisions like *Resident Marine Mammals* in protecting environmental rights may not be as significant as they seem.[60]

[51] *Oposa v Factoran*, G.R. No. 101083, 30 July 1993.

[52] ibid.

[53] D Gatmaytan, 'Artificial Judicial Environmental Activism: *Oposa v Factoran* as Aberration' (2007) 17 *Indiana International & Comparative Law Review* 1, 1–2.

[54] D Gatmaytan, 'The Illusion of Intergenerational Equity: *Oposa v Factoran* as Pyrrhic Victory' (2003) 15 *Georgetown International Environmental Law Review* 457, 480.

[55] R Puno and D Gatmaytan, 'Environmental Activism by the Philippine Supreme Court: Initiatives and Impediments' (2024) 27 *Asia Pacific Journal of Environmental Law* 10, 23.

[56] *Resident Marine Mammals of the Protected Seascape Tañon Strait v Reyes*, G.R. Nos. 180771 & 181527, 21 April 2015.

[57] ibid.

[58] Rules of Procedure for Environmental Cases, Rule 8, A.M. No. 09-6-8-SC, 13 April 2010.

[59] Puno and Gatmaytan (n 55) 35.

[60] ibid.

Relatedly, another power of the Supreme Court that has facilitated public interest litigation concerning human rights is its 'rule-making' function under the 1987 Constitution. The Supreme Court is empowered by the constitution to 'promulgate rules concerning the protection and enforcement of constitutional rights,' among other spheres of concern.[61] Among the rules promulgated by the Supreme Court through this mandate are the rules on the protective Writs of *amparo*[62] and *habeas data*[63] against threats to life, liberty, or security. The Supreme Court similarly promulgated the RPEC under this constitutional power. While the protective writs of *amparo* and *habeas data* were judicially crafted as a response to the spate of extrajudicial killings and disappearances of political dissidents,[64] the rules themselves also govern acts or omissions by private individuals or entities.[65] Be that as it may, these writs 'will not issue to protect purely property or commercial concerns'[66] even if the purported act or omission was allegedly done by a private corporation. In one case, the Supreme Court dismissed a petition seeking the issuance of the writ of *habeas data* against a company when the alleged threats concerned the conditions of the petitioner's employment – an issue 'inarguably lodged by law' with labour quasi-tribunals.[67]

Meanwhile, the RPEC provides for remedies other than the aforementioned continuing mandamus, including the availability of SLAPP suit defence and the Writ of *Kalikasan* (Writ of Nature). The Writ of *Kalikasan* is envisioned as an 'extraordinary remedy covering environmental damage of such magnitude that it will prejudice the life, health or property of inhabitants in two or more cities or provinces.'[68] In one case, a community of urban residents sought the issuance of the Writ of *Kalikasan* against the Manila Electric Company for an alleged breach of their right to a balanced ecology and right to health arising from the construction of electric poles and transmission lines.[69] Another example where a civic group attempted to secure a Writ of *Kalikasan* against a corporate entity was in the case of *AGHAM v Japan Tobacco International (Philippines)* for the supposed environmental harms caused by the improper destruction of certain seized tobacco products.[70] Petitioners were not successful in obtaining the writs in both cases. In fact, the Writ of *Kalikasan* 'is seldom granted, with petitioners having a difficult time meeting its requirements,'[71] that is, clearly showing acts or omissions that violate environmental laws and individual rights. Sta. Maria adopts a more optimistic view of the use of judicially-promulgated rules, in that the RPEC has 'increasingly become a popular form of recourse for claimants who have been adversely affected by socially and environmentally harmful business activities,' thereby innovating 'domestic business and human rights law' at the same time.[72]

[61] 1987 Constitution, Art VIII, s 5(5).

[62] Rule on the Writ of Amparo, A.M. No. 07-9-12-SC, 24 October 2007.

[63] Rule on the Writ of Habeas Data, A.M. No. 08-1-16-SC, 2 February 2008.

[64] A Lorem Ramos, 'The Writs of Amparo and Habeas Data: Judicial Approaches to Human Rights Implementation in the Philippines' [2011] *LAWASIA Journal* 87, 87.

[65] Rule on the Writ of Amparo, s 1; Rule on the Writ of Habeas Data, s 1.

[66] *Tapuz v Del Rosario*, G.R. No. 182484, 17 June 2008.

[67] *Manila Electric Co. v Lim*, G.R. No. 184769, 5 October 2010.

[68] Puno and Gatmaytan (n 55) 26.

[69] *Dela Cruz v Manila Electric Co.*, G.R. No. 197878, 10 November 2020.

[70] *Alyansa ng mga Grupong Haligi ng Agham at Teknolohiya para sa Mamamayan v Japan Tobacco International (Philippines), Inc.*, G.R. No. 235771, 15 June 2021.

[71] Puno and Gatmaytan (n 55) 35.

[72] B Sta. Maria, 'Rule-Making for Rights Protection in the Philippines: The Judiciary's New Powers for Environmental Regulation and Access to Remedy for Business-Related Rights Abuses' in M Mohan and C Morel (eds), *Business and Human Rights in Southeast Asia* (Abingdon, Routledge, 2014) 227.

The robust human rights and social justice framework of the 1987 Constitution mirrors its unique quality of being a post-dictatorship, 'transformative' foundational law.[73] More than the main article on the Bill of Rights, the reformist spirit that animated the drafting history of the constitution is evident in its 'array of provisions on social and economic welfare, rights and equity,'[74] so much so that Article XIII is considered the 'heart of the charter.'[75] Formally speaking, the Philippines' judicial infrastructure led by the Supreme Court may be seen as a receptive forum for the assertion of human rights claims, which could also include cases involving corporations and businesses. Since the ratification of the 1987 Constitution, the Philippines has, after all, experienced some form of 'counter legal mobilisation' from peoples' groups against elite economic interests.[76] In the same vein, civil litigation presents a useable platform for vindicating human rights abuses committed by both public and private actors.

C. Civil Litigation for Human Rights Abuses and the Liabilities of Business Enterprises

If an individual wishes to assert human rights claims through civil litigation in the Philippines, the main legal vehicle for such a claim would be filing a suit under the 'Human Relations' chapter of the Civil Code of the Philippines.[77] The Civil Code's Human Relations torts espouse a 'broader' notion of tort liability, such that there are causes of action available to 'to cover other possibilities, including those arising from intentional actions.'[78] In the United States, constitutional torts refer to wrongdoing by a government official that has resulted to compensable individual injury.[79] Constitutional torts in the United States belong in the class of 'public torts' which also include 'public international torts' drawn from the Alien Tort Act.[80] Litigation using the Alien Tort Act has, for some time, allowed for human rights claims to be brought before courts, even against multi-national corporate entities.[81] The reference to American public tort principles is essential in discussing Philippine tort law, as some aspects of Human Relations torts in the Civil Code were adopted from the notion of torts in the United States.[82]

The Philippine Supreme Court has not doctrinally articulated parts of the Civil Code's Human Relations chapter as 'constitutional torts' *per se* even in their traditional sense. However, authors writing on the Human Relations torts have referred to a specific provision – Article 32 of the Civil Code – as constitutional torts.[83] The provision textually provides for the liability of 'any

[73] S Chopra, 'The Constitution of the Philippines and Transformative Constitutionalism' (2021) 10 *Global Constitutionalism* 307.

[74] ibid 314.

[75] ibid 318.

[76] Bedner and Berenschot (n 38) 88.

[77] Republic Act No. 386 or 'An Act to Ordain and Institute the Civil Code of the Philippines' (30 August 1950).

[78] G Bautista Fernandez et al, 'The Philippines: Civil Vindications for Uncivilised Wrongs' in E Aristova and U Grušić (eds), *Civil Remedies and Human Rights in Flux: Key Legal Developments in Selected Jurisdictions* (Oxford, Hart Publishing, 2022) 274.

[79] JJ Park, 'The Constitutional Tort Action as Individual Remedy' (2003) 38 *Harvard Civil Rights-Civil Liberties Law Review* 393, 398.

[80] NJ Miller, 'Human Rights Abuses as Tort Harms: Losses in Translation' (2016) 46 *Seton Hall Review* 505, 536.

[81] ibid 506.

[82] A Carpio, 'Intentional Torts in Philippine Law' (1972) 47 *Philippine Law Journal* 649, 669.

[83] Pangalangan (n 18) 122; FT Hilbay, 'The Philippine President as Tortfeasor-in-Chief: Establishing Civil Liability for Constitutional Negligence' (2009) 4 *Asian Journal of Comparative Law*; T Aquino, 'Constitutional Torts' (2022) 4 *University of Asia and the Pacific Law Journal* 1, 2.

public officer or employee, or any private individual, who directly or indirectly obstructs, defeats, violates or in any manner impedes or impairs [the] rights and liberties of another person.'[84] Article 32 then proceeds to list a set of constitutional rights that are actionable, and states that any action under the provision may proceed as an independent civil action regardless 'whether or not the defendant's act or omission constitutes a criminal offense.' Other than Article 32, the Civil Code provides for other bases of independent civil actions under the Human Relation chapter.[85]

Victims of human rights violations may use independent civil actions to vindicate their claims and make use of their built-in advantage. First, independent civil actions do not require criminal culpability before the award of damages. Next, the quantum of evidence is preponderance of evidence – a lower threshold than proof beyond reasonable doubt.[86] Therefore, instead of filing criminal cases – the usual, primary route for human rights violations victims – civil litigation may provide another route, even as against private persons. However, civil claims as a pathway to accountability for human rights violations 'has not been used extensively by human rights defenders in the Philippines' given their cost and the burden to be discharged by the plaintiff.[87] Litigating human rights claims using torts is distinct from public interest litigation, as public tort-based cases restore 'the link between right and remedy … by seeking damages derived from the harm suffered.'[88] On this principle, utilising public torts could strongly emphasise the liability of the perpetrator of violations.

Other Human Relations torts in the Civil Code include 'catch-all provisions' that contemplate 'possibilities not specifically provided for in the laws' and therefore expand the range of what are considered civil wrongs under Philippine law.[89] These torts are covered by Articles 19, 20 and 21 of the Civil Code:

> ARTICLE 19. Every person must, in the exercise of his rights and in the performance of his duties, act with justice, give everyone his due, and observe honesty and good faith.
>
> ARTICLE 20. Every person who, contrary to law, wilfully or negligently causes damage to another, shall indemnify the latter for the same.
>
> ARTICLE 21. Any person who wilfully causes loss or injury to another in a manner that is contrary to morals, good customs or public policy shall compensate the latter for the damage.

These provisions have been invoked in a litigation involving a private individual and a foreign corporation. In *Saudi Arabian Airlines v Court of Appeals*, the Supreme Court resolved the question of whether a case brought under Articles 19 and 20 should be entertained by the Philippines as a forum when the alleged tortious act of illegal dismissal happened abroad.[90] The plaintiff in the case was Milagros Morada, a former flight attendant of Saudia Air. During a layover in Jakarta, Indonesia, other male flight crew staff attempted to rape Morada, resulting in the deportation of the men from Indonesian soil. Several years after the incident, Morada was summoned by Saudia Air officers and was then made to appear before a Saudi court. Morada received a sentence of imprisonment and 286 lashes, ostensibly for violating Islamic tradition. After the Prince of Makkah dismissed Morada's case and declared her to be wrongfully convicted, she was sent home to the Philippines and promptly terminated by Saudia Air. Morada brought a civil case under Articles 19 and 20 for abuse of right. Saudia Air contested the choice of the Philippines

[84] Civil Code of the Philippines, Art 32.
[85] Civil Code of the Philippines, Arts 32, 33, 34 and 2176.
[86] Fernandez et al (n 78) 277.
[87] Global Rights Compliance (n 7) 29.
[88] Miller (n 80) 532.
[89] Fernandez et al (n 78) 275.
[90] *Saudi Arabian Airlines v Court of Appeals*, G.R. No. 122191, 08 October 1998.

as a forum. The Supreme Court held that the Philippines is a proper forum in this case because 'the over-all harm or the fatality of the alleged injury to the person, reputation, social standing and human rights of complainant' concerns an individual residing and working in the country.[91] Therefore, for purposes of bringing the civil claim, the Philippines is the 'state of the most significant relationship' to the case's factual context.[92]

Saudi Arabian Airlines v CA's resolution of the choice of forum issue could form the basis of filing civil cases against corporations anchored on human relations torts against corporations when breaches of human rights are potentially involved. The Supreme Court's decision in *Saudi Arabian Airlines v CA* may help settle conflicts of law issues especially if the party involved is a foreign corporation. The CHR institutionally recognises the use of civil cases for the filing of human rights claims. A commission-wide memorandum issued in 1998 lays down the basis for the initiation of investigations of 'violations of human rights not yet defined as criminal offenses.'[93] The memorandum specifically states that human rights violations victims may file an action for civil damages 'Articles 20, 21 and 32 of the Civil Code,'[94] aligning with cases decided by the Supreme Court.

Despite the promise of civil litigation for bringing human rights claims, there are accompanying procedural and resource challenges that may sometimes be insurmountable for human rights defenders. These include expensive filing fees, delays in trials, and enormous paperwork required of plaintiffs.[95] Even when litigants are able to claim the status of an 'indigent party'[96] and therefore be exempt from the payment of filing fees, there is no uniform practice to guide this litigation strategy. Further, 'acquisition of the status to litigate as an indigent does not exempt a party from payment of other necessary amounts arising from litigation' such as reproduction of documents, transportation expenses, notarisation, and other miscellaneous costs.[97]

Access to remedies is one of the pillars of the Guiding Principles. Making available effective judicial and non-judicial remedies constitute part of a state's duty to guard against business-related human rights.[98] The CHR has called for the reduction of barriers to access to justice in the context of business-related human rights cases, including 'costs of filing a lawsuit' and 'the lack of legal representation, of communities and vulnerable groups like the women and the indigenous people.'[99] Thus, while the possibility of bringing civil suits to bring human rights claims in the Philippines has already been recognised in scholarship and by human rights thinktanks, practical challenges abound in filing such cases.

A basis for bringing suits against corporations is textually found in the confines of the Revised Corporation Code of the Philippines.[100] Corporations incorporated under the Revised Corporation Code may be sued in their corporate name.[101] It remains to be settled in Philippine law what is the appropriate mechanism where the corporate act already amounts to human rights

[91] ibid.

[92] ibid.

[93] CHR Memorandum No. JRC-M-22B98-83, 'Civil Cases as Violation of Human Rights' (22 May 1998).

[94] ibid.

[95] Global Rights Compliance (n 7) 30.

[96] 2019 Rules of Civil Procedure, rule 3, s 3: 'A party may be authorized to litigate his action, claim or defense as an indigent if the court, upon an *ex parte* application and hearing, is satisfied that the party is one who has no money or property sufficient and available for food, shelter and basic necessities for himself and his family.'

[97] International Commission of Jurists, 'Access to Justice: Human Rights Abuses Involving Corporations (Philippines)' (International Commission of Jurists, 2010) 15.

[98] Guiding Principles, Pillar III (n 35).

[99] Commission on Human Rights of the Philippines, 'Guiding Document on Business and Human Rights' (Commission on Human Rights of the Philippines, 2020) 13.

[100] Republic Act No. 11232, or 'An Act Providing for the Revised Corporation Code of the Philippines' (23 February 2019).

[101] Revised Corporation Code, Art 35(a).

violations.[102] Prior to the passage of the Revised Corporation Code, the CHR sought to introduce elements of the Guiding Principles to the proposed amendments to the old corporation law.[103]

The CHR emphasised in their Position Paper twin human rights responsibilities of businesses. First, business must avoid causing or contributing to negative human rights impacts through their own actions and address any such impacts that arise. Second, they must try to prevent or lessen negative human rights impacts directly connected to their operations, products, or services through their business relationships, even if the business itself did not cause the harm.[104] Specific recommendations in the CHR Position Paper included human rights impact assessments, express human rights commitments included in articles of incorporation, and reparations for gross human rights violations from corporate acts.[105] The Revised Corporation Code's final text did not adopt the CHR recommendations.

Meanwhile, one legislative measure taken up in the Philippine Congress pertaining to greater corporate accountability is a proposed 'Corporate Social Responsibility Act' that seeks to amend the Revised Corporation Code and include a 'developed framework for the promotion and implementation' of CSR.[106] A closer examination of the proposed law reveals, however, the lack of a human rights orientation. Senator Raffy Tulfo's version in the 19th Congress, for instance, only provides for tax incentives and an awards scheme for business that adopt what appears to be a superficial engagement with corporate social responsibility.[107] Opposition to the measure from other members of Congress point to the possibility of corrupt practices and abuse of tax loopholes by corporations.[108]

III. Illustrative Thematic Areas of Business and Human Rights in the Philippines

Significant gaps remain unfilled in the Philippines' legal framework with respect to business and human rights in the Philippines.[109] There appears no legal basis yet to severely penalise corporations for human rights breaches and no durable single, identifiable mechanism for making corporations liable.[110] Additionally, there remains difficulties when it comes to the piercing the corporate veil, especially given complex corporate structures that may facilitate evasion of responsibility.[111] Despite these specific limitations, jurisprudence involving corporate liabilities for what may be characterised as harms affecting human rights continue to grow.

[102] Fernandez et al (n 78) 283.

[103] Commission on Human Rights of the Philippines, 'Position Paper on the Amendment of the Corporation Code of the Philippines: Incorporating the United Nations Guiding Principles on Business and Human Rights in the Corporation Code of the Philippines', cdn1.chr.gov.ph/wp-content/uploads/2018/04/08174156/Position-Paper-on-the-Amendment-of-the-Corp-Code-of-the-PH.pdf.

[104] ibid 2.

[105] Commission on Human Rights of the Philippines, 'CHR Position Paper on the Amendment of the Corporation Code' (n 103).

[106] 19th Congress, Senate Bill No. 2722.

[107] ibid.

[108] J Mangaluz, 'House Bill Incentivizing Corporate Social Responsibility Passes Final Reading' *Philippine Daily Inquirer* (29 May 2023) newsinfo.inquirer.net/1776555/house-bill-incentivizing-corporate-social-responsibility-passes-final-reading.

[109] Madrona (n 9) 4.

[110] ibid.

[111] International Commission of Jurists (n 97) 27.

Three thematic areas of concern illustrate these legal developments: extractive industries and 'mega' infrastructure projects, labour rights of precarious workers, and corporate policies relating to gender equality. Examples from these thematic areas may help demonstrate the application and opportunities to better integrate the Guiding Principles in the Philippines.

A. Extractive Industries and Mega Infrastructure Projects

The 2006 Interim Report of Special Representative John Ruggie identifies the 'extractive sector' mainly made of the 'oil, gas and mining' industries as the biggest perpetrator of abuses in the conduct of their businesses.[112] Types of violations include acts committed by security forces in guarding company assets and property, corruption, labour violations, and abuses in relation to local communities.[113] Human rights violations related to the extractive sector are so pervasive and 'widely acknowledged' that the UN Committee on Social, Economic and Cultural Rights took note of them in the 2017 General Comment No. 24 on Business and Human Rights.[114]

The extractive sector's expansion comes hand-in-hand with the construction of facilities and infrastructure that may also drive the perpetration of abuses and violations. The Philippine Mining Act of 1995,[115] a domestic statute that facilitates the conduct of extractive mining, allows mining companies to 'build necessary infrastructure on private lands as well as water and timber rights within the mining areas.'[116] With these statutory grants, large-scale mining became increasingly aggressive 'at the expense of the people and communities affected by their operations.'[117]

One of the most affected sectors of extractive industries in the Philippines are indigenous peoples' communities. Indigenous communities are historically situated in 'most peripheral areas of the Philippine archipelago' that are incidentally some of the most resource-rich locations in the country.[118] As a result, indigenous peoples are vulnerable to different forms of violence and physical displacement. Internal armed conflict in the areas where ancestral lands are located at times would, at times, force indigenous communities to evacuate. Forced displacement of indigenous communities from their ancestral land make it easier for 'development aggression' projects of extractive industries to enter and take over.[119] Past examples such as the Chico River dam construction, Jalaur River dam system project, and MacroAsia mining exploration saw outright disregard for the free, prior, and informed consent procedure[120] mandated by the Indigenous Peoples' Rights Act.[121] Human rights defenders – which may include activists, lawyers, journalists,

[112] J Ruggie, 'Interim Report of the Special Representative of the Secretary-General on the Issue of Human Rights and Transnational Corporations and Other Business Enterprises' (United Nations Commission on Human Rights, 2006) E/CN.4/2006/97, para 25.

[113] ibid.

[114] I Feichtner, M Krajewski and R Roesch, 'Introduction' in I Feichtner, M Krajewski and R Roesch (eds), *Human Rights in the Extractive Industries*, vol 3 (London, Springer, 2019) 2.

[115] Republic Act No. 7942, or the 'Philippine Mining Act of 1995' (3 March 1995).

[116] A Aytin, 'A Social Movements' Perspective on Human Rights Impact of Mining Liberalization in the Philippines' (2016) 25 *New Solutions: A Journal of Environmental and Occupational Health Policy* 535, 538.

[117] ibid 539.

[118] O Paredes, 'Between Rights Protection and Development Aggression' in MR Thompson and E Vincent C Batalla (eds), *Routledge handbook of the contemporary Philippines*, 1st edn (Abingdon, Routledge, 2018) 348.

[119] ibid 349.

[120] ABE Bayot, 'Free, Prior, and Informed Consent in the Philippines: A Fourth World Critique' in Feichtner, Krajewski and Roesch (n 114) 299.

[121] Republic Act No. 8371, or 'The Indigenous Peoples Rights Act of 1997' (29 October 1997).

and community organisers, academics, or ordinary citizens[122] – are also at risk of harm because of their opposition to development aggression projects by extractive industries.[123]

In spite of the difficulty in securing a Writ of *Kalikasan*, the Supreme Court has, on occasion, issued the writ in favour of a community affected by extractive activities. The Department of Environment and Natural Resources (DENR) suspended the activities of Zambales Diversified Metals Corporation and the Benguetcorp Nickel Mines, Inc. in 2016 by virtue of the Writ of *Kalikasan* issued by the Supreme Court upon the petition of filed by the concerned citizens of Santa Cruz, Zambales.[124] In 2023, the Supreme Court also issued the writ against Ipilan Nickel Corporation and Celestial Nickel Mining and Exploration Corporation, two mining operators in Mt. Mantalingahan, Palawan for their tree-cutting activities. The petition was filed by the Indigenous Cultural Communities of BICAMM Ancestral Domain, Brooke's Point, Palawan, likewise impleading the DENR and the Mines and Geosciences Bureau.[125]

B. Platform-based Work and Labour Rights

Another emerging critical area for the protection of rights vis-à-vis business practices is the plight of precarious platform workers in the Philippines. Platform workers offer services and labour through online, digital technologies operated by tech companies. The Philippines is one of the leading sources of online digital labour,[126] a reality that has birthed regulatory and governance issues as the phenomenon comes into contact with the rights-grounded constitutional policy on labour.[127] Regulatory framework and policy discussions on platform work only came 'after the fact' once the rapid growth of this kind of labour became apparent.[128] Current limitations built in the Philippines' domestic labour laws only guarantee full protection to workers where an employer-employee relationship subsists; platform workers are instead governed by contract law as contractors, in accordance to what their independent contracts stipulate.[129]

Aside from the usual benefits enjoyed by workers encompassed by an employer-employee relationship, such regular workers are clearly entitled to the more political aspects of work, namely the right to organise and bargain collectively. These rights are fundamental civil and political liberties guaranteed by the 1987 Constitution and conventional international human rights law. Due to such limitation, the ability of platform workers to jointly demand better conditions of work are severely limited, if not curtailed.[130] Further, platform workers suffer from precarity and vulnerability due to the lack of security of tenure, little to no insurance and social benefits, and

[122] Commission on Human Rights of the Philippines, 'Report on the Situation of Human Rights Defenders in the Philippines' (Commission on Human Rights of the Philippines, 2020) 2.

[123] AI Valdez, 'Defending the Defenders: Upholding the Right to Effective Remedy of Environmental Defenders in the Philippines' (2021) 66 *Ateneo Law Journal* 176, 186.

[124] Department of Environment and Natural Resources, 'DENR Suspends Two Mining Firms in Zambales' (8 July 2016) r7.denr.gov.ph/news-events/denr-suspends-two-mining-firms-in-zambales/.

[125] *Indigenous Cultural Communities of BICAMM Ancestral Domain, Brooke's Point, Palawan v Office of the Secretary of the DENR, et al.*, G.R. No. 268140, 15 August 2023.

[126] CR Soriano, 'Digital Platform Labor in the Philippines: Emerging Configurations and Policy Implications' (2021) 5 *Japan Labor Issues* 56, 56.

[127] 1987 Constitution, Art XIII, s 3.

[128] J Gamboa, 'Adopting Miller's First Principles for Online Food Delivery Platforms' Labor Regulation in the Philippines' (2022) 2021 *Philippine Journal of Public Policy: Interdisciplinary Development Perspectives* 203.

[129] ibid 202.

[130] AC Presto and R Rosselle Tugade, 'Finding Policies That Work: Examining the Case of Filipino Freelancers' (Friedrich Naumann Foundation for Freedom, 2023) 8.

impacts on physical and mental wellbeing.[131] With the government promoting platform work to plug in the national unemployment problem, more workers become exposed to exploitation and pernicious corporate practices.[132]

The International Labour Organization (ILO) has increasingly addressed and mainstreamed the unique issues facing platform workers. In the ILO's initial studies on decent work in the platform economy, the body recognised that there is yet no international legal framework 'of comprehensive application to digital labour platforms.'[133] Still, there are various existing conventional international law or soft law standards provide guidance on the crucial dimensions of platform work. The ILO identified issues such as humane terms and conditions of work, exploitation and forced labour in platforms, equal opportunity, social security, and fair remuneration. The Philippines has signed and/or ratified a number of instruments cited by the ILO's study on platform work as follows: (1) Freedom of Association and Protection of the Right to Organise Convention; (2) Equal Remuneration Convention; (3) Labour Inspection Convention; (4) Promotional Framework for Occupational Safety and Health Convention; (5) Employment Policy Convention; (6) Protection of Wages Convention; and (7) Violence and Harassment Convention.

Labour occupies a prominent place in the social and economic rights constitutional framework. To this end, Article XIII of the 1987 Constitution guarantees 'full protection to labor'[134] and balances the interests of labour on the one hand and industry and private enterprise on the other. Maintaining industrial peace is a 'shared responsibility' and there is equal recognition of the 'right of labor to its just share in the fruits of production and the right of enterprises to reasonable returns on investments.'[135] The viability of civil suits to vindicate abusive and inhuman treatment of employees is already well-established in Philippine jurisprudence, specifically on the use of Human Relations torts.[136] On the other hand, with platform work not yet fully captured in the traditional framework of labour laws in the Philippines, there is fertile ground for the use of civil suits to forward claims against businesses in violation of basic rights.

The Supreme Court may go beyond the nomenclature of the contractual agreement between workers and corporate entities, for instance, and instead look at the 'factual situations of the engagement' to rule upon legal questions surrounding workers' rights.[137] Platform workers in the Philippines have made headway in their struggle for better treatment and greater respect for their rights. The Supreme Court has had the chance to examine the labour claims of delivery riders of an e-commerce platform and came up with the determination that the workers in those cases were entitled to monetary benefits as regular employees.[138] Thus, there is some prospect for fortifying the social and economic rights of platform workers against abuse by big tech corporations through strategic suits filed in courts.

[131] ibid 3.

[132] Soriano (n 126) 58.

[133] International Labour Organization, 'Realizing Decent Work in the Platform Economy' (International Labour Organization, 2024) 29.

[134] 1987 Constitution, Art XIII, s 3.

[135] ibid.

[136] *Globe Mackay Cable and Radio Corp. v Court of Appeals*, G.R. No. 81262, 25 August 1989.

[137] Gamboa (n 128) 209.

[138] *Ditiangkin v Lazada E-Services Philippines, Inc.*, G.R. No. 246892, 21 September 2022; *Borromeo v Lazada E-Services Philippines, Inc.*, G.R. No. 265610, 3 April 2024.

C. Corporate Policies Impacting Gender Equality

The gendered implications of corporate policies are well-recognised and integrated in the Guiding Principles and its subsequent commentaries.[139] When it comes to the Southeast Asian context, there are marked 'significant differences with regards to gender equality,' though the Philippines fares relatively ahead of its neighbouring states.[140] Within the 1987 Constitution's states policies and social justice framework, gender equality is articulated as the guarantee of 'fundamental equality before the law of women and men'[141] and the provision of 'safe and healthful working conditions'[142] for women. Yet despite the Philippines' image and status as a gender-equal country, there is still no comprehensive national law that addresses acts of discrimination on the basis of sexual orientation, gender identity and gender expression (SOGIE).[143] The legislative agenda for SOGIE equality has languished in Congress since 2000 and largely remained in the primary deliberations phase.[144] An anti-discrimination national legislation will provide a fuller framework for protection in place of local ordinances that are limited in territorial scope and application.[145]

Internal corporate policies on awareness about discrimination on the basis of SOGIE is particularly deficient when it comes to the experiences of LGBTI employees.[146] Multinational companies are ahead when it comes to implementing LGBTI-inclusive policies, with domestic companies or the public sector often unaware of emerging standards on gender equality.[147] One area of disparity concerns the availability of support for LGBTI employees to organise themselves inside domestic companies.[148] Unlike the textual guarantee of the 1987 Constitution for equality on the basis of sex, finding a constitutional policy to cover gender-based discrimination will have to be derived from other human rights policies in the charter. Additionally, the absence of a comprehensive SOGIE equality law may constrain litigants to find causes of action in statutes.

Philippine jurisprudence on corporate policies impacting gender has, so far, only dealt with discrimination against women in the enjoyment of benefits. The Supreme Court voided a provision on mandatory retirement in a collective bargaining agreement between Philippine Airlines and its employees' union as the clause was discriminatory against female cabin crew.[149] In an earlier case, the court awarded damages and monetary compensation to female cabin crew of Saudia Air who were unlawfully terminated on the sole basis of their pregnancy.[150] International human rights law and the 1987 Constitution's social justice policies framed the tenor of the aforementioned decisions of *Halagueña v PAL* and *Saudia v Rebesencio*. To this end, the Supreme Court directly quoted the provisions of the Convention on the Elimination of All Forms of

[139] K Dovey, 'Why Gender Matters for the Business and Human Rights Agenda in Southeast Asia' in M Mohan and C Morel, *Business and Human Rights in Southeast Asia*, 1st edn (Abingdon, Routledge, 2014) 64.
[140] ibid 58.
[141] 1987 Constitution, Art II, s 2.
[142] 1987 Constitution, Art XIII, s 14.
[143] AC Presto, 'Contradictions in Gender Inclusivity and Discrimination: Experiencing the Paradoxical Workplace in the Philippines. Sexuality, Gender & Policy' (2025) 8(3), e70014,. onlinelibrary.wiley.com/doi/pdf/10.1002/sgp2.70014.
[144] TM Ildefonso, 'SOGIE Equality Bill Deliberations in the 18th Congress of the Philippines: A Persisting Battle against Discrimination' (2024) 32 *South East Asia Research* 95, 96.
[145] ibid 105.
[146] United Nations Development Programme and International Labour Organization, 'LGBTI People and Employment: Discrimination Based on Sexual Orientation, Gender Identity and Expression, and Sex Characteristics in China, the Philippines and Thailand.' (United Nations Development Programme, 2018) 33.
[147] ibid.
[148] ibid 37.
[149] *Halagueña v Philippine Airlines, Inc.*, G.R. No. 243259, 10 January 2023.
[150] *Saudi Arabian Airlines (Saudia) v Rebesencio*, G.R. No. 198587, 14 January 2015.

Discrimination against Women (CEDAW), a core human rights treaty, and Article XIII of the 1987 Constitution.

IV. Assessing the Place and Relevance of the Guiding Principles in the Philippines

As of the writing of this chapter, a consolidated NAP for business and human rights has yet to materialise in the Philippines. The absence of 'a clear commitment to a NAP development process' and, thus an organised strategy at the institutional level, is at the crux of the setback.[151] While the constitution provides for an independent Commission on Human Rights to oversee the protection and fulfilment of the state's human rights obligations, the responsibility of formulating a national human rights action plan is lodged with the President Human Rights Committee (PHRC) – an executive office.[152] An examination of previous national human rights action plans emanating from the PHRC shows the inclusion of specific chapters on economic, social, and cultural rights, but these do not make explicit endorsements on crafting a NAP to integrate the Guiding Principles. The Third National Human Rights Action Plan covering 2018–2022 loosely frames the scheme for progress and development using the International Covenant on Economic, Social, and Cultural Rights and Sustainable Development Goals.[153]

The role that businesses play in the Philippines' national development goals is not directly addressed by the national human rights plan, thereby leaving a huge gap as to acknowledging the human rights impact of these businesses. On top of the top-down formulation of the national human rights plan, other policy instruments of national scope like the Philippine Development Plan do not expressly tackle the reality of gross violations of human rights aided or facilitated by business enterprises. Additionally, the absence of a human rights policy within the Revised Corporation Code feeds into the state's deflection of Business and Human Rights issues on the ground. As a result, the Guiding Principle's fundamental recommendation to lay down coordinate processes for prevention, mitigation and remediation of business-related human rights abuses is sidelined, if not spurned. A key institutional deficiency of this scale affects the Philippine state's fulfilment both of its international human rights obligations and the full enforcement of the robust constitutional framework on human rights. In effect, the state may run the risk of defeating its constitution's own goal of effecting distributive justice.[154]

Recognising the extent to which business operations have affected the fulfilment of the state's human rights obligations is necessary in considering present laws and remedies for breaches of human rights. Commentaries to the second pillar of the Guiding Principles articulate this benchmark: 'the responsibility to respect human rights is a global standard of expected conduct for all business enterprises wherever they operate.'[155] Yet because the Philippines has not concretely integrated the Guiding Principles in a single policy plan, it cannot be fully determined if existing institutions and processes are sufficient to deal with the human rights impacts of business activities.

[151] Asia Centre (n 8) 14.

[152] Administrative Order No. 163, 'Strengthening and Increasing the Membership of the Presidential Human Rights Committee, and Expanding Further the Functions of Said Committee' (8 December 2006).

[153] President Human Rights Committee, 'An Agenda for Protecting Human Lives, Uplifting Human Dignity, & Advancing People's Progress: The Philippines Human Rights Action Plan 2018–2022' (President Human Rights Committee, 2018).

[154] Chopra (n 73) 308.

[155] Guiding Principles, Pillar II (n 35).

The sampling of legal disputes filed in Philippine courts paints a sufficiently clear picture of how corporations and enterprises infringe on the rights of individuals in different ways. Extractive industries have resulted in a host of violations of life, liberty and property and corporate employment regulations may result in discrimination or even exploitation. Civil litigation strategies and the wider public interest litigation and advocacy culture in the Philippines – while contemporarily vigorous – may suffer in the long term once they are met with the outer limits of the available remedies and legal frameworks.

Nevertheless, it is important to note the significant policy milestones that have arisen out of strategic human rights cases concerning private industries. For instance, the Philippine Congress is the first legislative body in the world to take up a bill providing for a 'legal framework for climate loss and damage accountability.'[156] The proposed Climate Accountability Act (CLIMA), if it passes into law, will 'opens up the possibility for corporate climate accountability' as a pioneering measure. Legislative push for CLIMA partially finds its origins in the 'Carbon Majors' petition before the CHR and the wider trend of climate litigation elsewhere in the world.[157] Creating tangible policies and laws in this way would ensure that the more creative legal strategies initially taken up by civil society would not end up as pyrrhic nor symbolic victories.

V. Conclusion

Lawyers and litigants alike have relied on innovative legal strategies to secure favourable judicial decisions that address different human rights issues. Gaining such positive legal outcomes still rely on the courts' ability and willingness to make reasonable, rights-based interpretations of law that go beyond the rigid and traditional conception of human rights. The state action doctrine that relies on the public-private divide remains a cornerstone in Philippine human rights law, albeit narrow exceptions being carved out in several cases.[158]

In the areas of the environment, labour, and – to a limited extent – gender, the Supreme Court has shown its disposition to adopt the language of human rights as against private enterprise. The reality persists that that business and human rights concepts and the Guiding Principles themselves remain 'implied' within various instruments and policies.[159] At the same time, judicial or quasi-judicial remedies are fragmented and are not bound by uniform practice. Crafting solid legal frameworks that directly tackle corporate accountability for human rights violations must be in lockstep with enriching mechanisms for redress then appears to be the way forward, where both processes fortify each other. This way, the area of business and human rights in the Philippines may be able to intersect with the state's enduring and overarching framework of social justice.

[156] Greenpeace, 'Philippine Congress Files World's First Climate Accountability Bill' (*Greenpeace Philippines*, 4 December 2024) www.greenpeace.org/philippines/press/63109/philippine-congress-files-worlds-first-climate-accountability-bill/.

[157] E Bradeen, T Chan and C Higham, 'Philippines Climate Accountability Bill: Loss and Damage in Domestic Legislation' (*LSE Grantham Research Institute on Climate Change and the Environment*) www.lse.ac.uk/granthaminstitute/news/philippines-climate-accountability-bill-loss-and-damage-in-domestic-legislation/.

[158] Pangalangan (n 18) 107.

[159] Asia Centre (n 8) 38.

10

Thailand

SHAATI CHANDRAMOUR

The theme of this book and the topic of this chapter set this author two challenging tasks, namely to write about the current scene and to write about the future scene of the subject matter at hand. This author claims the relevance and the worthiness of the future scene due to the uncertain coverage of human rights and the interactions of multinationals either from paradigmatic, positional, and material perspectives. In other words, human rights in this chapter are defined to broadly cover both abstract and concrete ideas of human rights, and both present and future sets of rules, norms and practices. There may be a comprehensive discussion which subsists beyond positive law. For example, this author posits a thesis on the commonality between democracy and consumer protection. While both concepts are undoubtedly applied in two distinct areas of public and private law, they are distinct from one other but are overridden by broad homocentric considerations. The two terms are only instrumental for the communication of such an idea into language. To place this in a legal academic context, this author would like to translate both abstract and concrete ideas of human rights into three main questions, which are discussed in this chapter. How do human rights overarch the application of law either from a philosophical or policy point of view? Where are human rights located hierarchically prior to their operation? Finally, can and how do human rights directly complete and/or complement substantive rules and norms?

Human rights may interact with aspects of multinationals in a variety of scenes, where commitments incurred by these actors come centripetally from directions regardless of soft or hard normative values. The present landscape of law requires these actors to be mindful of human rights internally and externally, privately and publicly, substantively and procedurally, and economically and non-economically, among other spectra. In legal disciplines, the interrelationship can be found especially in, but not limited to, international economic law, domestic public law (constitutional and administrative law), international commercial law, conflict of laws, and civil and commercial law, all of which are connected to the main idea of this chapter and are quite relevant to Thailand, at least from this author's point of view. In effect, the extent of the discussion can go beyond the main instrument of this book, the United Nations Guiding Principles on Business and Human Rights (UNGPs), and perhaps can be fragmented into monographs, depending on the perspective writers may be taking. In other words, although the comprehensive framework of the UNGPs is able to deal with legal problems, a wide range of legal issues should be subjected to more specific dialogues.

Admitting the extent and limit of the UNGPs, together with the dynamism of the subject matter, human rights and corporations in a cross-border context, this author insists on using this instrument as a starting point for the discussion. Further steps discuss the instrument together with comparable efforts, and then mention the regulatory framework, and whether it exists or not.

I. The Soft Rules within a Domestic Context

A. The Development of the Domestic Framework

The UNGPs was officially recognised in the country soon after its conception. As per the Human Rights Council Resolution 17/4 adopted in 16 June 2011, the Human Rights Council of Thailand expressly held the instrument as a guiding framework for interventions against human rights violations as a result of business operation. The implementation of this global instrument is not possible without the assistance of some authority whereby the principles could be properly contextualised in this ecosystem from abstract and concrete points of view. In this regard, the Department of Rights and Liberties Protection (DRLP), Ministry of Justice, was assigned by the Thai cabinet on 31 January 2017 to take up the role as the central agency to transform ideas, concepts and principles into domestic possibilities, which may publish its final version in either hard or soft instrument, or either legal or non-legal measure.[1] The primary task of this authority is to draft the National Action Plan (NAP) on business and human rights. During the few years after its designation, the DRLP quickly arranged studies, meetings, and seminars. Collaborations and contributions were obtained from a variety of public and private sectors, including public officers, legal practitioners, academics, international organisation officers, and business operators, among others. The DRLP finally found the proper model for the country as evidenced in the issuance of the First National Action Plan on Business and Human Rights (NAP), which was enacted on 29 October BE2562 (2019). This domestic instrument was effective from BE2562 (2019) to BE2565 (2022). Thanks to the expedient processing by the central agency in conjunction with other collaborators, Thailand has become the first country in Asia to transpose the UNGPs into its domestic framework.[2] The Second National Action Plan on Business and Human Rights ensued in BE 2566 (2023). This is effective during 2023 and 2027.

Both the First and the Second NAPs cover the three pillars as specified in the UNGPs, which concerns State, Business and Remediation. The current NAP, the second, contains 168 pages, which are covered in four chapters:[3]

- First Chapter – Historical Background.
- Second Chapter – Drafting Process of the Second NAP.
- Third Chapter – Core Content of the Second NAP.
- Fourth Chapter – Supervision, Monitoring, Reporting and Evaluation.

The second NAP does not differ from the first. Both NAPs address four key issues, which include:

- Labour;
- Community, Land, Natural Resources and the Environment;

[1] First National Action Plan on Business and Human Rights (2019–2022).

[2] See www.undp.org/asia-pacific/bizhumanrights/publications/first-national-action-plan-business-and-human-rights-thailand.

[3] Second National Action Plan on Business and Human Rights (2023–2027).

- Human Rights Defenders; and
- Cross-Border Investments and Multinational Enterprises.

The priority given to these four areas is not a coincidence, but a result of deliberations by the draftsmen, relying on the current situation in the country. While the first three are domestic by nature, the last is transnational and definitely related to the main idea of this chapter. The coverage of human rights interventions for the last should not be understood to be limited by the scope of the first three key issues. In other words, human rights as a subject of protection for the last issue, in a transnational context, may be detailed and protected far beyond the first three issues. For example, if the process of assessing human rights due diligence is being conducted within a transnational corporation, all possibilities of human rights violations, not only the issues of labour, environment and human rights defenders, are counted in such a procedural requirement.

Of much relevance is that the NAPs are made in alignment with other pre-existing and surrounding instruments. These are the National Strategy BE 2561-2580 (2018–2037), the Reform Plan, the 13th National Economic and Social Development Plan BE 2566-2570 (2023–2027), the National Security Policy and Plan BE 2566-2570 (2023–2027), and the 3rd Human Rights Plan BE 2566-2570 (2023–2027). International instruments were also observed when the NAPs were being drafted. These include the Sustainable Development Goals, the Universal Periodic Review, the ratified multilateral human rights conventions (such as the ICCPR,[4] the CRC[5] and the CEDAW[6]), and other globally renowned instruments (such as the OECD Guidelines for Multinational Enterprises), among others.

There are no new general concepts in the First and Second NAPs. It is not an exaggeration to describe the instruments as old wine in a new bottle. The only difference is the elaboration of the code of conduct assumed by business operators.

B. Social and Structural Coherence

The UNGPs is a broad framework containing good practices to protect human rights in the course of business operation. This global instrument appears to bridge the two distinct disciplines, business and human rights, which used to be treated as separate institutions of law and were governed by different sets of rules and norms in the modern ages of the Thai legal system concerning its reception of western legal products. Briefly speaking, the traditions of the civil law system and the dual-court system[7] of the country, which partition law into disciplines and subject them to distinct procedures, require the translation of human rights into the language of the individual sets of rules and norms. In other words, the treatment of human rights in a transnational business context requires multidimensional processes of collaboration of public and private sectors in the country. Of course, in doing so, one could anticipate some challenges in the course of the aforesaid bridging of the two institutions, which will be detailed in the following sections.

It is not an overstatement to characterise the country's reaction to this instrument as responsive and enthusiastic. There are a series of seminars, workshops, and studies that have been

[4] 1966 International Covenant on Civil and Political Rights.

[5] 1989 Convention on the Rights of the Child.

[6] 1979 Convention on the Elimination of All Forms of Discrimination against Women.

[7] Please see further in C Boonyawan and A Phetsiri, 'Legislative Process of Thailand: An Historical Perspective' in S Thanitcul and S Imaizumi (eds), *Legislative Process in Thailand: Qualitative and Quantitative Analysis* (The Institute of Developing Economies, Japan External Trade Organization (JETRO) of Japan and the Faculty of Law, Chulalongkorn University Thailand, 2010) 71–73.

arranged in order to raise awareness and prepare public and private sectors to serve as collaborators and catalysts for the implementation of this instrument in the domestic sphere.[8]

As a soft law instrument, the UNGPs enables the country to exercise its discretion to transpose the principles contained in the instrument into domestic legal measures. The public sectors do not confront the bottleneck in terms of the dualistic approach of the country,[9] which usually requires some necessary steps before its accession or ratification to legally binding instruments, such as treaties, conventions, etc. Primarily, this may concern the provision of the Constitution, Section 178,[10] which requires approval by parliament of the treaties, the implementation of which is to be done through the enactment and enforcement of a legislative act. For example, some human rights conventions may require criminal sanctions, which necessarily make up part of the enforcement of a legislative act. Second, for some kinds of treaties, which do not fall into the Section 178 category, the final decision to accede or ratify may be preceded by deliberations of the incumbent Ministries as well as of the Cabinet. Working groups may be established, public hearings may be arranged, and other processes may be realized, dependent on the subject matter of such a treaty.

From a formal point of view, the UNGPs does not face these procedural hurdles. In other words, the DRLP is given much space and time to proceed with its own plans whereby the global instrument is to be contextualised in the domestic system. Legal and non-legal measures are to be crafted upon deliberations by the domestic authorities. In this sense, subsidiarity is satisfied, which may make a soft law instrument even more powerful than a hard law instrument.

From a substantive point of view, human rights can be appreciated in the societal contexts of the country. It is claimed that the abstractness of human rights can find its accommodation in the east no less so than in the west.[11] This author claims that the east accepts human rights more readily than the west. Considering the timeframe, it took hundreds of years for the acclimatisation of human rights concepts and principles to take place in the west, most of the eastern concepts took less than half a century. The introduction of western philosophy may speed up the process. But

[8] For arrangements before the launch of the first NAP, please see The First NAP (n 1) 3. For relevant activities thereafter, please see, eg, www.manushyafoundation.org/coalition-building-workshop-report; www.freiheit.org/southeast-and-east-asia/business-and-human-rights-training-parliamentarians-and-political-party; www.ilo.org/meetings-and-events/thailand-training-social-dialogue-decent-work-and-human-rights-due.

[9] Please compare จตุรนต์ ถิระวัฒน์, *กฎหมายระหว่างประเทศ* (พิมพ์ครั้งที่ 3, วิญญูชน 2555) 78–79. (J Tirawat, *International Law*, 3rd edn (Winyuchon BE2555, 2012) 78–79.]

[10] Section 178. 'The King has the Royal Prerogative to conclude a peace treaty, armistice, and other treaties with other countries or international organisations.

Any treaty which provides for a change in Thai territories or external territories over which Thailand has sovereign right or jurisdiction under a treaty or international law, or which requires the enactment of an Act for implementation, and other treaties which may have wide scale effects on the security of economy, society, or trade or investment of the country must be approved by the National Assembly. In this regard, the National Assembly shall complete its consideration within sixty days as from the date of receipt of such matter.

If the National Assembly does not complete the consideration within such period of time, it shall be deemed that the National Assembly has given approval.

Other treaties which may have wide scale effects on the security of economy, society, or trade or investment of the country under paragraph two are treaties pertaining to free trade, common customs union, or the authorisation of natural resources utilisation, or which cause the country to lose rights over natural resources, in whole or in part, or on any other treaties provided by law.

There shall also be a law prescribing procedures for the public to participate in the expression of opinions and to obtain necessary remedy from the effects of conclusion of a treaty under paragraph three.

Where a question arises as to whether any treaty constitutes a case under paragraph two or paragraph three, the Council of Ministers may request the Constitutional Court to render a decision thereon. The Constitutional Court shall complete its decision within thirty days as from the date of receipt of such request.'

[11] L Henkin, 'The Universality of the Concept of Human Rights' (1989) 506 *The Annals of the American Academy of Political and Social Science* 14–15.

there are also other inherent factors. Notably, the embeddedness of religions in eastern societies supports rather than contests the abstractness of human rights. Of course, there are incoherence and inconsistency between the two institutions. That is to say, a reasoning based on human rights may challenge aspects of religions and vice versa. But coherence and consistency seem to take hold in many respects, and hence human rights concepts and principles can be transformed into parts of the domestic law of the east. Though admittedly the west has a more developed and structured system that monitors and enforces human rights,[12] the observation of the east is based on a sociological point of view for the purpose of discussion in this chapter.

This author concurs with the statement above. While not agreeing with situations in other eastern jurisdictions, this author insists that the description above is valid for Thailand. Human rights gain collective consciousness in the country if one observes from past to present, and from one sector to another. Some examples are selected especially for an external audience to appreciate the scene in this spatial limit.

The historic landmark widely known to the domestic and external audience may be the emancipation of slaves by King Rama V,[13] which was achieved with neither violence nor civil war. The best interest of the child, a concept which it is claimed was developed by the west especially in US case law,[14] and which was then transformed into an internationally recognised principle,[15] was practised in Thailand more than a century before its appearance in the CRC. Something similar to BHR has been realised in a project of the Ministry of Industry in that the incentive for environment and human rights protection is increased through the awarding systems.[16] The country's justice fund is the landmark project launched by the Ministry of Justice with the aim to assist the people with the financially limited access to the judicial process.[17] The recent enactment of the marriage equality bill is also proof of the country's reaction to the marginalisation of gender minorities.[18] The work of the judiciary is also evident. From time to time, the Court explicitly references human rights principles in solidifying its arguments in deciding cases.[19]

From the observation of this author, the awareness of human rights by private individuals and corporations came later than the public authorities. It is much increased at the moment as attributable to three leading factors, at least as claimed by this author. First, social media plays a leading role in breaking both sides, the service provider and the consumer, from maltreating one another. Second, the economic gain or loss of a company as a result of human rights violations in a variety of forms is contemplated more by such a company in relation to the treatment of internal and external people. For example, the probability of being sued is reduced if the company exercises due diligence on the employees or on the possible effects of its business operation to

[12] This can be attested at least by the existence of the US Supreme Court and of the European Court of Human Rights, which have entertained a high degree of compliance and respect.

[13] DM Engel, *Law and Kingship in Thailand During the Reign of King Chulalongkorn* (Ann Arbor, University of Michigan Press, 2020) 96–98.

[14] LM Kohm, 'Tracing the Foundations of the Best Interests of the Child Standard in American Jurisprudence' (2008) 10 *Journal of Law and Family Studies* 1, 3.

[15] ibid 15.

[16] The first award was given in 2003, which precedes the BHR. Please see industryaward.industry.go.th/th/source.

[17] Please see info.go.th/procedure/94e56d2d-155f-460b-8a0e-c1219b6a4703/view?lat=&lng=; thailand.go.th/issue-focus-detail/001_01_233.

[18] S Pongruengphant, 'Thailand's Marriage Equality: A Huge Step, But the Journey Continues' (*UNDP Thailand*, 13 February 2025) www.undp.org/thailand/blog/marriage-equality-law-journey#:~:text=Thailand%20just%20made%20history!,social%20transformation%20towards%20true%20inclusion. The law has made Thailand the first country in Southeast Asia that recognises the LGBTI family status as equal to the hetero couple.

[19] SCJ720/2515, for example, recognises the right to establish family of the stateless persons. ACJ18776/2561 recognises the marital status of a same-sex couple, which was established abroad. The decision was rendered before the enactment of the marriage equality act.

external people nearby. Costs in business operation can be reduced accordingly. This suggests that humanist considerations can be linked to the economic stability of the company.[20] Third, religion plays an important role. As a Buddhist society, the rule of karma is usually asserted by one against another,[21] and respecting human rights finds resonance with such a concept.

The systems of the Environmental, Social and Governance (ESG) and the Human Rights Due Diligence have gained traction with business operators since they are now having real implications. The ESG is assessed by banks usually when the loan is requested by a company. Non-compliance with the ESG standard could lead to problems in the process of injecting funds. The human rights due diligence as required by the UNGPs, Principle 17, is currently implemented by the Securities and Exchange Commission (SEC) through a soft mode of regulation. That is to say, sanctions may be realised by the shareholders when non-compliance with a human rights standard by the company is shown in the Form 56-1 One Report. In the meantime, this author is unaware of disputes brought to the Court in relation to misalignments under either of the systems.

Admittedly, there are some aspects of human rights that are considered to be big challenges in the country. Criticism of the situation in Thailand usually revolves around certain subject matters, including freedom of expression, assembly right, forced disappearance, and attacks on the activists.[22]

C. Thailand as an Emerging Economy: Host and Home State?

When the term 'multinationals' appears, some early questions may revolve around the definition and aspects of 'multinationals', and questions concerning the regulatory framework may come later. 'Multinational' involves a company the corporate structure of which has contact with more than one jurisdiction. Hence, some situations which seem to be those of multinationals, but actually are not, should be excluded otherwise the scope of discussion would be too broad. For example, certain international transactions including an international sales contract, an international distributorship contract, a payment transaction, and a carriage of goods by any cross-border means, is not to be discussed in this chapter. The corporate structure is the standpoint for a company to be multinational. At this point, there are two types of multinationals involved, namely multinationals in Thailand and Thai multinationals in a foreign country.

The first one, multinationals in Thailand or foreign direct investments, has been apparent for quite some time. As a third world country, similar to its neighbours in Southeast Asia and other developing nations, Thailand is known as a host of foreign direct investments, and the number of foreign direct investments is seen as a good indicator for the economic growth of the country. Recent decades have seen the new face of Thailand as a sender of foreign direct investments or as a home state, as the jargon suggests.[23] The number of Thai multinationals is increasing significantly as evidenced in statistics. It is one of the largest outward investors in Southeast Asia.[24]

[20] Please compare, eg, K Marslev, *Doing Well by Doing Right?: Exploring the Potentials and Limitations of a Business Case for Human Rights* (The Danish Institute for Human Rights, Denmark's National Human Rights Institution, 2020) 23–24; The Jakarta Post, 'Human Rights Violations Can Be Costly for Business' (Jakarta, 14 June 2013) www.thejakartapost.com/news/2013/06/14/human-rights-violations-can-be-costly-business.html.

[21] J Leeka, 'The Role of Karma in Thai Society: A Philosophical and Socio-Political Analysis' (2024) 1(3) *Journal of Modern Academic Social Science* (Online) 64, 66.

[22] www.hrw.org/world-report/2024/country-chapters/thailand.

[23] Please see JW Salacuse, *The Three Laws of International Investment: National, Contractual, and International Frameworks for Foreign Capital* (Oxford, Oxford University Press, 2013) 22.

[24] https://thailand.opendevelopmentmekong.net/topics/foreign-direct-investment-in-thailand/. Foreign direct investments from Thailand are usually found in Cambodia, Laos, Myanmar, and Vietnam.

The outgoing capital of Thai multinationals covers a range of business sectors, namely medical services, chemical industries, construction services, hospitality and hotel management, property management, and banking industry, among others. This has caused the country to rethink its vision and the current system. In the meantime, the soft mode of regulating the subject matter is realised in the NAP. Further development should also be made for the hard law, and this is clearly relevant to the operation of the conflicts mechanism. While a lawsuit is brought against the Thai multinational Mitrphol trying to invest in Cambodia, in the *Mitrphol* case, the court is confronted with the insufficiency of conflicts rules applicable to the legal problems at hand.

II. The Transposition of Human Rights Principles or Concepts in the Legal Mechanism of the Country

The previous section evaluated the possibility of having the UNGPs integrated into the country. This author finds the situation quite positive, considering the responses from both public authorities as well as business sectors. This section explores the legal mechanism inside the country. Subsection A discusses the existence of basic rights as per the awareness of the country. Subsection B shifts to talk about practices in the judicial mechanism. As a former human rights activist, this author claims that it does not suffice to mention the judicial mechanism in order to reflect real situations. The mechanisms to enhance human rights protections involve the operation of various public authorities as well as private arrangements. The judicial mechanism is stressed here. Since it is the ultimate source of authority, judicial decisions usually gain traction by both public authorities and private sectors.

A. The Ascertainment of the Basic Rights in the Legal System

In the Thai legal system, it is hard to name a term which represents the entire concept being discussed here. Human rights itself is not enough as a connotation. From the observation of this author, the ideas and objects of the UNGPs are more than a thin version of human rights. When reference is made to the thin version of human rights, this author actually means those that are contained in the human rights instruments. These instruments are the global achievement as a result of relentless negotiations and arrangements by diplomats, international organisation officers, and other participants. Hence, one should bear in mind limits of law making in such a global platform, where a principle or concept is not to be conjured at whim. In addition, the existing rights can be more detailed, modified, and repealed. New rights can be further developed, and not only from the global arena. To reflect the real objective of the UNGPs as well as the trajectories of the country, this author prefers to use the terms 'thick version of human rights' and 'basic rights.' However, he confesses his irritation over both terms and finds that there may be a better one to replace them in the future.

To render the analysis more precise, one may begin the discussion by having a close look at the rights, the rules, and the concepts as they appear in both written and unwritten sources of law and later have a glimpse of other rights, rules, and concepts which are evolving. The thick version of human rights, so to speak, may be contained in, but not limited to, human rights treaties,[25] humanitarian law instruments, labour rights instruments (especially of the ILO), and

[25] For example, ICCPR, CEDAW, and CRC, which have been mentioned.

environmental law treaties. Also, of relevance are those that are claimed as customary international law or general principles of law. These are considered to be rules of hard law. It should be noted that, in this chapter, mention may be made of some topics that are not directly related to human rights, but are of relevance. Environmental law, for example, is not a discipline or a branch of human rights law. But, when some rules or provisions as contained in international or domestic environmental regulations are breached, the violation of human rights occurs as a consequence.

The constitutional appearance of basic rights requires much attention because in many cases it can lead to real protection in the country in a better way than its mere existence in an international instrument. The basic rights as they appear in the treaties are reflected in the Constitution of Thailand. For example, the right to non-discrimination (Section 27), the right to life (Section 28), the right to privacy (Section 32), and the freedom of expression (Section 34) are the reflections of the ICCPR, Articles 26, 19 and 17.

For the reiteration of basic rights in the Constitution, mention should be made on a limit of the Constitution of the country. Unlike the Basic Law of Germany (Grundgesetz), the Thai Constitution does not have its part containing elaborate provisions describing the basic rights of all human beings. Only Section 4-5 of the Constitution provides for a very broad idea of protecting human beings. Section 4 paragraph 1 reads, '[[h]uman dignity, rights, liberties and equality of the people shall be protected.' Section 5 paragraph 2 reads, '[w]henever no provision under this Constitution is applicable to any case, an act shall be performed or a decision shall be made in accordance with the constitutional conventions of Thailand under the democratic regime of government with the King as Head of State.' Briefly speaking, Section 4 contains the general idea of human rights as applicable to all human beings without elaborate provisions. Section 5 indicates the 'constitutional conventions' as a source of rules, norms and practices. The term 'constitutional conventions' is translated from 'ประเพณีทางปกครองของประเทศไทย', which can be transliterated rather as 'Thai administrative customs', but since this term is put in the constitutional text, its location suggests the constitutional rank of such customs or conventions.

Perhaps to the surprise of non-Thai readers, the elaborate provisions on basic rights (human or fundamental rights) are contained in Chapter III, which is titled 'Rights and Liberties of the Thai People.' When reading all provisions in this Chapter, one may appreciate a parallel version of international human rights rules. They are unfortunately elaborate provisions for the Thai people, not for human beings in general.

The explicit separation between the rights and liberties of the Thai people, and those of human beings (regardless of the nationality) has some implications. First, when the subject is Thai, the elaborate provision simply applies to the case. But, if the subject is foreign, whether and which rule is applicable is necessarily subjected to interpretation, and there are a number of ways to do this, which are namely to apply Chapter III provisions analogously, to seek general principles of law, to reference the constitutional conventions, and/or to employ rules of international law for Section 4 interpretation.[26] This suggests that the Constitutional Court or other public authorities have a range of discretion to choose an applicable rule when the legal problem at hand concerns rights of a foreigner. There can be a normal case in which victims of human rights violation are residing abroad. And, a further inquiry may be whether such constitutional rules, albeit not yet

[26] This may be compared with the Constitutional Court Ruling No 12/2555 (2012), which involves the reference of the relevant rules under the ICCPR and UDHR for the application of the presumption of innocence principle as acknowledged by Section 39 of the Constitution BE 2555 (2012). Although this case is not the dispute of a foreigner, such application is logical and possible. As a useful fact for non-Thai readers, Thailand has not ratified the Optional Protocol to the ICCPR, which would give the authority of investigation to the ICCPR Committee. As a result, the Constitutional Court has its full authority to review the consistency of legislations with the ICCPR. The same applies to other human rights treaties. Other Optional Protocols, for example, to the CEDAW and the CRC are opted out of by the country. In this regard, the Constitutional Court has the role of protecting constitutional rights as well as human rights.

clarified, have a long reach to intervene in the human rights violation that occurs in a foreign country.

An interesting, yet peculiar question is, whether it is logical to reference constitutional rules of a foreign country. The quick answer is negative. The role of the Thai Court to apply a foreign law is given by the source of authority, which is the Conflict of Laws Act BE 2481 (1938), and applicable foreign rules are restrained only by the substantive rules applicable to the private law relationship. In most of the cases, this concerns foreign substantive or conflicts rules applicable to the legal problem. Foreign constitutional rules can be relevant if it has already been transformed into a legislative provision, and the Thai conflicts rules allow the application of such a (foreign) legislative provision. If this is the case, some foreign constitutional rules, the source of transformation, may be employed to interpret the legislative provision(s) at hand. Humbly admitted that a clearer and better concept of human rights may exist in a foreign constitution, and its reference can be of relevance in resolving the cases of multinationals submitted to the Thai Court, but yet the Thai Court does not have the authority to directly refer to it due to the structural limit as just explained. If this idea (compare the constitutional provisions of both countries, and pick a better one) may be useful in practice, the second version of the UNGPs or a future treaty may elaborate on this concept. In other words, the suggested operation in the domestic mechanism can be rendered from the level of international law.

Notwithstanding some limits as already mentioned, it is fortunate, at least, that these explicit rules as they appear in the Constitution can be referenced directly by the Constitutional Court, the Administrative Court, and the Court of Justice.

A bottleneck in the country is the horizontal effects or third effects[27] of constitutional rules, or, so to say, the reference of constitutional rules for the private law relationship. This is an ongoing debate in the country. There are affirmation and opposition from both academics and practitioners as to the existence of such horizontal effects. Some jurisdictions, such as Germany, admit the existence of horizontal effects while academic views are split into two, namely those that endorse direct effects, and those that endorse only indirect effects of constitutional rules.[28] The usage of horizontal effects could help the attorney and/or the judge to construct a solid argument especially when the relevant legislative provision does not exist or exist in an ambiguous form, and hence an abstract rule such as constitutional provision should be employed for a better application or interpretation of law. Given that further investigation on horizontal effects in the country is required, there are both cases that overlook the idea and those that explicitly accept it.

In SCJ4893/2558 (2015), the plaintiff attorney pleaded the constitutional rule (Constitution BE2540 (1997), Section 34) as a basis for the tort claim concerning the violation of the right to privacy, which does not appear in any elaborate provision of the CCC. The Supreme Court does not affirm any such constitutional/ third effect, but rather applies the default rule of tort under the CCC, Section 420, and awards the plaintiff the compensation. Although referencing the Constitution, Section 34 can solidify the argument of the Court, this is finally abandoned. Another case gives a positive answer to the third effects of constitution. In ACJ18776/2561 (2018), the civil partnership status of a homosexual couple established under the English law was recognised by the Appellate Court. The Court applies Sections 4 and 27 of the Thai Constitution BE 2560 (2017), which concerns non-discrimination on the basis of sex. Further, the Court refers to the Universal Declaration of Human Rights (UDHR) to affirm its endorsement of non-discriminatory rules.

[27] F Hufen, *Staatrecht II: Grundrecht* (Munich, CH Beck, 2009) 101; CD Classen, 'Die Drittwirkung der Grundrechte in der Rechtsprechung des Bundesverfassungsgerivhts' (1997) 122(1) *Archiv des offentlichen Rechts* 65, 65; P Badura, *Staatsrecht, Systematische Erläuterung des Grundgesetzes* (Munich, CH Beck, 2003) 110.

[28] ibid.

As evidenced in the recent case, the employment of constitutional rules for clarifications in private law relationships is possible at this stage of legal practice. The overriding factor is unavoidably the consciousness of individual judges, which can lead to an affirmative or negative result, and this can cause uncertainty as asserted in the two cases above that split away their judicial reasoning.

The abstract nature of constitutional rules should be briefly mentioned, which is relevant to this author's further discussions. Constitutional rules, or even human rights rules (in constitutional provisions) can definitely be useful, as previously mentioned. But, in context, the abstract nature of constitutional rules usually prevents judges from reaching a single direction. The principle of non-discrimination based on gender and sex may cast doubt, for example, on whether private law should be aware of only direct discrimination or both direct and indirect forms[29] of discrimination, and many other problems. The cases that concern interaction between two or three constitutional sets of rules, which are at opposite sides of the spectrum can be a difficult task for the Court, such as the balance of natural resources conservation and of community rights, concerning the provisions of Sections 43 and 57. Therefore, the way in which ways of referencing constitutional or human rights rule can lead to certain results requires further consideration by the Court. The long-term development of the system is necessary while the present solution already exists.

B. Interventions against the Violation of Basic Rights Committed by Multinationals

Basic rights can be claimed and interventions can operate in a number of mechanisms, including the Constitutional Court, the Administrative Court, the Special Committees, the Public Authorities, and even the Private Sectors. Emphasis is placed on the judicial mechanism by the Court of Justice of the country, with a discussion of other mechanisms only if any of them are involved in some aspect of the intervention. In the judicial procedure itself, there can be a variety of cases concerning basic rights violations, which can be submitted thereto. These are namely general tort, product liability, labour rights abuses, corruption, discrimination, environmental damage, and privacy rights claims, among others. Each concerns a particular set of problems, answerable by distinct rules and provisions. Some types of litigations are briefly exemplified below before the analyses of rules.

The first hypothetical example concerns the liability of products imported from a foreign country which have caused injuries to consumers in Thailand, and so a class action is instituted. The plaintiffs find it necessary to have the parent company located in the foreign country as a defendant, and to have some foreign laws applicable to some problems in making their case successfully because the foreign law perhaps explicitly accepts psychological damage as a result of the product liability, while the issue is very controversial in Thailand[30] and the mere application of Thai law may not lead to the coverage of adequate remedies. In this case, human rights may be consulted as a ground for extending the liability to the parent company based on its own law.

[29] J Clifford, 'Equality' in D Shelton (ed), *The Oxford Handbook of International Human Rights Law* (Oxford, Oxford University Press, 2013) 438.

[30] วารี นาสกุล, *คำอธิบายกฎหมายแพ่งและพาณิชย์ ลักษณะละเมิด จัดการงานนอกสั่ง และลาภมิควรได้* (พิมพ์ครั้งที่ 5, บริษัท กรุงสยาม พับลิชชิ่ง จำกัด 2563) 135–50. (W Nasakul, *Lecture on the Civil and Commercial Code: Tort, Management of Affairs without Mandate and Undue Enrichment* (Krungsiam Publishing BE 2563, 2020) 135–50.)

For the second hypothetical example, a transnational corporation has chosen Thailand as a host state for manufacturing its products because labour law and pollution control regulations in Thailand are much less strict than the law in its own country. As a result, the loosely regulated working conditions have caused a large number of employees to become severely sick with an incurable disease. The tort law of Thailand actually holds the employer responsible, but the awarded compensation is unreasonably low compared to that which would be awarded by the law of the country where the parent company is incorporated.

The third hypothetical example is similar to the second. Unlike the second, this example is real and concerns a Thai multinational Mitrphol, which has its subsidy in Cambodia. Its subsidy obtained a concession from the Cambodian government to build a sugar factory. Reportedly, the installation of the factory has caused deforestation by fire and other means, and also the displacement of humans and animals. Hundreds of villagers are the victims as a result of the establishment of the Mitrphol subsidy. The victims decided to bring a lawsuit against the parent company in Thailand.

Hypothetical example number four concerns a bank in Thailand which provides a loan for a Thai multinational which is reportedly involved with an industry that produces weapons used in civil wars in Myanmar. This story is actually reported in the news,[31] yet there is no claim brought in the Thai Court or elsewhere. What if the claim is brought by the victims against the Thai multinational as well as the Thai bank? Are both considered to be wrongful and hence liable together for the injuries as a result of the civil war? Suppose that this case is brought to the Thai Court some decades in the future, and the Thai tort law holds the corporation and the bank jointly liable?

Consider that all four hypothetical examples are litigations instituted in Thailand. The first two are similar in that they are claims against foreign transnational corporations, which have been brought to the Thai Court. The third and fourth examples concern Thai multinationals that have invested in a foreign country. As mentioned above, these claims are distinct by nature, and are subject to different sets of conflicts and substantive rules.

Notwithstanding such a distinction, on this premise, where the so-called thick version of human rights is taking hold in the process of applying conflicts and substantive rules, as the theme of this volume and this chapter claim, the straight application of conflict rules may not be a good choice for the settlement of these four examples, or others. Admittedly, the CLA has been enacted for almost 100 years, the draftsmen obviously were not aware of legal problems of multinationals, and this legislative act does not contain any provision which is employable for the cases of multinationals. The application of the existing old rules may lead to an unfair decision. For example, the double-actionability requirement as contained in the CLA, Section 15[32] could prevent a foreign law from its application to protect victims of human rights violations. The strict reliance on the prescription requirement as per the Thai domestic law may cause the defendant to gain an unfair advantage, as the case will be dismissed immediately.

Another direction is a favourite path for, so to speak, most human rights defenders found in groups of civil society, such as academics, lawyers, and even public authorities in all countries. This direction is to agree to all questions as regards direct and indirect interventions based on

[31] H Regan, K Olarn and M Mitsanas, 'Thailand Is Now the Myanmar Junta's Favored Banking Destination as Military Attacks Ramp up, UN Expert Says' (*CNN World*, 27 June 2024) edition.cnn.com/2024/06/27/asia/myanmar-junta-weapons-thailand-banks-intl-hnk.

[32] Please see further explanation in ชาติ จันทรามูร์, *คำอธิบายกฎหมายระหว่างประเทศแผนกคดีบุคคล* (โครงการตำราและเอกสารประกอบการสอน คณะนิติศาสตร์ มหาวิทยาลัยธรรมศาสตร์ 2568) 152. (S Chandramour, *Treatise on the Private International Law* (Treatise and Course Material Project, Faculty of Law, Thammasat University BE 2568, 2025) 152.)

hard or soft rules of human rights to all legal problems. This author coins the term, 'human-rights-trump-in-all-cases' solution, model or approach.

In the case of Thailand, this seems to be a radical approach, and it can be easily overturned by the Thai Court. This is because the judicial decision usually involves, apart from the application of law, the balance of interests and ideologies, which requires policy considerations. While European countries are cognisant of the margin of appreciation as asserted in the European Convention on Human Rights (ECHR), the Thai Court is unavoidably aware of public policy. This approach is also subject to the structural limit of the country. That is to say, the consultation of human rights in private law cases usually involves the identification and application of rules. There are cases where basic rights can be referenced by the Court of Justice for direct or indirect interventions in its deliberations for the problems of multinationals. There are also cases where basic rights can only be asserted through the review process of the Constitutional Court of Thailand, which could lead to a modification or a repeal of some provision(s) in the legislative act.[33] In addition, regard shall also be sufficiently paid to due process. The human-rights-trump-in-all-cases model may lead to a result-orientated ruling by the Court, which can shake due process and rule of law in the country. This is simply because a radically strong inclination towards the victims may prejudice the multinationals either from a conflict, procedural or substantive point of view.

The current stage of the country sees the situation of Normenmangel [de][34] or, for example, lack of conflicts and substantive norms for this subject matter. An efficient long-term solution is to amend the CLA to create a better version that provides more elaborate and functional rules and provisions for the Court. At the onset of developing such a legal model, it is necessary to assist the judiciary in developing a proper direction of judicial decisions, which is to be detailed below. As aforementioned, protection of human rights in this context is to find out the possibilities of valid interventions against human rights violations in the context of multinationals. While this academic work is trying to find or develop conflicts, substantive or procedural rules, it shall strike good balances from philosophical and policy perspectives.

III. Conflicts and Procedural Aspects of Law

A. Holding the Multinationals Accountable[35]

In the context of multinationals, human rights interventions through the judicial functioning may change the landscape of the Thai judiciary. As a system, the Court of Justice usually pursues some direction, and is required to consult a set of policies and laws. The UNGPs itself is not the hard law, which would task the country to do something in particular. But, when this soft law instrument is read with the national action plans, the domestic regulations, and the international commitments of the country, adjustments are necessary in the landscape of the judiciary.

[33] ธีระ สุธีวรางกูร, *คำ วินิจฉัยและผลของคำ วินิจฉัยของศาลรัฐธรรมนูญ* (กองทุนวิจัย คณะนิติศาสตร์ มหาวิทยาลัยธรรมศาสตร์ 2560) 108–11. (T Suteewarangkul, *Decisions of the Constitutional Court and their Effects* (Research Fund, Faculty of Law, Thammasat University BE 2560, 2017) 108–11.)

[34] Please compare J Kropholler, *Internationales Privatrecht: Einschließlich der Grundbegriffe des Internationalen Zivilverfahrensrechts* (Tübingen, Mohr Siebeck, 2006) 22.

[35] This subject matter is discussed elsewhere under the topic of attribution. Please see A Reyes, 'The Use of Domestic Law to Regulate the Conduct of Individuals, Corporations and Governments Extraterritorially' (2024) 441 *Recueil des Cours* 353, 367–409.

Here, emphasis is placed on an internationalist approach.[36] The reason of this rests on the logic that the country has international commitments under rules of public international law, and the violation of rules can lead to a state responsibility.[37] As a state organ, the Court is hence required to satisfy the rules of treaty, customary international law, and general principles of law.

Simply speaking, exercising of the judicial authority shall not cause Thailand to be liable or to be sued in any international tribunal. In this stage of analysis, this author proposes to split human rights interventions into two groups, namely those requiring or concerning clear involvements of the Thai Court (especially by the rules of international law) and those pertaining to an unclear circle. The first group includes, for example, human rights violations that incur the universal jurisdiction upon the Thai Court, and that concern explicit international commitments of Thailand vis-à-vis the human rights victims in the process of business operation by the multinationals. The second group usually gives a wide range of discretion to the judges to make decisions and, if necessary, to develop precedence.

For the first group, if the subsidiary of a Thai parent company is involved in an international crime taking place in a foreign country, the Thai Court can basically establish jurisdiction to hear the (civil) proceedings against the subsidiary and/or its parent company. For example, a Thai company has supplied weapons to the military junta in Myanmar, acknowledging the final usage of these weapons for a massacre. This scenario makes the basis for bringing the lawsuit against such the Thai company clear. The judicial direction of some cases remains unclear despite the universality of international crimes. For example, a Thai bank has lent money to a corporation in Myanmar despite insufficient compliance with human rights due diligence. It turns out that the foreign corporation is assisting in the process of killings.[38] Questions on *ratione materiae* and conflicts rules for this hypothetical scenario are left to judicial deliberations.

For the second group, this author references, as an example, the aforementioned second hypothetical example, which involves a foreign multinational that chose to establish a subsidiary in Thailand. Suppose that the health regulations of Thailand do not take precautions on the creeping adverse effects on health of the workers in the factory, which may occur after their retirement from the company, as it is too hard to prove the causation as required under the Thai tort law. Clearly, the human rights commitment of the country is unclear. Rules of public international law have not yet indemnified Thailand if the Thai Court has not applied the law of the home state of the company, which protects health of the workers better than the Thai law. Hence, the Thai Court obtains a range of discretion to decide the jurisdictional and the choice-of-law matters. In this regard, the UNGPs may be employed as a hortatory instrument while elaborate decisions can be of course be rendered by the Thai judges.

Apart from the international commitments of the country, an important prerequisite for Thailand, which can turn the case upside down, is possible alterations of embedded values the Thai judiciary pursues as a matter of course. This can concern a variety of topics from abstract to concrete questions. Should a cost allocation approach be employed more intensively in the

[36] It is a typical dialogue in conflicts scholarship that internationalism shall be balanced with unilateralism in some ways. While internationalism is easy to approximate, unilateralism is usually left for the Court to decide. The latter may be reliant on the public policy or the interests of the country. Another approach is functionalism that may involve the development of principles, rules and methods that lead to the long-term benefits of all while the ongoing process of developing such principles, rules and methods finds a good balance of all. For the discussion of internationalism and unilateralism, please see especially Y Loussouarn, P Bourel and P de Vareilles-Sommières, *Droit International Privé*, 10th edn (Paris, Dalloz, 2013) 126–43. For the functionalism or the functional analysis approach, please see A von Mehren, 'Choice-of-Law Theories and the Comparative-Law Problem' (1975) 23(4) *The American Journal of Comparative Law* 751, 755.

[37] Tirawat (n 9) 480–500.

[38] Regan, Olarn and Mitsanas (n 31).

process of deciding the liability of a corporation? What makes the threshold for holding the parent company liable for an action or omission of the subsidiary, which is located in a different country? Should the regime of awarding the remedies be changed? Should Thailand have a cross-border tort (substantive) legislation instead of conflicts rules? Should Thailand be inclined to take a business-friendly, victim-friendly approach, or fall somewhere in the middle?

Admittedly, in the meantime, the country does not have clear answers to these questions. As a result, in the context of applying conflicts rules, cases can turn out to be more complicated and the clients will face a lot of uncertainty, especially because the Court obtains a wide range of discretion to deliberate in steps of judicial procedure. The Court is bound to decide whether to finally apply the domestic or foreign law, and, if necessary, to decide whether and how to apply basic rules and principles in the judgment. In this stage of analysis, as proposed by this chapter, issues can be developed from two angles: from the victims' perspectives and from the multinationals' perspectives. These are discussed respectively in the following paragraphs.

From the victims' point of view, cost allocation or distribution[39] can be a fundamental question in most cases either from contractual or tortious aspects of multinational responsibilities, because a frequently asked question is usually how and to what extent the parent company can be held liable in a more extensive fashion. If this is possible, in all courses of multinational operation the victims can benefit from conflicts and substantive law. Some concrete questions are raised here. For contract conflicts, is the parent company liable for abuses in the course of an employment contract signed between the subsidy and the employee, which are unfortunately justified under the domestic law of the country where the subsidiary is established? As related to tort conflicts, what if an allegedly unusual regime of a foreign tort law, which extends the liability of the parent company, involves a cost allocation approach, which could be viewed by the Thai Court as disproportionate?

From a doctrinal point of view, this is a melting pot between human rights and economic analysis of law. While this requires a number of judges, if not all, to leave their comfort zones, which find contract and tort problems in a large dimension of corrective justice,[40] it is more easy to appreciate in some other jurisdictions. In the US, for example, law and economics takes hold to a greater extent, legal matters can be evaluated by the concept of efficiency, which can lead to the sacrifice of corrective justice. The reputation of this country as a tort litigation heaven[41] puts victims in a more favourable position when it comes to tort litigation. The plaintiff has a higher chance of success in a US Court than in Thailand. Simply speaking, the Thai Court regularly puts much effort into striking a balance between the rights of victims and of tortfeasors in aspects of litigations. In two examples at least, the Thai law is not held to have a long arm of enforcement, and punitive damages are accepted in quite limited circumstances in comparison to the US. In this regard, if the thick version of human rights is welcome as suggested by this author and in the course of transposing the UNGPs into the legal system, it is necessary for the judiciary to find a new way of striking a balance between corrective justice and efficiency. In other words, it turns out to be a task of the Thai judiciary as well as the legislature to develop a regulatory framework of protecting the absolute rights of the victims in transnational contexts while due process is maintained, especially in the course of applying conflicts rules.

[39] Please compare SC Symeonides, *Choice of Law* (Oxford, Oxford University Press, 2016) 177–78.

[40] Please see S Shavel, *Foundations of Economic Analysis of Law* (Cambridge MA, The Bell Knap Press of Harvard University Press, 2004) 3, 599 and 600.

[41] กิตติวัฒน์ จันทร์แจ่มใส, *คำอธิบายกฎหมายระหว่างประเทศแผนกคดีบุคคล เล่ม 2: วิธีพิจารณาความระหว่างประเทศ* (โครงการตำราและเอกสารประกอบการสอน คณะนิติศาสตร์ มหาวิทยาลัยธรรมศาสตร์ 2567) 85. (K Chunchaemsai, *Private International Law Book 2: International Procedure* (Treatise and Course Material Project BE 2567, 2024) 85.)

From the multinationals' perspectives, a realistic scene can be understood whereby multinational corporations find it necessary to select a proper place to locate a business activity or a transaction. Such a decision of the multinationals may be aimed at simply maximising benefits or escaping from an unfriendly ecosystem. The corporate and transactional designs may involve the business circle, and/or the supply chains, the marketing and the distributorship. As long as the decision of multinational corporations as regards the selection of places finds logic from some angle(s), the autonomy of the multinationals shall be respected from public authorities of any jurisdiction, including the Thai Court. Such an extended form of party autonomy is never disregarded by private international law. Admittedly, in some cases, the choice of place may be aimed at the manipulation of connecting factors, and may cause distortions. These include, but are not limited to, anti-competitive behaviours, offshore jurisdictions, money laundering, and environmental degradation, all of which may have repercussions in the form of human rights violations. Some of these aspects are regulated by settled rules of public international law,[42] which shall be considered especially when the Thai Court is tasked to define international public policy of the country as well as to decide on the problem concerning evasion of law. Of course, unacceptable modes of designing corporate structure and transactions shall be subject to scrutiny, and a putative decision may ensue if the Court finds it appropriate. Yet, in the conflicts dimension, the yardstick to mark the borderline between acceptable and unacceptable decisions of multinationals remains unclear since there is no proposal made in any judgment or scholarly work.

B. Jurisdiction

In the meantime, the country does not have a legislation that comprehensively deals with problems of the international competence of the Thai Court. Principally, Sections 3–7 of the Civil Procedure Code are employed by the Court to decline or establish jurisdiction. Although these provisions are designed to rather deal with domestic disputes, they serve as general rules applicable in international cases as well. The drawback in the eyes of conflicts scholars is that the jurisdiction of the Thai Court under those provisions is criticised as excessive when it comes to establishing or declining the international jurisdiction of the Thai Court. Briefly speaking, the international jurisdiction of the Thai Court is not restricted to the domicile of the defendant and the situs of the property, but also the nationality or the domicile of the plaintiff.[43] Situs of immovable property makes cases special because, if it is espoused with other elements, a foreign Court may have an exclusive jurisdiction, and the Thai Court has no choice but to dismiss the case.[44] Notwithstanding a broad range of competence of the Thai Court, the CPC, Sections 3–4 connecting factors only provides for the minimum contacts between the Thai Court and the case.

[42] Rules of international law are contained in a number of treaties, including, but not limited to, the 1992 United Nations Framework Convention on Climate Change, the 2000 UN Convention against Transnational Organized Crime, and the 2003 UN Convention against Corruption.

[43] The CPC, Section 4ter. 'Any other plaint than those provided in section 4 bis in the case where the defendant does not have a domicile in the Kingdom and the grounds of action do not exist in the Kingdom, shall, if the plaintiff is a Thai national or has a domicile in the Kingdom, be submitted to a civil court or the court within whose jurisdiction the plaintiff has a domicile.

The plaint under paragraph one may, if the defendant has the property, whether temporarily or permanently, which may be subject to execution in the Kingdom, be submitted by the plaintiff to the court within whose jurisdiction the property is situated.'

[44] The exclusive jurisdiction of either the Thai or foreign Court is assumed in cases where the immovable is located in any country conditional on the fact that the defendant is not a domiciliary of Thailand. Please see a detailed explanation in Chandramour (n 32) 193.

The establishment or decline of jurisdiction is finally dependent on the deliberations of the Thai Court, and the guidelines for exercising such competence are neither detailed nor exhausted in any instrument.[45] This allows the Thai Court to consider abstract or concrete rules and principles. In this regard, to convince the Court either to establish or decline jurisdiction, the plaintiff or the defendant may plead PIL rules or principles, which convince the Thai Court. And, of course, in so doing, human rights principles may influence the Thai Court when it tries to develop the judicial policy in the subject matter.

Whether a subject matter is arguable before the Court can be a problem. If it fails to satisfy the criteria of the Civil Procedure Code, Section 55, the Court has no choice but to dismiss the petition either partially or wholly.

Section 55 reads, '[w]hen any dispute arises in relation to the right or duty of any person under the civil law or any person is to exercise his or her right through a court, such person shall be entitled to submit his or her case to a civil court having jurisdiction in accordance with the provisions of the civil law and this Code.'

The key element is the existence of 'dispute' that involves a situation where a subjective right of the person is contested.[46] The contestation criterion requires the Thai Court to consult existing rules and provisions, which usually pertain to a legal discipline in the Thai legal system. From conflicts and comparatist points of view, there are disputes that could be dismissed by the Thai Court simply because the subject matters are unknown to Thai law. For example, the anticipatory damage in foreign environmental laws that concerns the situation where a physical injury has not yet occurred to anyone, is unknown in the eyes of Thai environmental law. If a purely domestic case is brought to the Thai Court, this case shall be absolutely dismissed. The question here concerns the judicial treatment of cases with a foreign element. Of course, a subject matter in such international litigation is unknown to the Thai Court, and some conflicts rules can be deployed to make the case admissible. This involves especially the application of 'adjustment' (as a conflicts rule),[47] which allows the Thai Court to pursue a flexible direction in establishing jurisdiction. But the scenario is not that easy. The establishment of jurisdiction is a matter of public policy, which requires judicial deliberations, and this is unavoidably an arbitrary decision. It turns out that concepts of human rights render such cases less sophisticated. In detail, human rights can be perceived as another set of public policy that comes to interweave with another pre-existing notion. In effect, the discretion of the Thai Court is henceforth reduced.

International disputes concerning multinationals therefore have great uncertainty. This Section does not aim to provide a concrete solution on this subject matter, but rather to discuss some possibilities to deal with the problems. There are at least two scenarios. First, the subsidiary or the agent is located in Thailand, and the parent company in a foreign jurisdiction. Second, the parent company is established in Thailand, and the subsidiary or the agent in a foreign country.

Considering the basic rules of international jurisdiction as discussed in the previous paragraph, if one of the connecting factors is satisfied, the Thai Court has the standing to establish or decline jurisdiction. The foreign status of the defendant company does not provide an obstacle in the eyes of the Thai Court as asserted in SCJ1096/2505 (1962), which recognised the *ratione personae* of foreign corporations. Therefore, either the subsidiary or the parent company which is established in a foreign jurisdiction can be sued in the Thai Court. Also, the *ratione personae* of domestic corporations for the abuses committed by them that occur in a foreign country can

[45] In this regard, this author also means internal communications in the judiciary.
[46] SCJ2671/2550 (2007).
[47] Or Anpassung in German term. Please see Kropholler (n 34) 234–35.

provide a legal basis for bringing the litigation in the judicial procedure, and this is affirmed in the *Mitrphol* case, the first case concerning GVC and human rights of the country as the home state of the investor.

In the meantime, albeit not comprehensively elaborated on, blackletter law can be found in a few subject matters that can be relevant to multinationals and human rights and they warrant a brief discussion here. These are (i) choice-of-court agreement and (ii) class action.

The choice-of-court agreement is recognised in a particular matter, namely multimodal transportation under Section 65 paragraph 1 of the Multimodal Transport Act BE 2548 (2005),[48] while it is not found in other specific matters. Human rights can be involved in litigations brought for or against multinationals that are related either to contractual or non-contractual matters. For example, in a case where chemical substances explode during the course of transportation causing injuries to people and there is a choice-of-court contained in all contracts, the important questions concern the extents of liability of carriers and of the damages sustained by the victims. Some concepts of human rights may be employed to reinforce arguments of the attorneys or the judges as regards the extent and limit of the choice-of-court agreement.

The class action is now possible in the Thai legal system since the addition of Sections 222/8–222/49 to the Civil Procedure Code, which broadly deal with litigations concerning any subject matter, including consumer protection, environment, securities and labour, among others. The petitioner is generally required to be a member of the group as per Section 222/8. This can however be exempted in specific cases that are accommodated by specific legislations. Civil societies, for example, can bring a consumer case to the Court for a group of consumers under Section 19 of the Consumer Case Procedure Act BE 2551 (2008), which requires the status of such civil societies to be recognised by the Consumer Protection Board. Environmental litigations are similar. Civil societies working on the issue can bring an environmental litigation against a corporation that has caused harm to the environment according to Section 8, paragraph 1(5) of the Enhancement and Conservation of National Environmental Quality Act BE 2535 (1992) (ECNEQ). Foreign civil societies can also represent the clients but are required to complete the process of registration under Section 7 of the same legislation.

In the meantime, the first and only case obtaining a foreign element that is brought to the Court is the *Mitrphol* case, which concerns the violation of environmental and human rights rules found in Cambodia.

Of much significance is flexibility, as can be appreciated in the Thai conflicts mechanism. It should be utilised while there is not yet comprehensive legislation on international civil and commercial procedure. There are two levels of flexibility that can be observed in this legal system. First, it is possible to plead PIL rules and principles to the Thai Court. In SCJ931/2545 (2002), for example, the concept of *forum non-conveniens* is assimilated in the case, whereby efficiency and due process are contemplated to the extent to which this concept is employed. In 8455/2559 (2016), the concept of good faith in the context of law circumvention and forum shopping was once pleaded in the Thai Court, and provides a solution to deal with *lis alibi pendens* in an international divorce case. Second, real practice suggests that conflicts rules are regularly employed as an escape device to serve the purpose of either the attorney or the judge in some direction. In SCJ15066/2555 (2012), for example, a judicial settlement rendered in a foreign jurisdiction was

[48] Section 65, para 1. 'The parties to the multimodal transport contract may agree, by stipulating such agreement on the multimodal transport bill of lading or contract of multimodal transport, that a court in any country which, according to the law of that country, has jurisdiction to consider civil claims arising from multimodal transport contract or tort shall be the competent court having jurisdiction to consider and adjudicate the case.'

classified by the attorney as a substantive instead of procedural problem, and such a classification is respected by the Thai Court.[49]

Optimistically, this author perceives the recently mentioned flexibility as a starting point for the development of judicial policy or framework to deal with cases concerning multinationals and human rights while the legislative framework is absent. If one takes the thick version of human rights that can serve up to the level of policy or meta-rule overarching deliberation of the Thai Court in developing PIL rules and principles on international jurisdiction, in a general sense, this may result in an establishment or a decline of jurisdiction, dependent on the case, say, when the inclination of the Thai Court goes toward the thick version of human rights. The decision of the Court in establishing jurisdiction over the *Mitrphol* case can be ascribed to such an inclination, although the detailed arguments are not yet accessible and should be observed in the judgment, which is to be published in the future.

The current stage of development already sees the inclusion of human rights in the international public policy of the country, and further detail should be put into the jurisdictional rules and principles concerning the establishment or decline of jurisdiction of either or both the subsidiary or the parent corporation as well as other basic questions on jurisdictional matters, including, *lis alibi pendens*, the multiparty litigation, and the enforcement of foreign judgments, among others. This author finds it quite early to discuss what should be good and best practices for the country in this chapter. This subject matter should be discussed more extensively in a separate research project.

C. Conflicts Rules

Similar to the topic of international jurisdiction, human rights may serve as a policy or meta-rule overarching deliberations of the Thai Court when it applies conflicts rules. In this section, this author claims that human rights rules can be employed to assist the attorneys and the Court in interpreting and applying conflicts rules, and this can lead to an easier route to human rights concepts.

The conflicts rules of the country can be subject to a wide range of interpretation. This interpretation is required, to a large extent compared to other systems, for a number of reasons. First, the legislation was enacted in 1938. Strict reliance on the 42 provisions contained in the legislation can render an absurd result. In the majority of cases, flexibility of applying conflicts rules is preferred. Second, when espoused with the adversarial rules of civil procedure of the country, the judgments rendered by the Court of the First Instance, the Court of Appeal and the Supreme Court result from the argumentation between the attorneys. The Thai Court has no authority to direct an attorney to plead a conflicts or foreign rule. The role of the judges is rather to contemplate the arguments of both, and choose to apply conflicts and substantive rules and provisions as recommended by the parties. The interpretation and application of conflicts rules can be appreciated in individual cases instead of the country's direction of caselaw or precedence. Notwithstanding this limit, some pattern can be appreciated not through the development of conflicts rules, but rather asserted judicial policy, and this can be the starting point for the discussion of conflicts rules in the context of human rights.

[49] Judicial settlements are treated under the Hague Convention as a judgment as its provision of Article 10 reads, '[judicial settlements] shall be enforced under this Convention in the same manner as a judgment.' Although Thailand is not a signatory to this Convention, such a classification finds logic in its conflicts system. However, whether this is classified as such depends on the argumentation of the attorneys. Please see the discussion in Chandramour (n 32) 91–92.

From the observation of this author, there is no single judgment made in the context of PIL that the judges disregard policy considerations. And, as claimed above, human rights can be employed either as policy or meta-rules for the attorneys and the Court in the interpretation and application of conflicts rules to the problems. Connecting this point to the flexibility of the Thai conflicts system as recently mentioned, conflicts rules can be interpreted and applied in such a way that advances the policy of the country in the eyes of the Thai Court. In the meantime, there is no single final judgment in which human rights rules or principles are employed to solve the problems of multinationals.

An unrelated, useful case is Appellate Court Judgment 18776/2561, which shows how human rights and constitutional rules and principles can direct the judges. This case concerns a same-sex couple who registered for same-sex marriage under the English law. The Englishman is deceased. The Thai spouse claimed that he is qualified as an interested person under the CCC, Section 1713, and requested the Court to appoint him as estate administrator under the same provision. In the timeframe, the country did not have a legislation on civil partnership or marriage equality. The Thai Court solved the problem by characterising the relationship as contractual instead of family status. In doing so, it explicitly referenced the provisions of Sections 4[50] and 27[51] of the Constitution. The International Covenant on Civil and Political Rights and the Universal Declaration of Human Rights are also cited though without specific provisions.

A major point of this chapter is whether the referencing of human rights rules or principles is possible in the context of multinationals. The simple answer is yes. This can be achieved by the utilisation of the flexible mode of the conflicts rules of this system. Two hypothetical examples relating to contract and tort conflicts are given below.

For contract conflicts, supposing that an employment contract is signed between the foreign multinational corporation A and the employee B and the chosen law is the law of Country A. The multinational A is located in Country A while the employee B usually works in Thailand. Clearly, the employment law of Country A provides for a higher standard of protection than that of Thailand. If there is a dispute between the multinational corporation and the employee, and the attorney or the Thai Court finds the law of Country A more consistent with the international human rights law, and would like to apply it, they need to plead and apply the Thai conflicts rules. Primarily, this requires the declaration of an internationally mandatory rule (IMR) by the Thai Court. To overcome the limit of the Thai labour protection law is to reduce its scope of application. The Court may simply apply the CLA, Section 13, which leads to the application of relevant rules and provisions as contained in the employment law of Country A. In other words, while not classifying the competing rules in the Thai employment law as the IMR, the conflicts rules can operate to an extent that escalates the protection of human rights, which is unknown to the

[50] Section 4. '<u>Human dignity, rights, liberties and equality of the people shall be protected.</u>

The Thai people shall enjoy equal protection under the Constitution.'

[51] Section 27. 'All persons are equal before the law, and shall have rights and liberties and be protected equally under the law.

Men and women shall enjoy equal rights.

<u>Unjust discrimination against a person on the grounds of differences in origin, race, language, sex, age, disability, physical or health condition, personal status, economic and social standing, religious belief, education, or political view which is not contrary to the provisions of the Constitution or on any other grounds, shall not be permitted.</u>

Measures determined by the State in order to eliminate an obstacle to or to promote a person's ability to exercise their rights or liberties on the same basis as other persons or to protect or facilitate children, women, the elderly, persons with disabilities or underprivileged persons shall not be deemed as unjust discrimination under paragraph three.

Members of the armed forces, police force, government officials, other officials of the State, and officers or employees of State organisations shall enjoy the same rights and liberties as those enjoyed by other persons, except those restricted by law specifically in relation to politics, capacities, disciplines or ethics.'

Thai legal system. In this regard, human rights can be regarded as the meta-rule that directs the interpretation and application of conflicts rules of the country.

Tort conflicts can benefit from human rights in aspects. The contemporary case of *Mitrphol* is chosen for a brief discussion in this paragraph. There are some limits in the Thai tort conflicts. Criticism usually goes against the rule of *lex loci delicti*, and the double-actionability requirement under the CLA, Section 15. The place of wrong as the only connecting factor puts the utility of this provision in doubt. Today's tort conflicts are diversified into areas, *lex loci delicti* may do justice for some, but not other cases. The *Mitrphol* case can prove this claim, and this is clearly so for other typical cases of multinationals as well. Cases of this type usually involve the scenario that the law of place of commission is not capable of protecting the right of tort victims, and therefore the law of elsewhere claims its application. Reportedly, as the foreign direct investor (FDI), the company entertains privileges in establishing its business in Cambodia under the investment promotion scheme. The Cambodian law is suspected of being impartial, say, favouring the FDI. In this respect, the plaintiff tries to claim the application of the law of place where the parent company is located. Clearly, this is contradictory to the CLA, Section 15. Admittedly, a clear direction cannot be shown by the assistance of purely conflicts rules and methods. Rather the conflicts rules and methods that are espoused with human rights principles are capable of providing some solutions. Reference should be made to the two versions of the CLA, Section 15, thick and thin versions. That is to say, this provision can be reducibly interpreted, and hence is held as inapplicable to the case. As a consequence, Section 3 of the CLA can be consulted, which gives the parties and the Court some room to deliberate on policy and legal issues.

IV. Concluding and Residual Remarks

In the process of realising this academic work, this author has stressed two important activities, namely conceptualisation and contextualisation. Conceptualisation involves some steps aimed at identifying and assessing human rights concepts either as policies, meta-rules, principles, or rules, and at locating them somewhere in the system. In contextualising, this author has tried to elaborate human rights into concrete rules, provisions and models that are workable in Thailand.

However, the time is not ripe to conceptualise and contextualise unless distrustful feelings or assumptions remain. In this regard, there are some frequently asked questions. Could the permeation of human rights rules and principles in the area of private international law displace the division of labour (say, of legal disciplines and/or legal mechanisms), which usually takes hold in the civil law traditions of the country? Is subsidiarity[52] going to be dislocated from the legal system? Is due process as enshrined in the PIL mechanism of the country to be downgraded? This author is not going to answer these questions in this last section. Some of them are already answered explicitly or implicitly, and fully or partially. The emphasis here is placed on the basic finding of this academic work that human rights instead complement imperfect scenes of the PIL for past, present and future cases.

Where human rights concepts interweave with other aspects of public policy in multinationals contexts, more generosity – for the vulnerable, or the human rights victims – is attached to the processes of balancing ideologies, and developing rules and principles. This does not mean that human rights will trump other abstract ideas. The Court is still required to take into account all notions which are employed in applying conflicts rules and assessing public policy. Of particular

[52] D Shelton, 'Subsidiarity and Human Rights Law' (2006) 27 *Human Rights Law Journal* 4, 5.

significance is the clarity in argumentation, which can address two complex qualities of the Thai PIL, namely the vagueness of the conflicts provisions and the adversarial procedural rules. As discussed in this chapter, both of these qualities have caused a resolution of PIL problems to be unforeseeable. The flexible mode as it is called by this author – or the escape device as it is called in the US – is considered to be an unwanted, but usual phenomenon in the Thai legal system. Because of this, a degree of arbitrariness is maintained, and due process is shaken in the conflicts mechanism. From the observation of this author, human rights can tame this escape device phenomenon on the one hand. Interestingly, on the other hand, thanks to flexibility, human rights can also be embraced easily in Thailand. This conviction can be attested in the *Mitrphol* case in which the Court has established jurisdiction.

Since this chapter is not the last piece of PIL scholarship on the subject matter of multinationals and human rights, the discussion of procedural, conflicts and substantive rules and principles requires further and deeper exploration in future academic workings.

11

India

MANOJ KUMAR SINHA AND SWARIL DANIA

I. Introduction

The existence of human rights abuse across the globe is rampant because of the cost which is concomitant with the prevention of human rights violations. In order to seek profits, corporations completely disregard the standards of human rights, attempting to maximise their earnings and minimise their costs, even if it comes at the expense of gross violations of human rights of the individuals. Remedying the abuse of human rights entails expenditure to undo the damage done to the environment or to compensate for the industrial accidents and to provide for safe workplace environments and decent wages. However, profit-oriented businesses do not consider it wise to incur such expenditure. It could be owing to the lax enforcement of the human rights standards, or corruption,[1] that in many developing countries operating a workplace is cheaper, if compared with the cost of operating a workplace in developed countries. True, if the developing countries enjoyed well governed rule-of-law states, free of corruption, there would be less abuse of developing countries by developed nations. However, building 'rule of law states' out of the aftermath of colonial chaos is a challenging issue. Building the rule of law in developing and underdeveloped countries is a problem which can only be solved by these nations themselves. All the first world can do, therefore, is give examples and explanations and models for emulation. However, the first world has also sought to take advantage of loopholes in the legal systems in underdeveloped and developing nations, seeking to make quick profits.

The doctrine of human rights aspires to provide a common framework for determining the basic civil, economic, political, and social conditions required for all individuals to lead a minimally good life.[2] The use of the idea of 'national sovereignty' as a shield to opt out of fundamental human rights-based commitments by States cannot be allowed.[3] The moral justification

[1] Sometimes however third world corruption works *against* first world corporate interests. For example, Chevron had defended against extraterritorial claims made in the U.S. for its conduct in Ecuador, which it won on forum non conveniens grounds. The Court in Ecuador thereafter awarded a multi-billion-dollar judgment against Chevron for its polluting activities. Chevron claimed the Ecuadorian courts were corrupt – and so did the attorney litigating against. Should Chevron have been estopped from claiming corruption, having claimed the case should not have been litigated in the USA? Should the USA recognise or enforce damage awards from third world courts? See: *Chevron Inc. v Donziger*, 768 F.Supp.2d 581 (U.S. Dist. Ct. SDNY, 2011).

[2] U Baxi, 'From Human Rights to the Right to be Human: Some Heresies' www.researchgate.net/publication/254144900_From_Human_Rights_to_the_Right_to_be_Human_Some_Heresies.

[3] L Glanville, 'The Responsibility to Protect Beyond Borders' (2012) 12 *Human Rights Law Review* 1–32.

of human rights is thought to precede considerations of strict national sovereignty.[4] An underlying aspiration of the doctrine of human rights is to provide a set of legitimate criteria to which all nation-states should adhere.[5] Thus, the doctrine of human rights is ideally placed to provide individuals within a State with powerful tools for questioning the legitimacy of State, which denies fundamental rights to its citizens.[6]

The canon of human rights aims at identifying the fundamental prerequisites for each human being leading a minimally good life.[7] But human history has always witnessed the rights of the mighty. The poor have never had freedom from fear and want. Suppression of liberty, lack of equality, perennial hunger and malnutrition, morbidity and mortality, and deprivation of human dignity have plagued the poor throughout history.[8] People were never allowed to determine their destiny, either under the camouflage of religious beliefs or under coercion. People were forced to accept their suppression of freedom and lowering of human dignity as a *fait accompli*.[9] At the same time, history also witnessed the poor and marginalised protesting against the unjust social order whenever they suffered hardship.[10]

The enforcement of human rights depends to a great extent on legal provisions protecting these rights, contained in international and regional documents and treaties, as well as in national constitutions and laws.[11] Since 1945, a large number of human rights treaties were adopted, both at regional and international levels. On a universal plane, the Universal Declaration of Human Rights (UDHR), 1948, International Covenant on Civil and Political Rights (ICCPR), and the International Covenant on Economic, Social and Cultural Rights (ICESCR) were adopted.[12] The UDHR remains an important milestone in the development of national, regional and international human rights instruments.[13]

The rise of globalisation has caused the blurring of the boundaries between economies and society across the world. The corporations have, consequently, risen in economic, social and political power. The same is particularly true for transnational corporations. It is widely reported that these corporations are engaged in several human right violations. It is pertinent to note that to curb these violations, state action alone is not sufficient. Thus, this chapter makes an attempt to explore how the changes in the wake of globalisation have affected how individuals enjoy their human rights in relation to the activities of these corporations. It examines the question of human rights obligations of corporations at an international level, thereby trying to identify their obligations so as to ensure the protection of human rights of individuals.

The aim of this chapter is to examine the impact of Multinational Companies on human rights, environment and labour rights in India and suggest how far the Multinational Corporations (MNCs) adhered to domestic laws and international law while transacting businesses in India.

[4] R Falk, *Human Rights and the State Sovereignty* (New York, Halmes and Meiser Publishers, 1981).

[5] RP Claude and BH Weston, *Human Rights in the World Community -- Issues and Action* (Philadelphia, University of Pennsylvania, 1989).

[6] U Baxi, *The Future of Human Rights*, 3rd edn (New Delhi, Oxford University Press, 2008).

[7] MK Sinha, *Implementation of Basic Human Rights* (New Delhi, Manak Publications, 1999).

[8] TV Boven, 'Human Rights and Rights of People' (1995) 6 *European Journal of International Law* 1–17; PH Imbert, 'Rights of the Poor, Poor Rights? Reflections on Economic, Social and Cultural Rights' (1995) 55 *Review of the International Commission of Jurists* 85–99.

[9] D Banik (ed), *Rights and Legal Empowerment in Eradicating Poverty* (Farnham, Ashgate, 2008).

[10] PN Drost, *Human Rights as Legal Rights*, (Leiden, AW Sijthoff, 1965) 14–20.

[11] BG Ramcharan, 'Implementation of the International Covenant on Economic, Social and Cultural Rights' (1976) 23 *Netherland International Law Review* 151–62; EW Vierdag, 'The Legal Nature of the Rights Granted by the International Covenant on Economic, Social and Cultural Rights' (1978) *The Netherlands Yearbook of International Law* 69–105.

[12] Sinha (n 7).

[13] BG Ramacharan (ed), *Human Rights Forty Years After the Universal Declaration* (The Hague, Martinus Nijhoff, 1989).

Efforts will be made in this chapter to evaluate the decisions of the Supreme Court in protecting human rights and environment, in cases of infringement of these rights by the MNCs.

II. Human Rights and Business

The most prominent change in the twenty-first century which took place in relation to the human rights discourse, has been the recognition of the link between business and human rights.[14] Because of the emergence of the transnational corporations as the primary actor in the international sphere in the second half of the twentieth century, it became important to understand their role towards the observance of human rights obligations.[15] The significance of these corporations can be estimated from the fact that the revenue of some transnational corporations exceeds the gross national product of smaller European States, and in some cases, is even larger than many African States together. This gives transnational corporations ('TNCs') excessive influence over international market regulations and national legislative and political processes.[16]

There has been a global expansion of markets in recent decades especially since the 1990s owing to the multilateral trade agreements, bilateral investment treaties, and domestic liberalisation and privatisation policies adopted by the States.[17] Thus, the rights of TNCs have also become more securely anchored in national laws and increasingly defended through compulsory arbitration before international tribunals. There has been an impressive contribution to poverty reduction in major emerging market countries and overall welfare in the industrialised world, because of globalisation.[18] However, it has also imposed costs on people and communities. The many costs that are imposed by the pressures of globalisation include corporate-related human rights abuses.[19] What is important today is to harmonise economic growth with the protection and promotion of human rights.[20] It is a challenge, which, if met, can harness the great power of economic growth to the great principle of human dignity. Many companies find strength in their human rights records; others suffer the consequences of ignoring this vital part of corporate life. Today, human rights are a key performance indicator for corporations all over the world.[21] The next section discusses some of the most important judicial decisions which have been delivered by the Indian judiciary in the context of human rights violations by the transnational actors and corporations. They have been analysed so as to highlight the need for promoting the human rights obligations of these actors, which have gained major prominence in this era.

[14] R Sullivan (ed), *Business and Human Rights: Dilemmas and Solutions* (Sheffield, Greenleaf, 2003); Amnesty International, *Business and Human Rights: A Geography of Corporate Risk* (The Prince of Wales International Business Leaders Forum, 2002); R Mares, *Business and Human rights: A Compilation of Documents* (Leiden, Martinus Nijhoff, 2003); O De Schutter (ed), *Transnational Corporations and Human Rights* (Oxford, Portland, Hart Publishing, 2006).

[15] L Cata Backer, 'Multinational Corporations as Objects and Sources of Transnational Regulation' (2008) 14(2) *ILSA Journal of International and Comparative Law* 2–26.

[16] R Fagerfjäll, P Frankental and F House, *Human Rights – A Corporate Responsibility?* (Stockholm, Amnesty International, 2001).

[17] ibid.

[18] U Baxi, 'Globalization: A World Without Alternative?' available on upendrabaxi.in/.

[19] J Ruggie, Implementation of General Assembly Resolution 60/251of 15 March 2006 entitled 'Human Rights Council' Report of the Special Representative of the Secretary-General on the issue of human rights and transnational corporations and other business enterprises, A/HRC/4/35, 19 February 2007, see www.ohchr.org.

[20] Harvard Law School, *Business and Human Rights: An Interdisciplinary Discussion* (Harvard Law School, 1999).

[21] Sullivan (n 14).

III. Enforcing Human Rights Obligations Upon MNCs: Significant Judicial Decisions

A. Bhopal Tragedy Case

The Bhopal gas tragedy remains one of the most disturbing and devastating industrial disasters mankind has witnessed. The accident involved the massive leak of toxic methyl isocyanate (MIC) gas, which occurred during the night of 2–3 December 1984 at the Bhopal plant of Union Carbide, India, Ltd. (UCIL), a subsidiary of Union Carbide Corporation, a New York corporation with headquarters in Danbury, Connecticut. Union Carbide owns 50.9 per cent of the stock of its Indian subsidiary. The Indian Government's reports put the death toll at 2,347, over 1,600 of whom were killed as a direct result of the deadly gas leak, while the remaining casualties died because of its fatal effects over the next few months. Those seriously injured number between 30,000 and 40,000 and the Indian Government received 500,000 leak-related claims.[22] In order to provide remuneration to victims, and to create an institutional framework for disbursal of remedies, the Bhopal Gas Leak Disaster (Processing of Claims) Act (Act) 1985 was enacted by the Government of India on 20 February 1985. Through the Act, the Union government was granted the exclusive right to represent the claim on behalf of the numerous victims of the tragedy who were entitled to claim compensation. It also empowered the Central Government to initiate suits or other proceedings and to enter into a compromise. Consequently, the Bhopal Gas Leak Disaster (Registration and Processing of Claims) Scheme 1985 was framed in the exercise of powers conferred under section 9 of the said Act. Thereafter, several actions for compensation were brought in the United States District Court for the Southern District of New York against Union Carbide Corporation (hereinafter referred as 'UCC'). UCC was a New York based corporation which owned 50.9 per cent stock in UCIL at the time of the tragedy. UCC resisted the jurisdiction of the New York Court on grounds of *forum non conveniens*, claiming that it had subjected itself to the Courts of India. Judge Keenan allowed this plea *vide* order dated 10 June 1086 and dismissed the consolidated action on the basis of several factors, including the presence of witnesses and evidence in India. The order however recorded UCC's statement that it shall consent to submit to the jurisdiction of the Courts of India.

As would be expected, the company was eager to dissociate itself from all legal responsibility in the aftermath of the worst industrial accident in history. A settlement was reached between the UCC and the Government through the Supreme Court of India, and UCC accepted its moral responsibility and agreed to pay 470 million dollar in compensation, a relatively small amount based on significant underestimations of the long term health consequences of exposure and the number of people exposed.[23] The Bhopal gas disaster was a wake-up call for the State about the disastrous consequences of a potential industrial accident and it raised a number of questions related to the preparedness of the State to deal with such disasters. The disaster indicated a need for enforceable international standards for environmental safety to cope with any future disasters.

After the disaster, there has been a rapid growth of industrialisation in India, thus, multiplying the risk of other such potential accidents. Though there have been some positive changes in the government policy which has resulted in a change in the behaviour of a few industries, that

[22] VP Nanda, 'For Whom the Bell Tolls in the Aftermath of the Bhopal Tragedy: Reflections on Forum Non Conveniens and Alternative Methods of Resolving the Bhopal Dispute' (1987) 15(2) *Denver Journal of International Law & Policy* 235–34.

[23] *Union Carbide Corporation v Union of India* (1990) AIR 273.

has not sufficiently mitigated the threats to environment and people emerging out of the rapid and poorly regulated industrial growth. Widespread environmental degradation with significant adverse human health consequences continues to occur throughout India.

B. *Sundarajan v UOI*[24]

This matter concerned the setting up of a nuclear power plant at Kundankulam in the state of Tamil Nadu, which lies at the southeastern tip of the country. Apprehensions were raised regarding the environmental consequences of the project which led to the filing of the writ petition. The Supreme Court disposed of the case with the issuance of directions to various authorities of state, highlighting the need to balance economic benefit alongside the protection of environment and health of people. The Court observed that it is necessary to balance 'economic scientific benefits' with those of 'minor radiological detriments' on the touchstone of our national nuclear policy. The court asserted that economic benefit had to be viewed through the perspective of not just economic growth but on the parameter of poverty alleviation and employment generation. The Court also made a reference to the nuclear accidents which have occurred in different parts of the world such as the Three Miles Island Power Plant in the USA, Chernobyl in the Ukraine, Fukushima in Japan and the Union Carbide Bhopal incident. All these had been haunting the memory of the people living in and around Kudankulam, leading to large-scale agitation and an emotional reaction to the setting up of the Nuclear Power Plant (NPP). The nature of the potential adverse effect of ionising radiation adds to fears and unrest which might not have even been thought of by Enrico Fermi, a noble laureate in physics in 1938, who was responsible for the setting up of the first Nuclear reactor in a Doubles squash court, at Slagg Field, Chicago University, USA. India now has 20 Nuclear Reactors in place, and the world contains approximately 439 of them, but people still react emotionally, for more reasons than one, when a new one is being established.

The court in this case also examined the stand which has been taken by India on an international level on the matter of international nuclear treaties. Notably, India is not a signatory to the Nuclear Non-Proliferation Treaty (NPT). However, it is a party to various international conventions, namely: (a) the Convention on the Physical Protection of Nuclear Material 1979, (b) the Convention on Assistance in the Case of a Nuclear Accident or Radiological Emergency 1986, (c) the Convention on Nuclear Safety, (d) the Joint Convention on the Safety of Spent Fuel Management and on the Safety of Radioactive Waste Management 1997, and (e) the Convention on Early Notification of a Nuclear Accident 1986. Moreover, India has also entered into various bilateral Civil Nuclear Co-operations. An example is a cooperation agreement with France for the construction of ERR Power Plants (10,000 MWe) at Jethapur site in Maharashtra, which also comprises cooperation in the areas of research, safety and security, waste management, education etc, followed by various other commercial contracts. India and Canada have finalised the terms for their nuclear deal, which paved the way for Canadian firms to export Uranium to India in 2010. India has also signed a civil nuclear deal with Mongolia for the supply of uranium to India.[25]

[24] (2013) 6 SCC 620.

[25] See para 35 of the judgment. A Memorandum of Understanding was signed between the Department of Atomic Energy, Government of the Republic of India and the Nuclear Energy Agency, Regulatory Agency of the Government of Mongolia on Cooperation in the Field of Peaceful Use of Radioactive Minerals and Nuclear Energy was signed on 14 September 2009. See www.hindustantimes.com/delhi/india-inks-uranium-deal-with-mongolia/story-4DZUl04D77djmwyzVhKscO.html#google_vignette.

In addition, India and the US issued an Inter US Joint Statement in Washington on 18 July 2005 which located the final broad policy so as to actually facilitate and also outline the broad contours of a legally binding agreement. 'Nuclear 2007', an agreement for co-operation between India and the US concerning peaceful uses of nuclear energy (the 2007 Co-operation Agreement) laid down certain binding obligations between the two countries. India, however, is not a party to any of the Liability Conventions, specifically the IAEA Vienna Convention on Civil Liability for Nuclear Damage. India has enacted the Civil Liability for Nuclear Damage Act 2010 (Nuclear Liability Act) which aims to provide a civil liability for nuclear damage and prompt compensation to the victims of a nuclear accident through No-Fault Liability to the operators.[26]

C. *Novartis AG v Union of India*

The other aspect which is sometimes ignored in a human rights discussion is that of access to health care and the corresponding protection enjoyed by the medicine manufacturers in the form of the intellectual property regime. As is widely known, the TRIPS Agreement (The Agreement on Trade-Related Aspects of Intellectual Property Rights (TRIPS)) is the most comprehensive multilateral agreement which sets detailed minimum standards for the protection and enforcement of intellectual property rights. It is aimed at harmonising national intellectual property systems. All members of the World Trade Organization (WTO) are bound by the obligations under the TRIPS Agreement. India is one of the founding members of the General Agreement on Tariffs and Trade (GATT) and thus a member of the WTO from its inception from 1 January 1995, and is bound by the obligations under the TRIPS Agreement like all other members of the WTO. As a result of the international agreement, the law governing the grant of Patents in India, the Patents Act 1970, was subject to large scale changes in three stages. Further, the Patents (Amendment) Act 2005, deleted section 5 from the Parent Act (Patents Act 1970). Between 1 January 1995 and 1 January 2005, the Patents Act 1970 underwent wide ranging changes. The deletion of section 5 of the Patents Act opened the doors to product patents in the country.

One of the most significant judgments concerning the jurisprudence of intellectual property in India is the *Novartis* case. On 1 April 2013, the Supreme Court of India rendered judgment on an appeal filed by *Novartis*[27] against the decision of the Indian Patent office rejecting a product patent application for a specific compound, the beta crystalline form of *imatinib mesylate*. Imatinib mesylate is used to treat chronic myeloid leukemia and is marketed by Novartis as 'Glivec' or 'Gleevec'. The Apex Court upheld the rejection by the Indian Patent office, and confirmed that the beta crystalline form *of imatinib mesylate* failed the test of section 3(d).[28] Section 3(d) stipulates

[26] *Sundarajan v UOI* (2013) 6 SCC 620, para 42.

[27] *Novartis A.G. v Union of India* (2013) 6 SCC 1.

[28] In May 2006, Novartis had filed two writ petitions before the Madras High Court under Article 226 of the Indian Constitution to declare that section 3(d) of the Patents Act 1970 as substituted by the Patents (Amendment) Act 2005 is non-complaint with the World Trade Organization Agreement on Trade-Related Aspects of Intellectual Property Rights (TRIPS) and is unconstitutional, being vague, arbitrary and in violation of Article 14 of the Constitution of India, and consequentially to direct the Controller General of Patents & Designs to allow the Patent Application. The Challenges on TRIPS compliance and the constitutionality of section 3(d) were heard by the Madras High Court. The court held that it did not have jurisdiction to decide a case concerning the compliance of domestic law with an international treaty. The Madras High Court dismissed both writ petitions and the judgment was not appealed.

the conditions to be fulfilled for the patenting of an invention The *efficacy* criterion is discussed in the section as:

> For the purposes of this clause, salts, esters, ethers, polymorphs, metabolites, pure form, particle size, isomers, mixtures of isomers, complexes, combinations and other derivatives of known substance shall be considered to be the same substance, unless they differ significantly in properties with regard to efficacy.

The Court clarified that efficacy as contemplated under section 3(d) is therapeutic efficacy. The judgment has received severe criticism from a number of pharmaceutical companies on the ground that it has dealt a harsh blow against the future of innovation. However, the judgment is well-crafted and the Court took a balanced view of the matters brought before it. The issue of access to health care is essential for the realisation of human rights. At the same time, protection of intellectual property is significant to ensure that the inventors are incentivised to undertake research in the field of medicine. Striking a balance between the two is a major challenge, however the Indian judiciary has risen to the challenge and has time and again asserted its role as the champion of human rights.

D. *Centre for Environmental Law, WWF-I v U O I*

In another case, where a petition was filed in the matter of securing a safe habitat for the Asiatic Lion, the Supreme Court undertook an extensive survey of the development of environmental jurisprudence at the international level. In *Centre for Environmental Law, WWF- I v UOI*,[29] the petitioner approached the Supreme Court to decide the necessity of a second home for the Asiatic Lion, an endangered species, for its long-term survival and to protect the species from extinction. In this case, the Court extensively referred various international environmental treaties and their applicability at the national level while delivering the final judgment. The court observed how the environmental jurisprudence has evolved ever since the Stockholm Conference on Human Environment in 1972, in which India also participated. It was one of the first steps taken towards protection of the environment by the international community. As is now known widely, the outcome of the Conference was the adoption of the Stockholm Declaration which laid down the foundation of sustainable development and urged the nations to work together for the protection of the environment.[30] After 20 years, once again the international community met in Rio De Janeiro in 1992 and adopted Conventions on Biological Diversity. The Biological Diversity Convention recognised for the first time in International Law that the conservation of biological diversity is a common concern of humankind and is an integral part of the development process. As a consequence of the international deliberations, India also chose to enact the legislation for biodiversity conservation and the Indian Parliament also passed the Biological Diversity Act in 2002, which was followed by the National Biodiversity Rules in 2004. The main objective of the Act is the conservation of biological diversity, sustainable use of its components and fair and equitable sharing of the benefits arising out of the utilisation of genetic resources. Bio-diversity and biological diversity includes all the organisms found on our planet, ie plants, animals and micro-organisms, the genes they contain and the different eco-systems of which they form a part.

[29] (2013) 8 SCC 234.

[30] The Stockholm Declaration had an impact on the development of environmental law in India. The 42nd Constitutional Amendment has added Articles 48(A) and 51A(g) under the Indian Constitution. According to Article 48 and Article 51-A(g) of the Constitution of India, the State has a duty to protect and improve the environment and safeguard forests and wildlife in the country, a duty cast upon all the States in the Union of India.

At the international level, the next step was Rio +20, when the States renewed their commitment to sustainable development again, thereby promising to promote an economical, social and environmentally sustainable future for our planet and for present and future generations.[31] Countries also reaffirmed the principles enunciated at the 1992 meeting.

The International Union for Conservation of Nature (IUCN) has highlighted that the only living representative of lions once found throughout much of south-west Asia, is now available only in Gir Forest in India. IUCN has identified the Asiatic Lion as a critically endangered species on the IUCN Red List. The IUCN adopted a resolution of 1963 by which a multi-lateral treaty was drafted – the Washington Convention – also known as the Convention on International Trade in Endangered Species of Wild Fauna and Flora (CITES) 1973.[32] The Court observed that the Government of India in the light of Articles 48A and 51A(g), adopted various policies and legislations for the proper implementation of the Convention on Biological Diversity (CBD), IUCN and CITES.

The National Board of Wild Life (NBWL) was constituted by the Parliament to frame policies and advise the Central and State Governments on the ways and means of promoting wild life conservation and to review the progress in the field of wild life conservation in the country and suggesting measures for improvement. The Central and the State Governments cannot brush aside its opinion without any cogent or acceptable reasons.[33]

The judgments pertaining to environmental jurisprudence in India have shown a leaning towards an eco-centric approach as against the anthropocentric approach. Anthropocentrism places the focus on human interest, advancing the view that non-humans have only instrumental value to humans. In other words, humans take precedence and human responsibilities to non-humans are based upon their benefits to humans. On the other hand, eco-centrism is nature-centred, where humans are seen as a part of nature and non-humans are also recognised as having intrinsic value. In other words, human interest does not take automatic precedence and humans have obligations to non-humans independently of human interest. Eco-centrism is, therefore, life-centred, nature-centred where nature includes both humans and non-humans.[34] The Court, while examining the necessity of a second home for the Asiatic Lions, adhered to an eco-centric approach. It held that the Asiatic Lion currently exists as a single sub-population and is thus vulnerable to extinction from unpredictable events, such as an epidemic or large forest fire etc, and thus it is important to safeguard this endangered species because this species has a right to live on this earth, just like human beings.

E. Hindustan Unilever Limited: Kodaikanal Mercury Poison Case

This case related to a factory producing mercury thermometers in Kodaikanal (Tamil Nadu) in 1983. In 1987, Pond's India came into the Unilever fold through the larger corporate acquisition of Chesebrough-Pond's. Pond's India, and with it the thermometer factory, merged with Hindustan Limited in 1998. In 2001, demands were raised by NGOs against Unilever, the

[31] The United Nations Conference on Sustainable Development (Rio+20) was held in Rio de Janeiro, Brazil, on 20–22 June 2012, and adopted an outcome document entitled 'The Future We Want'.

[32] CITES entered into force on 1 July 1975, which aims to ensure that international trade in specimens of wild animals and plants does not threaten the survival of the species in the wild.

[33] *Centre for Environmental Law, WWF- I v UOI*, (2013) 8 SCC 234, para 28.

[34] ibid para 39.

Anglo-Dutch firm, to account for the mercury pollution that was detected in the vicinity of one of its mercury factories in India. Hindustan Unilever Limited was a subsidiary of Unilever Plc and manufactured mercury thermometers for export to the US and Europe, among other destinations. It was found by Greenpeace that they were dumping sites with mercury-containing wastes, both on the factory premises and beyond. Employees were said to have been exposed to the toxic metal for years. Environmental organisations Greenpeace and Tamil Nadu Alliance against Mercury (TAAM) insisted that Unilever clean up the sites, close down the factory and issue an apology. In 2001, Hindustan Unilever had to shut down its factory in Kodaikanal because of a case of mercury poisoning. Many families were affected due to the pollution and workers suffered from illness due to exposure to mercury.

After some years, in February 2006, some of the former employees of the Kodaikanal factory approached the Madras High Court seeking directions for conducting a fresh health survey and providing economic rehabilitation. This petition was filed more than four years after HUL had made a full and final settlement in November 2001. The severance package was significantly higher than the statutory requirement. The workers had been offered alternative jobs in another unit of the company. However, they opted out of service. The Ministry of Labour & Employment was also made a respondent in the matter filed by the ex-workers of the Kodaikanal factory in the Madras High Court. After almost four years of the earlier report being on Court record and without any objections to the report, the Ministry submitted a report at the end of 2011 to the Honourable Madras High Court. In 2011, the Government of India study on workers' health concluded that many workers suffered from illnesses caused by workplace exposure to mercury.

HUL filed its objections to the Ministry's report in January 2012. Hearings were held subsequently with the last one taking place in February 2013. At this last hearing, the presiding judge excused himself and directed the matter to be listed before the Chief Justice of the Madras High Court. HUL signed a settlement on humanitarian grounds with former workers on 4 March 2016. The Hon'ble High Court of Madras took the settlement agreement on record. As part of the agreement, HUL, with an objective to ensure long term wellbeing of its former workers, has agreed to provide ex gratia payments to 591 former workers/association members and their families to be used towards livelihood enhancement projects & skill enhancement programmes. The settlement has been considered a success story of a first ever litigation in India by industrial workers against exposure to toxic chemicals.[35] The exposé of the environmental abuse led to the closure of the factory in 2001 and opened up a series of issues in India such as corporate liability, corporate accountability and corporate negligence.

F. *Orissa Mining Corporation Ltd. v Ministry of Environment and Forests*[36]

An order was passed by the Ministry of Environment and Forests which rejected the Stage II clearance for diversion of forest area, which had been applied for by the Orissa Mining Corporation (OMC). The corporation, a State of Orissa Undertaking, approached the Supreme Court seeking a Writ of Certiorari to quash the order. The permission sought was for clearance for the diversion of 660.749 hectares of forest land for the mining of bauxite ore in Lanjigarh Bauxite Mines in the Kalahandi and Rayagada Districts of Orissa.

[35] *The Guardian*, 'Unilever Settles Dispute Over Mercury Poisoning' available at www.theguardian.com/environment/2016/mar/09/unilever-settles-dispute-over-mercury-poisoning-in-india.

[36] (2013) 6 SCC476.

A proposal was sent by the Orissa government in February 2005 to the Ministry, for diversion of around 661 hectares of forest land for mining bauxite ore ('the Bauxite Mining Project') in favour of the state-owned OMC in the Kalahandi and Rayagada Districts. On 2 March 2005 the Central Empowered Committee ('CEC') wrote to the MoEF stating that CEC was examining the project proposal for diversion of forest land and till CEC takes a final decision in this regard this matter should not be decided by MoEF. However, Vedanta Resources ('Vedanta') approached the Supreme Court seeking a direction to the MoEF to take a decision on the application for forest clearance for bauxite mining submitted by the State Government on 28 February 2005.

The question posed by the Court in deciding the application was whether Vedanta should be allowed to set up an Alumina Refinery Project ('the ARP') in Lanjigarh Tehsil of District Kalahandi. The CEC had objected to the grant of clearance sought by Vedanta on the ground that the ARP would be totally dependent on the mining of bauxite from Niyamgiri Hills, Lanjigarh, which was vital wildlife habitat and formed part of an elephant corridor. The CEC had also objected on the ground that the ARP would obstruct the proposed wildlife sanctuary and the residence of tribes like Dongaria Kondh. On 23 November 2007, the Court held that it was not agreeable to grant clearance to the ARP and disposed of Vedanta's application. However, the Court did grant liberty to Sterlite (a parent company of Vedanta) to move the Court if they would agree to comply with the conditions suggested by the Court. Sterlite, the State Government and OMC subsequently accepted the conditions suggested by the Court. The MoEF subsequently agreed in principle with the proposal forwarded to it by the State Government in April 2009 and granted environmental clearance to OMC ('Stage I approval'). Stage I approval was subject to various conditions, including a requirement for OMC to obtain the necessary forestry clearances under the Forest (Conservation) Act 1980 (India).

The State Government then forwarded the final proposal to the MoEF on 10 August 2009 stating that the user agency had complied with all the conditions stipulated in the letter of MoEF dated 11 December 2008. The final proposal was subsequently placed before the Forest Advisory Committee ('the FAC') on 4 November 2009. The FAC recommended that the final clearance should be considered only after the Gram Sabha had determined the community rights of forest dwelling scheduled tribes ('FDSTs') and other traditional forest dwellers ('TFDs') pursuant to section 6 of The Scheduled Tribes and Other Traditional Forest Dwellers (Recognition of Forest Rights) Act 2006.[37] After further expert investigations had taken place into the issue of community rights, the FAC opined that it was a fit case for applying the precautionary principle and recommended the temporary withdrawal of the in-principle Stage I approval accorded previously to OMC by MoEF. On 24 August 2010, MoEF considered the recommendations made by the FAC and decided to reject the request by OMC for Stage II clearance approval to divert around 661 hectares of forest land for the Bauxite Mining Project, making orders to that effect.

OMC through this petition sought to challenge the legality of these orders. The Court duly recognised in this case the customary and cultural rights of indigenous people and also made it clear that these rights were also the subject matter of various international conventions. It referred to various international instruments which emphasised the protection of social, political and cultural rights of indigenous population. The International Labour Organization (ILO)

[37] According to s 6(1) of the FR Act, the Gram Sabha was the authority with power or responsibility for initiating the process for determining the nature and extent of individual or community forest rights or both that may be given to FDSTs and TFDs within the local limits of its jurisdiction under the FR Act. Examples of such rights that could be determined by the Gram Sabha to exist included the right to use and collect forest products (including fish and other products from forest water bodies) and the right to occupy forests for habitation.

Convention on Indigenous and Tribal Populations Convention 1957 (No.107), ILO Convention (No.169) and Indigenous and Tribal Peoples Convention 1989 and United Nations Declaration on the rights of Indigenous Peoples (UNDRIP) 2007 were highlighted in this case. In addition to the abovementioned conventions, some other relevant instruments were also mentioned by the Court, which stressed the importance of the Convention on the Biological Diversity (CBA). The Biodiversity Convention highlights the necessity to preserve and maintain knowledge, innovation and practices of the local communities relevant for conservation and sustainable use of bio-diversity.[38]

The necessity to respect and promote the inherent rights of indigenous peoples which derive from their political, economic and social structures and from their cultures, spiritual traditions, histories and philosophies, especially their rights to their lands, territories and resources has adequately been provided for in the United Nations Declaration on Rights of Indigenous Peoples. Scheduled Tribes and other forest dwelling tribes residing in the Scheduled Areas have a right to maintain their distinctive spiritual relationship with their traditionally owned or otherwise occupied and used lands.

The Court gave direction to the state of Orissa to place these issues before the Gram Sabha and its decision should be communicated to the MoEF. MoEF shall take a final decision on the grant of Stage II clearance for the Bauxite Mining Project in the light of the decisions of the Gram Sabha within two months thereafter. The judgment echoes the need for inclusion of the indigenous communities in the policy-making process where such policies have an effect on environment and biodiversity. The rights of the indigenous population cannot be subject to demands of the profit seeking corporations and the judiciary displayed the same commitment to the protection of these rights through this judgment.

G. *Reliance India Limited and BG Exploration and Production India Limited v Union of India*[39]

The dispute was between the Union of India and Reliance India Limited and BG Exploration and Production India Limited and it arose out of two Production Sharing Contracts (PSCs). The detailed dispute resolution clauses of the contract provided that:

i. The substantive law governing the contracts was: Laws of India.
ii. The law governing the arbitration agreement was: Laws of England.
iii. The venue of arbitration was: London, England.

The matter had arisen in the context of the lease over the Panna-Mukta and Tapti oil fields. The companies involved in the matter had the right to extract the petroleum from the reserves in the area. As per the principles of international environmental law jurisprudence, the control over natural resources such as petroleum, and oil and natural gas fields vests with the government, however, owing to the production sharing contract, RIL and BG Exploration and Production India Limited were granted the rights to extract oil from the oilfields at their own cost. There would be a sharing of profits between the government and the contractors as per the Production Sharing contract. The dispute arose in relation to the law governing arbitration of the contract.

[38] *Orissa Mining Corporation Ltd. v Ministry of Environment and Forests*, (2013) 6 SCC 476, para 38.
[39] AIRONLINE2015 SC 28.

In the case of Reliance India Ltd., the substantive issue raised was with regard to the arbitrability of the production sharing contracts. As agreed to by the SCI in the judgment.[40]

> … where the law governing the conduct of the reference [law of the seat] is different from the law governing the underlying arbitration agreement, the court looks to the arbitration agreement to see if the dispute is arbitrable, then to the curial law to see how the reference should be conducted and then returns to the [law governing the arbitration agreement] to give effect to the resulting award.

Therefore, it was held by the court that the court had no jurisdiction to set aside an award made in London. This has been seen by academicians and scholars alike to be an arbitration friendly judgment. The pertinent issue raised here demonstrates the impact of globalisation and expansion of international trade which has led to the development of arbitration mechanisms at an international level to facilitate dispute resolution. This has however affected the traditional role of the State. Thus, the need for protection of human rights which also includes the right of the people over their natural resources is also to be seen from the perspective of the growing influence of multinational conglomerates which often resort to principles of international arbitration law for resolution of disputes. This might weaken the control of the domestic courts in matters of protection of rights of citizens and may require attention.

H. *Samson Maritime Ltd. v Union of India*[41]

A notification issued in pursuance of the 'Make in India' policy was challenged in this case before the Delhi High Court. The notification provided for according special preferential treatment to 'Indian Built Ships'. This notification was quashed by the High Court, on the ground that the same was in violation of the guarantee of equality which was enshrined under Article 14 of the Indian Constitution. It was argued by the petitioner that as a result of the notification, there was no incentive or preference available to Indian Ships in Indian business, due to which a ship which was originally built in India, but may be owned by a foreigner, would get first preference in Indian business. The counsel further added that the impugned notification introduced 'Indian Built Ships' as a concept extraneous/alien to the Merchant Shipping Act 1958 and by giving special preferential treatment to Indian Built Ships irrespective of the Flag of the ship, the concept of flagging/ownership had been arbitrarily destroyed which was outside the ambit of the provisions of the Act. Counsel on behalf of the respondents submitted that the notifications had been issued in respect of larger public interest under the 'Make in India' policy and did not violate any right of the petitioners and hence no irreparable and grave harm would be caused to the petitioners. The Court noted that the 1958 Act governs ownership of ships and not where the ship is built, and that this essential difference was not appreciated by the respondents. The Court cited the case of *Halliburton Offshore Services Inc. v Principal Officer of Mercantile Marine Department*[42] where the Supreme Court had held that nationality is bestowed upon a ship by means of registration which makes the Indian ship entitled to fly the Indian Flag and claim benefits and privileges under the 1958 Act. The Apex court further held that under customary international law, ships are regarded as part of the territory of the Flag State, ie, an extension of the country, and so registration extends nationality rights to the Ship. The Court elucidated that Indian Ships are a class

[40] M Mustill and S Boyd, *The Law and Practice of Commercial Arbitration in England*, 2nd edn (London, LexisNexis, 1989).

[41] 2019 SCC OnLine Del 8727.

[42] (2017) 14 SCC 238.

unto themselves and equalisation of Indian Ships with Foreign Flag Ships amounts to treating unequals equally which violates Article 14 of the Constitution of India. The bench pointed out that 'the effect of the impugned regime would be that the entire Indian trade would fall in the hands of Foreign Flag Vessels and Indian Ships would be rendered completely out of the market.'

I. *Karnataka State Pollution Control Board v B. Heera Naik and Ors*[43]

This case raised an important question as to whether the Commissioner of City Municipal Council and the Chief officers of City Municipal Council can be prosecuted under section 48 of the Water (Prevention and Control of Pollution) Act 1974 (Water Act). The Karnataka State Pollution Control Board challenged the judgment of the High Court of Karnataka of 16 February 2015. The respondents, who were working as Municipal Commissioner and Chief officers of the Municipal Council, approached the High Court under section 482 of the Code of Criminal Procedure, the appeal was allowed and the proceeding initiated for their prosecution by appellants under the Water Act 1974 was quashed. In this case, the Karnataka State Pollution Control Board filed a complaint in the Court of Metropolitan Magistrate at Bangalore for taking cognisance of the offence punishable under sections 43 and 44 of the Water (Prevention and Control of Pollution) Act 1974 (Water Act) against the accused persons and to punish them for the offences. The complaint highlighted that the Board had accorded a consent to the accused persons to discharge sewage effluent after treatment which expired on 30 June 2006 and thereafter the same was not renewed. The complaint stated that not obtaining consent after the expiry date and discharging the untreated sewage into the neighbouring water bodies constituted a violation of section 25 of the Water Act 1974, which was punishable under section 44 of the Act.

The Court observed that the concept of corporate criminal liability as contained in section 141 of the Negotiable Instruments Act 1881 would arise against a corporation and a company. Section 141 uses the term 'person' and refers it to a company. There is no trace of doubt that the company is a juristic person. In light of the above the Court examined the purpose and object of the Water Act 1974, and held that section 47 could be resorted to for offences by a body corporate. The Court observed that the Karnataka State Pollution Control Board, by filing a complaint before the Magistrate for taking cognisance of offences under section 49, did not commit an error. Section 49 embraces cognisance of all offences under the Act. Thus, in the event of any offence being committed by anyone, its cognisance can be taken under section 49. However, the Court reiterated that offences by a body corporate are to be covered by section 47, since in the event offences by body corporates are not covered by section 47, the benefit of the section 47(1) proviso shall not be available to those body corporate. The Court held that offences by bodies corporate like the City Municipal Council are covered under section 49, treating it as an offence by a company as provided in section 47, and held that the High Court erred in quashing the complaint filed by Karnataka State Pollution Control Board against the Respondents. The applications filed under section 482 of the Code of Criminal Procedure by the Respondents were dismissed and the Magistrate/Metropolitan Magistrate was allowed to proceed with the complaints in accordance with law. This decision by the Court reaffirms its deep commitment to ensuring effective implementation of laws related to protection of the environment. The case also sends a clear message to those who are holding responsible positions in the Municipality and Municipal Corporations to ensure that the environment is not damaged; otherwise they will be held responsible under

[43] AIR 2020 SC 2020.

various laws. The issue of liability of corporate personality for environmental harms is a significant one and judgments like these further the cause of responsible and ethical conduct by the corporations.

J. *Pappini Amman Traders v T.N. Pollution Control Board*[44]

In the case of *Pappini Amman Traders v T.N. Pollution Control Board*, a series of writ petitions were filed under Article 226 of the Constitution of India, challenging an order issued by the National Green Tribunal ('NGT') concerning charcoal manufacturing units operating in the southern states of India. The NGT's order required all charcoal units in the region to transition from the existing 'below ground level technology' to a new 'above ground level technology' approved by expert committees, aimed at reducing pollution. Until the new technology was adopted, the units were prohibited from operating under the old technology.

The petitioners, who were operators of charcoal units in Tamil Nadu's Tiruppur District, contested the NGT's order. They argued that their current method of converting coconut shells into charcoal using the old technology was safe and did not pose environmental risks. They asserted that they had obtained proper permissions and had taken measures to control emissions and pollution, such as installing water sprinklers, scrubbers, and chimneys. They claimed that they were not part of the proceedings that led to the NGT's order and therefore were unfairly affected by the decision. They emphasised their right to conduct business under Article 19(1)(g) of the Constitution and contended that the NGT's order infringed upon this right. Furthermore, they argued that the NGT's order should apply only to new units and not to existing ones.

In its judgment, the Madras High Court ('MHC') thoroughly examined the petitioners' arguments, with a particular focus on the application of international legal principles. The MHC stressed the importance of achieving a balance between economic development and environmental protection, citing the principles enunciated in *Vellore Citizens' Welfare Forum v Union of India*.[45] The doctrine of sustainable development was also referred to by the MHC. Sustainable development requires that the current needs must be met in such a manner that the ability of future generations to meet their needs is not compromised. It was asserted by the Madras High Court that sustainable development must be prioritised and that the right to a clean environment takes precedence over purely economic interests. Further, the MHC also acknowledged the doctrine of public trust, which designates certain resources as being held in trust by the government for the common good, as mentioned in the *Vellore Citizens' Welfare Forum* case. It highlighted the State's duty to protect the environment and natural resources for the benefit of all citizens.

The MHC also referred to notable international treaties and principles, underscoring its consideration of the broader legal landscape. Among these were the Stockholm Declaration of 1972, the Brundtland Report of 1987, and the Earth Summit held in 1992 at Rio de Janeiro. These international documents underscored the paramount importance of 'sustainable development' and the delicate equilibrium between economic progress and environmental preservation. The MHC astutely recognised that the judicious approach adopted by the NGT was in harmony with these foundational principles and past determinations. This measured stance by the NGT

[44] *Pappini Amman Traders v T.N. Pollution Control Board* (2022) SCC OnLine Mad 3538.
[45] *Vellore Citizens' Welfare Forum v Union of India case* (1996) 5 SCC 647.

permitted the charcoal units to continue their operations provided they adopted the new pollution-reducing technology.

The MHC concluded that the NGT's order harmonised with the tenets of sustainable development, the fundamental right to a clean environment, and the tenet of public trust. In this context, the MHC upheld the NGT's decision, concurrently offering a reasonable timeline for the petitioners to transition to the new technology. The MHC effectively emphasised the necessity of safeguarding the environment for both the present and future generations, thereby aligning itself with both the domestic and international legal framework's guiding principles.

K. *Gujarat Mazdoor Sabha v The State of Gujarat*[46]

In this writ petition, a notification of the government of Gujarat issued on 17 April 2020 under section 5 of the Factories Act was challenged. The impugned notification exempted the factories in the state of Gujarat from observing certain obligations, which were incumbent upon the employers towards upholding certain rights of the workmen employed in the factories, which were guaranteed by the Factories Act. The impugned exemptions pertained to weekly hours, daily hours and intervals of rest of adult workers in factories. The daily and weekly working hours of the workmen were extended and the overtime wages were to be fixed in proportion to the existing wages (as opposed to twice the existing wages as stipulated by the provisions of the Act) as per the impugned notification. The government justified its action on the ground that the COVID-19 induced lockdown disrupted the economy and as a result caused financial hardships for the industrial employers. A trade union named Gujarat Mazdoor Sabha which had a state-wide presence and another with a national presence approached the Supreme Court invoking writ jurisdiction under Article 32 of the Constitution and challenged the validity of the said notification. The main objective of the notification was to provide certain relaxations for industrial and commercial activities for a brief period starting from 20 April 2020 till 19 July 2020. Upon expiration of the notification on 20 July the State government extended it up to 20 October 2020. The petitioner alleged that the use of section 5 in the context of economic slowdown was mainly intended to benefit the factories by compelling the workers to work longer hours, without paying them their overtime wages as stipulated by the Act. However, it was argued on behalf of the State government that the COVID-19 pandemic is a 'public emergency' as defined in section 5 of the Factories Act. To deal with the impact of COVID-19, emergency measures were essential and these were required to protect the existence and integrity of the State of Gujarat. It was further argued by the state that the massive slowdown in economic activities caused by lockdown resulted in an internal disturbance in the state within the meaning of section 5 of the Factories Act. It was also argued by the defendant that section 5 of the Factories Act confers the power of exemption on the State government to exempt any factory or class of factories from its provisions. The State government has the prerogative to determine whether all or only a class or description of factories were to be exempted. The Court examined whether the notification of the government of Gujarat fell within the ambit of the power conferred by section 5 of the Factories Act.

Another issue which was also dealt by the Court was to ascertain whether the nationwide lockdown imposed due to the COVID-19 pandemic could qualify as a public emergency as defined in section 5. The nationwide lockdown was imposed by the Union government on 24 March 2020, and it was subsequently extended until 31 May 2020 to contain the spread of the virus. In

[46] AIR 2020 SC 4601.

determining whether public emergency existed, the Court referred to the 'explanation' portion of section 5 of the Factories Act. As per the 'explanation', public emergency means a grave emergency whereby India's security or any part of the territory thereof is threatened either by war or external aggression or internal disturbance. The state argued that the pandemic-induced lockdown severely disrupted economic activities, thereby leading to internal disturbance in the state. Reliance was also placed by the state upon the report of the Sarkaria Commission which lists grounds for invocation of emergency such as natural calamities, epidemics etc. The state therefore justified the exemptions as a means for revival of the economy by protecting the factories from the adverse effects of slowdown.

The Court observed that objective conditions establishing the existence of public emergency must exist. The emergency must be a grave emergency which threatens the country or any part of it. Upon fulfilment of this condition, a proportionality test determining the validity of state action infringing fundamental rights must be fulfilled. The proportionality test was laid down in *K.S. Puttaswamy v Union of India*.[47] Most importantly, the court observed that internal disturbance must be of the same gravity as that of war or external aggression. It was further observed by the court that state security and public order are not the same. Even if economic slowdown caused by the pandemic amounts to internal disturbance, it doesn't threaten State security for it to result in public emergency. As regards the Sarkaria Commission report, which was relied upon by the State, the court clarified that the report requires that natural calamity or an epidemic must be of a nature so as to hinder State's administration and State security, and economic slowdown hinders or threatens neither. As regards the object of the impugned notification, the court observed that it is entirely contrary to the object for which this Act was enacted in the first place. The court pointed out that the enactment of the Factories Act was almost contemporaneous with the framing of the Constitution and was the outcome of a long struggle of worker's unions to secure the right to human dignity in workplaces so as to ensure their safety and wellbeing. The notification issued by the government of Gujarat on 17 April 2020 had exempted all factories in the State from the applicability of sections 51, 54, 55 and 56, effectively overriding section 59 of the Factories Act. The Court observed that the need for protecting labour welfare on one hand and combating a public health crisis caused by the pandemic on the other, necessitates careful balancing. A statutory provision which permits the grant of an exemption to stipulated conditions must be resorted to sparingly and with the utmost of sincere intentions. Exemptions must not be employed to allow a free hand to the State to eliminate provisions promoting dignity and equity in the workplace in the face of unique challenges to the state administration. The workers were worst affected during the lockdown and taking note of their conditions the State should have taken more 'worker friendly' measures, instead of issuing notifications in question which heavily affected the legitimate claim of overtime wages of workers. The court while interpreting the Factories Act observed that the said Act is an integral part of the Indian Constitution, and the provisions of the Factories Act should be interpreted according to the relevant articles of the Constitution. The Court emphasised that the worker's right to life cannot be deemed contingent on the mercy of an employer and the State. The notification which denied the overtime wages provided by law clearly violates the worker's right to life and right against forced labour that are made available by Articles 21 and 23 of the Constitution. In the interest of justice and to ensure that employers pay overtime wages to workers from the first date of notification in accordance with the provision of section 59 of the Factories Act, the Court invoked Article 142 of the Constitution of India. This judgment once again firmly establishes that the Indian Judiciary is

[47] AIR 2017 SC 4161.

deeply committed to the promotion, protection and perpetuation of human rights, especially of the weaker and underprivileged sections of society.

L. *Omkar Mahadeo Supekar v Municipal Corpn. of Greater Mumbai*[48]

In this case, before the Bombay High Court ('BHC'), the significance of the Ramsar Convention on Wetlands came to the forefront, highlighting its application and role in environmental protection and regeneration. The petitioners in the case expressed concerns over the construction activities for a proposed cycling and jogging track within Powai Lake by the Municipal Corporation of Greater Mumbai ('MCGM'). They contended that the activities violated regulations and posed a threat to the ecological balance of the lake. Importantly, they invoked the Ramsar Convention's principles and provisions, asserting that the Powai Lake had been designated as a wetland in the National Wetland Atlas 2011, which was sponsored by the Ministry of Environment and Forest, Government of India, in line with the Ramsar Convention's objectives.

The Ramsar Convention on Wetlands, adopted in 1971 in Ramsar, Iran, seeks to promote the conservation and wise use of wetlands globally. It designates wetlands of international importance, also known as Ramsar Sites, to ensure their protection and sustainable use. The Powai Lake, being designated as a wetland in the National Wetland Atlas, carried implications under the Ramsar Convention. The significance of the Ramsar Convention's principles were acknowledged by Bombay High Court in this case. However, it also highlighted that while Powai Lake was designated as a wetland in the National Wetland Atlas, it had not been formally notified as a wetland under the notification dated 26 September 2017, issued by the Ministry of Environment, Forest and Climate Change, Government of India. The BHC's focus was on the specific notification requirement, underscoring the need for formal recognition.

The judgment emphasised the need for responsible development and ecological regeneration. It meticulously evaluated the proposed 'Gabion Technology' put forward by the MCGM as a sustainable means of construction. The BHC's scrutiny of the technology's efficacy and environmental implications reflected its commitment to ecological balance and regeneration. By interpreting the term 'construction' in the absence of a formal definition, the BHC demonstrated a dedication to promoting sustainable practices. The case underscored the importance of adhering to both international and domestic regulations to ensure environmental protection and regeneration. By addressing the Ramsar Convention in the context of formal notification and applying it to broader principles of ecological sustainability, the case highlighted the interconnectedness of global conservation efforts and local legal interpretations.

M. *Citizens for Green Doon v Union of India (UOI)*[49]

In the present case, the Supreme Court, while agreeing with the security needs of the country as highlighted by the Ministry of Defence (MOD), the bench of Justices DY Chandrachud, Surya Kant, and Vikram Nath had modified the Apex Court's decision of 8 September 2020 in which the Court directed the Ministry of Road Transport and Highways (MoRTH) to stick to its circular on the widening of the roads in hill terrain. On 23 December 2016, the Ministry of Road Transport

[48] *Omkar Mahadeo Supekar v Municipal Corpn. of Greater Mumbai* (2022) SCC OnLine Bom 1008.
[49] LL 2021 SC 737, available at www.livelaw.in/pdf_upload/citizens-for-green-doon-and-others-versus-union-of-india-and-others-405939.pdf.

and Highways (MoRTH), had announced the Chardham Mahamarg Vikas Pariyojna, aimed at widening the roads (around 900 km of national highways) in order to ensure safer, smoother, and faster traffic movement. These highways would connect the four religious places in the state of Uttarakhand, namely, Gangotri, Yamunotri, Kedarnath and Badrinath, which have been popularly known as the 'Chote Char Dham.' An original application was filed before the principal bench of the National Green Tribunal on 27 February 2018, in the public interest, contending that the construction would have a negative impact on the Himalayan Ecosystems. Taking note of the concern of the applicant, the NGT directed the constitution of an 'Oversight Committee' to monitor the environmental safeguards for the execution of the project. The order of the NGT was challenged before the Apex Court. The Court modified the order of the NGT and constituted a High-Power Committee (HPC). The HPC submitted a report to the Court on 13 July 2020. The Court noted that the conclusions of the report were unanimous, except for the issue relating to the width of the road. Another miscellaneous application was filed by the Union of India, through the Ministry of Defence, seeking modification of the Apex Court's order of 8 September 2020. The Court examined the specific issues in the context of the project in light of the relevant decisions of the Court and various circulars and guidelines that were issued in regard to the issues raised in this case.

In this case, the Court had an elaborate discussion on environmental law-related principles. The principle of sustainable development is deeply rooted in the jurisprudence of environmental law. The same was acknowledged by the court and it highlighted how sustainable development has emerged as a multifaceted principle, that does not prohibit development, but structures it around what is sustainable. The Court observed that there was a lack of consensus on how to ascertain whether a particular development project strictly adhered to the principle of sustainable development. The Court suggested that the appropriate way to overcome this problem is by adopting the standard of the 'environmental rule of law' to test governance decisions under which developmental projects are approved. The Court, after examining the various reports and guidelines, observed that the national highways will provide vital connections to the establishments of the Armed Forces. The importance of the requirement for double-laned highways has been emphasised, as it is necessary for the movement of trucks, equipment, and personnel of the Armed Forces. The Court opined that the HPC was mandated to assess the environmental and social impact of the project and that it was in no way competent to address the security needs of the country. Balancing the interests of defence against environmental considerations was outside the purview of the HPC. The Court did not shy away from expressing its dissatisfaction regarding the indifferent approach of the government in giving serious consideration to the HPC report, which highlighted that the project is riddled with environmental issues which need to be resolved in order to make it environmentally sustainable. The Court categorically stated that the general recommendations issued by the HPC should form the baseline and be implemented. The Court directed that the MoRTH and MoD be allowed to proceed with the project, subject to the fulfillment of the conditions that have been raised by the HPC and enumerated by the Court.

To ensure the effective implementation of the recommendation, the Court also constituted an 'Oversight Committee', which would report to the court directly. The Court carefully balanced the two important issues linked in this case: on the one hand, protection of the environment and, on the other hand, national security. The Court nicely carved out its decisions based on elaborate discussions related to the environmental rule of law and sustainable development.

N. *Perumatty Grama Panchayat v State of Kerala*[50]

The issue that was raised in this case for consideration was whether a Grama Panchayat could cancel the licence of a factory manufacturing non-alcoholic beverages on the ground of excessive exploitation of ground water. The Perumatty Village Council gave a licence to the company to commence production in 2000. In March 2000, Coca Cola, under its Indian subsidiary Hindustan Coca Cola Beverages Private Limited (HCCBPL), commenced operations at its bottling plant at Plachimada. Its main products were soft drinks and bottled drinking water. The said factory was established after obtaining permission from the Panchayat. It started commercial production in March 2000 after obtaining a licence from the petitioner Panchayat. The main raw material used in the manufacture of beverages is water. A substantial portion of the need for water is met by exploiting ground water through bore-wells. Allegations were raised that the excessive exploitation of ground water for the functioning of the said unit was causing a scarcity of drinking water and other severe environmental problems.

In connection with this, political and mass organisations started holding agitations. The agitation by the Adivasis opposite the gate of the company had been continuing for over a year. Taking into account the above circumstances, to prevent the excessive use of ground water and also the consequential environmental problems, the Panchayat took the decision of withdrawing the company's licence. Coca Cola drew around 510,000 litres of water each day from boreholes and open wells. For every 3.75 litres of water used by the plant, it produced one litre of product and a large amount of waste water. Over the next few years, the area surrounding the plant began to feel the plant's hazardous effects, as groundwater was contaminated and toxic waste was released. On 22 April 2002, the '*Coca Cola Virudha Janakeeya Samara Samithy*' (Anti-Coca Cola Peoples' Struggle Committee) began its protest against the plant, with over 1,500 people, mostly Adivasis, demanding the immediate shutdown of the plant owing to the severe detriment it was causing to their daily lives. Owing to the objections raised by people against the exploitation of ground water by the Company, the Panchayat passed a resolution on 7 April 2003, deciding not to renew the company's licence. The translation of that resolution reads as follows:

> As the excessive exploitation of ground water by the Coca-Cola Company in Plachimada is causing acute drinking water scarcity in Perumatty Panchayat and nearby places, it is resolved in public interest, not to renew the licence of the said Company. It is also resolved to inform about this decision to the Hon'ble Chief Minister of Kerala and the Hon'ble Minister for Industries, Kerala.

The company challenged this order in the Kerala High Court, which directed the litigants to approach the government's Local Self-Government Department (LSD). The LSD overruled the Panchayat's order banning the licence. The Panchayat again approached the High Court, which observed this time around that 'groundwater was a public property held in trust by a government and that it had no right to allow a private party to overexploit the resource to the detriment of the people.' However, the company was allowed to continue operation as long as it found alternative sources of water supply. Things came to a head when the Supreme Court, in 2005, issued a notice to the company allowing it to draw 5,00,000 litres of groundwater per day. The factory had been in lockdown since 2004, with the legal stalemate ensuring that the future of the company's operations in Plachimada remained uncertain. The 12-year-old case finally reached closure after much wrangling, when Coca-Cola relinquished its licence, stating in the Supreme Court that it did not intend to resume production from Plachimada.

[50] 2004 (1) KLT 731.

IV. Conclusion

It is beyond doubt that despite the advantages and benefits which are associated with foreign investment and corporate investors, the rise of Multinational Corporations can have a negative impact on individuals' enjoyment of their fundamental human rights. Such developments pose a challenge to the current normative framework. The rights of an investing corporation are often strengthened by investment agreements without taking their tripartite obligations to respect, protect and fulfil fundamental human rights into account, and consequently the rights of local populations. In this light, the obligations of corporations should also be strengthened in relation to the fundamental human rights of individuals and local communities. It is recommended that investment contracts and investment agreements must also include in their objectives the promotion and protection of fundamental human rights.[51] The same would imply that the interpretation of investment contracts or agreements would take place in the light of corporations' human rights obligations.[52] The Indian judiciary has exhibited a progressive and inventive stance in dealing with intricate legal matters, encompassing both domestic legislation and international legal standards, as seen by its interpretation. This methodology has resulted in noteworthy advancements in diverse fields of law, encompassing social equity, safeguarding of intellectual property, preservation of the environment, and handling of international business affairs. The aforementioned judicial rulings have successfully served to reconcile discrepancies within the national legal system and to align it with established international legal principles, hence facilitating the progress of international law's implementation in India. The aforementioned cases further underscore the importance of refraining from transgressions against *jus cogens* principles, which embody the most fundamental standards of international law that are inviolable under all circumstances. The proactive approach of the Indian judiciary in protecting these principles signifies a dedication to maintaining fundamental human rights and adhering to international legal standards. The ongoing process of harmonising national laws with international legal duties is subject to future consideration. The judiciary's proactive involvement in the interpretation of cases from multiple perspectives is crucial in facilitating this process of reconciliation. The anticipation arises from the ongoing evolution and adaptation of legal principles in response to shifting global dynamics, to achieve a peaceful coexistence between national laws and international legal standards. This would facilitate the achievement of a more efficient global legal framework and the attainment of the goals set forth by international law and global organisations. No company competing with integrity can justify collateral human rights damage in its endeavours to achieve its profit targets. Enlightened companies will therefore take a *rights-based approach*, that is, be willing to accept that its stakeholders have universally accepted human rights and take appropriate action to strive to respect these. Many of the deliverables that result from a *rights-based approach* can be seen as part of good management practices and thus make management a force for good corporate human rights commitment. In this pursuit of strengthening socially and ethically responsible and 'rights aware' corporations, the role of domestic courts is crucial. This chapter has sought to highlight these issues, illustrating judicial developments in India.

[51] UN Commission on Human Rights, *Human Rights, Trade and Investment, Report of the High Commissioner for Human Rights*, UN Economic and Social Council, U.N. Doc. E/CN.4/Sub.2/2003/9, 2 July 2003, 57.

[52] ibid.

PART III

Specific Issues

12

Environmental Damage and Climate Change – Climate Change Litigation between Private Parties in Asia

DANIEL LINDEN

I. Introduction

Climate change is a worldwide problem which has been dominating various aspects of our everyday life for several years, eg, media, science, national and international legislation, etc. On the one hand, greenhouse gases (GHGs), which absorb the radiation leaving the terrestrial surface and thereby preserve heat and energy in the atmosphere, are essential and necessary for the survival of plants, animals, human beings and all other parts of the complex biological systems as they exist on earth at this moment. On the other hand, the artificially higher atmospheric concentrations of GHGs due to emissions caused by humankind around the world, most predominantly including carbon dioxide (CO_2) emissions, lead to proportionally greater absorption and reflection of heat and energy in the atmosphere and therefore result in global warming.

Scientists have nominated global warming, as it is happening right now, one of the most threatening issues to humankind in the twenty-first century. Its impacts include a sharp increase in heat waves and other weather disasters, coastal flooding, etc, and are expected to lead to a drastic rise in climate-related deaths, either directly from weather disasters or indirectly from the effects of weather disasters on the worldwide access to nutrition.[1]

The Intergovernmental Panel on Climate Change (IPCC) has established itself as the preeminent authority in climate research and receives highest international recognition. Its recent reports illustrate that climate change is a serious current issue, and many recent weather disasters, eg, droughts, floods, storms, etc, are actually consequences directly resulting from global warming.[2] As per the IPCC's reports, the rise in the global average temperature so far already amounts to 1.1°C and is likely to increase by another 1.5°C even before 2040. In this case the upper limit, as stipulated in the Paris Agreement,[3] of an increase in temperature of

[1] M Rosso Grossman, 'Climate Change and the Individual' (2018) 66(1) *The American Journal of Comparative Law* 345, 346.

[2] D Hanschel and M Schultze, 'Menschenrechtliche Aspekte des Klimaschutzes' (2022) *Klima und Recht* 166, 167.

[3] Paris Agreement under the United Nations Framework Convention on Climate Change, adopted in 2015, 195 member states.

less than 2.0°C, while actually aiming for a 1.5°C-increase compared to pre-industrial levels,[4] will probably be reached well before the year 2050.[5] Subsequently, the coming years offer the last chance to get on the right track to comply with the limits set in the Paris Agreement.[6] To sum up, it can be seen as common knowledge that human behaviour enhances climate change and that the accumulation of GHG emissions in the atmosphere leads to global warming due to absorption and reflection of terrestrial radiation.[7] Therefore, in order to adhere to the internationally accepted goals of restricting global warming, as set out in the Paris Agreement, human behaviour has to change.

The reasons stated above have led to a still ongoing increase in court litigation related to climate change worldwide.[8] There are administrative climate change cases against governments and other state authorities as well as civil climate change cases between private parties, eg, companies, organisations, individuals, etc. This chapter will focus on litigation between private parties in Asia and put them into the context of climate change litigation worldwide. It will first provide a short explanation of the notion of climate change litigation in general as well as the specifics of cases between private parties. Then, in the third section of this chapter, an overview of all cases of climate change litigation between private parties in Asia will be given, ie, in Japan, in China, and in South Korea, as so far these are the only jurisdictions with relevant cases. For each country the situation of GHG emissions as well as its international commitments made and national legislation introduced will be briefly explained, before the relevant cases and main legal issues therein are analysed. The fourth section of this chapter will identify the characteristics of Asian climate change litigation between private parties by placing these cases in the context of international trends based on a few international landmark cases. Here, the relevant Asian cases and their characteristics and issues will be put in comparison to the international landmark cases. In the conclusion, the findings will be briefly summarised.

II. Notion of Climate Change Litigation and Specifics of Cases between Private Parties

A. Notion of Climate Change Litigation in General

The term 'climate change litigation' is neither a technical term nor does it have any widely accepted specific and clear definition.[9] Climate change litigation can describe any kind of litigation that has the objective of legal protection of the climate, eg, by forbidding activities whose impact

[4] M Rodi and M Kalis, 'Klimaklagen als Instrument des Klimaschutzes' (2022) *Klima und Recht* 5, 8.

[5] T Sonohara [苑原俊明], 'Climate Litigation and International Human Rights Law: Urgenda Foundation v State of the Netherlands [気候訴訟と国際人権法: Urgenda財団対オランダ王国事件]' (2021) 30(2) *Daitō Hōgaku* [大東法学] 119, 120.

[6] Rodi and Kalis (n 4) 5.

[7] ibid 5, 7; S Kubota [久保田修平], 'Corporate Legal Affairs and ESG Investments in the Era of Climate Change, SDGs: Taking Trends in Climate Change Litigation into Consideration [気候変動時代における企業法務とESG投資、SDGs: 気候変動訴訟の動向も踏まえて]' (2021) *Kankyō-hō Kenkyū/Ningen Kankyō Mondai Kenkyū-kai hen* [環境法研究/人間環境問題研究会 編] 46, 33.

[8] S Mundy, P Temple-West, K Talman and G Tett, 'Climate change activism heads to the courtroom' *Financial Times* (29 September 2021) at www.ft.com/content/b18ff95a-413b-4b2d-9f6f-8360648512db#:~:text=This%20week,%20Deutsche%20Umwelthilfe,%20a.

[9] Rodi and Kalis (n 4) 5, 6.

would harm the climate, by requesting specific climate-protective measures, or even by requesting compensation for damages caused by climate change. Such actions can be directed against the state government, other public authorities or against private companies or individuals.[10]

There are many kinds of climate change trials. In some cases, the plaintiffs aim to force governments towards regulatory actions. In other cases, they might be seeking remedies for harm suffered resulting from GHG emissions. Yet in other cases, the goal might be injunctions to prevent or stop such harm from occurring.

However, individual plaintiffs or environmental organisations suing on behalf of their members often face several administrative and other legal issues when they try to bring their cases before the competent courts.[11] These issues include standing, as plaintiffs in principle need to prove that they have a personal stake in the controversy.[12] This often creates a hurdle, as it is difficult to connect mostly objective environmental matters, eg, protection of the atmosphere and other community resources, with specifically subjective legal interests.[13] Furthermore, the derivation of a subjective right that can confer standing is a common issue in many jurisdictions.[14] Plaintiffs will often argue that a 'right to climate protection' or 'right to a healthy environment' derives from constitutional or international human rights, but in most jurisdictions the constitution clearly does not specifically mention such a right. Therefore, basing claims on such a right requires a substantive legal argument that ties into other parameters that are part of the constitution or international agreements.

Then, another issue widely faced by plaintiffs is the separation of powers.[15] In principle, important political questions need to be decided by parliaments or other legislative authorities. However, these are often only directly bound by a rather vague constitutional framework. Therefore, legislative authorities have the prerogative to assess[16] and make specific decisions on how to solve a certain problem.[17] And while executive authorities on the other hand are bound to national laws, they still often have broad discretion in their decision-making processes. Accordingly, judicial authorities always have to assess whether the questions placed before them are actually theirs to decide and if they are not overstepping the thin line between the three separate state powers by deciding them.[18] Where specific legislation is required or where executive authorities do have broad discretion in their decision-making, the scope of judicial review is very limited and courts may only overturn the status quo in cases of administrative abuses that can be qualified as evident.[19]

B. Specifics of Cases between Private Parties

In general, climate change litigation can be divided into administrative and civil cases depending on the defendant. In administrative cases, the defendant is the state, including the state government, relevant ministries, federal or local authorities. Possible goals of litigation may be to have an

[10] T Heymann, 'Klimaklagen – von grundrechtlichen Schutzpflichten und zivilrechtlicher Haftung' (2022) *InfrastrukturRecht* 60.
[11] Rosso Grossman (n 1) 345, 348.
[12] ibid 345, 353.
[13] Hanschel and Schultze (n 2) 166, 170.
[14] Rodi and Kalis (n 4) 5, 7.
[15] ibid 5, 6.
[16] Einschätzungsprärogative.
[17] Rodi and Kalis (n 4) 5, 7.
[18] Rosso Grossman (n 1) 345, 357.
[19] F Fellenberg, 'Rechtsschutz als Instrument des Klimaschutzes – ein Zwischenstand' (2022) *Neue Zeitschrift für Verwaltungsrecht*, 913, 914.

administrative decision declared invalid, eg, planning permission approvals granted by authorities, etc, or to force the administrative authorities to render specific decisions or even specific legislation to reach goals stipulated by international agreements by changing the regulatory framework.

Most administrative cases are filed on the grounds of human rights. As a relevant legal interest, human rights may be enshrined in national constitutions or legislation as well as in universal or regional human rights treaties. A 'right to a healthy environment' or a 'right to climate protection' seem to be gaining recognition around the globe in national as well as international legal systems.[20] To derive such a human right, plaintiffs generally argue from multiple other human rights or other parameters enshrined in national constitutions or international agreements, eg, the right to life, the right to freedom, provisions on environmental protection, etc.

In civil cases, on the other hand, the defendants are private companies or individuals, therefore constituting cases of litigation between private parties. Here, plaintiffs generally either claim for damages for the harm, which they have suffered from certain emissions, or they might seek injunctions to prevent such expected harm in the future. These cases are usually brought before courts under the respective nation's tort law.[21]

In cases between private parties, the burden of proof may become an issue and a hurdle for access to justice. The civil procedure law of most jurisdictions, in principle, imposes the burden of proof on the party whose legal position would benefit from the proof of the specific fact, ie, in most constellations of climate change litigation, on the plaintiff. Regarding the defendant's specific action and the harm suffered by the plaintiff, however, it is often very difficult to prove a direct causal connection. Without being able to prove such direct causation, many plaintiffs fail to provide the evidence deemed required to be successful in an action claiming for damages or seeking injunctions.[22]

III. Climate Change Litigation between Private Parties in Asia

There are cases of court litigation related to climate change in many jurisdictions across Asia, eg, in China, India, Indonesia, Japan, Nepal, Pakistan, Philippines, South Korea, Taiwan, Thailand, etc. Most of these cases involve state actors, including national governments, ministers, local or provincial governments, etc. However, this chapter will be focused on disputes between private actors, ie, companies, other entities, non-governmental organisations (NGOs) and individuals. In Asia, there has only been a handful of such court cases between civil parties so far. Up to date, civil court cases related to climate change can only be identified in Japan, China and South Korea.[23]

A. Japan

i. Situation of GHG Emissions and Anti-Measures in Japan

Coming after China, the United States, India and Russia, Japan ranks fifth in the world in GHG emissions. The reason for this is that most Japanese emissions originate from the energy sector which, for the most part, still depends on coal-fired power plants for the generation of energy.

[20] Hanschel and Schultze (n 2) 166, 167.
[21] Fellenberg (n 19) 913, 914.
[22] Rosso Grossman (n 1) 345, 360.
[23] See Sabin Center for Climate Change Law of Columbia Law School, *Global Climate Change Litigation by Jurisdiction*, at climatecasechart.com/non-us-jurisdiction/.

While this dependency had been declining slightly until 2010, the Tohoku Earthquake and Tsunami on 11 March 2011, paired with the Fukushima Daiichi Nuclear Disaster,[24] led to a drastic shift in Japanese energy policies. With the resulting shutdown of all nuclear power plants in Japan, the reliance was refocused on fossil fuels, especially coal-fired power plants. In Japan even new coal-fired power plants are in planning or under construction still nowadays, while other parts of the industrialised world are already in the process of gradually shutting down their coal-fired power plants and replacing them with sources of renewable energy in order to reduce national GHG emissions.[25]

Although there are still new plans for ongoing constructions of coal-fired power plants, Japan has signed and accepted the Paris Agreement and thereby committed itself to achieving the goal of net zero GHG emissions by 2050. Based on that, on the national level, Japan with its Nationally Determined Contribution (NDC) has furthermore committed to a 46 per cent reduction in its GHG emissions by 2030 compared to the peak of emissions in 2013. As for national legislation, the 2021 revision of the Act on Promotion of Global Warming Countermeasures[26] includes the legally binding goal of net zero emissions by 2050 as well. As per its content, this act moreover puts the obligation on state and local authorities, private citizens, businesses, and other private organisations to respect the goal of net zero GHG emissions and other objectives stipulated in the Paris Agreement and thereby makes them legally binding for all relevant actors in Japan.[27]

ii. *Climate Change Litigation in Japan*

In recent years, there have been several court cases litigated before Japanese courts in relation to climate change. All of these have been directed against the construction or operation of coal-fired power plants. Administrative court cases are directed against METI (Ministry of Economy, Trade and Industry) and its issuance of the Notice of Finalization of the Environmental Impact Assessment, by which the electricity suppliers' plans of construction and operation of the plants are approved. The two relevant administrative cases are the *Administrative Kobe* case[28] and the

[24] The Tohoku Earthquake and Tsunami on 11 March 2011, also known as 'Great East Japan Earthquake', *Higashi Nihon Dai-shinsai* [東日本大震災], in Japan, had a seismic magnitude of 9.0–9.1 and was the fourth most powerful earthquake worldwide and the most powerful earthquake in Japan since the beginning of modern record-keeping in 1900. Lasting for approximately six minutes with its epicentre in the Pacific Ocean less than 100 km off the coast of Japan's Tohoku area, the earthquake triggered an enormous tsunami that hit land shortly after, with earthquake and tsunami causing approximately 20,000 deaths and more than 200,000 people losing their homes. Furthermore, the tsunami caused a nuclear disaster at Fukushima Daiichi Nuclear Power Plant, which included the meltdown of three reactors and the discharge of large amounts of contaminated water and caused the evacuation of hundreds of thousands of residents in the surrounding areas.

[25] T Shimamura [島村健], S Sugita [杉田峻介], N Ikeda [池田直樹], M Asaoka [浅岡美恵] and J Wada [和田重太], 'Legal Arguments in Climate Litigation in Japan: Taking the Kobe Coal-Fired Power Case as an Example [日本における気候訴訟の法的論点: 神戸石炭火力訴訟を例として]' (2021) 71(2) *Kōbe Hōgaku Zasshi* [神戸法學雜誌] 1, 3.

[26] Act No. 117 of 9 October 1998, *Chikyū Ondanka Taisaku no Suishin ni Kansuru Hōritsu* [地球温暖化対策の推進に関する法律].

[27] Y Nishikawa, 'Guest Post: Climate Litigation in Japan: Citizens' Attempts for the Coal Phase-Out' (*Climate Law Blog*, 1 June 2022) blogs.law.columbia.edu/climatechange/2022/06/01/climate-litigation-in-japan-citizens-attempts-for-the-coal-phase-out/.

[28] *Citizens' Committee on the Kobe Coal-Fired Power Plant v Japan*, Osaka District Court, 15 March 2021 (平成30(行ウ)第184号); Osaka High Court, 26 April 2022 (令和3年(行コ)第46号); Supreme Court, 9 March 2023 (令和4年(行ツ)第198号, 令和4年(行ヒ)第215号). There is an administrative as well as a civil case against the same coal-fired power plants in Kobe. As the focus of this chapter lies on civil cases between private parties, the term 'Kobe Case' here in principle refers to the civil case, unless otherwise stated.

Yokosuka case.[29] On the other hand, civil court cases have been directed against the private operators, suppliers, etc. The goal of litigation is generally an injunction against the construction or operation of the relevant plants based on an alleged infringement of the plaintiffs' personal rights. Relevant examples here are the *Sendai* case[30] and the *Civil Kobe* case[31].[32]

Among the above, the most famous example of climate change litigation in Japan is the *Administrative Kobe* case, in which the plaintiffs lost in the first instance before the Osaka District Court as well as on appeal before the Osaka High Court.[33] The plaintiffs decided to request a final appeal before the Japanese Supreme Court, which was the first climate-change-related case to reach the highest court of Japan. However, in March 2023 the Supreme Court issued its decision rejecting the request for a final appeal and upholding the Osaka High Court's judgment due to inadmissibility according to procedural reasons.[34]

There are four main points that have been debated regarding the Japanese cases so far. As it is the case in administrative court actions in many other jurisdictions, the question in Japan has been whether plaintiffs lack standing to even bring their claims before the courts in response to a governmental action that may affect the climate. This is at issue in many climate change litigation cases. Often it may be questionable how the plaintiffs could be directly affected by the measures at issue.[35] Furthermore, the specific rights that confer standing on the plaintiffs can be problematic in matters related to climate change, as no explicit 'right to climate protection' nor anything comparable exists on the constitutional level or in any other national legislation. Therefore, such a right can only be derived from and interpreted on the basis of other rights and principles.

Another set of questions that has come up in Japan is how much discretion executive governmental bodies have with regard to their climate change policies and the specific measures they may take. To what extent are they bound by international law, eg, the Paris Agreement, or their self-imposed GHG reduction targets? And moreover, when may a court declare a measure invalid that the executive branch has taken? Due to these questionable points, the justiciability of the controversy is often at issue with the principle of separation of powers.[36]

Then, it is still unclear and a highly discussed topic in academia how and under which circumstances plaintiffs can address, through litigation, a parliament's failure to legislate, eg, if it has failed to implement measures consistent with international GHG emission goals. In particular, it seems questionable whether and in which cases courts of law can force legislative bodies to enact specific laws in this context.[37]

[29] *Yokosuka Citizens v Japan*, Tokyo District Court, 27 January 2023 (令和元年(行ウ)第275号, 令和元年(行ウ)第598号).

[30] *Sendai Citizens v Sendai Power Station*, Sendai District Court, 28 October 2020 (平成29年(ワ)第1175号); Sendai High Court, 27 April 2021 (令和2年(ネ)第372号).

[31] *Citizens' Committee on the Kobe Coal-Fired Power Plant v Kobe Steel Ltd., et al*, Kobe District Court, 20 March 2023 (平成30年(ワ)第1551号); Osaka High Court, 24 April 2025 (令和5年(ネ)第1029号).

[32] N Kojima [小島延夫], 'Worldwide Climate Litigation Today [世界の気候訴訟の今日]' (2022) *Jiyū to Seigi* [自由と正義] 73 (3), 18, 24; Shimamura, Sugita, Ikeda, Asaoka and Wada (n 25) 1, 3, 4.

[33] *Citizens' Committee on the Kobe Coal-Fired Power Plant v Japan*, Osaka District Court, 15 March 2021 (平成30(行ウ)第184号); Osaka High Court, 26 April 2022 (令和3年(行コ)第46号).

[34] *Citizens' Committee on the Kobe Coal-Fired Power Plant v Japan*, Supreme Court, 9 March 2023 (令和4年(行ツ)第198号, 令和4年(行ヒ)第215号).

[35] Shimamura, Sugita, Ikeda, Asaoka and Wada (n 25) 1, 87.

[36] M Asaoka [浅岡美恵], 'Worldwide Trends in Climate Change Litigation: Implications for the Climate Change Litigation in Japan [世界の気候変動訴訟の動向: 日本における気候変動訴訟への示唆]' (2019) 49(1) *Kankyō to Kōgai* [環境と公害] 31, 35.

[37] Kojima (n 32) 18, 25.

Lastly, in civil court actions between private parties, the issue frequently comes up what specific rights plaintiffs can base their tort claims on and what kind of evidence plaintiffs have to submit in order to prove a breach of a duty of care. Here, a clear distinction must be made between emissions of pollutants and GHG emissions. Since there are often concrete legal standards for the concentration of air pollutants, it is significantly easier in a tort case to prove violations of personal rights from air pollutants than from GHG emissions. The reason for that is that emitting an amount of air pollutants higher than the legally stipulated standards constitutes an illegal act and illegality is a requirement under most tort law provisions conferring claims or other rights to a damaged or potentially endangered party.

In yet another more recent case, ie, the *Youth Climate Case Japan for Tomorrow*,[38] in 2024, for the first time, a group of young plaintiffs has filed a suit that is not directed against a specific project, but against the responsibility of Japanese companies in the energy sector on the whole and their GHG reduction goals. They argue that the failure of major power companies to implement adequate and scientifically grounded GHG emission reductions constitutes a violation of their rights. However, this case is still pending before the Nagoya District Court.

a. *Sendai Citizens v Sendai Power Station*[39]

The first climate-change-related court action in Japan was filed in September 2017 before the Sendai District Court. Several citizens from Sendai requested an injunction against the operation of the newly built Sendai Power Station. They argued that the operation constituted violations of their personal rights[40] to life, health, and bodily integrity due to the emission of environmental pollutants, eg, sulfur oxides (SOx) and nitrogen oxides (NOx), as well as climate change, worsened by the GHG emissions expected from the power plant. Furthermore, the plaintiffs argued with their 'right to maintain biodiversity', based on Article 13 of the Japanese Constitution, which they regarded to be violated by the emission of hazardous substances.

During the process the arguments presented by the plaintiffs were modified significantly. Only tort claims based on the 'right to a peaceful life', a variant of personal rights, which was claimed to be violated by the environmental pollution, remained in the end. The court had determined that the 'right to maintain biodiversity' was not recognised under Japanese civil law and the plaintiffs had withdrawn their claim of violations of their personal rights caused by climate change, due to the difficulty of proving an illegal activity based on GHG emissions. Thus, the final judgment in October 2020 only dealt with the possible violation of the 'right to a peaceful life' caused by the emission of environmental pollutants. The Sendai District Court rejected the claim, concluding that the environmental pollution was not serious, and the evidence brought by the plaintiffs was insufficient. However, the court further mentioned the power station's operator's social accountability to consider the citizens' concerns regarding environmental pollution and do its best to relieve these concerns.

In December 2020, one of the citizens filed an appeal to the Sendai High Court. In his statement, the appellant claimed that the Sendai District Court, inter alia, should have considered the

[38] *Youth Climate Case Japan for Tomorrow*, Nagoya District Court, still pending; for an English summary see also Sabin Center for Climate Change Law of Columbia Law School, *Youth Climate Case Japan for Tomorrow*, at www.climatecasechart.com/document/youth-climate-case-japan-for-tomorrow_74f6?l=japan.

[39] *Sendai Citizens v Sendai Power Station*, Sendai District Court, 28 October 2020 (平成29年(ワ)第1175号); Sendai High Court, 27 April 2021 (令和2年(ネ)第372号); for an English summary see also Sabin Center for Climate Change Law of Columbia Law School, *Sendai Citizens v Sendai Power Station*, at climatecasechart.com/non-us-case/sendai-citizens-v-sendai-power-station/.

[40] *Jinkaku-ken* [人格権].

consequences of global warming as well as GHG emissions either as factors to weigh against the public necessity of the power plant or as aggravating factors of the tort, even though they could not be directly addressed as an illegal activity violating the plaintiffs' rights. He substantiated that the GHG emissions from this new power plant were not consistent with the widely accepted ideas in modern Japanese society and the Japanese government's national carbon neutral policies. Finally, he argued that, based on precedents and academic theories regarding personal rights and air pollution, the protection of personal rights outweighed the public necessity for a new power plant by far, claiming that such a necessity did not even exist due to the surplus of power already being supplied.

In the appeal judgment from April 2021, the Sendai High Court explained that the presence of surplus at one moment could not prove the lack of public necessity for the power plant, as power demand and supply were changing over time and heavily influenced by different factors. The court did briefly deal with the negative effects of GHG emissions on global warming and the ecosystem. However, it denied the existence of a concrete danger to global warming or biodiversity. The court, apart from that, found that the danger to health caused by the new power plant was still within socially acceptable limits, when balancing the level of damage, the social usability, public nature, and preventive measures, etc.

b. *Citizens' Committee on the Kobe Coal-Fired Power Plant v Kobe Steel Ltd., et al*[41]

In another case, in September 2018, a group of citizens filed a civil lawsuit seeking an injunction to stop the construction and operation of two coal-fired power plant units. The citizens are being represented by the 'Citizens' Committee on the Kobe Coal-Fired Power Plant.'[42] The same committee had also represented citizens in the *Administrative Kobe* case, which had unsuccessfully been filed against METI's Notice of Finalization of the Environmental Impact Assessment of the same two coal-fired power plant units and was the first climate-change-related case of litigation to reach the Japanese Supreme Court. In this civil case the plaintiffs filed their action against Kobe Steel Ltd., Kobelco Power Kobe No. 2 Inc. and Kansai Electric Power Co., Inc. as defendants. They claimed that the construction and operation of the new coal-fired units would lead to emissions of CO_2, as well as air pollutants, which violate their personal rights to life, bodily integrity, and health as well as the 'right to a peaceful life'. According to the plaintiffs' argumentation and interpretation, the 'right to a peaceful life' should include the 'right to enjoy a stable climate' as well as the 'right to clean air and a healthy and clean environment'. In addition to that, the plaintiffs addressed the general incompatibility of the construction of new coal-fired power plants with Japan's 2030 and 2050 GHG reduction targets. Another argument brought forward was the air pollution in adjacent residential areas, where the required standards of air quality were already not being met.

In March 2023, the Kobe District Court rendered a judgment regarding the requested injunction to stop the construction and operation of the two new coal-fired power plant units. At first, the court discussed a violation of the plaintiffs' personal rights to life, bodily integrity and health as well

[41] *Citizens' Committee on the Kobe Coal-Fired Power Plant v Kobe Steel Ltd., et al*, Kobe District Court, 20 March 2023 (平成30年(ワ)第1551号); Osaka High Court, 24 April 2025 (令和5年(ネ)第1029号); for an English summary see also Sabin Center for Climate Change Law of Columbia Law School, *Citizens' Committee on the Kobe Coal-Fired Power Plant v Kobe Steel Ltd., et al.*, at climatecasechart.com/non-us-case/citizens-committee-on-the-kobe-coal-fired-power-plant-v-kobe-steel-ltd-et-al/.

[42] *Kōbe no Sekitan Karyoku Hatsuden wo Kangaeru Kai* [神戸の石炭火力発電を考える会], see kobesekitan.jimdoweb.com/.

as a violation of the 'right to a peaceful life' caused by the emission of air pollutants, eg, SOx, NOx, mercury, etc, and denied the existence of a sufficiently concrete danger.

In a third step, the court assessed, if the aggravation of climate change caused by the construction and following operation of new coal-fired power plant units constituted a violation of the citizens' personal rights. Regarding this third argument, the court at first acknowledged that climate change is likely to affect the plaintiffs as well as people on the entire planet and that the plaintiffs may suffer damage from it. However, the court also found that the level of damage suffered from natural disasters and the specific population and places affected as well as the time of occurrence of such disasters were still uncertain factors. Furthermore, when determining the existence of a concrete danger, the court stated that this could not be equated to the likelihood of the global compliance with GHG emission reduction targets, as the concrete danger needed to be assessed based on the damage that each individual plaintiff would suffer from climate change. International reduction targets, however, had been established in order to prevent global warming on the entire planet and not for the specific individual plaintiffs. Moreover, the court found that stopping the operation of the two units in question was not a potential means for achieving the claimed global reduction targets. Therefore, finally, the court denied the existence of a concrete danger to the citizens' rights to life, bodily integrity and health. However, it admitted that there could be an abstract danger, as GHG emissions from coal-fired power plants could aggravate global warming and climate change.

In a last step, the court discussed a violation of the plaintiffs' 'right to a peaceful life' and 'right to a stable climate', which was claimed to be included therein, from climate change caused by GHG emissions. At first, it found that the possible damage to the claimed rights only constituted uncertain future dangers and therefore was not sufficiently serious. Secondly, it stated that a 'right to a stable climate' was not specifically legally protected and a concrete danger was not imminent. Finally, the court added that the responsibility for the claimed violations and dangers could not unilaterally be conferred on the two new coal-fired power plants unit, thereby denying a concrete causal relation. Overall, the court denied an injunction based on the absence of sufficient grounds.

In April 2023, the citizens lodged an appeal before the Osaka High Court. Once more, they requested an injunction against the operation of the coal-fired power plant units as well as an injunction against the instructions to generate electricity by Kansai Electric Power Co., Inc. In addition to that, the appellants requested a phased implementation of GHG emission reduction measures with the goal to annihilate all emissions by 2040 in accordance with the worldwide goal to eliminate all coal-fired power plant units by that year. They argued that a violation of their rights was already constituted, even without specific disasters, merely based on the fact that they had to 'live in a climate unstable world' and were continuously exposed to potential damages. Furthermore, the appellants admitted that GHG emissions were not in general illegal. But they postulated that emissions rendering the 1.5°C target impossible must be illegal and argued that this included the GHG emissions from the two relevant coal-fired power plant units.

In April 2024, while the Osaka High Court acknowledged that climate change and its side effects could possibly constitute violations of the appellants' personal rights to life, bodily integrity, and health, it still dismissed the appeal, as it denied the necessary legal causation between the specific emissions and the potential violations of appellants' personal rights from climate change due to the indirect and abstract relationship.

c. *Youth Climate Case Japan for Tomorrow*[43]

In 2024, 16 young plaintiffs from across Japan initiated legal proceedings in the Nagoya District Court against ten of the country's largest thermal power companies, including JERA Corporation. The plaintiffs seek an injunction to compel these corporations to reduce CO_2 emissions in line with internationally recognised scientific standards, specifically those necessary to limit global warming to a rise of 1.5°C compared to pre-industrial levels in accordance with the goals stipulated under the Paris Agreement. This litigation frames the climate crisis as a threat to the fundamental rights and future livelihoods of Japan's younger generations.

The plaintiffs argue that the defendants, collectively accounting for a significant proportion of Japan's energy-derived CO_2 emissions (in 2019, approximately 333 million tons or 33 per cent), have failed to adopt adequate emission reduction targets or effective decarbonisation strategies. Notably, the electricity generation sector as a whole is responsible for about 400 million tons of CO_2 emissions or 40 per cent of Japan's energy-related CO_2 emissions, placing 16th globally in terms of national emissions when this sector is considered independently. Despite these emission levels and international obligations, the defendants continue to invest in coal-fired generation and unproven decarbonisation technologies, eg, hydrogen or carbon capture and storage, etc, while lacking sufficiently ambitious 2030 and 2035 emission reduction targets. JERA, for instance, has set only a 40 per cent reduction target by 2035, thereby falling short of the IPCC's recommended benchmarks of a 48 per cent reduction by 2030 and a 65 per cent reduction by 2035 relative to 2019 levels.

Furthermore, the plaintiffs invoke recent international developments, eg, statements by UN Secretary-General António Guterres describing 'global boiling' and highlighting the danger of extreme heat to human life, as evidence for the urgent need for emission reductions. They call on the court to recognise a legal obligation for major emitters in industrialised nations, such as Japan, to reduce emissions in accordance with global climate science and multilateral commitments, including those from the IPCC, the International Energy Agency (IEA), and the G7, aiming for carbon neutrality of the electricity generation sector by 2035.

In conclusion, the plaintiffs contend that the defendants' inadequate response constitutes an infringement of their personal rights and seek judicial intervention to ensure alignment with the 1.5°C target. They also advocate for a structural transition by the defendant companies toward renewable energy production. The first hearing was held on 24 October 2024, during which the defendants indicated their intent to contest the claims. At this stage, the case is still pending before the Nagoya District Court.

B. China

i. *Situation of GHG Emissions and Anti-Measures in China*

China is the country consuming the most energy and emitting the highest amount of GHG in the world, as the energy sector is still heavily dependent on coal-fired power stations.[44] On the other

[43] *Youth Climate Case Japan for Tomorrow*, Nagoya District Court, still pending; for an English summary see also Sabin Center for Climate Change Law of Columbia Law School, *Youth Climate Case Japan for Tomorrow*, at www.climatecasechart.com/document/youth-climate-case-japan-for-tomorrow_74f6?l=japan.

[44] J Liu, 'China's renewable energy law and policy: A critical review' (2019) *Renewable and Sustainable Energy Reviews* 99, 212.

hand, China is also the largest producer of renewable energy worldwide, eg, hydroelectricity, solar power and wind power.[45]

China is a signatory party to the Paris Agreement and has pledged the targets to peak emissions before 2030 and reach carbon-neutrality before 2060.[46] The Chinese Renewable Energy Law[47] has been adopted into China's national law at the 14th Meeting of the Standing Committee of the 10th National People's Congress on 28 February 2005 and entered into force as of 1 January 2006. According to the decision of the 12th Meeting of the Standing Committee of the 11th National People's Congress of the People's Republic of China on 26 December 2009 the law has been amended, with the amendments entering into force on 1 April 2010. The law includes specific national renewable energy targets, arrangements for the funding of renewable energy generation as well as mandatory purchase policies.[48]

ii. Climate Change Litigation in China

In China, there are two cases of litigation against state-owned enterprises led by the NGO 'Friends of Nature Institute'.[49] Both cases concern the duty to purchase renewable energy in order to protect the environment under the Renewable Energy Law and the specific scope of this duty. One specific issue is if this duty to purchase renewable energy includes the duty to connect the purchased renewable energy to the grid. Another case led by the NGO Beijing Grassland Alliance Environmental Protection Center is directed against Xingyi Shangcheng Power Generation Company Limited questioning whether CO_2 emission and quota laws have been violated by the defendant.

a. *The Friends of Nature Institute v Gansu State Grid*[50]

In June 2017, the NGO Friends of Nature Institute filed a suit against the Gansu State Grid, which is a state-owned enterprise. The plaintiff claimed that Article 14 was violated due to high rates of wasted wind energy. While Article 2[51] defines the term 'renewable energy', Article 14[52] regulates that power grid enterprises shall: (1) purchase the full amount of electricity

[45] A Hove, 'Trends and Contradictions in China's Renewable Energy Policy' (2020), see www.energypolicy.columbia.edu/publications/trends-and-contradictions-china-s-renewable-energy-policy/.

[46] Y Yang and K Lo, 'China's renewable energy and energy efficiency policies toward carbon neutrality: A systematic cross-sectoral review' (2023) 35(1) *Energy & Environment* 491.

[47] *Zhōnghuárénmíngònghéguó Kězàishēng Néngyuán Fǎ* [中华人民共和国可再生能源法], see www.nea.gov.cn/2017-11/02/c_136722869.htm, English translation at english.www.gov.cn/archive/laws_regulations/2014/08/23/content_281474983043598.htm.

[48] S Schuman and A Lin, 'China's Renewable Energy Law and its impact on renewable power in China: Progress, challenges and recommendations for improving implementation' (2012) *Energy Policy* 51, 89.

[49] *Zìrán zhī Yǒu Huánjìng Yánjiūsuǒ* [自然之友环境研究所], see website at www.fon.org.cn/.

[50] *The Friends of Nature Institute v Gansu State Grid*, Lanzhou Intermediate People's Court, 14 August 2018, (2017)甘01民初434号; Gansu High People's Court, 28 December 2018, (2018)甘民终679号; Gansu Mining Area People's Court, 10 April 2023, (2019)甘95民初7号; for an English summary see also Sabin Center for Climate Change Law of Columbia Law School, *The Friends of Nature Institute v Gansu State Grid*, at climatecasechart.com/non-us-case/the-friends-of-nature-institute-v-gansu-state-grid/.

[51] Article 2(1): For the purpose of this Law, 'renewable energy' refers to non-fossil energies, such as wind energy, solar energy, hydroenergy, bioenergy, geothermal energy and ocean energy, etc.

[52] Article 14(3): Power grid enterprises shall conclude grid connection agreements with enterprises which generate electricity by using renewable energy resources and which have gone through the administrative licensing or archive-filing formalities according to the plan for the development and utilisation of renewable energy resources, purchasing in full amount the on-grid electricity of the grid-connected power generation projects which meet the grid connection

generated from renewable energy resources, and (2) 'provide services for bringing electricity generated by using renewable energy resources on grid'. The defendant had purchased the electricity from wind and solar power, but without connecting it to the grid. Gansu State Grid defended this by stating that Article 14 did not explicitly require power grid enterprises to connect all of the purchased renewable energy to the grid. The Friends of Nature Institute, on the other hand, requested holding the defendant responsible for the environmental damage caused by using coal-fired power instead of renewable energy based on Article 29,[53] although Article 29 explicitly requires 'economic losses'.

In August 2018, the Lanzhou Intermediate People's Court dismissed the plaintiff's claims on the grounds that the defendant did not cause any direct environmental pollution, but merely engaged in purchase, connection and distribution of electricity. Subsequently, the Friends of Nature Institute filed an appeal to the Gansu High People's Court, which overruled the lower court's decision to dismiss the action on procedural grounds in December of the same year and transferred the case to the Gansu Mining Area People's Court. In June 2019, the court started the proceedings, which were interrupted by the COVID-19 pandemic for an extensive amount of time. Finally, the parties settled the case by means of a mediation agreement supervised by the Gansu Mining Area People's Court. The agreement included the defendant's obligations to invest extensively into renewable energy sources and connect the generated electricity to the grid before 2025, to submit annual reports regarding the implementation of these measures, and to disclose general information on the consumption of electricity generated from renewable energy sources to the public.

b. *The Friends of Nature Institute v Ningxia State Grid*[54]

Shortly after filing its first lawsuit related to climate in January 2018, the same NGO also sued the Ningxia State Grid for its high rates of abandoned wind and solar energy, again claiming a violation of Article 14. Here, the defendant had not purchased the full amount of electricity from wind and solar energy. Therefore, the plaintiff sought that the full amount had to be purchased from renewable energy in the future. In addition, the Friends of Nature Institute requested a disclosure of any related information, an official apology as well as coverage of the litigation costs from Ningxia State Grid.

technical standards in the coverage area of their power grids. Electricity generating enterprises are obliged to cooperate with power grid enterprises in protecting grid security.

Article 14(4): Power grid enterprises shall strengthen the power grid construction, expand the scope of areas where electricity generated by using renewable energy resources is provided, develop and apply intelligent power grid and energy storage technologies, improve the operation and management of power grids, improve the ability for absorbing electricity generated by using renewable energy resources, and provide services for bringing electricity generated by using renewable energy resources on grid.

[53] Article 29: Any power grid enterprise violating Article 14 of this Law by failing to purchase the quantity of the electricity generated by using regenerable energy resources as required and thus causing economic losses to the relevant enterprise which uses regenerable energy resources to generate electricity shall be liable for such losses and be ordered by the State Electricity Regulatory Commission to make corrections within a specified time limit and, if it refuses to make corrections as required, be given a fine not exceeding the amount of the losses suffered by the relevant power enterprise.

[54] *The Friends of Nature Institute v Ningxia State Grid*, Yinchuan Intermediate People's Court, 4 April 2023; (2018)宁01民初109号; for an English summary see also Sabin Center for Climate Change Law of Columbia Law School, *The Friends of Nature Institute v Ningxia State Grid*, at climatecasechart.com/non-us-case/the-friends-of-nature-institute-v-ningxia-state-grid/.

In April 2023, the Yinchuan Intermediate People's Court decided that a violation of Article 14 could not be found. Although the court confirmed that power grid enterprises were, in general, obligated to protect the environment and purchase electricity generated from wind and solar energy under Article 14, this obligation could only stand where electricity coverage was confirmed and safe. So, in this case, the court found that a diversification of used energy resources was essential in order to assure grid stability due to the volatile nature of wind and solar energy. However, it also highlighted the power grid enterprise's social responsibility for facilitating energy transition plans towards carbon-neutrality as well as the NGO's efforts in this public interest matter and ordered the defendant to bear the litigation costs on these grounds. The Friends of Nature Institute has filed an appeal, which is still pending.

c. *Beijing Grassland Alliance Environmental Protection Center v Xingyi Shangcheng Power Generation Company Limited*[55]

In 2023, the NGO Beijing Grassland Alliance Environmental Protection Center, together with three other NGOs, filed a lawsuit against Xingyi Shangcheng Power Generation Company Limited, primarily addressing three issues: environmental damages, CO_2 emissions, and CO_2 quotas.

First, the plaintiff accused the defendant of engaging in prolonged activities that involved exceeding legally permissible limits in the emission of waste gases, dust, and other pollutants. Apart from that, the defendant was also alleged to have tampered with pollution monitoring data and neglected to maintain monitoring equipment. The plaintiff claimed that these actions constituted environmental tort and, therefore, sought the court to mandate injunction, restoration, compensation, and a public apology. In June 2024, the Court of Qianxinan Buyei and Miao Autonomous Prefecture rendered its decision and found that the defendant's sulfur dioxide and dust emissions did indeed exceed the legally permitted limits, establishing civil liability for environmental tort. However, the defendant had rectified the emissions prior to the lawsuit, which made no further restoration necessary. Finally, the court awarded the plaintiff 9,400 CNY for the loss of ecological services but denied requests for further remedies.

Second, the plaintiff argued that the defendant had exceeded permissible CO_2 emission limits. However, the court ruled that the plaintiff had failed to prove that the defendant's non-payment for additional CO_2 quotas had caused environmental harm. Nevertheless, the court emphasized the future risks associated with excess CO_2 emissions, urging stringent controls. Although CO_2 is not currently classified as a pollutant under Chinese law, the court underscored its potential environmental impact.

Lastly, the plaintiff contended that, despite exceeding allowable CO_2 emission limits, the defendant had failed to pay for more than 800,000 tons of CO_2 emission quotas during the first compliance period of China's carbon trading system. In this regard, the court ruled that the defendant had indeed not fully paid for the required CO_2 emission quotas. The court reaffirmed

[55] *Beijing Grassland Alliance Environmental Protection Center v Xingyi Shangcheng Power Generation Company Limited*, Court of Qianxinan Buyei and Miao Autonomous Prefecture, 7 June 2024, (2023)黔23民初19号; for an English summary see also Sabin Center for Climate Change Law of Columbia Law School, *Beijing Grassland Alliance Environmental Protection Center v Xingyi Shangcheng Power Generation Company Limited*, at www.climatecasechart.com/document/beijing-grassland-alliance-environmental-protection-center-v-xingyi-shangcheng-power-generation-company-limited_69c2?l=china.

the defendant's responsibility to purchase the necessary carbon credits, despite the plaintiff's inability to demonstrate direct environmental damage from the non-payment.

In conclusion, while CO_2 is not classified as a pollutant in Chinese law, its emissions are still subject to stringent regulations. The defendant's repeated failure to comply with carbon trading obligations was deemed unlawful and contrary to the broader goals of climate change mitigation and environmental protection. This decision highlights the evolving legal framework regarding CO_2 emissions and the responsibilities of corporations under China's emerging environmental and carbon trading systems.

C. South Korea

i. Situation of GHG Emissions and Anti-Measures in South Korea

According to data from the International Energy Agency, in 2017 South Korea's amount of emitted CO_2 ranked number seven worldwide.[56] South Korea's government ratified the Paris Agreement in 2016.[57] Based on the Paris Agreement, the goal to achieve carbon-neutrality in 2050 has been enshrined in the 'Carbon Neutral Frame Act' of 2021.[58] The reduction of GHG emissions by 40 per cent compared to 2018 levels by 2030 was part of the update to the 'Nationally Determined Contribution' in 2021.[59] Furthermore, the South Korean government targets 40 per cent of the energy to be generated from renewable energy sources by 2034.[60] One of the main measures that the South Korean government has introduced in order to control GHG emissions is the 'Korea Emissions Trading Scheme (K-ETS)'.[61] Furthermore, the 'Korean Green New Deal' was announced in 2020, including government funding of renewable energy production, eco-friendly infrastructure, comprehensive energy-saving, electric vehicles and clean hydrogen.[62]

ii. Climate Change Litigation in South Korea

In South Korea, there are numerous cases of constitutional court actions brought before the Constitutional Court by individuals against legislative or administrative bodies based on the 'constitutionally required protection of fundamental rights from the threat of climate change'. On the other hand, there are only three cases of court litigation against private corporations or individuals, among which two cases are still pending at this stage.

[56] J Smith and S Cha, 'Jobs come first in South Korea's ambitious "Green New Deal" climate plan' (2020) *Reuters*, at www.reuters.com/article/us-southkorea-environment-newdeal-analys-idUSKBN23F0SV/.

[57] Ministry of Foreign Affairs of the Republic of Korea, 'Korea's efforts to address climate change', at www.mofa.go.kr/eng/wpge/m_5655/contents.do.

[58] Ministry of Environment of the Republic of Korea, 'South Korea to move towards the goal of carbon neutrality by 2050', at eng.me.go.kr/eng/web/board/read.do?pagerOffset=0&maxPageItems=10&maxIndexPages=10&searchKey=&searchValue=&menuId=461&orgCd=&boardId=1516150&boardMasterId=522&boardCategoryId=&decorator=.

[59] Ministry of Foreign Affairs of the Republic of Korea, 'Korea's efforts to address climate change', at www.mofa.go.kr/eng/wpge/m_5655/contents.do.

[60] J Gabbatiss, 'The Carbon Brief Profile: South Korea' (2020) *Carbon Brief Clear on Climate*, at www.carbonbrief.org/the-carbon-brief-profile-south-korea/.

[61] The Korea Emissions Trading Scheme (K-ETS) is East Asia's first mandatory framework regulating and pricing GHG emissions and it covers approximately 74% of South Korea's national GHG emissions, including power, buildings, waste, transport and domestic aviation sectors.

[62] Gabbatiss (n 60).

a. *Kang et al v K-Sure and KEXIM (Tiwi)*[63]

In March 2022, members of the indigenous communities Larrakia and Jikilaruwu on the Tiwi Islands, Northern Territory of Australia, including one Korean citizen, applied for a preliminary injunction against the Korea Trade Insurance Corporation (K-Sure) and the Export-Import Bank of Korea (KEXIM) before the Seoul Central District Court. The defendants were South Korean state-owned financial institutions providing loans and guarantees for the 'Barossa Gas Project'[64] in the area.

The applicants sought a preliminary injunction in order to stop the defendants from providing any financial contribution to the project due to the expected significant environmental harm from the CO_2, that would be emitted in the process of gas production and consumption, as well as from the impact on the marine ecosystem in the area, which provides a habitat for unique species of sea turtles, etc. Then, the applicants stressed that the required consultation process with indigenous communities in the area had not been completed and that parts of the gas field were located within the EEZ[65] of Indonesia, which could lead to further disputes on the control over the gas fields. Furthermore, they claimed the incompatibility of developing new fossil gas wells with the GHG emission reduction targets under the Paris Agreement based on environmental rights under Article 35 of the Korean Constitution as well as the property rights of the inhabitants of the Tiwi Islands. The claims were also based on Article 100 of the Korean National Finance Act, according to which citizens may request measures in order to prevent unlawful spending of public funds. In May 2022, the Seoul Central District Court dismissed the application for a preliminary injunction.[66] However, later on, in February 2024, K-Sure decided to withdraw its insurance which was necessary to underwrite SK E&S's investment in the project.

b. *Kang et al v KEXIM and K-Sure (Mozambique)*[67]

In another case before the Seoul Central District Court, in April 2025, several South Korean citizens of a younger age and the environmental NGO Friends of Earth Mozambique applied for another injunction against KEXIM and K-Sure. In this case, the target is the Mozambique Coral North Floating Liquefied Natural Gas project. The plaintiffs seek to halt KEXIM and K-Sure from financing the project by providing loans or guarantees.

[63] *Kang et al v K-Sure and KEXIM*, Seoul Central District Court, preliminary injunction dismissed on 23 May 2022; for an English summary see also Sabin Center for Climate Change Law of Columbia Law School, *Kang et al. v KSURE and KEXIM*, at climatecasechart.com/non-us-case/kand-v-ksureandkexim/; see also J Bardon, 'Traditional owners vow to keep fighting Barossa gas field despite losing South Korean court battle' (*ABC News*, 2022) at www.abc.net.au/news/2022-05-25/nt-santos-barossa-gas-tiwi-larrakia-lose-southkorea-court-figh/101097372.

[64] The Barossa Gas Project is an offshore gas and condensate oil field in Australian waters north of Darwin, Northern Territory, under construction by Santos Limited. It is estimated that the project will be Australia's most carbon-intensive project of gas development, once constructions are completed (planned in 2025). The pipeline crosses through the Tiwi Islands, where the indigenous communities Larrakia and Jukilaruwu have been living with a strong cultural connection to the waters and marine species, eg, Australian flatback sea turtles and olive ridley sea turtles.

[65] Exclusive Economic Zone, an area of the sea in which a coastal state has sovereign rights for the purpose of exploring and exploiting, conserving and managing the natural resources, and with regard to other activities for the economic exploitation and exploration of the zone, in accordance with Article 56 UNCLOS.

[66] S Paul, 'S.Korea court dismisses plea to block loans to $3.6 bln Australian gas project' (*Reuters*, 2022) at www.reuters.com/article/australia-gas-southkorea-idAFL3N2XF1DD/.

[67] *Kang et al v KEXIM and K-Sure*, Seoul Central District Court, still pending; for an English summary see also Sabin Center for Climate Change Law of Columbia Law School, *Kang et al v KEXIM and KSURE*, at www.climatecasechart.com/document/kang-et-al-v-kexim-and-ksure_25c8?l=south-korea.

Also in this case, the plaintiffs argue with potential infringements of their rights to life, a healthy environment, and the protection of future generations under the Korean Constitution. Furthermore, they claim that financing the project would neither be in line with South Korea's self-set obligations under domestic law nor with its international GHG reduction commitments, as the amount of GHG emissions caused by the project is substantially high and cannot be weighed up by public interest. Furthermore, the project might lead to a stronger focus on fossil fuels in Mozambique with potential long-term implications for its energy sector. At this stage, the case is still pending before the Seoul Central District Court.

c. *Kim et al v POSCO*[68]

Then, there is another case of court litigation brought against the private corporation POSCO. In February 2025, several South Korean citizens applied for an injunction to halt the project of relining the No. 2 blast surface at Gwangyang Steelworks before the Daegu District Court. The applicants argue with a potential infringement of their right to a healthy environment and life under Article 35 of the Korean Constitution, as the project will lead to a focus on carbon-intensive steel production for at least 15 more years and increase GHG emissions accordingly. They, furthermore, claim that the impact on climate change caused by the project leads to irreversible harms which cannot be remedied by potential monetary compensation in the future. Moreover, the plaintiffs argue that the project is neither in line with POSCO's own ESG commitments nor with national carbon budgets or international GHG reduction obligations deriving from the 1.5°C target. They claim that POSCO could and should make use of low-carbon alternatives. Many of the applicants are directly impacted by the project as they live in direct vicinity to the furnace in question or other steel-producing regions and due to their young age.

Shortly after the filing of the case before the Daegu District Court, in March 2025, POSCO officially announced to change the planned project to a merely partial relining, which would lead to a shorter expected lifespan of the furnace of approximately eight years. The case is still pending at this stage.

IV. Comparison to Climate Change Litigation between Private Parties in Other Parts of the World

A. General Overview of Climate Change Litigation Worldwide

i. Short Overview of Cases

Climate change and global warming have led to a steady rise in climate-change-related litigation, not only in Asia but worldwide. In most cases between private parties, plaintiffs tend to sue powerful companies, which have an enormous impact on climate change due to their GHG emissions, eg, corporations in the automotive or energy industry.

[68] *Kim et al v POSCO*, Daegu District Court, still pending; for an English summary see also Sabin Center for Climate Change Law of Columbia Law School, *Kim et al v POSCO*, at www.climatecasechart.com/document/kim-et-al-v-posco_a7d0.

One notable example is the case *Luciano Lliuya v RWE AG*,[69] in which a Peruvian farmer has filed an action against Germany's largest electricity producer RWE in 2015. He is claiming for damages as well as a declaratory and injunctive relief, as RWE, so he argues, to some degree bears responsibility for mountain glaciers melting near his hometown in Peru, which has become an acute threat due to the immense expansion of a glacial lake. He argues that RWE's GHG emissions constitute 'nuisances'[70] under section 1004 of the German Civil Code causing him to take mitigation measures and therefore incurring considerable costs. Based on this, he is requesting reimbursement of a portion of the costs equivalent to RWE's share of global GHG emissions, being 0.47 per cent. The Regional Court of Essen, in the first instance, dismissed all claims as it could not find a clearly established causal chain between the emissions and the harm suffered. However, while the Higher Regional Court of Hamm had rendered the claim admissible for appeal proceedings, it finally dismissed the appeal based on expert reports regarding the specific threat and harm suffered as well as RWE's contribution thereto after a personal site visit. Based on these a concrete danger to the plaintiff's property could not be found. However, the court still admitted that, in principle, claims under section 1004 of the German Civil Code could be established, in case the GHG emissions in question led to a concrete danger. In this case, GHG emitters could be held accountable proportionally.

Another example is *Kaiser et al v Volkswagen AG*,[71] where Greenpeace Germany and Fridays for Future Germany took issue with Volkswagen's alleged failure to comply with the Paris Agreement's temperature goals by not committing to phase out sales of commercial vehicles with internal combustion engines by 2030. Claims were based on the 'fundamental right to climate protection' and the rights and freedoms of future generations as well as the carbon budget necessarily allocated to Volkswagen, which derives from German tort law and the Paris Agreement. The argumentation is in line with the German Federal Constitutional Court's decision in *Neubauer et al v Germany*,[72] which was based on the acceptance of limited GHG emission budgets. In *Neubauer et al v Germany*, the court had found that, considering the irreversibility of the effects of excessive GHG emissions on global warming and its impact on future generations' freedoms, it was constitutionally required to adhere to a limited national emission budget based on the internationally recognised goal of limiting global temperature increase to 1.5°C or at the most 2.0°C compared to pre-industrial levels as regulated in the Paris Agreement. Based on this argumentation, the plaintiffs calculated a specific GHG emission budget for the defendant and requested a list of specific measures that Volkswagen would need to follow in order to adhere to said budget. However, all claims were dismissed and the appeal was not admitted in this case.

[69] *Luciano Lliuya v RWE AG*, Landgericht Essen (Regional Court of Essen), 15 December 2016, 2 O 285/15; Oberlandesgericht Hamm (Higher Regional Court of Hamm), 28 May 2025, 5 U 15/17; for an English summary see also Sabin Center for Climate Change Law of Columbia Law School, *Luciano Lliuya v RWE AG*, at climatecasechart.com/non-us-case/lliuya-v-rwe-ag/.

[70] Beeinträchtigungen.

[71] *Kaiser et al v Volkswagen AG*, Landgericht Braunschweig (Regional Court of Braunschweig), 14 February 2023, 6 O 3931/21; for an English summary see also Sabin Center for Climate Change Law of Columbia Law School, *Kaiser, et al. v Volkswagen AG*, at climatecasechart.com/non-us-case/kaiser-et-al-v-volkswagen-ag/; for recent updates see also Greenpeace, 'VW-Klage vor Gericht', at www.greenpeace.de/klimaschutz/mobilitaet/vw-klage-gericht.

[72] *Neubauer et al v Germany*, Bundesverfassungsgericht (Federal Constitutional Court), Decision of the First Senate [Entscheidung des Ersten Senats], 24 March 2021, BvR 2656/18, BVerfGE 157, 30-177; engl. translation available at www.bverfg.de/e/rs20210324_1bvr265618en.html); for an English summary see also Sabin Center for Climate Change Law of Columbia Law School, *Neubauer, et al. v Germany*, at climatecasechart.com/non-us-case/neubauer-et-al-v-germany/.

Further, notable examples include lawsuits against Mercedes-Benz[73] and BMW,[74] in which the plaintiff is the German environmental organisation Deutsche Umwelthilfe (DUH),[75] over alleged insufficiency of the defendants' measures to decrease CO_2 emissions. In both cases, the DUH's argumentation was in line with that in *Kaiser et al v Volkswagen AG* based on *Neubauer et al v Germany*. So, it was argued that, by not committing to a phase out of sales of commercial vehicles with internal combustion engines by 2030, the defendants violated the 'fundamental right to climate protection' and the rights and freedoms of future generations, as the defendants both needed to phase out sales in order to adhere to their emission budgets based on German tort law and the Paris Agreement. In both cases, DUH requested a catalogue of specific measures for Mercedes-Benz and BMW to take in order to stay within their respective budgets. However, both the Regional Court and the Higher Regional Court of Stuttgart have dismissed the case in *Deutsche Umwelthilfe (DUH) v Mercedes-Benz AG*. In *Deutsche Umwelthilfe (DUH) v Bayerische Motoren Werke (BMW)*, the Regional and the Higher Regional Court of Munich dismissed the case in both instances as well. Therefore, DUH has now appealed before the Federal Supreme Court[76] in both cases, where the proceedings are still pending.

These cases in Germany show that, so far, courts have been resistant to transmitting the national emission budget, recognised as constitutionally binding by the Federal Constitutional Court, into specific emission budgets for individual companies. An important reason for this might be that the allocation of emissions within the national emission budget shall be free according to *Neubauer et al v Germany*. Furthermore, *Luciano Lliuya v RWE AG* shows that proving a direct causal link between harm suffered from global warming and emissions that can be ascribed to a specific company is considerably difficult.

One of the few examples of a civil action that has actually succeeded is the case *Milieudefensie et al v Royal Dutch Shell*[77] in the Netherlands, in which The Hague District Court ruled in the first instance that the oil corporation Shell was required to drastically reduce its GHG emissions in line with the Paris Agreement based on international human rights law.[78] The environmental group

[73] *Deutsche Umwelthilfe (DUH) v Mercedes-Benz AG*, Landgericht Stuttgart (Regional Court of Stuttgart), 13 September 2022, 17 O 789/21; Oberlandesgericht Stuttgart (Higher Regional Court of Stuttgart), 9 November 2023, 12 U 170/22; for an English summary see also Sabin Center for Climate Change Law of Columbia Law School, *Deutsche Umwelthilfe (DUH) v Mercedes-Benz AG*, at climatecasechart.com/non-us-case/deutsche-umwelthilfe-duh-v-mercedes-benz-ag/; for recent updates see also Deutsche Umwelthilfe, 'Klimaklage gegen Mercedes-Benz: Deutsche Umwelthilfe zieht vor den Bundesgerichtshof', at www.duh.de/presse/pressemitteilungen/pressemitteilung/klimaklage-gegen-mercedes-benz-deutsche-umwelthilfe-zieht-vor-den-bundesgerichtshof/.

[74] *Deutsche Umwelthilfe (DUH) v Bayerische Motoren Werke (BMW)*, Landgericht München (Regional Court of Munich), 7 February 2023, 3 O 12581/21; Oberlandesgericht München (Higher Regional Court of Munich), 12 October 2023, 32 U 936/23; for an English summary see also Sabin Center for Climate Change Law of Columbia Law School, *Deutsche Umwelthilfe (DUH) v Bayerische Motoren Werke AG (BMW)*, at climatecasechart.com/non-us-case/deutsche-umwelthilfe-duh-v-bmw/; for recent updates see also Deutsche Umwelthilfe, 'Klimaklage gegen BMW: Deutsche Umwelthilfe zieht vor den Bundesgerichtshof', at www.duh.de/presse/pressemitteilungen/pressemitteilung/klimaklage-gegen-bmw-deutsche-umwelthilfe-zieht-vor-den-bundesgerichtshof/.

[75] Can be translated as 'German Environmental Aid'.

[76] Bundesgerichtshof.

[77] *Milieudefensie et al v Royal Dutch Shell*, Rechtbank Den Haag (The Hague District Court), 26 May 2021, C/09/571932 / HA ZA 19-379, ECLI:NL:RBDHA:2021:5337; Gerechtshof Den Haag (The Hague Court of Appeal), 12 November 2024, 200.302.332/01, ECLI:NL:GHDHA:2024:2099; for an English summary see also Sabin Center for Climate Change Law of Columbia Law School, *Milieudefensie et al. v Royal Dutch Shell plc.*, at climatecasechart.com/non-us-case/milieudefensie-et-al-v-royal-dutch-shell-plc/; for recent updates see also Milieudefensie, 'Our Climate Case against Shell', at en.milieudefensie.nl/climate-case-shell.

[78] T Sonohara [苑原俊明], 'New Climate Litigation and International Human Rights Law: Dutch Branch of Friends of the Earth et al v Royal Dutch Shell [新たな気候訴訟と国際人権法： 地球の友オランダ支部ほか 対ロイヤル·ダッチ·シェル社 事件]' (2021) 31(1) *Daitō Hōgaku* [大東法学] 171, 172.

Milieudefensie[79] together with several other NGOs and citizens had sued Shell in 2019 alleging that Shell's immense amount of GHG emissions constituted a violation of the standard of care under the societal duty of care in Book 6 Section 162 of the Dutch Civil Code together with Articles 2 and 8 of the European Convention on Human Rights. This argumentation builds on the case *Urgenda Foundation v State of the Netherlands*,[80] in which the court had found a violation of the Dutch government's duty of care towards its citizens due to insufficient measures against climate change. In 2021, the Hague District Court ruled in favour of the plaintiffs and ordered Shell to reduce all GHG emissions, Shell's direct emissions as well as emissions of other companies from the use of Shell's oil, at least by 45 per cent until 2030 compared to the emission level in 2019. The court rendered a provisionally enforceable decision, which means that Shell is required to adhere to this decision even during appeal proceedings, as long as a different court decision has not been rendered. Subsequently, Milieudefensie reminded Shell of this fact in a public letter to the Board of Directors, requested strict and immediate compliance with the decision, and furthermore mentioned the possibility of the directors' personal liability for harm resulting from a failure to act immediately. Following this, Shell filed an appeal before The Hague Court of Appeal, which rendered its decision in November 2024. It basically followed the first instance decision's argumentation, but refused to impose specific rates of emission reductions. In February 2025, Milieudefensie announced its plans to file another appeal before the Supreme Court of the Netherlands in order to re-impose specific emission reduction rates. All in all, this case has had a very important impact on other cases of climate change litigation between private parties.

Based on this successful court action, Milieudefensie has decided to approach the ING Bank in *Milieudefensie v ING Bank*[81] with concrete plans to bring this issue to court, if ING Bank does not comply with their requests. In the beginning of 2024, the NGO issued a notice of liability to the bank, based on an alleged violation of the societal duty of care in Book 6 Section 162 of the Dutch Civil Code. The overall argumentation is in line with that in *Milieudefensie et al v Royal Dutch Shell*, but focuses on emissions indirectly caused by the bank, eg, emissions in the bank's value chain, especially emissions financed by the bank. Milieudefensie demands concrete GHG emission reduction targets to be set up by ING Bank, reporting commitments regarding its financed emissions as well as several other specific measures. ING Bank has replied to Milieudefensie's notice of liability, but according to them not in a satisfactory manner. Therefore, Milieudefensie served a formal summons on 28 March 2025, initiating a civil lawsuit before the Amsterdam District Court. The outcome needs to be awaited as 'financed emissions' could possibly be evaluated in a manner different from emissions deriving from oil directly produced by a company, as it is the case in *Milieudefensie et al v Royal Dutch Shell*.

These Dutch cases show that courts may actually derive specific emission limits as well as specific measures that are at least required in order to adhere to the emission limits for individual companies, based on human rights and the emission reduction goals stipulated in the Paris

[79] Dutch branch of Friends of the Earth.

[80] *Urgenda Foundation v State of the Netherlands*, Rechtbank Den Haag (The Hague District Court), 24 June 2015, C/09/456689 / HA ZA 13-1396, ECLI:NL:RBDHA:2015:7145; Gerechtshof Den Haag (The Hague Court of Appeal), 9 October 2018, 200.178.245/01, ECLI:NL:GHDHA:2018:2591; Hoge Raad (Supreme Court), 20 December 2019, 19/00135, ECLI:NL:HR:2019:2006; for an English summary see also Sabin Center for Climate Change Law of Columbia Law School, *Urgenda Foundation v State of the Netherlands*, at climatecasechart.com/non-us-case/urgenda-foundation-v-kingdom-of-the-netherlands/.

[81] *Milieudefensie v ING Bank*, Amsterdam District Court, still pending; for an English summary see also Sabin Center for Climate Change Law of Columbia Law School, *Milieudefensie v ING Bank*, at climatecasechart.com/non-us-case/milieudefensie-v-ing-bank/; for recent updates see also Milieudefensie, 'Our Climate Case against ING', at en.milieudefensie.nl/climate-case-ing.

Agreement. What is even more important to note is that this has happened for indirect emissions deriving from the consumption or use of the products of the company in question by others.

While plaintiffs have barely ever succeeded in climate change litigation proceedings with private parties due to the administrative and legal hurdles explained above, some cases might still serve different purposes. They attract public attention and can therefore both enhance major investments and lead to follow-up costs for the relevant companies regardless of the outcome of the lawsuit.[82] So, even if the plaintiffs are not immediately successful regarding the court decision, the mere matter of climate change litigation is still likely to influence the public discourse. That is why, in some cases, the ultimate goal of litigation may be to bring the issues into the public eye rather than actually win the specific case in question.[83]

ii. Characteristics and Issues of International Cases of Climate Change Litigation

The decisions in climate change litigation between private parties that have been successful so far show a clear trend. Rather than contesting specific projects of companies that affect GHG emissions, eg, construction or operation of specific coal-fired power plants, successful cases have argued with emission budgets for individual companies with immense amounts of GHG emissions based on national emission budgets under international agreements. They have based their arguments on the internationally accepted limits to temperature increases agreed upon in the Paris Agreement and enacted through national legislation in many countries. On the ground of these national emission budgets, there have already been several administrative cases against governments or other state authorities, in which legislation or other measures in line with the national commitments have been sought for and reached successfully. Considering the national emission budgets, plaintiffs now argue with approximate GHG emission budgets for individual companies, especially those with relatively high shares in overall worldwide emissions, which can be calculated as well. Based on these budgets, plaintiffs have demanded the enactment of rational plans and policies from the relevant companies.

However, one hurdle for climate change litigation internationally is the identification of plaintiffs' legal standing in order to have access to courts. In fact, due to these difficulties, in most cases NGOs act as plaintiffs. One reason for that is the NGOs' expertise in the field. Another is that access to justice in representative actions has been considerably facilitated under Article 7 of The Representative Actions Directive (EU) 2020/1828 based on Article 9 of the Aarhus Convention. Thereby, organisations may bring a representative action without proving an individually suffered direct harm, if they are qualified entities and the litigation is aligned with the objectives of the specific organisation.

Furthermore, most cases are filed against huge corporations with considerable emission shares. In doing so, the individual companies' responsibility for global warming can be brought into the public eye and companies might be pressured to take measures and required to reassess their policies due to the public discourse enhanced, regardless of the outcome in the relevant court action.

Further difficulties include proving a specific harm and a causal link between the harm and the emissions at question as well as the categorisation of GHG emissions as pollutants or nuisances in order to trigger remedies under national tort laws.

[82] Mundy, Temple-West, Talman and Tett (n 8).
[83] Fellenberg (n 19) 913.

B. Asian Characteristics in Comparison

Unlike many cases in other parts of the world, all the climate change litigation cases between private parties in Asia so far have concerned specific projects, eg, the construction and operation of specific coal-fired power plants, the purchase of electricity from renewable energy resources and its connection to the grid, or the financing of a gas development project. Although the plaintiffs in these cases have based their argumentations, inter alia, on the Paris Agreement as well as national legislation binding governments to net zero emission goals, it seems difficult to find a direct connection between a specific project and a national net zero emission goal, as the goal could still be reached, if emissions were reduced in other areas. Therefore, the question if companies engage in or financially support specific projects only impacts how the emissions are allotted within emission budgets, as long as the project's relevant emissions do not exceed the budget itself. The budgets argued with are usually derived from and calculated on the basis of national legislation in compliance with internationally accepted temperature limits. The only case of court litigation between private parties in Asia that places the impact of several companies on climate change and their GHG emission reduction goals on the whole at issue is the *Youth Climate Case Japan for Tomorrow*. However, this case is still pending and its outcome needs to be awaited.

Furthermore, the plaintiffs' legal standing in court is an issue in cases in Asia as well as in other parts of the world. It is difficult for plaintiffs to prove a specific harm or imminent danger to them, a causal link between such harm and the emissions in question, and to classify the legal nature of the emissions as a category that triggers remedies under the relevant national tort law, eg, nuisances or pollutants. Due to these hurdles, it is more common to bring representative actions led by NGOs or other organisations before the courts also in Asia. The organisations might have expertise in the relevant field or comprise a group of people who are specifically impacted by the project at question, eg, people living in the vicinity of a planned coal-fired power plant, etc.

V. Conclusion

In conclusion, one can summarise that climate change litigation between private parties in Asia is only at the beginning. Just like in other parts of the world, more cases will come in Asia, too. In addition to that, there will probably be more cases regarding not just a specific project, eg, the construction or operation of coal-fired power plants, the financial support of a gas development project, etc, but rather overall emission budgets and reduction plans and policies of individual relevant companies, like the *Youth Climate Case Japan for Tomorrow*.

However, it still remains to be seen on what basis plaintiffs can establish a legal standing to file claims over GHG emissions. It will depend on the plaintiffs' arguments as well as on the final reasoning of the courts. Future issues here will include proving the existence of a specific harm or danger to the plaintiffs, a direct causal connection between such harm and the GHG emissions in question, and the categorisation of GHG emissions under the relevant national tort law.

Japan, China, South Korea and other Asian states are also bound to the internationally accepted temperature limits, just like jurisdictions that have already experienced court rulings in favour of climate activists. Therefore, administrative suits against legislative or executive authorities based on internationally required temperature limits and national emission budgets, as they have already succeeded in other jurisdictions, may follow in Asia. In such future court actions legislative authorities may be asked to establish more concrete plans to comply with the goals of the Paris Agreement and to establish national emission budgets that do not overburden future generations with emission reduction measures, which could infringe on their freedoms in a way that would be disproportional compared to currently contemplated measures. Then, subsequently, cases against corporations based on specific emission budgets for them in order to establish concrete policies or to take specific measures might follow and maybe, depending on the legal environment and requirements at the time, be successful. However, it is difficult to predict how the landscape of climate change litigation in Asia will develop in the future. Negative impacts from global warming on everyday life, eg, natural disasters, unbearable temperatures, etc, might further enhance and accelerate this process, with regards to plaintiffs engaging in filing their actions as well as the judicial outcome.

13

Crime Against Humanity

JONATHAN IP AND JAY KOON

I. Introduction

The notion of crimes against humanity has been recognised as a matter of international law for (at least) almost 80 years after the end of World War II. Since then, these crimes have been enforced in various international tribunals,[1] and codified by and included into the Rome Statute of the International Criminal Court (the Rome Statute).[2] The concept has also received attention of the International Law Commission (the ILC), having been included in the 1950 Principles of International Law Recognized in the Charter of the Nürnberg Tribunal and in the Judgment of the Tribunal,[3] the 1954,[4] 1991,[5] and 1996[6] Draft Code of Offences against the Peace and Security of Mankind (the Draft Codes).

Recently in 2019, the ILC has adopted the Draft Articles on Prevention and Punishment of Crimes Against Humanity (The 2019 Draft Articles),[7] which is intended to serve as 'what would become a Convention on the Prevention and Punishment of Crimes against Humanity'.[8]

In light of the purpose of this publication, this chapter is not intended to serve as a comprehensive review and analysis of the law on crimes against humanity. Rather, while it would still set out the essential substance of the law and key episodes in the law's development, it would then review the circumstances of the implementation of the crimes against humanity specifically in the context of Asia.

[1] For example, the International Criminal Tribunal for the Former Yugoslavia, the International Criminal Tribunal for Rwanda, the Special Court for Sierra Leone, and the Extraordinary Chambers in the Courts of Cambodia.

[2] Rome Statute of the International Criminal Court (adopted 18 July 1998, entered into force 1 July 2002) 2187 UNTS 90, Art 7.

[3] ILC, 'Report of the International Law Commission on the Work of its 2nd Session' (5 June–29 July 1950) UN Doc A/1316, p 377, paras 120–124, Principle VI (c).

[4] ILC, 'Report of the International Law Commission on the Work of its 6th Session' (3 June–28 July 1954) UN Doc A/2693, p 150, Art 2, para 11.

[5] ILC, 'Report of the International Law Commission on the Work of its 43rd Session' (29 April–19 July 1991) UN Doc A/46/10, pp 103–104, Art 21.

[6] ILC, 'Report of the International Law Commission on the Work of its 48th Session' (6 May–26 July 1996) UN Doc A/51/10, pp 47–50, Art 18.

[7] ILC, 'Report of the International Law Commission on the Work of its 71st Session' (29 April–7 June and 8 July–9 August 2019) UN Doc A/74/10, paras 39–45.

[8] ibid pp 22–23, General Commentary (3).

II. Crimes against Humanity and Customary International Law

The term 'crimes against humanity' was first used by an American Civil War soldier turned minister George Washington Williams in a letter in 1890, describing the Belgian King Leopold's regime and their treatment of the Congolese people.[9] In the 1910s and in response to various events including the massacres by the Ottoman Empire of Armenians in Turkey and World War I, formal references were made to the concept again, with attempts to invoke it as a notion of criminal responsibility.[10]

In the aftermath of World War II, the notion of crimes against humanity was for the first time defined in international law.[11] Article 6(c) of the Charter of the International Military Tribunal[12] (referred to hereinafter respectively as 'the Nürnberg Charter' and 'the Nürnberg Tribunal') defined 'Crimes against humanity' as follows:

> murder, extermination, enslavement, deportation, and other inhumane acts committed against any civilian population, before or during the war, or persecutions on political, racial or religious grounds in execution of or in connection with any crime within the jurisdiction of the Tribunal, whether or not in violation of the domestic law of the country where perpetrated.

Specifically in Asia, a similar provision as also provided in Article 5(c) of the International Military Tribunal for the Far East Charter (referred to hereinafter respectively as 'the Tokyo Charter' and 'the Tokyo Tribunal'). The embedding of the notion of crimes against humanity in the Nürnberg Charter has been described as 'the landmark for the formation of customary international law'.[13]

As mentioned above, crimes against humanity have since been repeatedly addressed by the ILC, and enforced in various international tribunals. These crimes had been recognised under customary international law even before the adoption Rome Statute.[14] As identified in Commentary (5) to the Preamble of the 2019 Draft ILC Articles, 'the status of the prohibition on crimes against humanity as *jus cogens* has also been noted by' various regional, international and national courts.[15]

Despite the broad acceptance of their status as/in international law, there is 'a lack of uniformity of the text of crimes against humanity'[16] due to 'a multiplicity of conflicting definitions'.[17] These inconsistencies have far-reaching implications, as they go to, for instance, whether the offences must be 'linked to an armed conflict, or are to be considered as mere peace crimes'.[18]

For the present purpose, this chapter will use the definition of crimes against humanity under Article 7 of the Rome Statute as an illustration, given that it is still regarded as largely in line

[9] A Hochschild, *King Leopold's Ghost* (New York, Houghton Mifflin Company, 1998) 111–12.

[10] CK Hall and K Ambos, 'Article 7. Crimes against humanity' in O Triffterer and K Ambos (eds), *Rome Statute of the International Criminal Court: A Commentary*, 3rd edn (Munich, CH Beck, 2016) 152–53; C Byron, *War Crimes and Crimes Against Humanity in the Rome Statute of the International Criminal Court* (Manchester, Manchester University Press, 2009) 188.

[11] Byron (n 10) 189.

[12] Promulgated in the Agreement for the Prosecution and Punishment of the Major War Criminals of the European Axis (signed and entered into force 8 August 1945) 82 UNTS 279.

[13] Y Tan, *The Rome Statute as Evidence of Customary International Law* (Leiden, Brill, 2021) 145.

[14] ibid 137.

[15] ILC, 'Report of the International Law Commission on the Work of its 71st Session' (n 7) 24–25.

[16] Tan (n 13) 148.

[17] Byron (n 10) 189.

[18] Hall and Ambos (n 10) 154-155.

with and declaratory of the traditional conception of crimes against humanity under customary international law.[19]

III. Crimes against Humanity under the Rome Statute

The Rome Statute was entered into force on 1 July 2002, thereby creating the International Criminal Court (the ICC) and its governing framework. As of May 2025, there are 125 countries which are State Parties to the Rome Statute.

Article 7 of the Rome Statute sets out 11 acts which, when (i) 'committed as part of a widespread or systematic attack directed against any civil population' and (ii) 'with knowledge of the attack', would constitute crimes against humanity.[20] These acts include:

(a) Murder;
(b) Extermination;
(c) Enslavement;
(d) Deportation or forcible transfer of population;
(e) Imprisonment or other severe deprivation of physical liberty in violation of fundamental rules of international law;
(f) Torture;
(g) Rape, sexual slavery, enforced prostitution, forced pregnancy, enforced sterilisation, or any other form of sexual violence of comparable gravity;
(h) Persecution against any identifiable group or collectivity on political, racial, national, ethnic, cultural, religious, gender, or other grounds that are universally recognised as impermissible under international law, in connection with any act referred to in the article or any crime within the jurisdiction of the ICC;
(i) Enforced disappearance of persons;
(j) The crime of apartheid; and
(k) Other inhumane acts of a similar character intentionally causing great suffering, or serious injury to body or to mental or physical health.[21]

The above list of crimes largely accords with the understanding of crimes against humanity under customary international law, such that the latter should be taken into account when interpreting Article 7 of the Rome Statute; on the other hand, Article 7 is merely intended to provide for a definition applicable before the International Criminal Court, and should not be taken as changing the customary international law.[22]

Crimes against humanity may be distinguished from war crimes, which are set out under Article 8 of the Rome Statute, and genocides, which are set out under Article 6, in the following ways. First, whilst war crimes must be linked to an armed conflict,[23] no such pre-requisite exists

[19] ibid 158; Tan (n 13) 146.
[20] Rome Statute, Article 7(1).
[21] It is a residual category of Crimes against Humanity that requires the Court to determine whether 'inhumane acts' of a 'similar character' to those set out under Article 7 were carried out. 'Character' refers to the nature and gravity of the act: Elements of Crimes, Art 7(1)(k), fn 30. They include either loss of health or life, loss of fundamental rights or liberty, or attack on human dignity: Hall and Ambos (n 10) 237. This article must be interpreted conservatively and not be used to expand uncritically the scope of the crimes against humanity: *Prosecutor v Kenyatta & Ors* (Decision on the Confirmation of Charges Pursuant to Article 61(7)(a) and (b) of the Rome Statute) ICC-01/09-02/11 (23 January 2012) at para 269.
[22] Hall and Ambos (n 10) 158–59.
[23] Rome Statute, Art 8(2).

in relation to crimes against humanity, which may be committed in peacetime. Second, crimes against humanity differ from genocides in that the latter require an intent to destroy, in whole or in part, a national, ethnical, racial or religious group.[24] Such an intent is not necessarily required for crimes against humanity, even though the act of persecution may also amount to crimes against humanity.[25]

There are two contextual elements that must be present for an act to be qualified as a crime against humanity. First, it must be committed 'as part of a widespread or systematic attack directed against any civilian population'.[26] Second, the act must be done with knowledge of the attack.[27]

'Attack' directed against a 'civilian population' means a course of conduct involving the multiple commission of the acts, 'pursuant to or in furtherance of a State or organisational policy to commit such attack', and such acts need *not* be military in nature.[28] An attacks rather refers to a campaign or operation conducted against the civilian population which involves multiple (more than one) commission of acts set out in the list of crimes; in fact, an 'attack' involving a crime against humanity needs not occur in relation to any armed hostility or armed conflict.[29] The underlying acts said to constitute the offence must either occur as part of an attack, or constitute an attack itself.[30]

Remarkably, Article 7(2)(a) provides that the attack must be 'pursuant to or in furtherance of a State or organizational policy to commit such attack'.[31] The Trial Chamber of the International Criminal Tribunal for the Former Yugoslavia noted in *Tadić* that the policy requirement is a result of distinguishing crimes against humanity, as 'a deliberate attempt to target a civilian population', from 'isolated, random acts of individuals'.[32]

A 'policy' means that the State or organisation must have actively promoted or encouraged such an attack against a civilian population.[33] Hence, there is no requirement that the policy must be formally adopted or expressly declared.[34]

It suffices where the state or organisation actively promotes or encourages such an attack, and, in exceptional circumstances, where there is a deliberate failure (as opposed to mere absence) to take action, which is consciously aimed at encouraging such attack.[35]

While a 'policy' may be of a State or of an organisation as expressly recognised by Article 7(2)(a), there is controversy as to what kind of non-state entities would count as an 'organisation' for that purpose.[36] While it is not doubted that an entity holding *de facto* authority over a territory would amount to an 'organisation',[37] there exists disagreement whether the organisation must be 'State-like' and partake of some characteristics of a State, or it is already sufficient that the

[24] Rome Statute, Art 6.
[25] Rome Statute, Art 7(1)(h).
[26] Rome Statute, Art 7(1).
[27] Rome Statute, Art 7(1).
[28] Elements of Crime, Art 7(3).
[29] Hall and Ambos (n 10) 165–66; Byron (n 10) 191, 194–95.
[30] Hall and Ambos (n 10) 165.
[31] It is controversial whether this requirement exists under the customary international law (as opposed to under the Rome Statute); see Hall and Ambos (n 10) 244; Byron (n 10) 202.
[32] *Prosecutor v Tadić* (Opinion and Judgment) IT-94-1-T (7 May 1997) at para 653.
[33] Elements of Crime, Art 7(3).
[34] Hall and Ambos (n 10) 245; Byron (n 10) 130; ILC, 'Report of the International Law Commission on the Work of its 71st Session' (n 7) 39, Commentary (26) to Article 2 of the 2019 Draft Articles; *Prosecutor v Katanga* (Judgment pursuant to Article 74 of the Statute) ICC-01/04-01/07 (7 March 2014) at paras 1108–1113.
[35] Elements of Crime, Art 7(3).
[36] Hall and Ambos (n 10) 246.
[37] *Prosecutor v Kupreškić* (Judgment) IT-95-16-T (14 January 2000) at para 552.

organisation has the capability to commit a widespread or systematic attack against a civilian population.[38]

A 'population' may be considered as 'civilian' notwithstanding the presence of some non-civilians, as long as it is predominately civilian in nature, while the term 'civilian' covers all persons who have taken no active part in hostilities or are no longer doing so.[39] That said, the 'population' must share some common attributes, in that they must be linked geographically or by some other common features or shared characteristics.[40]

As to the requirement of the attack being 'widespread or systematic', a 'widespread' attack means an attack committed on a large scale and directed at a multiplicity of victims.[41] It could be indicated by the number of victims and the scale of the attack.[42] On the other hand, 'systematic' is recently understood to refer to the 'organised nature of the acts of violence and the improbability of their random occurrence',[43] such that 'a preconceived policy or plan' is an indicator of the 'systematicity' of the attack, but not a legal element of the crime.[44] Accordingly, isolated and random acts are excluded from the ICC's jurisdiction.[45] It must, however, be noted that while the 'attack' has to be widespread or systematic, the individual acts of the accused said to constitute the offence, which may be part of the attack as mentioned above, need not.[46]

As regards the element on intent or knowledge, the perpetrator must be shown to have known that the conduct charged was part of or have intended the conduct charged to be part of a widespread or systematic attack against a civilian population, in addition to the *mens rea* requirement for the underlying acts (which must fall within the list of crimes set out in Article 7(1)), as required by Article 30 of the Rome Statute.[47]

Notwithstanding that the perpetrator must have known or intended the conduct charged to be part of the collective 'attack', the element does not require proof that the perpetrator had knowledge of all characteristics of the attack or the precise details of the plan or policy of the state or organisation. In the case of an emerging widespread or systematic attack, the element is satisfied if the perpetrator intended to further such an attack.[48]

Under the Rome Statute, the ICC has jurisdiction over natural persons, and a person who commits a crime shall be individually responsible and liable for punishment accordingly.[49] The Rome Statutes shall apply regardless of the individuals' official capacities,[50] whilst commanders and superiors (in non-military relationships) may be responsible for the acts committed by the persons under their effective authority and control.[51] *Insofar as private multinationals (such as multi-national corporations) are concerned, this would be of significant importance, given that in*

[38] See Hall and Ambos (n 10) 246–50; ILC, 'Report of the International Law Commission on the Work of its 71st Session' (n 7) 40–42, Commentaries (29)–(33) to Art 2 of the 2019 Draft Articles.

[39] *Prosecutor v Kordić and Cerkez* (Judgment) IT-95-14/2-T (26 February 2001) at para 180; Hall and Ambos (n 10) 174–75.

[40] Hall and Ambos (n 10) 172.

[41] Byron (n 10) 193; Hall and Ambos (n 10) 167–69; ILC, 'Report of the International Law Commission on the Work of its 71st Session' (n 7) 32, Commentary (12) to Art 2 of the 2019 Draft Articles.

[42] *Prosecutor v Kunarac, Kovac and Vukovic* (Judgment) IT-96-23-T and IT-96-23/1-T (22 February 2001) at para 428.

[43] Hall and Ambos (n 10) 170–71; ILC, 'Report of the International Law Commission on the Work of its 71st Session' (n 7) 33–34, Commentaries (15)–(16) to Article 2 of the 2019 Draft Articles; *Katanga* (n 34) at para 1123.

[44] Hall and Ambos (n 10) 171.

[45] Hall and Ambos (n 10) 156–57; *Tadić* (n 32) at paras 644 and 648.

[46] Hall and Ambos (n 10) 171.

[47] Hall and Ambos (n 10) 174–75.

[48] Elements of Crime, Arti7(2); Hall and Ambos (n 10) 176.

[49] Rome Statute, Arti25(1)–(2).

[50] Rome Statute, Art 27.

[51] Rome Statute, Art 28.

specific cases, a resourceful and locally powerful multi-national corporation may be regarded as capable of committing a widespread or systematic attack against a civilian population, such that the corporation's officers, employees, servants and/or agents may commit acts which constitute crimes against humanity.

On the other hand, it should be noted that while there was a deep divergence of views as to the advisability of including criminal responsibility of *legal persons* in the Rome Statute, it ultimately *did not contain such a provision.*[52] The development of the Rome Statute would suggest that it only addresses liability of natural persons.[53]

IV. Historical Special Tribunals in Asia on Crimes against Humanity

The prosecution of crimes against humanity in Asia has been shaped by several landmark tribunals established to address systemic atrocities. These institutions, though varied in structure and scope, reflect the region's complex engagement with international criminal justice. While they advanced accountability, their legacies also underscore enduring challenges, including political resistance, jurisdictional limitations, and the tension between international norms and domestic sovereignty. This section examines three pivotal tribunals: the Tokyo Tribunal, the Extraordinary Chambers in the Courts of Cambodia, and the Special Panels for Serious Crimes in East Timor.

A. The International Military Tribunal for the Far East (The Tokyo Tribunal) (1946–1948)

The International Military Tribunal for the Far East (IMTFE), commonly known as the Tokyo Tribunal, was convened by the Allied powers in 1946 to prosecute Japanese political and military leaders for atrocities committed during World War II. Established under the authority of General Douglas MacArthur, Supreme Commander for the Allied Powers, the tribunal aimed to address crimes spanning Japan's invasion of Manchuria in 1931 to its surrender in 1945.[54]

Modelled after the Nuremberg Trials, the Tokyo Tribunal's charter granted jurisdiction over three categories of crimes, namely: (i) crimes against peace, (ii) war crimes, and (iii) crimes against humanity.[55]

28 high-ranking officials, including Japan's Hideki Tōjō, Japan's Prime Minister during World War II, were indicted. The tribunal's charges highlighted atrocities such as the Nanjing Massacre, forced labour campaigns, and the mistreatment of Allied prisoners of war.[56]

The Tokyo Tribunal faced criticisms for its perceived 'victors' justice,' as it excluded Emperor Hirohito and other imperial family members from prosecution – a decision influenced by

[52] ILC, 'Report of the International Law Commission on the Work of its 71st Session' (n 7) 81, Commentary (43) to Art 6 of the 2019 Draft Articles.

[53] O Triffterer and M Bohlander, 'Article 1. The Court' in Triffterer and Ambos (eds) (n 10) 19.

[54] 'The Nuremberg Trial and the Tokyo War Crimes Trials (1945–1948)' (*Office of the Historian, Foreign Service Institute, United States Department of State*) history.state.gov/milestones/1945-1952/nuremberg.

[55] The Charter of the International Military Tribunal for the Far East, Article 5. Crimes against humanity were provided under Article 5(c).

[56] 'International Military Tribunal for the Far East – Judgment of 4 November 1948' (*ICC Legal Tools Database*) www.legal-tools.org/doc/8bef6f/.

political pragmatism to ensure Japan's post-war stability.[57] Additionally, the narrow framing of crimes against humanity, which required a nexus to armed conflict,[58] limited its applicability to peacetime atrocities. In fact, no persons were convicted of the crime against humanity by the Tokyo Tribunal.[59] Despite these shortcomings, the tribunal established foundational principles for holding individuals accountable for state-sanctioned violence, influencing later developments in international criminal law.

B. Special Panels for Serious Crimes (East Timor) (2000–2006)

Following Indonesia's withdrawal from East Timor in 1999, the United Nations Transitional Administration (UNTAET) established the Special Panels for Serious Crimes, also called the East Timor Tribunal, to address, among others, crimes against humanity committed during the occupation. These hybrid panels, composed of both international and local judges, operated alongside a Serious Crimes Unit, which is a prosecutorial body tasked with investigations and indictments.[60]

The Special Panels were established under 'Regulation No. 2000/11 on the Organization of Courts in East Timor',[61] under which sections 10.1 and 10.2 provided the District Court in Dili with exclusive jurisdiction over various serious offences genocide, war crimes, crimes against humanity, murder, sexual offences, and torture committed in East Timor or by/against East Timorese citizens between 1 January 1999 and 25 October 1999. Pursuant to section 10.3 thereunder, panels established to exercise this jurisdiction shall be composed of both East Timorese and international judges.

Section 5 of 'Regulation No. 2000/15 on the Establishment of Panels with Exclusive Jurisdiction over Serious Criminal Offences'[62] adopts a definition of crimes against humanity which largely reflected the customary international law position. Section 22 thereunder prescribed that the Special Panels shall be composed of two international judges and one East Timorese Judge.

Over their tenure, the Special Panels indicted nearly 400 individuals, including high-ranking Indonesian military officials and militia leaders. However, a major challenge was Indonesia's refusal to extradite suspects, which meant that only 88 defendants-mostly low-level Timorese militiamen-were actually tried. Of these, 84 were convicted, while four were acquitted.[63] The panels conducted 55 trials, addressing incidents such as the Liquiçá Church Massacre, where a large number of civilians seeking refuge in a church were killed. Despite the gravity of the crimes, many of the most responsible individuals remained beyond the reach of the tribunal due to Indonesia's non-cooperation,

[57] See, eg, RH Minear, *Victors' Justice: Tokyo Crimes Trial* (Princeton, Princeton University Press, 1971).

[58] Article 5 of the Charter of the International Military Tribunal for the Far East only granted personal jurisdiction over 'Far Eastern criminals who as individuals or as members of organizations are charged with offences which include Crimes against Peace', and subject matter jurisdiction over several acts constituting crimes against humanity committed 'before or during the war' or as 'persecutions on political or racial grounds in execution of or in connection with the jurisdiction of the Tribunal'.

[59] ILC, 'Report of the International Law Commission on the Work of its 71st Session' (n 7) 50, fn 184 under Commentary (12) to Art 3 of the 2019 Draft Articles.

[60] C Reiger and M Wierda, *The Serious Crimes Process in Timor-Leste: In Retrospect* (International Center for Transitional Justice, March 2006) 12–14.

[61] UNTAET, 'Regulation No. 2000/11 on the Organization of Courts in East Timor' (6 March 2000) UNTAET/REG/2000/11.

[62] UNTAET, 'Regulation No. 2000/15 on the Organization of Courts in East Timor' (6 June 2000) UNTAET/REG/2000/15.

[63] Reiger and Wierda (n 60) 28.

despite the fact that the UNTAET and the Indonesian Government agreed on a Memorandum of Understanding for cooperation in legal, judicial, and human rights-related matters.[64]

The Special Panels' work was further hampered by resource constraints and the eventual withdrawal of UN funding. When the panels and the Serious Crimes Unit ceased operations in 2006, there were still 514 outstanding cases for which investigations had been conducted but no indictments issued, as well as 50 cases for which no investigations had yet been conducted.[65]

A report conducted by an independent Commission of Experts found that the judicial process before the Special Panels 'was not effective in delivering justice for the victims of serious violations of human rights and the people of Timor-Leste. The failure to investigate and prosecute the defendants in a credible manner has not achieved accountability of those who bear the greatest responsibility for serious violations. Many aspects of the ad hoc judicial process reveal scant respect for or conformity to relevant international standards'.[66]

Insofar as multinationals are concerned, the Special Panels, like most other international criminal tribunals, did not have criminal jurisdiction over legal persons, as opposed to natural persons.[67]

C. Extraordinary Chambers in the Courts of Cambodia (2007–2022)

The Extraordinary Chambers in the Courts of Cambodia ('the ECCC'), often referred to as the Khmer Rouge Tribunal, was a hybrid national-international court designed to address some of the gravest crimes committed in Asia during the twentieth century. The ECCC was established to prosecute senior leaders of the Khmer Rouge regime and those most responsible for atrocities committed between 17 April 1975 to 6 January 1979 – a period during which an estimated 1.7 million Cambodians died from execution, starvation, forced labour, and disease under the rule of Democratic Kampuchea led by Pol Pot.[68]

The origins of the ECCC can be traced to 1997, when Cambodia officially requested United Nations assistance in establishing a tribunal to hold Khmer Rouge leaders accountable.[69] The 'Law on the Establishment of Extraordinary Chambers in Courts of Cambodia for the Prosecution of Crimes Committed during the Period of Democratic Kampuchea' ('the ECCC Law'),[70] a Cambodian law, was initially promulgated in 2001. However, the Cambodian government and the United Nations were only able to reach an agreement in 2003,[71] with corresponding legislative amendments to the ECCC Law promulgated in 2004.[72]

[64] Reiger and Wierda (n 60) 21-22.

[65] UNSC 'Report to the Secretary General of the Commission of Experts to Review the Prosecution of Serious Violations of Human Rights in Timor-Leste (then East Timor) in 1999' (26 May 2005) in 'Letter Dated 24 June 2005' (15 July 2005) UN Doc S/2005/458, p 30, at para 107.

[66] UNSC 'Summary of the report to the Secretary-General of the Commission of Experts to Review the Prosecution of Serious Violations of Human Rights in Timor-Leste (then East Timor) in 1999' in 'Letter Dated 24 June 2005' (15 July 2005) UN Doc S/2005/458, p 6, at para 19; see also UNSC 'Report to the Secretary General of the Commission of Experts to Review the Prosecution of Serious Violations of Human Rights in Timor-Leste (then East Timor) in 1999' (n 65), p 118, at para 515.

[67] ILC, 'Report of the International Law Commission on the Work of its 71st Session' (n 7) 81, Commentary (43) to Art 6 of the 2019 Draft Articles.

[68] Dd Scheffer, 'The Extraordinary Chambers in the Courts of Cambodia' (*Cambodia Tribunal Monitor*) cambodiatribunal.org/wp-content/uploads/2013/08/history_history-analysis-scheffer_english.pdf.

[69] S Lamb, 'Reconciliation v. Accountability: The Extraordinary Chambers in the Courts of Cambodia' (2015) FICHL Policy Brief Series No. 34, fn 1, www.toaep.org/pbs-pdf/34-lamb.

[70] NS/RKM/0801/12.

[71] Agreement between the United Nations and the Royal Government of Cambodia concerning the Prosecution under Cambodian Law of Crimes Committed during the Period of Democratic Kampuchea (adopted 6 June 2003, entered into force 29 April 2005) 2329 UNTS 117.

[72] NS/RKM/1004/006.

The ECCC was a hybrid court (including both Cambodian and international judges, prosecutors, and staff) consisted of three judicial chambers (Pre-Trial, Trial, and Supreme Court), two investigatory offices (Co-Investigating Judges and Co-Prosecutors), and an Office of Administration.[73] Foreign judges are nominated by the Secretary-General of the United Nations.[74] The Court's jurisdiction extended to crimes under Cambodian law, as well as genocide, crimes against humanity, and war crimes as defined by international conventions and customary law.

Article 5 of the ECCC Law adopts a definition of crimes against humanity which largely reflected the customary international law position.

The ECCC's work spanned more than a decade, with its first judges sworn in during 2006 and its final decision delivered in 2022. Ultimately, the tribunal indicted five individuals for genocide, crimes against humanity, and/or war crimes. Three were convicted and sentenced to life imprisonment, including Khieu Samphan, the former head of state of Cambodia.

Critically, the ECCC's hybrid model has been both praised and critiqued. On one hand, it demonstrated that international and domestic legal actors could collaborate to address mass atrocity crimes, setting important precedents for victim participation and the application of international law in a national context. On the other hand, the court's limited number of convictions, high operational costs, and susceptibility to political influence have raised questions about its efficiency and legacy.

Despite these challenges, the ECCC has contributed significantly to transitional justice in Cambodia, fostering public awareness, supporting survivors, and reinforcing the principle that even the most powerful perpetrators can be brought to justice.

V. The International Criminal Court

The substantive content of the offence of crimes against humanity has been discussed in Part C above. This Part will primarily address the institution, jurisdiction and procedure of the ICC, as well as participation by Asian states therein.

A. The ICC's Institutional Background and Setup

The ICC is established by the Rome Statute. It is the first permanent international criminal court, which has a 'full-time' character.[75] As prescribed by Article 1 of the Rome Statute, the ICC has power to exercise its jurisdiction that is 'governed by the provisions of this Statute'. Article 4(1) provides that the Court shall have international legal personality.

Historically, the United Nations General Assembly ('the UNGA') invited the ILC 'to study the desirability and possibility of establishing an international judicial organ for the trials of persons charged with genocide' in 1948,[76] and requested the ILC to address the question of establishing of a permanent international criminal court in 1989.[77]

[73] M Baaz, 'Extraordinary Chambers in the Courts of Cambodia (ECCC)', *Max Planck Encyclopedias of International Law* (April 2020) opil.ouplaw.com/display/10.1093/law-mpeipro/e1713.013.1713/law-mpeipro-e1713?d=%2F10.1093%2Flaw-mpeipro%2Fe1713.013.1713%2Flaw-mpeipro-e1713&p=emailAkunz2XTMqMkc.

[74] See Article 11 new of the ECCC Law as amended in 2004.

[75] Triffterer and Bohlander (n 53) 18.

[76] Prevention and punishment of the crime of genocide, UNGA Res 260 (III) (9 December 1948.

[77] International criminal responsibility of individuals and entities engaged in illicit trafficking in narcotic drugs across national frontiers and other transnational criminal activities: establishment of an international criminal court with jurisdiction over such crimes, UNGA Res 44/39 (4 December 1989) UN Doc A/RES/44/39.

In the 46th session of the ILC in 1994, the ILC adopted a draft statute for an international criminal court consisting of 60 articles with commentaries, and decided to recommend the same go the UNGA.[78] The United Nations Diplomatic Conference of Plenipotentiaries on the Establishment of an International Criminal Court (the Rome Conference) was convened in Rome between 15 June to 17 July 1998, and resulted in the adoption of the Rome Statute on the last day. The Rome Statute came into force on 1 July 2002.

Under Article 34 of the Rome Statute, the ICC composed of (a) the Presidency; (b) an Appeals Division, a Trial Division and a Pre-Trial Division; (c) the Office of the Prosecutor; and (d) the Registry.

The ICC has 18 judges, who are elected by secret ballot by the Assembly of State Parties.[79] They hold office for a term of nine years, and are ineligible for re-election.[80] The President and the First and Second Vice-Presidents are elected by an absolute majority of the judges.[81]

Judges are assigned to the Appeals, Trial and Pre-Trial Divisions by the President.[82] Under Article 39(1) of the Rome Statute, the Appeal Division shall be composed of the President and four other judges; the Trial Division shall be composed of not less than six judges; and the Pre-Trial Division shall be composed of not less than six judges.

The judicial functions of the ICC are carried out in each division by Chambers:[83]

(a) All members of the Appeals Divisions are members of the Appeal Chamber.[84]
(b) The functions of the Trial Chamber shall be carried out by 3 judges of the Trial Division.[85] A Trial Chamber is constituted by the Presidency when referring a case to it.[86]
(c) The functions of the Pre-Trial Chamber shall generally be carried out either by 3 judges of the Pre-Trial Division, even though certain functions may be carried out by a single judge of that division.[87] Permanent Pre-Trial Chambers with fixed compositions are constituted by the Presidency.[88] When the Prosecutor has informed the Presidency of a situation as required by Regulation 45(1), the Presidency shall assign the situation to a Pre-Trial Chamber as soon as being informed.

While the functions of the Appeals Chamber and the Trials Chambers are relatively straightforward, the Pre-Trial Chamber exercises a variety of powers provided for by the Rome Statute:

(a) Under Article 56 of the Rome Statute, where the Prosecutor considers an investigation to present a unique investigative opportunity, the Prosecutor shall so inform the Pre-Trial Chamber. In that case, the Pre-Trial Chamber may take such measures as may be necessary to ensure the efficiency and integrity of the proceedings and, in particular, to protect the rights of the defence.[89]

[78] ILC, 'Report of the International Law Commission on the Work of its 46h Session' (2 May–22 July 1994) UN Doc A/49/10, p 26, paras 88–89; the draft statute and the commentaries were reproduced in the report at pp 26–74.
[79] Rome Statute, Art 36(6)(a).
[80] Rome Statute, Art 36(9)(a).
[81] Rome Statute, Art 38(1).
[82] Rome Statute, Art 39(1); The Rules of Procedure and Evidence, Rule 4*bis*(2).
[83] Rome Statute, Art 39(2)(a).
[84] Rome Statute, Art 39(2)(b)(i).
[85] Rome Statute, Art 39(2)(b)(ii).
[86] The Rules of Procedure and Evidence, Rule 130.
[87] Rome Statute, Art 39(2)(b)(iii).
[88] The Regulations of the Court, Regulation 46(1).
[89] Rome Statute, Art 56(1).

(b) Under Article 57, the Pre-Trial Chamber may also: (i) issue orders and warrants required for investigative purposes, (ii) provide for the protection and privacy of victims and witnesses, the preservation of evidence, the protection of persons who have been arrested or appeared in response to a summons, and the protection of national security information; (iii) authorise the Prosecutor to take specific investigative steps within a State Party's territory without having secured the cooperation of that State concerned;[90] and (iv) seek cooperation of States to take protective measures for the purpose of forfeiture, in particular for the ultimate benefit of victims.[91]
(c) Article 58 covers the Pre-Trial Chamber's powers to issue a warrant of arrest or a summons to appear. A warrant of arrest may be issued, upon application of the Prosecutor, where there are reasonable grounds to believe that the person has committed a crime within the ICC's jurisdiction, and such arrest appears necessary.[92] As an alternative to seeking a warrant of arrest, the Prosecutor may submit an application requesting the Pre-Trial Chamber to issue a summons for the person to appear. This is applicable where there are reasonable grounds to believe that a summons is sufficient to ensure the person's appearance.[93]

B. Jurisdiction; Complementarity; Gravity

Subject to the issue of complementarity and admissibility, the ICC may exercise jurisdiction over crimes against humanity in three circumstances, namely:

(a) When committed on the territory of a State Party;[94]
(b) When committed by a national of a State Party;[95] and
(c) When referred to by the United Nations Security Council.[96]

The ICC's jurisdiction is not subject to any statute of limitations.[97] Further, the ICC may still exercise its jurisdiction after a State Party withdraws from the Rome Statute, as long as the subject conduct took place prior to such withdrawal.[98]

One of the underlying principles on the ICC's jurisdiction is the principle of complementarity. Under the Rome Statute, each State Party has a responsibility to exercise its own criminal jurisdiction over international crimes,[99] and the ICC is complementary to the national jurisdictions.[100] Accordingly, a case will be inadmissible, and the ICC will not exercise its jurisdiction, where a State Party which has jurisdiction over the matter is investigating or prosecuting the case, or

[90] Where the Pre-Trial Chamber has determined in that case that the State is clearly unable to execute a request for cooperation due to the unavailability of any authority or any component of its judicial system competent to execute the request for cooperation.
[91] Rome Statute, Art 57(3).
[92] Rome Statute, Art 58(1).
[93] Rome Statute, Art 58(7).
[94] Rome Statute, Art 12(2)(a).
[95] Rome Statute, Art 12(2)(b).
[96] Rome Statute, Art 13(b).
[97] Rome Statute, Art 29.
[98] A notable example being the arrest of Rodrigo Duterte, the former president of the Philippines. The Pre-Trial Chamber, in issuing the Warranty of Arrest, held that 'while the Philippines' withdrawal from the Statute took effect on 17 March 2019, the Court retains jurisdiction with respect to alleged crimes that occurred on the territory of the Philippines while it was a State Party': *Rodrigo Roa Duterte* (Warrant of Arrest) ICC-01/21 (7 March 2025), para 6.
[99] Rome Statute, Preamble, para 6.
[100] Rome Statute, Art 1.

has already done so,[101] unless the State is/was unwilling or unable to genuinely carry out the investigation or prosecution.[102]

Another pre-requisite for the ICC to exercise jurisdiction is that the case must be of sufficient gravity to justify further action by the ICC.[103] According to the Prosecutor, in determining the issue, the relevant factors include the scale of the crimes, the nature of the crimes, the manner of their commission and their impact.[104] It should not however be assessed only by reference to the number of victims.[105] In the *Situation in the Democratic Republic of Congo* case, while the Appeals Chamber held the reasoning of the Pre-Trial Chamber I (which required the Prosecutor to focus only on the most senior leaders) to be flawed, and held that making an assessment of the particular role of the suspect varies 'considerably depending on the circumstances of the case' and thus such an assessment should not be carried out 'excessively on formalistic grounds'.[106] Unfortunately however, the Appeals Chambers did not lay down a comprehensive test to be applied, leaving it for the different chambers to decide.[107]

On the assessment of complementarity and gravity, the assessment and the level of rigour varies depending on the stage of proceedings before the Court.[108]

C. Procedural Framework

A case before the ICC may take the following stages from start to finish.

Preliminary Examinations and Investigations

a. A case is started by preliminary examination by the Prosecutor. The Office of the Prosecutor may initiate the process on the basis of (i) information sent by individuals or groups, States, intergovernmental or non-governmental organisations, (ii) referral from a State Party of the United Nations Security Council, or (iii) a declaration accepting the exercise of jurisdiction by the Court lodged by a State which is not a party to the Rome Statute.[109]
b. At this stage, the Prosecutor shall consider (i) jurisdiction (temporal, material, and either territorial or personal), (ii) admissibility (complementarity and gravity), and (iii) the interests of justice.[110]
c. Where the Prosecutor concludes that there is a reasonable basis to proceed with an investigation, they will submit to the Pre-Trial Chamber a request for authorisation of an investigation, together with any supporting material collected.[111] At this stage, victims may also make representations to the Pre-Trial Chamber.[112]

[101] Rome Statute, Arti17(1)(a)–(c).
[102] Rome Statute, Art 17(1)(a)–(b), 17(2)–(3). When assessing unwillingness and inability, the Prosecutor will consider whether any factors would vitiate the genuineness of the proceedings taken out by the national authority: Office of the Prosecutor, *Policy Paper on Preliminary Examinations* (November 2013), p 14 at para 58.
[103] Rome Statute, Art 17(1)(d).
[104] Office of the Prosecutor, *Report on Prosecutorial Strategy* (14 September 2006), p 5 at para 2(b).
[105] *Prosecutor v Abu Garda* (Decision on the Confirmation of Charges) ICC-02/05-02/09 (8 February 2010) at para 31.
[106] *Situation in the Democratic Republic of the Congo* (Judgment on the Prosecutor's appeal against the decision of Pre-Trial Chamber I entitled 'Decision on the Prosecutor's Application for Warrants of Arrest, Article 58') ICC-01/04 (13 July 2006), paras 68–82.
[107] WA Schabas and MM El Zeidy, 'Article 17. Issue of Admissibility' in O Triffterer and K Ambos (eds) (n 10) 813–14.
[108] ibid 814–15.
[109] Office of the Prosecutor, *Policy Paper on Preliminary Examinations* (November 2013) 2.
[110] ibid 2.
[111] Rome Statute, Art 15(3).
[112] Rome Statute, Art 15(3).

d. If the Pre-Trial Chamber, upon considering the request and supporting material, considers that there is a reasonable basis to proceed, it will authorise the commencement of the investigation. Where the Pre-Trial Chamber concludes that there is not a reasonable basis, the Prosecutor is not precluded from submitting a fresh application.[113]
e. The Pre-Trial Chamber may also, upon the Prosecutor's application, issue a warrant of arrest or summons to appear, where there are reasonable grounds to believe that the person has committed a crime within the ICC's jurisdiction.[114]

<u>Confirmation of Charges and Pre-Trial Stages</u>

a. Where a suspect is surrendered or voluntarily before the ICC, they are first brought before the Pre-Trial Chamber. At the initial appearance, the Pre-Trial Chamber shall satisfy itself that the person has been informed of the allegations against them, as well as their rights.[115] They may also apply for interim release pending trial.[116]
b. A Confirmation of Charges Hearing would be held within a reasonable time after the surrender or voluntary appearance.[117] At the hearing, the Prosecutor needs to support each charge with sufficient evidence to establish substantial grounds to believe that the person committed the crime charged,[118] and the defendant may object to the charges or challenge the evidence presented by the Prosecutor (including presenting evidence themselves.[119]
c. Upon hearing the argument and considering the evidence, the Pre-Trial Chamber will decide whether there is sufficient evidence to proceed and to commit the person to trial.[120] Once the charges have been confirmed, a Trial Chamber will be constituted and become responsible for the conduct of subsequent proceedings.[121] The Trial Chamber may, if necessary, refer preliminary issues to the Pre-Trial Chamber or another pre-trial judge.[122]

<u>Trials and Appeals</u>

a. The trial will be held before a Trial Chamber of three judges, which has a variety of functions and powers to conduct the proceedings.[123] The trial shall be held in public, whilst special circumstances may require that certain proceedings be in closed session.[124]
b. At the trial, the burden of proof is on the Prosecutor, and the Court must be convinced of the guilty beyond reasonable doubt in order to convict the accused.[125] The accused also has a number of rights including, *inter alia*, the right to remain silent.[126] The parties may submit evidence relevant to the case, and the Court also has authority to request the submission of all evidence that it considers necessary for the determination of the truth.[127]

[113] Rome Statute, Art 15(5)–(6).
[114] Rome Statute, Art 58.
[115] Rome Statute, Art 60(1).
[116] Rome Statute, Art 60(2).
[117] Rome Statute, Art 61(1). The Confirmation of Charges Hearing may also be held *in absentia*: Rome Statute, Art 61(2).
[118] Rome Statute, Art 61(5).
[119] Rome Statute, Art 61(6).
[120] Rome Statute, Art 61(7).
[121] Rome Statute, Art 61(11).
[122] Rome Statute, Art 64(4).
[123] Rome Statute, Art 39(2)(b)(ii), Article 64.
[124] Rome Statute, Art 64(7).
[125] Rome Statute, Art 66.
[126] Rome Statute, Art 67.
[127] Rome Statute, Art 69(3).

c. The Rome Statute also sets out protections of the victims and witnesses and their participation in the proceedings.[128] A State may also apply for necessary measures in order to protect its agents and confidential/sensitive information.[129]
d. The Trial Chamber will issue a verdict after considering all the evidence and arguments. In the event of a conviction, the Court may impose a sentence up to 30 years of imprisonment,[130] and a life sentence under exceptional circumstances.[131] The Court may also order reparations to victims.[132]
e. Decisions of acquittal, conviction, and sentences may be appealed, either by the Prosecutor or the convicted person.[133] The victims and the convicted person may appeal against an order for reparations.[134] Certain decisions at the pre-trial stages may also be appealed.[135] The appeals will be heard before an Appeals Chambers which is composed of all the judges of the Appeals Division.[136]
f. Apart from the appeals procedure, the Appeals Chamber may also, upon application, revise the final judgment of conviction or sentence on the grounds that (i) sufficiently important new evidence has been discovered that was not available at the trial, (ii) decisive evidence that was considered at trial was found to be false, forged, or falsified, or (iii) the judge(s) of the case committed an act of serious misconduct or seriously breach of duty.[137]

D. Asian State Participation

The Asia-Pacific region remains the most underrepresented region among the State Parties.[138] As of June 2025, there are only 19 Asia-Pacific State Parties of the Rome Statute.[139] Notably, the Philippines withdrew from the ICC in 2019,[140] and some geopolitically significant states such as China, India, Indonesia, Pakistan, Vietnam, and Thailand remain outside the Rome Statute.

As a result, there have been few ICC cases and investigations directly concerning Asian States. As of 2025, only the following investigations have commenced in relation to Asian States:

a. Afghanistan: In 2020, the Prosecutor commenced an investigation into alleged war crimes and crimes against humanity in relation to the situation in Afghanistan since 2002.[141]

[128] Rome Statute, Art 68.
[129] Rome Statute, Art 68(6).
[130] Rome Statute, Art 77(1).
[131] Where a term of life imprisonment is justified by the extreme gravity of the crime and the individual circumstances of the convicted person: Rome Statute, Art 77(1).
[132] Rome Statute, Art 75.
[133] Rome Statute, Art 81.
[134] Rome Statute, Art 82(4).
[135] Rome Statute, Art 82(1)–(3).
[136] Rome Statute, Art 39(2)(b)(i). There are 5 judges in the Appeals Division.
[137] Rome Statute, Art 84.
[138] M Takeuchi, 'Asian Perspectives on the International Law Commission's Work on Crimes Against Humanity' (2020) 6(2) *African Journal of International Criminal Justice* 151, 159.
[139] Afghanistan, Bangladesh, Cambodia, Cook Islands, Cyprus, Fiji, Japan, Jordan, Kiribati, Maldives, Marshall Islands, Mongolia, Nauru, Republic of Korea, Samoa, State of Palestine, Tajikistan, Timor-Leste, and Vanuatu.
[140] See the notification of withdrawal by the Government of the Republic of the Philippines: Depository Notification C.N.138.2018.TREATIES-XVIII.10.
[141] *Situation in the Islamic Republic of Afghanistan* (Judgment on the appeal against the decision on the authorisation of an investigation) ICC-02/17 OA4 (5 March 2020).

Two applications for arrest warrants were made in 2025, and such applications are still pending.[142]

b. Bangladesh/Myanmar: In 2019, the Prosecutor started an investigation for the alleged crimes in Bangladesh/Myanmar concerning the Rohingya crisis.[143] An application for arrest warrant was made in 2024 and is now pending.[144]
c. Philippines: In 2021, the Prosecutor commenced an investigation of crimes allegedly committed in Philippines between 2011 to 2019 in the context of the so-called 'war on drugs' campaign.[145] The former president of the Philippines, Rodrigo Duterte, was arrested in 2025, and the Confirmation of Charges hearing is now pending.[146]
d. Palestine: An investigation over the situation in Palestine was commenced in 2021.[147]

VI. Domestic Implementation of Crimes against Humanity in Asia

While international treaties and customary law set the framework for prosecuting and preventing crimes against humanity, the effectiveness of these norms depends largely on their translation into national law and practice. Without enacting national implementing legislation, State Parties to the Rome Statute have limited ability to investigate and prosecute core international crimes and to cooperate with the ICC.[148]

Currently, the incorporation of crimes against humanity into domestic legal frameworks is marked by significant gaps, inconsistencies, and a patchwork of legal reforms that reflect both the diversity of legal systems and the varying degrees of political will across the region. Unlike the crime of genocide or war crimes, which are often explicitly criminalised due to the widespread ratification of the Genocide Convention and the Geneva Conventions, there is no specific international convention covering crimes against humanity.[149]

As a result, crimes against humanity have not been systematically incorporated into the domestic legal codes of most Asian states, even among those that are parties to the Rome Statute.[150] The table below shows the current status regarding the Asian States.[151]

[142] Office of the Prosecutor, 'Statement of ICC Prosecutor Karim A.A. Khan KC: Applications for arrest warrants in the situation in Afghanistan' (*International Criminal* Court, 23 January 2025) www.icc-cpi.int/news/statement-icc-prosecutor-karim-aa-khan-kc-applications-arrest-warrants-situation-afghanistan.

[143] *Situation in the People's Republic of Bangladesh/Republic of the Union of Myanmar* (Decision Pursuant to Article 15 of the Rome Statute on the Authorisation of an Investigation) ICC-01/19 (14 November 2019).

[144] Office of the Prosecutor, 'Statement of ICC Prosecutor Karim A.A. Khan KC: Application for an arrest warrant in the situation in Bangladesh/Myanmar' (*International Criminal* Court, 27 November 2024) www.icc-cpi.int/news/statement-icc-prosecutor-karim-aa-khan-kc-application-arrest-warrant-situation-bangladesh.

[145] *Situation in the Republic of the Philippines* (Decision on the Prosecutor's request for authorisation of an investigation pursuant to Article 15(3) of the Statute) ICC-01/21(15 September 2021).

[146] *Prosecutor v Rodrigo Roa Duterte* (Order on the conduct of confirmation proceedings) ICC-01/21-01/25 (17 April 2025).

[147] Office of the Prosecutor, 'Statement of ICC Prosecutor, Fatou Bensouda, respecting an investigation of the Situation in Palestine' (*International Criminal Court*, 3 March 2021) www.icc-cpi.int/news/statement-icc-prosecutor-fatou-bensouda-respecting-investigation-situation-palestine.

[148] DJ Birkett, 'Twenty Years of the Rome Statute of the International Criminal Court: Appraising the State of National Implementing Legislation in Asia' (2019) 18 *Chinese Journal of International Law* 353, 390.

[149] See subsection G below.

[150] Birkett (n 147) 369–70.

[151] Takeuchi (n 138) 160–61.

Table 1 Asian States' Engagement with Crimes Against Humanity

	Countries	**Signatory to Rome Statute**	**Domestic Legislation Adopting Crimes Against Humanity**
East Asia	China		
	Japan	○	
	North Korea		
	South Korea	○	○
	Mongolia	○	
Southeast Asia	Brunei		
	Cambodia	○	○
	Indonesia		○
	Laos		
	Malaysia		
	Myanmar		
	Philippines		○
	Singapore		
	Thailand		
	Vietnam		△[152]
South Asia	Afghanistan	○	
	Bangladesh	○	○
	Bhutan		
	India		
	Maldives	○	
	Nepal		△[153]
	Pakistan		
	Sri Lanka		△[154]
Central Asia	Kazakhstan		△[155]
	Kyrgyzstan		○[156]
	Tajikistan	○	
	Turkmenistan		
	Uzbekistan		

[152] Focusing on genocide.

[153] Focusing on enforced disappearance.

[154] Covering enforced disappearance only.

[155] Covering enforced disappearance only.

[156] In Kyrgyzstan, following a major criminal legal reform in 2017, criminal responsibility for the commission of crimes against humanity is established: Criminal Code of the Kyrgyz Republic, Chapter 52, Article 381. However, it has been noted that there are gaps in the definition of the crime as compared with the formulation under the Rome Statute: Rustam Atadjanov, 'Domestic Implementation of Crimes against Humanity in Central Asia' (2022) 17(2) *Asian Journal of Comparative Law* 268.

As shown above, a number of Asian State Parties to the Rome Statute[157] do not explicitly criminalise crimes against humanity in their respective domestic laws.[158] On the other hand, some States not being a party (or withdrew from) to the Rome Statute have criminalised crimes against humanity under their domestic laws.[159]

For those States which have domestically implemented crimes against humanity, the contents of such legislation vary a lot and they do not necessarily mirror the formulations under the Rome Statute. 'Under-inclusiveness' and omissions could be seen as a common issue among many Asia States.[160]

In respect of the crime against humanity of persecution,[161] the grounds on which persecution may be committed vary from State to State. For example, Bangladeshi law omitted a number of grounds (e.g. nationality and gender), limiting the crime to 'political, racial, ethnic or religious grounds'.[162] In another example, many states did not incorporate the 'policy requirement'[163] into their domestic legislation.[164]

Such lack of comprehensive domestic implementation and inconsistencies may create barriers not only to domestic prosecutions but also to regional cooperation in investigating and extraditing suspects. Whilst Asian states have developed mutual legal assistance frameworks for certain transnational crimes, similar mechanisms for crimes against humanity are still largely absent, at least until the 2019 Draft Articles become a major treaty.

VII. Draft Articles on Prevention and Punishment of Crimes against Humanity

In 2019, the International Law Commission submitted Draft Articles on Prevention and Punishment of Crimes Against Humanity[165] to the UN General Assembly (ie, 'the 2019 Draft Articles' as defined above), representing a significant effort toward a potential new convention.

A. Structure and Scope of the 2019 Draft Articles

The 2019 Draft Articles comprise 15 substantive provisions, a draft preamble, and an annex, accompanied by detailed commentaries explaining their rationale and intended interpretation. The articles are designed to be comprehensive, addressing both the prevention and punishment of crimes against humanity, and are intended to apply universally to all states.

[157] See eg Afghanistan, Japan, Jordan, Maldives, Mongolia, Palestine, and Tajikistan.
[158] Birkett (n 148) 369–70.
[159] See eg Indonesia, Philippines.
[160] Birkett (n 148) 371–72.
[161] Rome Statute, Art 7(1)(h).
[162] The International Crimes (Tribunals) Act 1973 (Bangladesh), s 3(2)(a).
[163] ie the element that 'Attack directed against any civilian population' means a course of conduct involving the multiple commission of acts against any civilian population, pursuant to or in furtherance of a State or organisational policy to commit such attack: Rome Statute, Art 7(2)(a).
[164] Birkett (n 148) 372.
[165] ILC, 'Report of the International Law Commission on the Work of its 71st Session' (n 7) 11–21.

The Preamble sets out the moral and legal imperatives underlying the draft, recalling the suffering caused by crimes against humanity throughout history, affirming their status as crimes of concern to the international community, and recognising the duty of every state to exercise criminal jurisdiction over such acts.

B. Key Provisions and Innovations

Definition of Crimes Against Humanity – The 2019 Draft Articles define crimes against humanity as any of a list of acts (including murder, extermination, enslavement, deportation, torture, rape, persecution, enforced disappearance, apartheid, and other inhumane acts) when committed as part of a widespread or systematic attack directed against any civilian population, with knowledge of the attack.[166] This mirrors the ICC definition but is intended for universal application, regardless of whether a state is a party to the Rome Statute.

General Obligations of States – States are obligated not only to refrain from committing crimes against humanity but also to prevent and punish them.[167] This dual focus is a central innovation of the 2019 Draft Articles, reflecting the recognition that effective prevention is inseparable from the elimination of impunity. States must take legislative, administrative, judicial, and other measures to prevent crimes against humanity within any territory under their jurisdiction or control.[168]

Criminalisation and National Implementation – A core element of the 2019 Draft Articles is the obligation for states to criminalise crimes against humanity in their domestic legal systems. States must ensure that their laws cover all acts constituting crimes against humanity, adopt definitions consistent with the 2019 Draft Articles, and establish penalties that reflect the gravity of these crimes.[169] This article aims to close the 'impunity gap' that persists in many national jurisdictions, where crimes against humanity may not be specifically criminalised or may be subject to statutes of limitation or immunities.

Jurisdiction – The 2019 Draft Articles require states to establish jurisdiction over crimes against humanity committed in their territory, by their nationals, or against their nationals. Importantly, they also encourage the exercise of universal jurisdiction-the ability to prosecute offenders present in a state's territory, regardless of where the crime was committed or the nationality of the perpetrator or victim.[170]

Non-Refoulement – One of the most progressive features of the 2019 Draft Articles is the inclusion of a non-refoulement obligation: states may not expel, return, or extradite a person to another state where there are substantial grounds for believing that they would be in danger of being subjected to crimes against humanity.[171] This aligns with similar protections in the Convention Against Torture and reflects the seriousness of the risk posed by crimes against humanity.

Extradition and Mutual Legal Assistance – The 2019 Draft Articles contain detailed provisions on extradition and mutual legal assistance, requiring states to cooperate in the investigation,

[166] ibid 12–13, Art 2 of the 2019 Draft Articles.
[167] ibid 13, Arts 3 to 4 of the 2019 Draft Articles.
[168] ibid 13, Art 4 of the 2019 Draft Articles.
[169] ibid 13–14, Art 6 of the 2019 Draft Articles.
[170] ibid 14, Art 7 of the 2019 Draft Articles.
[171] ibid 13, Art 5 of the 2019 Draft Articles.

prosecution, and punishment of crimes against humanity.[172] States must either prosecute offenders found in their territory or extradite them to another state with jurisdiction (the principle of *aut dedere aut judicare*).[173]

Fair Treatment and Victims' Rights – The 2019 Draft Articles emphasise the right to a fair trial for alleged offenders and include safeguards for the treatment of suspects, such as access to legal counsel and consular assistance.[174] They also recognise the rights of victims, witnesses, and others affected, including the right to participate in proceedings, receive protection, and seek reparations.[175]

Statutes of Limitation and Immunities – The 2019 Draft Articles stipulate that statutes of limitation do not apply to crimes against humanity,[176] and prohibit the invocation of official capacity (such as head of state or government) as a defence or ground for immunity from prosecution,[177] mirroring the Rome Statute.[178]

C. Commentary and Rationale

The ILC's commentaries to the 2019 Draft Articles[179] provided detailed explanations of each provision, drawing on state practice, judicial decisions, and the experience of existing international treaties. The commentaries noted that by having a global convention on prevention and punishment of crimes against humanity, it could draw further attention to the need for prevention and punishment and help States to adopt and harmonise national laws relating to such conduct, thereby opening the door to more effective inter-State cooperation on the prevention, investigation and prosecution of such crimes.[180]

It is also stated that codification of existing law is not the objective of the 2019 Draft Articles. Rather, the objective is the drafting of provisions' that would be both effective and likely acceptable to States, based on provisions often used in widely adhered-to treaties in addressing crimes, as a basis for a possible future convention.[181]

D. The Path Toward a Crimes against Humanity Treaty

The ILC's adoption of the 2019 Draft Articles was widely hailed as a major step forward, but the road to a binding treaty remains challenging.

The 2019 Draft Articles were transmitted to the UN General Assembly's Sixth Committee, the primary forum for legal questions, which began substantive consideration and debate on their content and the process for treaty negotiation. Nearly 80 UN member states from all regions have expressed support for moving forward, but a small number of states remain

[172] ibid 16-18, Arts 13 to 15 of the 2019 Draft Articles.
[173] ibid 15, Art 10 of the 2019 Draft Articles.
[174] ibid 15, Art 11 of the 2019 Draft Articles.
[175] ibid 16, Art 12 of the 2019 Draft Articles.
[176] ibid 14, Art 6(6) of the 2019 Draft Articles.
[177] ibid 14, Art 6(5) of the 2019 Draft Articles.
[178] cf Rome Statute, Arts 27 and 29.
[179] ILC, 'Report of the International Law Commission on the Work of its 71st Session' (n 7) 22–140.
[180] ibid 22, General Commentary (2).
[181] ibid 22–23, General Commentary (3).

opposed or cautious, citing concerns about sovereignty, definitions, or the impact on national legal systems.

In December 2022, the General Assembly established a two-year process to further consider the ILC's recommendation, and in autumn 2024, the Sixth Committee is expected to decide whether to initiate formal negotiations for a convention based on the 2019 Draft Articles. In December 2024, the General Assembly adopted a Resolution which established a process for further consideration, with the aim of eventually convening a Conference of Plenipotentiaries in 2028 and 2029 to negotiate a treaty based on the 2019 Draft Articles.[182]

Civil society organisations, legal experts, and human rights advocates have called on states to fully support the adoption of a treaty, emphasising its potential to close legal gaps, strengthen prevention, and provide justice for victims.

E. Significance for Asia

For Asia and other regions where crimes against humanity have occurred or remain a risk, the adoption of a dedicated treaty would have far-reaching implications. As many Asian states have not ratified the Rome Statute, and domestic implementation of crimes against humanity remains patchy, a universal treaty would:

(a) Provide a clear legal framework and obligations for the states;
(b) Facilitate cooperation in investigation and prosecution across borders;
(c) Strengthen the capacity of national legal systems to address crimes against humanity and support victims; and
(d) Enhance prevention by signalling a global commitment to accountability and justice.

However, whilst most Asian States have constantly shown support for and understanding of the ILC's work on crimes against humanity,[183] the States' responses to the 2019 Draft Articles and how to proceed with it have been mixed.[184]

While some states (eg, Japan and South Korea) have expressed support for the 2019 Draft Articles,[185] some other states have raised concerns. Notably, most of the concerns were related to the scope of criminalisation and the establishment of national jurisdiction.[186] Concerns were also raised regarding the liability of legal persons for crimes against human as provided in the 2019 Draft Articles.[187] The States' reactions to the 2019 Draft Articles reflect their traditional position based on respect for national sovereignty and non-interference in other States' internal affairs.[188]

In progressing the 2019 Draft Articles and facilitating the negotiations, the ILC has taken an inclusive approach. Whilst the 2019 Draft Articles seek to contribute to the implementation of

[182] United Nations Conference of Plenipotentiaries on Prevention and Punishment of Crimes against Humanity, UNGA Res 79/122 (4 December 2024) UN Doc A/RES/79/122.

[183] Takeuchi (n 138) 154.

[184] Takeuchi (n 138) 154.

[185] Asian-African Legal Consultative Organization (AALCO), 'Verbatim Record of Discussions, Fifty-Fifth Annual Session' (17-20 May 2016) AALCO/55/NEW DELHI (HEADQUARTERS)/2016/VR, p 127; AALCO, 'Verbatim Record of Discussions, Fifty-Eighth Annual Session' (21–25 October 2019) AALCO/58/DAR ES SALAAM/2019/VR, pp 149–50.

[186] Takeuchi (n 138) 155.

[187] ibid 155. See ILC, 'Report of the International Law Commission on the Work of its 71st Session' (n 7) 13–14, Article 6 of the 2019 Draft Articles. See also the discussion in paras 13.24–13.25 above.

[188] Takeuchi (n 138) 157.

the principle of complementarity under the Rome Statute, they also aim to provide obligations that may be undertaken by States regardless of whether they are parties to the Rome Statute.[189] Since it is unlikely that Asian States will ratify the Rome Statute in large numbers in the near future, it would be imperative for the 2019 Draft Articles to be elaborated into a treaty as a means address the 'legal vacuum' of states in Asia.[190]

[189] ILC, 'Report of the International Law Commission on the Work of its 71st Session' (n 7) p. 23, General Commentary (4).

[190] Takeuchi (n 138) 160.

14

Corporate Crime, Compliance Programmes, and Criminal Law – The UN Guiding Principles on Business and Human Rights in Japan and China

SHIN MATSUZAWA AND ZIQING RUAN

I. Introduction

The objective of this chapter is to elucidate the manner in which the Guiding Principles on Business and Human Rights are reflected in the criminal legislation of Asian countries. 'The UN Guiding Principles on Business and Human Rights' (the UNGPs) is a document that was adopted by the UN Human Rights Council in 2011. It comprises three fundamental elements: the obligation of states to protect human rights, the responsibility of business to respect human rights, and access to remedies.

In today's business environment, the social responsibility of companies is a significant and growing concern. Previously, responsibility for ensuring human rights was borne solely by the state. However, the role of companies in society has grown significantly, and they are now expected to act as the primary entity responsible for guaranteeing human rights. Furthermore, companies are now required to align their activities with the Sustainable Development Goals (SDGs), which cannot be achieved without ensuring human rights. In this context, companies are expected to conduct their business operations in accordance with the UNGPs.

In the course of corporate activities, various scandals can occur. Of these, the most serious problems are caused by corporate crimes. The UNGPs is thought to have the function of preventing the occurrence of corporate scandals through the guarantee of human rights by companies. This raises the question of how the prevention of corporate crimes is achieved through this principle.

This chapter examines Japanese and Chinese responses to corporate crime and then considers what the UNGPs mean in the criminal law systems of the two countries. From a comparative legal perspective, it will be interesting to see how the principles are reflected in the legal systems of two Asian economic powers with different economic and state regimes.

The structure of this chapter is as follows. First, the situation in Japan is presented (section II), followed by the situation in China (section III). The content to be examined in each is as follows: (1) theories of corporate criminal liability; (2) the significance of compliance programmes and criminal law; and (3) how the UNGPs are embodied in criminal law. This situation regarding these issues is interesting because it reflects the state of society within each country.

This chapter is co-authored by Japanese Professor Shin Matsuzawa of Waseda University, and Chinese doctoral student Ziqing Ruan of Waseda University. Matsuzawa wrote introduction and section II on Japan, Ruan wrote section III on China and the Conclusion. Matsuzawa later made further amendments.

II. Japan

A. Theories of Corporate Criminal Responsibility in Japan

i. The Question of whether a Corporate Body has the Capacity to Commit a Crime has been the Subject of Debate in Japan

The prevailing theory has traditionally been that it does not have capacity. This is due to the influence of German law, which denies that a judicial person (in German: juristische Person) has the capacity to commit a crime, on the development of Japanese jurisprudence.[1]

The arguments for 'negative theory' are as follows:

(1) It is a fundamental principle of criminal law that an act is the essential element of a crime. Corporate body, on the other hand, is not capable of acting. This is because acts arise as an expression of the will and are grounded in psychological facts. The corporate body is not a living creature and therefore cannot have such a psychological state.
(2) Punishment is a form of disciplinary action taken against the individual in question. For the censure to have meaning, there must be an entity that is able to understand and be sensitive to the implications of the punishment. The corporate body does not have the necessary entity to make the sensitising power of the punishment meaningful.
(3) It is sufficient to deal with crimes committed by corporate bodies involving more than one person by using the provisions for complicity.
(4) It is inappropriate to use a penal system centred on imprisonment sentences for the corporate body.

Each of these reasons has a certain logic to it. The Japanese Penal Code was enacted with the objective of punishing natural persons. Accordingly, the position that does not recognise the criminal capacity of a legal person has historically been the dominant view.

However, more recently, a number of scholars have put forth a view that affirms the criminal responsibility of legal persons. The 'positive theory' is now considered to be the dominant view, as evidenced by the following arguments:

(1) It is true that crimes are committed by acts and have psychological facts as their basis. However, a corporate body also makes decisions and determines activities by its representational body, and its activities can be seen as acts. It is also possible to see the activities of natural persons belonging to the representational body as acts of the legal person.
(2) Persons belonging to a corporate body can reflect on their own economic activities when criminal penalties are imposed on a company. In addition, they can change activities and its position in society. Therefore, imposing penalties on a legal person has practical significance.

[1] The Japanese Penal Code was made under the strong influence by the German Criminal Theory. See S Matsuzawa, *Essays on Criminal Law in Japan* (Tokyo, Seibundo, 2024) ch 6.

(3) In modern society, business companies play a very important role, and it is not sufficient to control them through the application of the complicity provisions of the Criminal Code, which presupposes individual punishment.
(4) Penalties against business entities can be addressed primarily by fines.

From the above, it is considered that criminal liability can be affirmed for a corporate body. This chapter develops the following argument from the standpoint of positive theory.

ii. Dual Criminal Liability Provision (Ryobatsu-kitei)

The Japanese Penal Code does not include any provisions for punishing corporate bodies as such. This is due to the fact that the Japanese Penal Code has historically been influenced by German law. It should be noted, however, that many special criminal laws include provisions for dual criminal liability. A dual criminal liability provision is a legal mechanism that holds both natural persons and legal persons responsible for illegal actions carried out in the course of business activities.

A dual criminal liability provision usually takes the following form: 'If a natural person commits an offence in connection with the business of the corporate body, the natural person shall be punished and the corporate body shall also be fined.'

In accordance with these provisions, both natural persons and legal entities may be subject to penalties in Japan. Because of the existence of such penal provisions, it is theoretically superior to affirm the criminal liability of the legal person and allow the corporate body itself to be punished. Therefore, in order to explain such punishment in a more theoretical form, the theory described in the next section was developed.

iii. Theoretical Models

There are two main types of theoretical models proposed in Japanese criminal law studies.[2] The first is a theory that censures the organisational body itself for causing the illegal outcome and attempts to deter crime. This can be called 'the corporate body deterrence model'. The other is a theory that censures the individuals involved in the operation of the organisational body, thereby deterring crime. This is called 'the individual deterrence model'.

a. Corporate Body Deterrence Model

The corporate body deterrence model is based on the premise that the corporate body is regarded as a tangible and operational entity. It is true that the corporate body is made up of its constituent parts. Consequently, in previous eras, the corporate body was regarded as a conceptual entity rather than a tangible entity. However, in the present day, the corporate body is increasingly recognised as a real entity from the perspectives of sociology and management studies. In light of the above, the theory of deterring crimes by punishing illegal acts committed by the corporate body itself is a reasonable one.

[2] For the following, see T Imai, 'Kigyo no Keiji Sekinin' (Corporate Criminal Liability) in K Kai (ed), *Kigyo katsudo to keiji kisei* (Business Activities and Criminal Regulation) (Tokyo, Nippon Hyoronsha, 2008) 11. Also, for a comprehensive study on this issue, see R Higuchi, *Hojin Shobatsu to Keihou Riron* (Corporate Punishment and Criminal Law Theory) (Tokyo, daigaku shuppansha, 2009).

The corporate body deterrence model can be divided into two types in terms of its theoretical structure.

The first model is 'the aggregation model'. This model assumes that the will of each member of a corporate body is aggregated, and that the corporate body can be punished when the decisions made by the aggregated will result in illegal outcomes. This model focuses on the decision-making of corporate bodies. However, it only considers it as the aggregation of the intentions of individuals. Theoretically, this view cannot conceive of a corporate body's own decision making that is separate from each individual's decision, since the accumulated will can be reduced to the will of the individual.

The second model is 'the separate self-identity model'. This model aims to deter criminal activity by directly addressing the decision-making processes by the corporate body itself. The fundamental premise of this model is that each corporate body possesses its own unique ethos. This is also referred to as a 'corporate culture'. Indeed, it is evident that such a culture exists within a corporate body. Despite fluctuations in employee turnover, the distinctive atmosphere of a company tends to persist. Decisions that align with this culture are regarded as decisions of the corporate body and are therefore subject to penalties. These decisions are not merely the aggregation of individual choices; they are shaped by the unique corporate culture.

b. Individual Deterrence Model

The individual deterrence model is based on the idea that even a corporate body is composed of individuals, and that the corporate body should be punished by focusing on the individual who controls the corporate body and censuring them. If the corporate body deterrence model is based on holistic considerations, the individual deterrence model is based on analytical thinking.

The individual deterrence model can also be further divided into two models in its theoretical structure.

The first is called 'the vicarious liability model'. In this model, individuals acting on behalf of a corporate body are held responsible for the illegal consequences of the corporate body, and those individuals are punished. In this case, the individual is punished on behalf of the corporate body, hence the term 'vicarious liability model'. The disadvantage of this model is that, in the case of vicarious liability, the individual acting on behalf of the corporate body must be held liable, even if they are not at fault.

The second model is 'the self-identification model'. In this model, the acts of individuals who identify with the corporate body are considered to be those of the corporate body, and the corporate body is held responsible and punished for the illegal results caused by these individuals. This model is based on the recognition that the corporate body is controlled by a small number of individuals who belong to the executive branch. The actions of individuals on the executive committee ultimately move the employees within the company, which in turn moves the corporate body. In this sense, this model is consistent with reality.

c. Discussion

Of the above models, the authors believe that, basically, the corporate body deterrence model is the appropriate one. This is because, as long as the corporate body is punished, the organisation itself should be the object of reprimand. In the individual deterrence model, the methodology of trying to reduce the problem to individual responsibility is understandable. And if this were a case of ordinary complicity, it would therefore be interpreted as such. However, since the

corporate body itself is being punished here, the corporate body deterrence model is more in line with the actual situation.

In the corporate body deterrence model, an interesting conclusion can be reached by analysing the behaviour of individuals within the corporate body. For example, let us consider a case in which some individuals within an organisation disagree with a decision made by the organisation as a whole. In this case, even if the corporate body's activities resulted in an illegal outcome, the corporate body would be excused if there were dissenting opinions within the corporate body and some preventive measures were taken in response to those dissenting opinions. Even if complete exoneration is not granted, a reduction in sentence may be possible. One example of a consequence-prevention measure would be the implementation of a so-called compliance programme.

B. The Significance of Compliance Programmes and Criminal Law in Japan

i. The Development of a Compliance Programme

A compliance programme is a programme that defines the norms to be followed by a company.[3] Compliance programmes were originally developed mainly in the United States. In Japan, the importance of compliance programmes has been recognised since the beginning of the 2000s.

Previously, Japanese companies were managed in a familial atmosphere, reflecting the distinctive Japanese cultural context. In other words, the management of a company was conducted under a kind of family-like structure, with the manager acting as the father figure and the employees as the children. The president is the sole authority for determining work content, which employees are required to follow. However, employees are afforded significant protection by management. The lifetime employment system in Japan is a case in point. As a result, internal corporate scandals were often handled discreetly within the company. However, since the beginning of the 2000s, Japanese society has undergone a transformation towards a social structure based on transparent and fair rules. This period also saw the emergence of discussions around globalisation in Japanese society. In response to these social changes, Japanese companies have been required to implement compliance programmes. In the 2020s, it is now considered standard practice for companies in Japan to have robust compliance programmes in place and to adhere to them strictly.

ii. The Function of Compliance Programmes in a Criminal Law Context

In Japan, it has been theorised that compliance programmes have several legal functions under the criminal law.[4] Those functions can be divided into approximately four categories. The first is that the implementation of a compliance programme justifies corporate misconduct. The second function is that the implementation of a compliance programme excuses a company from

[3] On the significance of compliance programmes, see K Kai, 'Corporate Governance to keiji kise' (Corporate Governance and Criminal Regulation) in K Kai (ed), *Kigyou Katsudo to Keiji Kisei* (Corporate Activities and Criminal Regulation) (Nippon Hyoronsh, 2008) 204.

[4] See Kai (n 3) 209. For a comprehensive study by Professor Kai on criminal law theory and compliance programmes, see K Kai, *Kigyo Hanzai to Keiji Compliance* (Corporate Crime and Criminal Compliance) (Tokyo, Seibundo, 2018).

any wrongdoing. The third function is that the implementation of a compliance programme immunises the company from prosecution.

Since 2000, Japanese criminal law scholars have examined each of these functions under this theoretical framework. If a compliance programme has these functions, it can motivate companies to develop effective compliance programmes. However, it is difficult to draw directly the conclusion that, if a corporate crime occurs and damages are caused, the company should not be punished simply because it had strictly implemented a compliance programme. Of course, the implementation of a compliance programme will make corporate crimes less likely to occur. However, once damage occurs, the question arises as to whether the damage could have been avoided. The fact that a compliance programme has been implemented can only be one of the factors for finding avoidability of consequences. There are cases in which a company should be severely punished even if it had a compliance programme in place. Therefore, in Japan, the discussion on the criminal law function of compliance programmes has been stagnant for some time.[5]

What the authors think is important here is to consider the function of a compliance programme that reduces a company's sentence. Japanese criminal law scholarship has devoted a great deal of time and effort to examining whether the conduct in question is or is not a crime. On the other hand, few Japanese criminal law scholars have studied the appropriate level of punishment for offenders after determining that an act is a crime. The reason for this is that the Japanese Penal Code, enacted in 1905, does not contain general provisions on sentencing. In any case, considering the sentence for corporate crimes is an important issue. In this case, a reference point is whether or not a compliance programme is in place.

When considering the function of compliance programmes in sentencing, it may be useful to consider the types of compliance programmes. Professor Katsunori Kai of Waseda University divides compliance programmes into three types.[6] The first is the compliance programme common to all companies. This would be the one that defines the most basic norms when conducting corporate activities (general compliance programme). The second is a compliance programme that is required to be established for each type of business. Each industry may have different norms to follow (specialised compliance programme). The third is a compliance programme that each company is required to establish on its own. By establishing its own code to be followed by each company and ensuring that employees comply with it, the company can fulfill its corporate social responsibility at the same time (customised compliance programme).

Of these, customised compliance programmes are likely to be centred on company-specific norms, and it is difficult to bring these into the theory of sentencing in general. On the other hand, it should be possible to categorise the contents of general compliance programmes and customised compliance programmes to some extent and clearly position the elements of each. By clarifying in advance the degree to which such typified compliance programmes will be treated favourably in terms of punishment, it can be expected that companies will be motivated to formulate and implement compliance programmes. Of course, punishment is very

[5] Professor Kawasaki presented a detailed discussion of the excuse function of compliance programmes. See T Kawasaki, *Kigyo no Keiji Sekinin* (Corporate Criminal Liability) (Tokyo, Seibundo, 2004). This was a very significant and useful discussion in the Japanese academic community at the time. However, it became a limited argument in Japanese criminal law theory, as it only had a limited impact on the recognition of corporate negligence.

[6] See Kai (n 3) 206.

damaging to a company, but knowing that there is a way to recover from it as quickly as possible would be an incentive. It is hoped that such research will continue in Japan in the future.

C. Embodying the Guiding Principles on Business and Human Rights (UNGPs) in Japan

i. Introduction

The UNGPs were adopted by the UN Human Rights Committee in June 2011. More than a decade after their enactment, the UNGPs are now globally accepted as guiding principles for formulating policies on business and human rights. The task of this publication is to examine the question of how the UNGPs have been accepted and implemented as concrete policies in Asian countries. The purpose of this chapter is to identify and assess how the principles have been embodied in the field of criminal law in Japan and the People's Republic of China.

Japan has recognised the importance of the UNGPs and has sought to develop more concrete policies. Then, on 16 October 2020, the Japanese government released 'the Action Plan on Business and Human Rights (2020–2025)'. We will analyse Japan's efforts regarding criminal law in this Action Plan.

ii. Overview of the Action Plan

Chapter 2 of the Action Plan sets forth specific issues that the government should address. First, 'cross-sectoral challenges' which are issues that should be addressed across sectors, are listed. Next, three major areas that should be addressed individually are listed.

a. The Cross-sectoral Challenges

The following items are listed as cross-sectoral challenges: (i) labour (promotion of decent work), (ii) protection and promotion of children's rights, (iii) human rights associated with the development of new technologies, (iv) the rights and role of consumers, (v) equality before the law (persons with disabilities, women, sexual orientation and gender identity, etc), and (vi) acceptance and enforcement of foreign judgements. Particularly relevant to criminal law are: (i) the protection and promotion of children's rights, and (ii) human rights associated with the development of new technologies. The goals here are to take concrete measures to address the following crimes: (i) trafficking of children, sexual exploitation of children, and violence against children, and (ii) defamation, hate speech, and invasion of privacy on the Internet.

b. Three Individual Areas to be Addressed

The following three areas have been identified as areas that should be addressed individually: (i) efforts related to the obligation of states to protect human rights, (ii) efforts by governments to promote corporate responsibility to respect human rights, and (iii) efforts related to access to remedies. Most of these are not directly related to criminal law, but for (i), the elimination of gangs is included as a goal of the initiative. As for (iii), the IT of civil lawsuits is included as a goal, but recently, the IT of criminal lawsuits has also been discussed, and this will be taken into account as a future goal.

iii. Examples of Embodiment

Let us briefly discuss some of the new provisions that have been enacted in the Japanese Penal Code since the Japanese government announced its 'Action Plan' for 2020. The first is an increase in the statutory penalty for insult. The second is the strengthening of the protection of children from sexual crimes.

First, we begin with the crime of insult. Several years ago, an incident occurred in which a female victim committed suicide due to repeated slander on the Internet. This incident triggered a debate about the crime of insult. Until then, the statutory penalty for insult was detention or a fine. The question arose as to whether this penalty was too light in comparison with the actual damage. In the past, insulting acts were committed in front of the victim, and the emotional damage was transitory. However, with the spread of the Internet, the form of damage has changed. As a result, in 2022, the maximum penalty was increased to imprisonment for up to one year. Rather than raising the penalty for the purpose of crime prevention, it should be considered that the penalty was adjusted to be better reflect the actual harm.

Next, we discuss the strengthening of the protection of children from sex crimes. It is an international trend that revisions have been made in recent years regarding sex crimes. This is due to the fact that the reality of the damage has become more apparent. In Japan, the provisions on sex crimes were substantially revised in 2023. Among them, the introduction of a provision to punish sexual acts without consent attracted the most public attention. Here, however, we shall discuss the strengthening of child protection in relation to the 'Action Plan' mentioned above. Children under the age of 16 are considered vulnerable to sexual crimes due to their sexual immaturity. Therefore, the so-called 'sexual grooming offence' was stipulated. Under this provision, the act of demanding a visit from a person under 16 years of age for sexual purposes is punishable (maximum penalty is imprisonment of up to one year). Actual visitation is more severely punished (maximum penalty is imprisonment of up to two years). In addition, those who demand that a person under 16 years of age transmit images of their sexual behaviour to them will also be punished (maximum penalty is imprisonment of up to three years). These acts have been punishable as crimes of intimidation or coercion. However, by defining these acts as sex crimes, they are now more in line with the reality of the damage and send a message to society about the wrongfulness of the acts concerned.

III. China

A. Theories of Corporate Criminal Responsibility in China

i. Development of Criminal Legislation in China

a. Provisions in Criminal Code in China

In 1997, China amended its Penal Code. As a result, the Penal Code now provides for the punishment of corporate bodies. A crime committed by a corporate body is called a 'unitary crime'（単位犯罪）when the Chinese term is translated directly into English. In this chapter the term 'corporate crime' will be used.

An explanation of provisions for corporate body punishment in the current Chinese criminal law is as follows:

(1) Article 30 of the Chinese Criminal Law stipulates that: 'A company, enterprise, institution, organisation, or group which commits an act endangering society that is considered a crime

under the law shall bear criminal responsibility.'[7] In other words, 'Corporate organisation' in the context of corporate crime refers to companies, enterprises, business entities, institutions, or associations. Entities[8] that do not have the status of a legal person are also recognised as entities of corporate crime.

(2) Article 31 of the Chinese Criminal Law stipulates that: 'An entity responsible for a criminal act shall be fined. The person in charge and other personnel who are directly responsible shall also bear criminal responsibility. Where there are other stipulations in the Special Provisions of this Law or other laws, those stipulations shall apply.'[9] That means, when a corporate crime is committed, as a general rule, the corporate organisation shall be fined, and at the same time, the individuals responsible for the corporate organisation shall also be subject to punishment. In special circumstances where there are separate regulations, only the individual responsible may be held criminally liable.

(3) The number of corporate crimes stipulated in the Criminal Code is 128. This represents more than 30 per cent of the total number of crimes stipulated by the Penal Code.

(4) There are two approaches to the penalties for those responsible and other responsible persons in corporate organisations: One is to impose penalties on those responsible and other responsible persons in corporate crimes by referring to the statutory penalties for natural person crimes. The other is to prescribe independent statutory penalties (usually lighter than those for natural crimes) for those responsible for the abovementioned crime.

b. Trends in Amendments to the Chinese Penal Code Concerning Punishment of Corporate Body

Since the new Chinese Penal Code came into effect in 1997, it has been amended 12 times. The scope of punishment for crimes committed by business organisations has been gradually expanded.

The first notable one is the Criminal Code Amendment (11) of 2021. Among them, the punishment of the responsible person and other responsible persons in the case of corporate crime was unified in comparison with that in the case of natural person crimes, and the statutory penalties for both were unified. Furthermore, there is the Criminal Code Amendment (12), which came into effect in March 2024. Here, the amendment of the crime of bribery of business organisations shows a tendency to make the punishment of business organisations even more severe.

ii. Practical Issues Concerning Punishment of Corporate Body

Corporate crimes differ significantly from natural person crimes in the criminal decision-making process and the form of the burden of responsibility. Therefore, since the implementation of the new Chinese Penal Code, judicial practice has encountered a variety of problems in identifying and punishing corporate crimes.

[7] Criminal Law of the People's Republic of China [2023] No.5 adopted by the Second Session of the Fifth National People's Congress on 1 July 1979, revised by the Fifth Session of the Eighth National People's Congress on 14 March 1997, and amended for the twelfth time at the 7th Session of the Standing Committee of the 14th National People's Congress on 29 December 2023 (Chinese Criminal Law) www.lawinfochina.com/display.aspx?id=43140&lib=law&SearchKeyword=&SearchCKeyword=#, Article 30. See English version.

[8] In China, the term 'organisation' generally refers to a legal entity that is formed by individuals with a common purpose, operating with independent finances and regulations, and eligible for government approval and registration.

[9] Article 31 Criminal Law [2023].

a. Scope of Entities of Corporate Crime

Article 30 of the Chinese Penal Code defines all companies, enterprises, business entities, institutions, and organisations as entities of corporate crime. Under current judicial practice, private enterprises that do not have the status of a legal person are excluded from the scope of entities of corporate crime. On the other hand, the 'Interpretation of the Standing Committee of the National People's Congress on Article 384, Paragraph 1 of the Criminal Law,' promulgated in 2002, treats all organisations as business organisations with respect to the interpretation of 'those who misappropriate public funds and attribute them to personal use.

In other words, while the legislative interpretation broadly interprets the scope of corporate bodies, the judicial interpretation tends to strictly interpret the subject scope of corporate bodies and narrow the scope of punishment for corporate bodies.

b. Decision-making of Corporate Body

When a natural person belonging to a corporate body commits a crime, do we attribute the crime to the corporate body or to the individual actor themselves? The most important question to answer is whether the corporate crime was committed as a result of a decision made by the corporate entity. This is regarded as a rather complex question in practice.

There are two main opinions in traditional practice regarding the approach to recognising the decision-making of a corporate body.

The first is the opinion that the two requirements of 'using the name of the corporate body to commit the crime' and 'attributing the illegal income to the corporate body' must be satisfied simultaneously. In the past, this view was generally supported in judicial practice. However, if these criteria are adopted, it may be difficult to confirm the definition of a corporate crime in the following situations: (1) a corporate crime with no illegal income, (2) a natural person within the corporate body commits a crime in the name of the corporate body for some personal purpose and subsequently donates the illegal income to the corporate body, (3) where the illegal income is attributed to the corporate body, but the corporate crime was not committed in the name of the corporate body.

The second is the opinion that following two conditions must be met at the same time: 'in the interest of the business organisation entity' and 'a decision by the decision-making body or responsible person of the business organisation entity.' In current court practice, this view also remains influential.

However, the following problems remain with these criteria as well: (1) Generally, it is considered that 'a crime committed by a responsible person within a corporate entity who uses the corporate body as a tool' should be regarded as a crime by a natural person and excluded from the scope of corporate crime. However, since the line between the will of the individual responsible and the will of the corporate body is unclear, it is extremely difficult to envision a crime committed by a responsible person within the corporate body using the corporate body as a tool. (2) The scope of punishment for corporate crimes may be excessively limited. For example, even in cases where the supervision and management system of a business entity is seriously flawed and ordinary employees within the business entity carry out business activities in accordance with the business entity's management objectives, code of conduct, and organisational culture, resulting in serious infringement of legal interests, the lack of a decision by the decision-making body or responsible person of the business entity may not. In general, the establishment of a 'corporate crime' cannot be affirmed. (3) Generally speaking, the conversion of the will of a natural person into the will of the corporate body through a specific decision-making procedure, namely 'a decision by the decision-making body or responsible person of the corporate body,' is possible only in the case of an intentional crime. Therefore, if the two conditions mentioned above are considered as requirements for the establishment of a corporate crime, it will be difficult to punish the negligent commission of a corporate crime. (4) In large corporations, the complexity of the organisation makes it difficult to communicate within the corporation, making managerial control difficult. As a result, if the responsible party cannot be identified, it becomes difficult to hold the corporation as a whole responsible.

Statistics show that in recent years, corporate crimes have been punished at an extremely low rate in judicial practice, accounting for less than 1/1,000 of all criminal convictions.[10] In addition, there has been a particularly high number of environmental pollution crimes in recent years, but few of these crimes were directly carried out by the decision-making by corporate bodies. Therefore, it has been pointed out that in the area of environmental pollution crimes, provisions for the punishment of a corporate body are basically ignored.[11]

c. Proportionality of Sentences and Preventive Effects

According to a study on the sentencing of natural persons responsible for corporate crimes, the proportion of suspended sentences has reached 74 per cent of the total.[12] The question has been raised as to whether there is a preventative effect regarding such sentences.

In addition, the type of punishment for a corporate body is limited to fines only, which raises questions as to whether this is enough to satisfy the demand for retribution and prevention of corporate crimes. Although the Chinese Criminal Law does not specify the number of fines that can be imposed on a corporate body, judicial practice tends to impose relatively light fines on corporate bodies. And in some cases, the fines imposed on corporate bodies are lighter than the fines for administrative penalties, and sometimes even lower than the revenues illegally obtained.[13]

There is also the question of whether punishing those responsible within the corporate entity will deter corporate crime if only these people are punished. Some scholars have pointed out that if only individuals are punished without punishing the corporate body as a whole, the corporate body may achieve its criminal objectives at the expense of the members of the organisation.[14]

iii. Academic Debate on Corporate Criminal Responsibility

Since the definition and punishment provisions for corporate crimes were created in the new Chinese Penal Code, there has been much debate over the interpretation of these provisions. The details of these debates must be omitted here. However, the debate that is currently most concerning is the one regarding the basis for corporate criminal liability. This issue is discussed here.

[10] See L Hong, Zuzhiti xingshi zerenlun jiqi yingyong 'The Theory of Criminal Liability of Organization and Its Application' (2020) 2 *Faxue yanjiu* 71.

[11] For a detailed analysis of this issue, see the following articles: G Jianing, Wuran huanjing zui qiye zuzhiti xingshi zeren de keguan guishu quxiang jiqi heli Xianzhi 'On the Orientation of Objective Imputation of Corporate Criminal Liability for Crime of Environmental Pollution and Its Reasonable Limitation: An "Inherent Liability" Solution' (2018) 9 *Zhengzhi yu falv* 39.

[12] See L Bencan, Renzui renfa congkuan chuli jizhi de wanshan 'Perfection of Legal System of Leniency Based on Confession: From the Perspective of Corporate Crime' (2018) 3 *Faxue pinglun* 111.

[13] See W Pengxiang, Danwei fanzui de lifa quexian jiqi wanshan 'On the Legislative Drawbacks and Its Perfection of Corporate Crime' (2009) 4 *Faxue zazhi* 95.

[14] See L Hong, Wanshan woguo danwei fanzui chufa zhidu de sikao 'Reflections on Improving the Punishment System for Corporate Crimes in China' (2011) 1 *Fashang yanjiu* 80.

a. Theories of Criminal Responsibility of Corporate Body

There is currently no clear theoretical conclusion as to why corporate crime, in which legal personality is mimicked, acquires the capacity to act as a criminal subject under criminal law. However, this issue is inevitably raised when discussing the recognition of decision-making in corporate crime, the grounds for the dual criminal liability provisions, and the mens rea of corporate crime.

In academic theories, the view that focuses on the acts of natural persons within the corporate body as the representative view of the theory of criminal responsibility of a corporate body has had a significant impact on the academic and practical world in the past.

Some scholars have argued for a view that influences the decision-making mechanism of a corporate body and the punishment of a corporate crime by looking at the difference between a corporation as an organisation and the natural persons who are its members. This view[15] is as follows: corporate bodies are entire social systems with personalities. Corporate crime is a crime of the corporate body with its own characteristics, not of individual members. The relationship between a corporate body and its members is one of whole and part. The reason why the dual punishment provision not only imposes punishment on the corporate body but also on the natural persons who belong to the corporate body is that there are two entities of corporate crime and punishment: the corporate body and the individual.

For a long time, however, this debate stalled and progress became difficult. Thus, 'the negative theory',[16] which had been asserted in the past, reemerged. This view is as follows: corporate crimes are in fact crimes committed by the members of a corporate body. The criminal responsibility of a corporate body is merely a shifting of the responsibility of its members. This view points out that the criminal responsibility of corporate body is not a matter of logic, but rather a matter of criminal policy.

It should be noted that in recent years some scholars have also argued for a new view[17] that focuses on the systemic nature and independence of organisational entities, and in particular on the relationship between the organisation itself and its members.

b. Criminal Policy Theory of Corporate Crime

In response to the increasing number of corporate crimes, recent criminal legislation in China has increasingly expanded the scope of punishment for corporate crimes and tended to make the penalties more severe. However, when holding a corporate body responsible, courts have tended to take a careful stance and limit the scope of punishment. The reality of society creates doubt that corporate crime is being allowed to go unchecked.

A new trend in corporate crime governance in the US after the *Enron* case is the development of the so-called DPA/NPA system, which has been attracting international attention. In China, some scholars have also begun to review the criminal policy of corporate crime and pursue effective preventive measures. One scholar argues for a dualistic approach to criminal policy for

[15] See H Bingsong, Danwei(Faren) fanzui de gainian jiqi lilun genju: Jianping xingshi liandai zerenlun 'The Concept of Corporate Crime and Its Theoretical Basis: A critique of the Doctrine of Criminal Joint Liability' (1998) 2 *Faxue yanjiu* 91.

[16] See Z Kewen, Nizhi fanzui he nizhi xingshi zeren: Faren fanzui foudinglun zhi huigui 'Fictional Crime and Fictional Criminal Liability: The Return of the Denial Theory of Corporate Crime' (2009) 3 *Faxue yanjiu* 39.

[17] Regarding this claim, I would like to share the following representative articles: C Zhonglin and X Ruo, Danwei fanzui de qiantao zerenlun 'On Nested Criminal Responsibility of Corporate Crime' (2017) 2 *Xiandai faxue* 110. For further analysis, see L Hong, Zuzhiti xingshi zerenlun jiqi yingyong 'The Theory of Criminal Liability of Organization and Its Application' (2020) 2 *Faxue yanjiu* 71.

corporate crime, distinguishing between the punishment of natural persons within the corporate organisation and the punishment of the corporate body itself, and adopting different criminal policies for each. Furthermore, the scholar advocates promoting reform of China's corporate crime governance, drawing also on the US DPA/NPA system.[18]

The shift from retribution to prevention and cooperation in crime prevention between state agencies and corporations has gradually become the focus of criminal policy discussions on corporate crime. These have become the theoretical basis for subsequent debates and institutional reforms related to compliance programmes.

B. The Significance of Compliance Programmes and Criminal Law in China

i. Process of Introducing the So-called 'Compliance Non-indictment System'

In 2012, the 'Some Opinions on Building a Culture of Chinese Enterprises Abroad' was released to promote overseas management and outward investment by Chinese companies. The document aims to promote the sustainable development of Chinese enterprises operating overseas, and it proposed goals for building a compliance programme culture for those enterprises. Since then, under the supervision of the State-owned Assets Supervision and Administration Commission, compliance programmes have been promoted within state-owned enterprises, and are gradually spreading to private enterprises as well.

In 2018, ZTE was heavily fined for violating US export control laws. Other Chinese companies also came under criminal investigation and prosecution abroad. These incidents have made it increasingly important to improve compliance systems within companies. In response to this, a series of documents was successively published in China to guide companies in building their compliance structures.[19] Thus, 2018 was also known as the first year of corporate compliance in China.

In 2018, an amendment to the Chinese Criminal Procedure Code introduced a system in which sentences are reduced if a private enterprise admits guilt and cooperates with the investigation（認罪認罰從寬制度）. In November of the same year, the Supreme People's Procuratorate proposed a way of applying this system in criminal trials of private enterprises for the sake of sound economic development. This allowed for preferential criminal treatment to be given to those private enterprises that actively cooperate with investigations and evidence collection, truly repent their crimes, and voluntarily accept punishment.

After the introduction of this system, since March 2020, the Supreme People's Procuratorate began a trial of this system in six key people's prosecutors' offices. 'The compliance and non-indictment system' refers to the fact that, when certain conditions are met, the prosecuting authority will take the initiative to encourage the improvement of the compliance management

[18] See L B, Qiye fanzui chengzhi zhong liangyuanhua xingshi zhengce de goujian: Jiyu qiye fanzui chengzhi fu waibu xiaoying kefu de sikao 'The Construction of a Dual Criminal Policy in Corporate Crime Punishment: Reflections on Overcoming the Negative Externalities of Corporate Crime Sanctions' (2014) 5 *Anhui daxue xuebao (Zhexue shehui kexue ban)* 132.

[19] For example, in 2017, the 35th meeting of the Central Leading Group for Comprehensively Deepening Reform reviewed and approved the 'Opinions on Regulating Overseas Operations of Enterprises'. In 2018, the National Development and Reform Commission, Ministry of Foreign Affairs, Ministry of Commerce, People's Bank of China, State-owned Assets Supervision and Administration Commission, State Administration of Foreign Exchange, and All-China Federation of Industry and Commerce jointly issued the 'Guidelines for Compliance Management of Enterprises' Overseas Operations'.

system of the companies involved in the case, and if they can pass a supervisory inspection after a certain period of time, the case will not be prosecuted. Thus, compliance programmes have acquired new significance in corporate crime governance in recent years.

While there have been various developments since then, it is important to note that in July 2023, the CPC Central Committee and the State Council issued 'Opinions on Promoting Private Economic Development and Growth,' which clearly called for deepening the compliance reform of companies involved in cases and promoting compliance structuring. Furthermore, it is proposed here that the system be advanced from the prosecution stage to the trial stage.

ii. Current Status of 'the Compliance and Non-indictment System'

Since the introduction of the compliance and non-indictment system, the system has been widely used in corporate crime governance. In August 2023, the Supreme People's Court issued a 'Research Report on Case-Involved Corporate Compliance Reforms' by the People's Court. According to this report, in the first half of 2023, courts across the nation handled 495 cases in the first instance and 13 cases in the second instance, for a total of 508 cases.

iii. The Academic Debate on the Significance of Compliance Programmes and Criminal Law

a. Compliance Programmes and Criminal Policy Transformation

As mentioned earlier, there is a certain tension between the expansion of the legislative scope of punishment and harsher penalties for corporate crimes and lenient treatment by the courts. In recent years, some scholars have pointed out that from the perspective of penal purposes, the need for moral censure of corporate crime is relatively low, and the public expects corporations to maintain their normative service to society rather than to punish them severely. Therefore, the goal of crime prevention should be emphasised and criminal policies for corporate crime should be transformed into more effective and positive ones.[20]

An important goal of the shift in criminal policy for corporate crime is to effectively achieve the objective of deterring corporate crime by providing certain rehabilitation opportunities to the companies. In this context, the compliance non-indictment system is seen as a new strategy for corporate crime governance, since it also includes principles such as the shift from ex post punishment to ex ante prevention, cooperation in crime prevention between state agencies and private corporations, and corporate social responsibility. Some scholars have also pointed out that under the compliance non-indictment system, in order for the companies to obtain preferential treatment, they must actively restore the legal interests that have been violated and repair social relations through communication. Therefore, the compliance non-indictment system is also considered to include the idea of restorative justice.[21]

[20] See C Xuequan and T Langxiao, Qiye fanzui sifa qinghuanhua beijing xia woguo xingshisifa zhi yingdui 'The Answers of China's Criminal Judicial System in the Judicial Mitigation of Enterprise Crime' (2021) 2 *Zhengfalunye* 117; S Guoxiang, Danwei fanzui de xingshi zhengce zhuanxing yu qiye hegui gaige 'The Transformation of Criminal Policy of Corporate Crime and the Reform of Corporate Compliance' (2021) 6 *Shanghai zhengfa xueyuan xuebao* 21.

[21] See H Ting and Y Zemin, Xiufuxing sifa linian zai qiye fanzui futiaojian buqisu zhong de yinru yu yingyong 'The Introduction and Application of Restorative Justice Concept in Conditional Non-prosecution for Corporate Crimes' (2022) 6 *Fazhi shehui* 46.

b. Compliance Programme and Criminal Responsibility of Corporate Body

Clarifying the relationship between the responsibility of the corporate body itself and the responsibility of natural persons within it has always been a difficult issue. In recent years, with the introduction of the compliance and non-indictment system, Chinese academics have once again been engaged in a debate about the criminal responsibility of corporate bodies. The compliance programme has caused a certain change in perspective in this debate. In other words, the liability of a corporate body is not simply the responsibility of the natural persons within it that is transferred to the legal entity. It stems from the attitude of the corporate body itself, including its defective supervision and control system, its violation of its obligation to prevent crime, and its acceptance, acquiescence, and support of the criminal acts of its internal employees. Recently, Chinese academia has paid great attention to the close connection between these arguments and compliance programmes. It has also had an impact on court practice.

Currently, the prevailing academic theory holds that the liability of a corporate body and the liability of natural persons within it are independent and separate. On the other hand, there is a growing discussion of corporate negligence crimes in the academic community. In this context, many scholars advocate the use of the status of a compliance programme as a criterion for determining whether there has been a breach of a company's supervisory duty.[22]

c. The Sentencing Significance of Compliance Programmes

Discussions on the sentencing significance of compliance programmes have been limited to the introduction of practices in other countries and have not been discussed in much detail in China. However, since the issuance of the 'Opinions on Promoting Private Economic Development and Growth' in 2023, compliance reforms have been promoted from the prosecution stage to the trial stage. And the sentencing significance of compliance programmes has come to be emphasised.

However, it is not clear at this time what kind of significance compliance programmes may have on the sentencing of corporate crimes.

Some scholars argue that compliance programmes should be incorporated into criminal law as a statutory sentencing circumstance.[23] However, the logical basis for the impact of compliance programmes on the sentencing of corporate crimes has not yet been fully discussed. At the same time, while the establishment and improvement of a compliance programme is generally accepted as a reason for reducing the sentence, it is debatable whether an aggravated sentence is permissible when a company fails to adhere to its compliance programme. In addition, the creation of a probationary system for corporate organisational entities that focus on the establishment and improvement of compliance programmes has recently been discussed.[24]

[22] For this view, see the following representative articles: S Guoxiang, Xingshi hegui de linian, jineng he zhongguode jiangou 'The Concept and Function of Criminal Compliance and Its Construction in China' (2019) 2 *Zhongguo xingshifa zazhi* 3; G Jjianing, Danwei guyou xingshi zeren de tichang ji moshi de fansi 'Promotion of Corporate Inherent Criminal Liability and Its Doctrinal Forms' (2020) 6 *Zhengzhi yu falv* 1489; C Xian, Zuzhi jinhua shiye xia dui qiye xingshi guize moshi de fansi 'The Reflection on Model of Attributing Criminal Liability to Enterprises from the Perspective of the Evolving Organization' (2021) 3 *Zhengzhi yu falv* 57; J Yizhen, Danwei guoshi fanzui guize moshi zhi jianshi: Yi qiye hegui wei shijiao 'Inspecting the Accountability Mode of Organization Negligence Crimes: From the Perspective of Enterprise Compliance' (2021) 3 *Jiangxi jingcha xueyuan xuebao* 77.

[23] See C Weidong, Qiye hegui congkuan chuli de shijian yangtai yu jiangou lujing 'On the Practical Patterns and Constructive Paths in Using Leniency to Deal with Corporate Compliance' (2023) 2 *Faxue pinglun* 100. See also S Yanan, Shenpan jieduan tuijin shean qiye hegui gaige de fali yu lujing 'The Legal Theory and Path of Promoting the Compliance Reform of the Involved Enterprises in the Trial Stage' (2024) 1 *Faxue pinglun* 29.

[24] For a discussion on the probation system for organisations, see the following article: P Wenhua and X Haoyu, Xingshi hegui shiye xia woguo qiye zuzhi huanxing zhidu de jiangou 'The Construction of Probation System for Organizations in China under the View of Criminal Compliance' (2024) 5 *Hebei faxue* 63.

C. Embodying the Guiding Principles on Business and Human Rights (UNGPs) in China

i. Initiatives Required of Companies to Respect Human Rights

It is now internationally recognised that corporate activities may infringe on human rights. Even within the global scope, there have been tragic cases of worker suicides due to mental illness caused by long working hours and power harassment, deaths of consumers due to manufacturing defects, and environmental degradation and destruction caused by economic activities that exceed the resilience of nature.

Based on this common international understanding, the Guiding Principles on Business and Human Rights (the UNGPs) were agreed upon by the UN Human Rights Council in June 2011, clarifying that companies have a responsibility to respect human rights.

In China, the following initiatives are being undertaken to embody the UNGPS.

ii. Initiatives by Chinese Companies to Respect Human Rights

In China, there originally were regulatory laws, such as the Labour Standards Law, to prevent negative impacts on the human rights of its workers and others. In recent years, consumer protection rules for financial transactions have been enacted. Furthermore, human rights protection has been emphasised in areas such as environmental protection and data security. Thus, the responsibility of companies to respect human rights has been attracting a great deal of attention in China. However, at this point, regulatory laws that require companies to take measures to prevent negative impacts on the human rights of stakeholders in general, including those in their supply chains, have not yet been developed.

Meanwhile, China has been gradually strengthening its regulations on the management activities of Chinese companies operating overseas since the publication of the UNGPs. Specifically speaking, in recent years China has issued a series of legal regulations and policy documents on corporate social responsibility. These documents serve as guidelines for companies expanding overseas to prevent and manage the risk of human rights infringement.

For example, guiding principles emphasising corporate social responsibility have been published. Namely, in 2015, China established GB/T 36000-2015 'Social Responsibility Guidelines'. Furthermore, the General Administration of Quality Supervision, Inspection and Quarantine of China and the State Administration of Standardization released GB/T 35770-2017 'Compliance Management System Guidelines'. This is intended to mitigate compliance risks faced by enterprises and provide guidance to help various organisations implement compliance management. These guides are intended to help companies of all types establish and effectively operate compliance management systems. Specifically, the guides are designed to provide guidance for identifying, analysing, assessing, addressing, and managing compliance risks. This will enable companies to mitigate the risk of legal sanctions, while at the same time fulfilling their social responsibilities and avoiding human rights infringements.

There is also a specialised document that stipulates requirements for human rights protection. In September 2014, the Ministry of Commerce promulgated the 'Regulations for the Administration of Foreign Investment'. This requires companies with overseas investments to fulfill their social responsibilities and make appropriate efforts to protect the environment, labour rights, and build a corporate culture. In January 2017, the State-owned Assets Supervision and Administration Commission of the State Council promulgated the Regulations on Supervision and Management of Overseas Investment by Central Enterprises. This clearly stipulates that in their overseas investments, central enterprises shall comply with the laws, business regulations, and cultural practices of China and the target countries, strengthen overseas investment risk management, and actively fulfill their social responsibilities.

Furthermore, the National Human Rights Action Plan (2016–20) released by the State Council on 29 September 2016, states that 'respect and protection of human rights will be an important consideration for both domestic and foreign investment,' and that 'Chinese companies expanding overseas must comply with the laws and regulations of the host country and fulfill their social responsibilities in foreign economic and trade cooperation, assistance, and investment.'

The National Human Rights Action Plan (2021–25), released on 9 September 2021, also stipulates that 'Chinese enterprises shall promote responsible business behaviour in the global supply chain and fulfill their social responsibility to respect and protect human rights in foreign economic and trade cooperation and investment in accordance with the UNGPs.' This is the first time that China has made a national human rights commitment. and incorporated a requirement for compliance with the UNGPs into its national human rights action plan. As a nation, China is demonstrating its commitment to corporate human rights responsibilities and its willingness to fulfill its international obligations.

Looking at the status of Chinese companies' efforts regarding respect for human rights, the number of Chinese companies that have established policies on human rights has been increasing since 2011. In particular, the rate of increase has accelerated since 2020. In addition to the full range of workers' rights, most Chinese companies' policies cover a wide range of human rights, including non-discrimination (including gender equality), guarantees of indigenous rights, guarantees of freedom of speech, guarantees of privacy rights, and even environmental human rights. Many also state that corporate human rights responsibilities extend to suppliers and supply chains. Others establish effective control measures and usually include a basic approach to human rights, education and training, human rights due diligence, information disclosure, dialogue, and remedies. In addition, a number of companies have also proposed mechanisms to review and update these policies.

As noted above, Chinese companies are increasingly aware of their human rights responsibilities.

iii. 'UNGPs' and their Relevance to Trends in the Punishment of Corporate Bodies in China

In recent years, illegal and criminal acts by corporations in areas such as financial transactions, environmental protection, food safety, and data security have resulted in serious violations of the fundamental rights of consumers and the general public, including property rights, life, health, and privacy rights. In response to this situation, stricter social responsibility is legally mandated in these industries to ensure that companies respect and protect human rights. Even at the criminal legislative level, there is a trend toward a broader scope and stricter penalties for corporate organised crime in these sectors.

When a company is involved in human rights infringements, it may be accused by society, its reputation may be severely damaged, and its corporate value may be damaged, for example, by being excluded from the supply chain or being held liable for damages by its business partners. Ultimately, the burden imposed on the corporation by the penalty may be passed on to innocent shareholders or consumers. However, simply mitigating corporate organisational punishment through lenient judicial treatment is clearly not enough to balance the twin goals of crime prevention and protection of corporate interests.

As noted earlier, China began to make rapid progress in establishing a corporate compliance system in 2018. Since then, China has learned from the experience of other countries in introducing compliance programmes in corporate crime governance. Companies are consciously fulfilling their social responsibilities and aiming to prevent crime by establishing and improving effective compliance systems. By incorporating specific requirements regarding respect and protection of human rights into corporate compliance systems, and by using criminal justice incentive measures to promote the establishment and improvement of compliance, companies can achieve both the realisation of corporate social responsibility and the protection of corporate value. In fact, by providing remedies and protection in criminal proceedings to corporations that have consciously fulfilled their social responsibilities, China may be said to be embodying the UNGPs in the area of corporate organisational punishment.

IV. Conclusion

In summary, this chapter introduces the current state of theory and practice of corporate criminal responsibility in Japan and China, examines the criminal law significance of compliance programmes to prevent corporate crime, and discusses how the UNGPs are embodied in the criminal law systems of both countries, particularly in the regulation of corporate crime.

Indeed, because of the differences in economic and national regimes, it is not surprising that the two countries' responses do not coincide in their treatment of the provisions for the punishment of corporate crimes and their understanding of the grounds for the punishment of corporate bodies. Rather, it should be noted that since the beginning of the twenty-first century, and especially since the UNGPs were issued, corporate social responsibility, and more specifically, stricter social responsibility for companies to respect and protect human rights, has increasingly become a legal obligation in both countries.

Underlying this is the fact that the development of theories on the punishment of corporate bodies in both countries shows a common trend. In other words, there is a trend toward holding a corporate body itself criminally responsible. The connection between compliance programmes, which are an important tool for the realisation of corporate social responsibility and the protection of corporate value, and corporate criminal responsibility is becoming more and more important. In this sense, it is very important to consider the question of how to incorporate specific requirements regarding the respect and protection of human rights into the compliance system and what effect the development and improvement of the compliance system will have in terms of criminal law. In both countries, compliance programmes will play a central function in embodying the UNGPs in order to regulate corporate crime.

In both countries, however, although there has been considerable discussion regarding the criminal law significance of compliance programmes, the substantive criminal law has not yet been clearly institutionalised in legislation. Therefore, a review of criminal law theory, including the grounds for corporate criminal responsibility and the purposes of punishment for corporate crimes, seems necessary. The authors intend to further examine this issue in the future.

15

Conclusion

JASON HO CHING CHEUNG AND YURI MUKOJI

I. Introduction

The underlying series on *Studies in Private International Law* proposes that there is an underlying assumption that private international law in different jurisdictions follows broad but discernible patterns. This book is no exception, in that its goal is to discern an 'Asian' legal pattern on human rights laws via analysing the need for the drafting of and the follow-up implementation of the 2011 UN Guiding Principles on Business and Human Rights (UNGPs).[1] While perhaps much has already been said about the implementation of the UNGPs in the European/Western context, it is intriguing to know whether such principles fit into the Asian environment. And if they do (or do not), why so?

II. Lessons Learned

Throughout this volume, the individual chapters have examined the evolving landscape of business and human rights in Asia from multiple legal, institutional, and cultural perspectives. Whilst diverse in approach and focus, the chapters commonly highlight the need to move forward from the ordinary approach, being conscious of a binary between public and private international law.

A. Global Awareness of Human Rights and International Protection

Part I of the book started with the conceptual discussion of multi-nations and human rights in a global and regional context. The legal and normative system of Business and Human Rights (BHR) has evolved little by little, although it has also encountered many difficulties. In the Asian-Pacific Region and on the global stage, corporations accountable for abuses of human rights are facing both structural and strategic obstacles.

Chapter two elaborates on a detailed case study of the Barossa Gas Project in Northern Australia, illustrating how Japanese, Korean, and Australian financial institutions continued to disregard the principle of Free, Prior and Informed Consent (FPIC) prompting Indigenous communities to bring legal claims and engage in transnational advocacy. It emphasises the

[1] UN Human Rights Council, *Guiding Principles on Business and Human Rights: Implementing the United Nations 'Protect, Respect and Remedy' Framework*, UN Doc A/HRC/17/31 (21 March 2011).

potential to make the BHR structure even stronger and the way to link between the legal rules, investors' strategies, and rights of the indigenous, by showing us their advocacy beyond the conventional legal measures and the nations. Based on the comparison analysis of the Asian civil procedure in this chapter, the issues highlighting why it is so hard to accomplish the enforcing of human rights against multinationals, are the complex and multi-layer supply chains, informal labour arrangements, information asymmetries, and weak domestic regulatory frameworks. In a response to these matters, the authors suggest establishing the stronger role of institutional investors, particularly public pension funds. As the idea of the Environment, Social, and Governance investment (ESG investment) is becoming more widespread, the investors' accountabilities toward human rights would help to promote the multinational corporations (MNCs) to ensure transparency and sustainability throughout their operations and to implement FPIC in all relevant stakeholders' engagements. The chapter ultimately links legal norms, investor strategy, and Indigenous rights in demonstrating how business and human rights frameworks can be strengthened in the Asia-Pacific context.

Chapter three explores the theoretical baseline of human rights jurisdiction and how to ensure access to remedy and enforce protection against corporations in a cross-border legal context. The author conducted a comparative analysis of national rules on international jurisdiction in the US, with special attention to the doctrine of *forum non conveniens*, and landmark cases such as *Vedanta*,[2] *Chevron*[3] and *Chiquita*.[4] The author analysed the scope and limits of universal jurisdiction, including the Koblenz trial in Germany and the Lafarge corporate complicity case in France, while also addressing political criticisms of neo-colonialism. While the discussion on neo-colonialism as a separate political science subject is outside the scope of this book, it does raise the concern of whether an application of universal jurisdiction is automatically presumed to be the best approach. This chapter also explored the extraterritorial application of national law, including mandatory human rights due diligence regimes (eg, EU Corporate Sustainability Due Diligence Directive (CSDDD), France's duty of vigilance), supply chain liability, and climate cases like *Urgenda*. The role of private international law in shaping access to judicial remedies – such as conflict-of-law rules, public policy exceptions, and recognition and enforcement of foreign judgments – are also explored. It concludes with a comparative analysis of regional approaches across Asia, identifying distinct 'remedy models' in Japan, South Korea, China, India, Singapore, Taiwan, and ASEAN, and reflecting on the convergence pressures created by EU legislation and global ESG standards. This chapter demonstrates that the reasons for enforcement of human rights across jurisdiction require a multi-layered approach with a combination of various legal tools such as universal jurisdiction, sanctions, private law safeguards, extra territorial application etc. It demonstrates that multi-nation and human rights require analysis from multifaceted legal and cultural aspects.

Chapter four shows the journey of the drafting of UNGPs, as an attempt to solve the puzzles of the muti-layered approach as shown in the previous chapter. This chapter's examination of the UNGPs demonstrates both the normative breakthrough and the structural limitations of soft-law frameworks in regulating multinational corporate conduct. The UNGPs succeeded in establishing a shared vocabulary and a foundational architecture – most notably the concept of human rights due diligence. However, 15 years on, their implementation remains uneven and largely aspirational. Despite widespread endorsement by states and companies, empirical evidence shows a troubling disconnect between policy rhetoric and operational reality: the vast majority of

[2] *Vedanta Resources PLC v Lungowe* [2019] UKSC 20, [2020] AC 1045.
[3] *Chevron Corp v Yaiguaje* 2015 SCC 42, [2015] 3 SCR 69.
[4] *Doe v Chiquita Brands International Inc*, Case No 08-cv-01916 (SD Fla filed 2008).

corporations still fall short of even the most basic UNGP benchmarks. This persistent implementation gap reflects not only the non-binding nature of the UNGPs but also the structural power imbalance between affected communities and corporate actors, particularly in jurisdictions with weak legal enforcement. The chapter concludes that while the UNGPs have succeeded in shaping global discourse and influencing regulatory initiatives, they have not delivered meaningful improvements in corporate respect for human rights. Drawing on the World Benchmarking Alliance's 2024 assessment, the chapter underscores that approximately 90 per cent of major global corporations continue to fall short of the minimum expectations set by the UNGPs.[5] This reflects structural shortcomings in the framework itself: its reliance on voluntary compliance, lack of enforcement mechanisms, and limited engagement with affected communities. The chapter also notes that while the UNGPs have inspired legislative and policy reforms – such as the EU's due diligence directive – their foundational weaknesses remain unresolved. Without stronger institutional backing and clearer accountability mechanisms, the chapter suggests, the UNGPs will struggle to fulfil their original promise. The chapter concludes by calling for a future regulatory framework that addresses the normative weaknesses of the UNGPs, especially their non-binding nature, limited accountability mechanisms, and lack of meaningful participation from affected communities. These lessons are vital as the UN explores new treaty-based solutions through its Open-ended Intergovernmental Working Group.

The subsequent chapter five offers a tempered but insightful reflection on the progress and limits of the UN treaty process on business and human rights. While acknowledging the diplomatic momentum generated by procedural innovations such as the formation of the Friends of the Chair group and the adoption of UNHRC Decision 56/116, the chapter underscores that fundamental disagreements persist within the Open-ended Intergovernmental Working Group.[6] While various steps (.ie, details of how Ecuador has shifted its approach in recent years, seeking compromise through procedural innovations like the 'Friends of the Chair' group, draft language revisions, and most recently, the UNHRC's Decision 56/116, which enables intersessional consultations supported by legal experts) have generated cautious optimism – including from prior sceptics such as the EU and the US – the chapter makes it clear that major points of contention persist, especially regarding whether the treaty should apply only to transnational corporations or to all businesses, and how human rights due diligence (HRDD) should be regulated. Key tensions also include divergent views on the treaty's scope – particularly whether it should apply universally to all business entities or remain limited to transnational corporations – and the extent to which binding human rights due diligence obligations should be imposed. These unresolved issues continue to stall broad consensus. Nonetheless, the chapter emphasises that the treaty negotiations have produced consequential normative and political shifts. Beyond the formal drafting process, the broader ecosystem of regulatory change – especially the development of mandatory due diligence regimes such as the CSDDD – is influencing global corporate accountability frameworks in meaningful ways. For Asian jurisdictions in particular, the chapter highlights that engagement with these evolving standards is becoming increasingly necessary. Ultimately, the authors suggest that even if the treaty remains in draft form for the foreseeable future, the process itself has become a catalyst for reshaping how states, businesses, and civil society approach the regulation of human rights in global commerce. Although binding treaty consensus remains elusive, the chapter concludes that the treaty process itself, and the

[5] E Birchall, 'The UN Guiding Principles: A Significant Step but not yet Delivering the Promised Corporate Respect for Human Rights' in ch 4 of this volume, n 71.

[6] UN Human Rights Council, Decision 56/116 on the intersessional consultation on business and human rights, UN Doc A/HRC/DEC/56/116 (11 July 2024).

surrounding regulatory evolution, are reshaping the landscape of corporate accountability, with implications extending well beyond the formal outcome of the treaty.

Chapter six focuses on comparative studies in the Asian context. The comparative approach in analysing the EU's CSDDD and its projected impact on human rights and environmental standards in Southeast Asia explored the realm of whether a Western driven approach in human rights jurisprudence can be transplanted to the Asian context, in particular that in ASEAN. The chapter reveals that ASEAN legal systems often lack clarity, certainty, or enforceability, especially around child labour, union rights, and environmental damage. These issues are compounded by the 'ASEAN Way' – a regional legal culture that prioritises non-interference and state discretion, limiting robust legal commitments and public accountability. The author raises concerns about procedural limitations on access to remedies, but notes emerging innovations, such as environmental litigation in the Philippines, which may offer a partial blueprint. Ultimately, the chapter questions whether a European-style regulatory framework can be transplanted into Southeast Asia without significant adaptation, engagement, and public-private coordination. For instance, issues arise as to whether the common value in the EU can be shared in non-EU companies operating in the ASEAN region. Companies also require long-term business relationships that may have to start with providing guidance to its business partners alongside information on compliance of human rights agendas. The chapter suggests that in the ASEAN context, trust-building, capacity development, and industry-wide cooperation may prove more effective than strict contractual compliance alone.

B. Influences on Asian Countries

Part II of the book proceeds with country specific discussions. Our discussion commenced with Japan in chapter seven. The Japanese case highlights the complexity of embedding human rights norms within a legal system that showcases formalism, judicial restraint, and voluntary compliance. While Japan has made visible progress in recent years – through non-binding human rights due diligence guidelines, inclusive disability legislation, and increasing civil society engagement – the enforcement gap remains significant. Domestic courts are only beginning to grapple with hard questions around corporate liability, and judicial inconsistency persists, particularly in emerging areas such as LGBTQ+ rights. Japan's cautious approach to extraterritorial regulation contrasts sharply with recent European developments, revealing a deeper reluctance to impose direct obligations on multinational parent companies. Nonetheless, the chapter points to growing recognition, both within government and the private sector, of the reputational and legal risks associated with inaction. The Japanese experience underscores the importance of multi-level reform: clearer legislative mandates, expanded stakeholder participation, and judicial openness to transnational legal developments will be crucial if Japan is to move from principled aspiration to effective implementation. As global norms on corporate accountability evolve, Japan's future contribution will depend on its willingness to internalise these standards and reimagine its human rights architecture in a more proactive and binding form.

Chapter eight discusses South Korea. On the aspects of corporate governance, the authors conclude that Korea is incrementally developing toward a more robust, transnationally relevant regime for corporate human rights accountability – though legal uncertainty and fragmentation remain major hurdles. Turning to ESG-specific laws, the chapter covers: Korea's fragmented sectoral approach to ESG governance, The Environmental Damage Relief Act which lowers the burden of proof in tort claims for pollution victims, The Serious Accidents Punishment Act, which imposes direct criminal and civil liability on senior executives; and ongoing legislative proposals to codify mandatory human rights and environmental due diligence. In the second half, the chapter moves into private international law, offering one of the most comprehensive overviews in the volume. It addresses jurisdictional doctrines (including anchor defendants, *forum non conveniens*, and emergency jurisdiction), conflict of laws and choice-of-law issues in tort claims against Korean parent companies for extraterritorial harms, and recognition and enforcement of foreign judgments involving punitive or non-compensatory damages. Drawing on recent Supreme Court judgments and legislative initiatives, the authors conclude that South Korea is incrementally developing toward a more robust, transnationally relevant regime for corporate human rights accountability – though legal uncertainty and fragmentation remain major hurdles. One intriguing point the chapter suggests is the announcement in April 2024 of the forthcoming release of the Korean Sustainability Disclosure Standards (KSDS) by the Financial Service Commission. The intention is to reduce the reporting burden on Korean companies subject to international ESG regulation including the EU's Corporate Sustainability Reporting Directive (CSDR). This showcases the attempts of South Korea (as one of the Asian jurisdictions) to take into account the development of ESG regulation overseas, though perhaps with localisation.

Chapter nine on the Philippines explores the Philippine legal framework and practice in addressing business-related human rights violations, providing one of the most comprehensive jurisdictional studies in the volume. Despite lacking a formal National Action Plan (NAP) on business and human rights, the Philippines demonstrates a fragmented but dynamic approach, combining constitutional protections, civil litigation, environmental rules, and public interest advocacy. It is suggested that the state action doctrine that relies on the public-private divide remains a cornerstone in Philippine human rights law, while in areas of environment, labour and gender there have been adoption of languages of human rights against private enterprise. The chapter then ends with the notion that judicial or quasi-judicial remedies are fragmented with no uniform practice. The chapter concludes that while Philippine courts, NGOs, and institutions have developed a creative ecosystem for enforcing business and human rights principles, the lack of systematic policy integration of the UNGPs and structural barriers (eg, high litigation costs, fragmented access to remedies) remain major obstacles to corporate accountability. In discussing sector-specific challenges, this chapter raises the issue of displacement of indigenous peoples, and environmental damage. Reflecting on challenges faced by the indigenous population in Australia as enshrined in chapter two, this perhaps highlights the activities of multinationals affecting populations across the Asian jurisdiction.[7] This chapter also slightly touches upon an intriguing issue on gender equality in which the author suggested 'multinational companies are ahead when it comes to implementing LGBTI-inclusive policies, with domestic companies or the public sector often unaware of emerging standards on gender equality.'[8]

The Thailand chapter (chapter ten) uniquely delves into Thailand's legal culture and socio-religious context, arguing that the abstract ideals of human rights find resonance in Thai legal and cultural frameworks. For example, historic milestones like the peaceful abolition of slavery under King Rama V are cited as early manifestations of human-rights-aligned statecraft. Despite this progress, the chapter acknowledges limits. The NAPs, while institutionally coordinated, are largely non-binding and may represent 'old wine in new bottles' – lacking substantive innovations in enforcement. The chapter also realises that the Thai Court is still required to weigh the balance of all notions when utilising the human rights concept in Thai jurisprudence in light of the complex qualities of Thai private international law (PIL), and the vagueness of the

[7] K Matsuki and A Burke, 'Litigation Against Corporations: Why Enforce Human Rights Against Multinationals?' in ch 2 of this volume.

[8] R Tugade, 'The Philippines' in ch 9 of this volume, section III(C).

conflicts provisions and the adversarial procedural rule. The author nonetheless stresses that their symbolic and procedural value – especially in promoting cross-sectoral collaboration – should not be underestimated. The conclusion lies in the reflection on Thailand's potential to shape an 'eastern' model of corporate accountability in a Buddhist society. Perhaps, one that blends legal formalism, institutional responsiveness, and cultural legitimacy.

The last country covered is India in chapter eleven. This chapter posits that the Indian judiciary is proactive and a rights-based approach be seen as part of good management practices and make management a force for good corporate human rights commitment. Through an impressive collection of landmark cases – including the *Bhopal Gas* case,[9] Hindustan Unilever's mercury poisoning in Kodaikanal[10] and litigation involving Coca-Cola's water extraction in Kerala – the authors demonstrate how courts have grounded their judgments in both domestic constitutional guarantees and international instruments (eg, the United Nations Declaration on the rights of Indigenous Peoples (UNDRIP),[11] the Endangered Species of Wild Fauna and Flora (CITES),[12] the Convention on Biological Diversity (CBD),[13] The Agreement on Trade-Related Aspects of Intellectual Property Rights (TRIPS)[14] and the Ramsar Convention[15]). These cases also exemplify India's increasing move from an anthropocentric to an ecocentric jurisprudence, emphasising intrinsic environmental rights. Other key highlights include the interpretation of labour protections during the COVID-19 pandemic in *Gujarat Mazdoor Sabha v State of Gujarat*,[16] doctrinal developments in corporate criminal liability and regulatory enforcement under environmental laws and the judiciary's evolving approach to arbitration and sovereign resource rights, especially where MNCs invoke international investment law to limit state oversight. The chapter argues that the Indian Supreme Court and High Courts have become key actors in translating international human rights norms into enforceable obligations, often ahead of statutory reform. The conclusion stresses the importance of harmonising domestic investment law with international human rights duties, and makes a normative case for embedding human rights clauses in investment contracts.

C. Human Rights Litigation and Actions in Practice

Part III of the book focuses on three different non-exhaustive examples of human rights issues. Chapter twelve on climate change discusses how administrative suits against legislative or executive authorities based on internationally required temperature limits and national emission budgets may follow in Asia. This chapter then presents a jurisdiction-by-jurisdiction survey of private climate litigation in Japan, China, and South Korea. In Japan, plaintiffs have pursued injunctions against coal-fired power plants (eg, the *Sendai* and *Kobe* cases), arguing violations of personal rights and the 'right to a peaceful life.' Japanese courts have so far rejected these claims, citing lack of concrete danger and insufficient causation.[17] In China, the NGO *Friends of Nature*

[9] M Sinha and S Dania, 'India' in ch 11 of this volume.
[10] Tugade (n 8).
[11] United Nations Declaration on the rights of Indigenous Peoples (13 September 2007).
[12] Endangered Species of Wild Fauna and Flora (Geneva, 3 March 1973).
[13] Convention on Biological Diversity (Rio de Janeiro and New York, 5 June 1992–4 June 1993).
[14] The Agreement on Trade-Related Aspects of Intellectual Property Rights (Marrakesh, 15 April 1994).
[15] Ramsar Convention on Wetlands of International Importance Especially as Waterfowl Habitat (Ramsar, 2 February 1971).
[16] Tugade (n 8) and S Chandramour, 'Thailand' in ch 10 of this volume.
[17] D Linden, 'Environmental Damage and Climate Change: Climate Change Litigation between Private Parties in Asia' in ch 12 of this volume; *Sendai Citizens v Sendai Power Station*, Sendai District Court, 28 October 2020

has brought civil lawsuits against state-owned power grid companies for failing to purchase or connect renewable energy as required under the Chinese Renewable Energy Law. While one case settled through mediation with compliance obligations, others were dismissed due to narrow readings of legal duties.[18] In South Korea, the *Barossa Gas Project* case saw Indigenous plaintiffs from Australia seeking an injunction against Korean state-owned lenders. Although the application was dismissed, the case reflects growing transnational strategies and environmental due diligence expectations.[19]

The chapter concludes by comparing these Asian cases with prominent international examples, such as *Lliuya v RWE* (Germany) and *Milieudefensie v Shell* (Netherlands).[20] It identifies a trend: successful cases tend to be those that link corporate emission targets to national or international climate goals, such as the Paris Agreement, and focus on systemic rather than project-specific remedies. Despite the current limitations in Asia – including restrictive standing rules, lack of emission-based liability frameworks, and weak judicial recognition of environmental rights – the chapter predicts a growing wave of climate litigation against private actors. Future cases may increasingly adopt budget-based claims and rely on corporate due diligence duties under international climate commitments.

Chapter thirteen analyses the law of crime against humanity. The authors turn to Asia's historical contributions to international criminal justice through an examination of three key case studies: the International Military Tribunal for the Far East (the Tokyo Tribunal), the Special Panels for Serious Crimes in East Timor, and the Extraordinary Chambers in the Courts of Cambodia (ECCC).[21] Each example illustrates both the institutional innovations and limitations of hybrid justice in Asia. The Tokyo Tribunal, while foundational in principle, ultimately failed to convict any individual for crimes against humanity due to the requirement of nexus with armed conflict. The East Timor Panels faced challenges with political non-cooperation and resource limitations, leading to an incomplete accountability process. The ECCC, while securing landmark convictions, was plagued by high costs, political interference, and a limited caseload. These case studies collectively demonstrate the political and legal fragility of transitional justice mechanisms in the region, while also underscoring their symbolic significance. The chapter further addresses the implementation gap within domestic legal systems in Asia. Drawing on a jurisdictional matrix, the chapter demonstrates that many Asian states – even those that are party to the Rome Statute – have not incorporated crimes against humanity into their national criminal codes, or have done so in a limited and inconsistent manner. Definitions often diverge from those in the Rome Statute, omitting key grounds for persecution or the policy requirement. This patchwork of legal provisions severely undermines domestic enforcement and restricts cross-border cooperation. The chapter notes that while some mutual legal assistance frameworks exist in Asia for certain transnational

(平成29年(ワ)第1175号); Sendai High Court, 27 April 2021 (令和2年(ネ)第372号); *Citizens' Committee on the Kobe Coal-Fired Power Plant v Kobe Steel Ltd., et al*, Kobe District Court, 20 March 2023 (平成30年(ワ)第1551号).

[18] Linden (n 17); *The Friends of Nature Institute v Gansu State Grid*, Lanzhou Intermediate People's Court, 14 August 2018 (甘01民初434号).

[19] Linden (n 17).

[20] Linden (n 17); *Luciano Lliuya v RWE AG*, Landgericht Essen (Regional Court of Essen), 15 December 2016, 2 O 285/15; *Milieudefensie et al v Royal Dutch Shell*, Rechtbank Den Haag (The Hague District Court), 26 May 2021, C/09/571932 / HA ZA 19-379, ECLI:NL:RBDHA:2021:5337.

[21] J Ip, 'Crimes Against humanity' in ch 13 of this volume; Promulgated in the Agreement for the Prosecution and Punishment of the Major War Criminals of the European Axis (signed and entered into force 8 August 1945) 82 UNTS 279; UNTAET, 'Regulation No. 2000/11 on the Organization of Courts in East Timor' (6 March 2000) UNTAET/REG/2000/11; UNTAET, 'Regulation No. 2000/15 on the Organization of Courts in East Timor' (6 June 2000) UNTAET/REG/2000/15; cambodiatribunal.org/wp-content/uploads/2013/08/history_history-analysis-scheffer_english.pdf.

crimes, they are largely absent in the context of international crimes such as crimes against humanity.

The chapter concludes by turning to the 2019 Draft Articles on the Prevention and Punishment of Crimes Against Humanity, adopted by the International Law Commission (ILC) as a blueprint for a future treaty.[22] It analyses key provisions of the Draft Articles – including obligations to criminalise, prevent, and cooperate; the rejection of immunity and statutes of limitations; and the incorporation of victims' rights – and underscores their potential to fill the current legal vacuum. The chapter highlights the mixed reactions from Asian states, some of which have expressed concern over jurisdictional and definitional scope, particularly regarding the criminal liability of legal persons. Nevertheless, the authors argue that, in a region where Rome Statute ratification is limited, the Draft Articles present a promising and politically realistic avenue for improving accountability. With diplomatic momentum building toward a Conference of Plenipotentiaries in 2028 or 2029, the chapter urges greater Asian participation in shaping the contours of a future universal treaty.

Chapter fourteen is a relatively unique chapter due to its focus on criminal law instead of the orthodox international human rights law perspective. The chapter identifies and assesses how UNGPs have been embodied in the field of criminal law in China and Japan, particularly in the context of regulation of corporate crime. It posits that stricter social responsibility for companies to respect and protect human rights has become a legal obligation in both countries. In addressing the Japanese jurisprudence, the chapter explores two competing models of criminal liability: 'The corporate body deterrence model', which views punishment as targeting the organisation itself, especially where a distinct 'corporate culture' facilitates wrongdoing, and 'the individual deterrence model', which sees corporate crimes as reducible to actions by natural persons within the entity. It also addresses the legal role of dual criminal liability provisions, which allow both natural and legal persons to be prosecuted, and examines how compliance programmes – once rare in Japan – are now widely adopted, particularly since the early 2000s. These programmes are increasingly viewed as relevant to justification, excuse, and sentencing mitigation, although formal legislative recognition remains underdeveloped. In China, corporate criminal liability has been formally recognised since the 1997 revision of the Penal Code, with over 128 offences now applicable to legal persons. However, in practice, enforcement remains limited due to unclear attribution of decision-making, judicial reluctance, and lenient sentencing. Notably, China has introduced an innovative system known as the 'compliance and non-indictment mechanism', initially piloted in 2018 and expanded in 2023. Under this system, prosecutors may defer or drop charges against companies that implement effective compliance programmes in response to criminal investigations. This reflects a shift toward incentivising preventative measures over punishment. While this framework has grown in significance, it remains largely administrative and discretionary, without fully integrating human rights-based standards or aligning with the UNGPs' emphasis on transparency and access to remedy. Both jurisdictions reflect a broader shift from retributive to preventive and restorative models of criminal justice, where corporate compliance programmes are increasingly seen as integral to fulfilling the UNGPs' third pillar: access to remedy. The chapter concludes by noting that while legislative reforms are uneven, compliance mechanisms – if tied explicitly to human rights obligations – can become central tools for regulating and rehabilitating corporate actors in Asia.

[22] Ip (n 21); ILC, 'Report of the International Law Commission on the Work of its 71st Session' (29 April–7 June and 8 July–9 August 2019) UN Doc A/74/10, para 39-45.

III. Challenges Solved?

A. What is the (Scope of the) Law?

This volume commenced with the celebration of the coming 15th anniversary of the UNGPs as an introduction. It is said the UNGPs apply to all business enterprises, regardless of size, location, ownership, or structure.[23] The author shall not recite the UNGPs here as this was comprehensively discussed in chapter four.[24] Rather, the author would like to take a macro view in light of the UNGPs principle to distill in the realm of international human rights law to what extent was the traditional notice of international law (being that states have no right to intervene in other states' internal affairs) reinterpreted (if at all).[25] In fact, the scope of the law in the field of business and human rights in Asia defies rigid classification. The chapters in this volume collectively show that the scope of the law governing multinationals and human rights in Asia cannot be captured by a single doctrinal tradition or normative system. Rather, it reflects a fragmented and evolving patchwork of international treaties, soft-law instruments, domestic legislation, judicial activism, and policy experimentation. In other words, the legal landscape consists not of a singular, codified regime but of a constellation of overlapping and sometimes competing legal sources, ranging from soft-law instruments like the UNGPs, to binding constitutional norms, domestic statutes, administrative guidance, and emerging international treaty initiatives.

As the Thailand chapter insightfully notes, human rights in the context of transnational business are both abstract value systems and concrete regulatory framework, which require a multidimensional process of coordination across public and private actors.[26] This complexity underscores what the UNGPs describe as the 'state duty to protect,' 'corporate responsibility to respect,' and 'access to remedy' – a tripartite framework that assumes shared but differentiated roles between governments, businesses, and civil society. Several chapters such as those on India, Japan, and China further illustrate how international human rights norms have been selectively internalised into domestic systems, sometimes through constitutional interpretation, sometimes through regulatory guidance, and increasingly through hybrid mechanisms like corporate compliance programmes or multi-stakeholder frameworks.[27] The Japanese and Chinese chapters reveal how state actors adopt regulatory innovations – such as human rights due diligence guidelines or compliance-based prosecutorial discretion – not through explicit human rights mandates, but as pragmatic responses to international pressure and economic necessity. In India, constitutional and judicial discourse has created limited openings for the recognition of business-related human rights violations, though full incorporation remains to be achieved.

Chapter three's doctrinal analysis underscores that the reach of law is also defined procedurally: rules on jurisdiction, *forum non conveniens*, and enforcement shape whether and how victims can access remedy across borders.[28] Meanwhile, chapter five reminds us that attempts to define a global legal scope through treaty-making efforts have been shaped as much by political compromise as by normative ambition, with deep divisions over whether binding obligations

[23] R Smith, *International Human Rights Law*, 10th edn (Oxford, Oxford University Press, 2022) 458.
[24] Birchall (n 5) section IV.
[25] JHC Cheung, 'Introduction' in ch 1 of this volume.
[26] Chandramour (n 16).
[27] T Nakamura, 'The EU Corporate Sustainability Due Diligence Directive: Challenges and Potentials in the ASEAN Context' in ch 6 of this volume.
[28] D Ishii, 'International Jurisdiction, Universal Jurisdiction, Extraterritoriality and the Enforcement of Human Rights Across Borders (including the use of sanctions)' in ch 3 of this volume.

should apply to all business enterprises or only to transnational corporations.[29] Even the UNGPs, while hailed as a conceptual breakthrough, remain formally non-binding and heavily dependent on voluntary implementation. As chapter four noted, this weak normative basis has contributed to their uneven uptake and limited accountability.[30]

Taken together, the chapters reveal that the 'scope of the law' in this area cannot be measured solely by textual commitments or legislative coverage. It is also contingent on institutional capacity, political will, and the strategic interactions between international frameworks and local legal cultures. Law in this field is negotiated, plural, and often deliberately ambiguous – expanding through guidance, compliance, and soft norm diffusion rather than through direct compulsion. The real challenge, as many contributors observe, lies not only in defining the boundaries of legal obligation, but in building the mechanisms – both public and private – through which those obligations may be meaningfully realised. What emerges is a legal field that is not static but negotiated – a dynamic, pluralist landscape where the boundary between public international law and private regulation is increasingly porous.

B. 'Who' are the Parties?

The chapters in this volume collectively complicate the traditional state-centric paradigm of international law by showing how both non-state actors (particularly MNCs) and individuals, including indigenous communities, have come to occupy legally significant roles in the business and human rights landscape. While orthodox international law has long denied corporations and individuals formal legal personality, the past several decades have seen a reimagining of legal subjecthood in both treaty regimes and normative practice. Chapter two, for instance, begins with a grounded account of the legal battle involving indigenous Tiwi Islanders seeking redress for climate inaction under international human rights mechanisms as a case that underscores the increasing visibility and legitimacy of non-state voices in transnational legal fora.[31] This narrative finds a regional echo in chapter twelve, which situates the *Kang et al v K-Sure and KEXIM* litigation within a broader frame of climate justice claims initiated by Korean youth and activists.[32] These cases demonstrate that not only private individuals, but also indigenous and local communities (across both developing and developed jurisdictions) are asserting participatory claims in the enforcement of environmental and human rights standards.

This theme resurfaces in chapter nine on the Philippines, where the evolving role of civil society actors, including victims and community groups, highlights how individuals are increasingly positioned as both rights-holders and agents of accountability.[33] The Indian chapter adds an important dimension by referencing the *Orissa Mining Corporation Ltd. v Ministry of Environment and Forests*, where the Supreme Court affirmed that 'the rights of the indigenous population cannot be subjected to the demands of profit-seeking corporations,' thereby signalling a jurisprudential commitment to recognising indigenous groups as distinct legal constituencies whose rights must be protected even against economic imperatives.[34] Viewed alongside chapter two's

[29] A Tang, A Crockett and J Sendut, 'A Decade of UN Business and Human Rights Treaty Negotiations: Something to See Here?' in ch 5 of this volume.

[30] Nakamura (n 27).

[31] Matsuki and Burke (n 7).

[32] Linden (n 17); *Kang et al v K-Sure and KEXIM*, Seoul District Court, 23 March 2022.

[33] Tugade (n 8).

[34] Linden (n 17); *Orissa Mining Corporation Ltd vs Ministry Of Environment & Forest &Ors.*; on 18 April, 2013 (Supreme Court of India).

account of how Australian indigenous communities have engaged international law, these examples challenge the notion that international legal protections are reserved solely for individuals in conflict or authoritarian settings – they show that even within advanced democracies, marginalised communities are repositioning themselves as key parties in rights-based litigation.

At the same time, several chapters point to the growing expectation that corporations themselves become bearers of human rights obligations. Chapter four outlines the conceptual foundation for this shift in the UNGPs, which treat business enterprises as having a responsibility to respect human rights, irrespective of state action.[35] Chapter five furthers this trajectory by situating corporations within ongoing treaty negotiations, where the scope and binding nature of their obligations remain one of the most contested issues.[36] Chapter six discusses the evolving understanding of legal parties by demonstrating that corporations, especially in ASEAN countries, are increasingly held to substantive obligations even outside formal treaties. For instance, EU CSDDD shows how global standards are prompting companies to engage with human rights and environmental norms through supply chain contracts and stakeholder consultation practices. These developments illustrate an expanding recognition that businesses are more than economic actors – they are subject to normative expectations that frame them as duty-bearers in the human rights arena.[37]

Together, these contributions show that in Asia, the identity of the 'parties' in business and human rights is undergoing gradual but meaningful transformation. Legal systems are beginning to recognise that both corporate actors and non-state individuals, including the historically excluded, have roles to play not only as objects of law, but as active participants in its development and enforcement.

C. 'How' to Protect?

Protection of human rights in the context of multinational business activity remains deeply contested and structurally uneven across Asia. As Bantekas and Oette observed, multinationals benefit from a web of legal rights while often evading equivalent obligations, due to jurisdictional gaps, contractually imposed limits, and the fragmented application of international law. The chapters in this volume offer both a diagnosis and a partial remedy.[38] Chapter three maps the procedural architecture of transnational litigation – including doctrines of jurisdiction, enforcement, and forum non conveniens – that often determine whether corporate human rights abuse can be meaningfully redressed.[39] Chapter four presents the UNGPs as a soft-law framework that articulates the 'protect, respect, remedy' pillars, while also acknowledging their limitations in the absence of binding enforcement.[40] Chapter five traces the evolving treaty negotiations under the Human Rights Council, where protection is sought through progressive codification, but remains mired in normative and political disagreement.[41]

Legal protection also hinges on state capacity and willingness to regulate, as reaffirmed by the recent International Court of Justice's Advisory Opinion of 23 July 2025 on *States' obligations*

[35] Birchall (n 5).
[36] Tang, Crockett and Sendut (n 29).
[37] Nakamura (n 27).
[38] JHC Cheung, 'Introduction' in ch 1 of this volume; I Bantekas and L Oette, *International Human Rights Law and Practice*, 4th edn (Cambridge, Cambridge University Press, 2024).
[39] Ishii (n 28).
[40] Birchall (n 5).
[41] Tang, Crockett and Sendut (n 29).

concerning climate change.[42] Although directed at states, the Opinion underscores the duty to control private actors' harmful conduct, reinforcing the logic of due diligence regulation already reflected in instruments like the EU's CSDDD. In this regard, chapter six contributes a distinct perspective by examining how human rights protections are increasingly being diffused through private contractual mechanisms in global supply chains, particularly within ASEAN states.[43] Drawing on examples from the apparel sector, the chapter reveals how European due diligence requirements are pressuring corporations in Southeast Asia to implement child labour safeguards, forced labour prevention measures, and environmental protections, even when local enforcement regimes remain underdeveloped. This 'contractual compliance' approach reflects a shift in how human rights protection can operate: indirectly, extraterritorially, and via private governance regimes.

Yet, as noted in chapter twelve, Asia still has 'only a handful of such court cases between civil parties', suggesting a critical gap between normative expectations and enforceable protections, particularly for victims of climate and human rights harms.[44] Chapter nine on the Philippines and Chapter ten on Thailand explore how domestic institutions may supplement this gap through national human rights mechanisms, ombuds offices, or localised administrative remedies.[45] In addition, chapter fourteen contributes a distinct model of protection through corporate criminal accountability, examining how countries like China are experimenting with compliance-driven non-prosecution schemes to incentivise human rights adherence.[46] The Indian chapter offers a complementary judicial model, where courts have occasionally prioritised constitutional rights and environmental justice over commercial interests, as seen in the *Orissa Mining* case.[47] This judicial activism positions the judiciary itself as an institutional actor of protection, even in the absence of strong regulatory mandates. Finally, chapter two reminds us that protection need not flow solely through courts or regulatory enforcement. The chapter highlights how ESG investment frameworks driven by investor demands and reputational pressures have become an important private ordering mechanism.[48] These frameworks increasingly incentivise corporate actors to integrate human rights considerations not just for compliance, but for long-term business sustainability.

Earlier it is mentioned that chapter nine slightly discussed gender equality in which it was suggested multinational companies are more ahead in the implementation of LGBTI-inclusive policies. As a side note to this chapter nine, the authors would like to mention that in 2023, the Japanese Supreme Court declared an important judgment which is that Article 3, paragraph 1, item 5 of the 'Act on Special Cases in Handling Gender Status of Persons with Gender Identity Disorder'[49] is unconstitutional.[50] This provision required, as one of the conditions for filing a petition to change legal gender, that the individual 'does not have reproductive glands or is in a state where the function of the reproductive glands is permanently lost.' In other words, in order to realise the significant legal interest of being treated under the law in accordance with one's gender identity, individuals were effectively compelled to undergo surgery, forcing those

[42] International Court of Justice, *Advisory Opinion on the Obligations of States in respect of Climate Change* (23 July 2025).

[43] Nakamura (n 27).

[44] Linden, (n 17).

[45] Tugade (n 8).

[46] S Matsuzawa, 'Corporate Crime, Compliance Programmes, and Criminal Law – the UN Guiding Principles on Business and Human Rights in Japan and China' in ch 14 of this volume.

[47] MK Sinha, 'India' in ch 11 of this volume.

[48] Matsuki and Burke (n 7), section I(A) and (B).

[49] In 2019, the WHO replaced the term 'Gender Identity Disorder' with 'Gender Incongruence'; however, Japanese legislation still uses the term 'Gender Identity Disorder.'

[50] Japan Supreme Court, 25 October 2023, p 1792, 77-7 Volume, Minshu (民集第77巻7号1792頁).

with gender incongruence into an extremely harsh dilemma. The fact that Japan's judiciary, often regarded as conservative, struck down this provision as unconstitutional and allowed gender change without requiring removal of reproductive glands was truly a bolt from the blue. Similarly, in Hong Kong, in September 2023, the Court of Final Appeal ruled that the government's failure to establish a legal framework for recognising same-sex couples was unlawful and ordered the government to create such a framework.[51]

Whilst it is difficult to assert that progressive multinational corporations directly contributed to these outcomes, it can be said that liberal multinationals, by often driving social change and significantly influencing public consciousness, have indirectly played a role in these developments. Taken together, protecting human rights in Asia today depends on a mosaic of tools: litigation, regulatory reform, corporate accountability, supply chain leverage, ESG-driven private governance, and judicial courage.

D. Is it Working in Asia?

The Thailand chapter's author stated 'the east receives human rights easier than the west'.[52] One interesting discussion raised but which remains unexplored is the concept of karma under the Buddhist society of Thailand in which human rights finds resonance in the legal jurisprudence.[53] India takes an eco-centric approach but not an anthropocentrism way.[54] In the Philippines, the state action doctrine is based on the distinction between public (state/government) and private (individuals/companies) spheres, holding that constitutional remedies for human rights violations are, in principle, applicable only to acts committed by the state.[55] A key feature of China is its state-led corporate governance. This governance model involves deep involvement of the government – particularly the Communist Party and state-owned capital – in corporate management and strategy. It differs significantly from Western shareholder primacy and market-driven governance models, as corporate objectives and decision-making are closely linked to national policies and social goals.[56] The conclusion is that there is no conclusion. Asia is a vast land, as with their legal challenges and culture. Indeed, whilst globalisation has required Asian countries to undergo certain transformations, they are not entirely abandoning their traditional characteristics and values. Rather, they are seeking a kind of sublate of these elements. Therefore, no single pattern can be generalised, as each country is taking its own distinct path.

These reflections underscore a deeper truth: that no single model or jurisprudence can claim universal applicability across Asia. The region's diversity of legal cultures and socio-political traditions necessarily produces different configurations of rights protection, even when engaging with shared international norms. Thailand and the Philippines, for instance, both implemented a NAP on Business and Human Rights, yet their approaches diverge substantially in both process and substance, shaped respectively by Buddhist-influenced legal pluralism and a constitutionally

[51] *Sham Tsz Kit v Secretary for Justice* [2023] HKCFA 28.

[52] S Chandramour, 'Human Rights, Multinationals and Conflicts Law – An Ongoing Story of Thailand' in ch 10 of this volume.

[53] ibid para 21; J Leeka, 'The Role of Karma in Thai Society: A Philosophical and Socio-Political Analysis' (2024) 1(3) *Journal of Modern Academic Social Science* (Online) 64, 66.

[54] Tugade (n 8).

[55] Birchall (n 5).

[56] Y Yang, 'Lessons and challenges of China's state-led and party-dominated governance model', 1 November 2023, Wiley Online Library, available at onlinelibrary.wiley.com/doi/10.1111/1758-5899.13274.

limited state-action doctrine. Similarly, chapter fourteen's comparison of China and Japan reveals how even economically advanced states pursue distinct paths: China through state-led corporate governance, where human rights compliance aligns with national policy goals; and Japan through a compliance-based prosecutorial approach, where non-indictment incentives aim to encourage internal corporate reform.[57]

Rather than pointing to convergence or fragmentation, these examples suggest a pluralist but dynamic regional evolution. As global norms like human rights due diligence become increasingly formalised through instruments such as the EU CSDDD, the real question is not whether Asian countries will 'adopt' Western models wholesale, but how they will translate and internalise these obligations within their own legal and institutional vocabularies. What this volume makes clear is that protection and progress are taking place, but on terms negotiated locally through courts, civil society pressure, state intervention, ESG frameworks, and cultural values. In this sense, 'Is it working in Asia?' may resist a binary answer. It is working – but not in any one way.

IV. The Action Plan

By way of conclusion, the book attempts to offer an action plan for implementing the UNGPs and their principles in Asia. It is said that the ongoing process of rising awareness of supply chains, business practice, and working conditions is a success of implementation of UNGPs.[58] Nevertheless such success shall only be sustained if there is conscious awareness to ensure multinationals contribute to the promotion and protection of human rights.

The authors boldly suggest there may be three non-exhaustive ways to achieve the goal of sustainability of protection and promotion of human rights in multinational context: (A) education, (B) lobbying and involving human rights as political agendas, and (C) cross border litigation and other dispute resolution mechanisms.

A. Education

Education serves as the foundation for realising respect for human rights at all levels: corporate, governmental, and civil society. Within the UNGPs' 'Protect, Respect and Remedy' framework, in particular the pillar of 'Respect' as it pertains to businesses can only function meaningfully through internal transformation and the dissemination of knowledge.

In universities and law schools, a comparative and regionally grounded approach is essential to understanding human rights risks associated with corporate activities. This includes legal structures surrounding human rights and corporate social responsibility (CSR) in Asian jurisdictions. In Asia especially, despite the rapid expansion of MNCs both in terms of attracting foreign investment and expanding overseas, legal and ethical literacy concerning business and human rights remains insufficiently widespread.

Within corporations, internal education is also critical. Human rights training should be implemented not only for departments which are directly involved, such as supply chain management, legal, and CSR divisions, but also at the executive level. Senior management must fully

[57] Matsuzawa (n 46).
[58] Smith (n23) 459.

understand the content of the UNGPs and the expectations of the international community. This is particularly important in the current context where ESG investment is gaining traction, and institutional investors are increasingly recognising that investing in companies indifferent to human rights poses a significant financial risk.[59]

B. Lobbying and Involving Human Rights as Political Agendas

Situating the relationship between corporate activity and human rights not merely as a matter of voluntary efforts or ethical responsibility, but as a political and institutional issue, is essential for achieving sustainable progress. In some Asian countries, structural human rights violations against workers, indigenous peoples, and migrant laborers persist, yet such issues are rarely elevated to the level of political discourse. For instance, while Japan is home to the indigenous Ainu people in Hokkaido, serious governmental efforts to protect their rights have only emerged in recent years.[60] This stands in stark contrast to the comparatively more robust protections afforded to indigenous communities in Australia.

To make the first pillar of the UNGPs (ie, States' duty to protect) truly effective, governments must embed human rights considerations into their legislation and policy frameworks. In this process, civil society, NGOs, the media, and even responsible businesses themselves must play an active role in lobbying for institutional reforms that safeguard human rights. For example, institutional investors demanding mandatory human rights due diligence and greater corporate disclosure at the policy level can be a powerful catalyst for regulatory reform. This mirrors developments in Europe, such as the CSDDD, and similar momentum is anticipated across the Asian region.

C. Cross Border Litigation and Other Dispute Resolution Mechanisms

One of the most noteworthy means of enhancing the effectiveness of the UNGPs in the Asian context is cross-border dispute resolution. MNCs operate supply chains that span multiple jurisdictions, and in many cases victims residing in one country face significant obstacles in seeking effective legal remedies against such companies.

In these circumstances, courts in the home states of the parent companies (typically located in Europe or North America) have increasingly become venues for holding corporations accountable for human rights abuses. Such cross-border litigation has emerged as an important complement to the third pillar of the UNGPs: access to remedy. As noted above, landmark cases such as *Vedanta* in the UK, *Nevsun* in Canada, and *Shell* in the Netherlands exemplify this trend. Meanwhile, even in domestic cases lacking a cross-border element, such as the recent case of *Torres Strait Islanders v Commonwealth of Australia*[61] before the Federal Court of Australia, we are beginning to see attempts to hold governments accountable for climate change and environmental harms experienced by Indigenous communities, linking such harms to failures in public

[59] Matsuki and Burke (n 7).

[60] Ainu Policy Promotion Headquarters, Cabinet Secretariat, Government of Japan, 'Overview of Ainu Policy in Japan', www.kantei.go.jp/jp/singi/ainusuishin/policy.html.

[61] *Pabai v Commonwealth of Australia (No 2)* [2025] FCA 79, www.judgments.fedcourt.gov.au/judgments/Judgments/fca/single/2025/2025fca0796#_Ref203402748.

policy.[62] While these cases differ from corporate liability litigation, they are nonetheless significant in demonstrating the growing scope of legal accountability through international public law perspectives, particularly concerning state omissions in protecting human rights. In addition, the development and utilisation of non-judicial grievance mechanisms, such as National Contact Points under the OECD Guidelines, corporate grievance procedures, and international arbitration, are also practical and essential pathways to securing access to remedy in line with the UNGPs.

In this light, the integrated use of both private law mechanisms (such as tort claims and contractual liability) and public law mechanisms (such as basic environmental laws and constitutional human rights protections) is critical to enhancing the effectiveness of corporate and state accountability. This integrated approach also serves as a concrete and pragmatic response to the question posed at the outset of the book:[63] is the traditional division between private and public international law truly necessary in the field of human rights?

[62] J Vincent, 'Duty of care – Those three little words that mean so much (or do they?)' (23 July 2025), always happy never satisfied, ahns.substack.com/p/duty-of-care?r=181yn9&utm_campaign=post&utm_medium=web&triedRedirect=true.

[63] Cheung (n 38).

INDEX

www.ingramcontent.com/pod-product-compliance
Ingram Content Group UK Ltd.
Pitfield, Milton Keynes, MK11 3LW, UK
UKHW051534061026
15470UKWH00029B/1620

9 781509 980406